ETHICS

in

Theory and Practice

ETHICS
in
Theory and Practice

THOMAS E. HILL

Professor of Philosophy
Macalester College

THOMAS Y. CROWELL COMPANY

New York - 1956

Preface

THIS BOOK HAS three major objectives, corresponding to its three parts: (1) to give the student a somewhat more adequate and intelligible view of the significant literature of moral philosophy than is usually furnished by introductory textbooks; (2) to assist the student to arrive at a working ethical theory by using the best methods that recent philosophical thought affords; and (3) to refine and fulfill the basic purposes of such a theory by applying its principles and methods to some of the more pressing practical problems of our day.

Since critical understanding of the best thinking of others is prerequisite to one's own best thinking, Part One is devoted to the exposition and criticism of each of the more significant types of ethical theory. That the theories may appear in intelligible order, they are arranged, not in historical sequence, but according to major types and subtypes in terms of the central problem of the meaning of "right." In each case the writer who is the most characteristic representative of the theory is considered regardless of his place in the historical sequence. The critical analysis that follows each exposition, though cast in the form of definite statements for the sake of brevity, is intended to stimulate rather than to conclude discussion.

Critical study of ethical theories has as its principal value its contribution to the clarification of a satisfactory theory in terms of which the student may think and act. Although many introductory textbooks adhere to older methods, leading moral philosophers now tend to agree that this clarification can best be achieved through careful analysis of the meanings of moral terms. Accordingly, Part Two outlines a working theory designed to help the student arrive at such an interpretation of moral terms as may illuminate the whole of moral experience. He is encouraged to draw suitable suggestions from other theories and to examine the data carefully, using the best methods of current moral philosophy. Although the working theory outlined here is the one that in the judgment of the author best fits the available data, it is by no means final. Many

v

questions remain open, and the sketch presented is intended to stimulate the student to achieve his own theoretical basis for moral thought and action.

Although ethical theory is often intrinsically interesting, no one ever fully understands what an ethical theory implies until he sees it applied to practical problems.   Hence, in Part Three the attempt is made to indicate the most significant practical ethical principles and methods implicit in the working theory sketched in Part Two and to apply them to important contemporary moral problems. Since definitive solutions of many of these problems would require the cooperation of experts in the fields concerned, together with much more thorough investigation than can be undertaken here, the present inquiries in practical ethics are not to be regarded as substitutes for the more extensive efforts often needed.   Rather, they are meant to throw some light upon the problems considered, to indicate how other problems could be approached, and to suggest points at which expert assistance is required.

The size and arrangement of this volume are designed to encourage considerable supplementary reading in the significant literature of ethics, and to this end appropriate readings have been suggested at the close of each chapter.   In order to facilitate maximum use of these suggestions the readings have been confined to four well-known books of readings, one systematic study, and an inexpensive collection of historical documents.*   In addition, ample references to a much wider literature suitable for use in special studies are also given.   A further study help at the close of each chapter consists of provocative questions designed to focus attention, stimulate thought, and encourage class discussions.

One significant theory, the unique good theory of G. E. Moore, has been deliberately omitted from the theories presented in Part One.   The reason is that Moore's thought has been followed in the main in most of Part Two and has furnished many of the criticisms in Part One.   The points at which the thought of Part Two differs materially from that of Professor Moore are the insistence that an intrinsic good is always a conscious experience and the distinction of some senses of "good" and "right" in addition to those with

---

* In case the other suggested books cannot conveniently be made available to students, A. I. Melden's *Ethical Theories* (2nd ed., New York: Prentice Hall, 1955) and R. D. Heffner's *A Documentary History of the United States* (New York: New American Library, 1952) will serve most of the purposes of the reading lists.

which Moore is primarily concerned. Other influences that have helped to shape the thought of this book are my early training in practical Christian ideals; the patient efforts of a succession of able teachers including Professors M. E. Sentelle, Kenneth Foreman, B. C. Holzclaw, E. T. Thompson, W. T. Thompson, Norman Kemp Smith, A. E. Taylor, and especially R. B. Perry and C. I. Lewis; the writings of such authors as Perry, Lewis, Nicolai Hartmann, Durant Drake, John Dewey, A. K. Rogers, J. B. Pratt, and many others whose works I had occasion to consider carefully in connection with the preparation of an earlier volume. I wish to express special gratitude to Professor Brand Blanshard of Yale University for reading my manuscript and making many helpful suggestions, and to my wife for typing the manuscript.

THOMAS E. HILL

St. Paul, Minnesota
January, 1956

Contents

PART ONE

Ethical Theories

PART TWO

A Working Theory

PART THREE

Practical Ethics

Contents

ETHICS

in

Theory and Practice

1

Introduction

THE NATURE OF ETHICS

A TRUCK LOADED WITH SOLDIERS is speeding down a narrow mountain road when just ahead the driver sees a child playing in his path. To try to turn aside will be to risk the lives of all of the soldiers, but not to do so will be to kill the child. What ought the driver to do? [1] A physician is asked by a critically ill patient what her chances are. To tell her the whole truth will be to add to the danger; not to do so will be to deceive her. What is the right course of action for the physician? A legislator is requested to do a special favor for a person who has contributed substantially to his campaign funds. To refuse might be to be ungrateful, but to accede might be to be unfair to others. What, in such circumstances, would a good man do? Ought a graduating college senior to follow his own desire to go on into graduate work if his parents wish his financial help at home? Should a person ever kill or lie or steal? Are truthfulness, justice, and kindness always good? Is it ever right to "squeal" on a friend who has done wrong or to hurt one person in order to help another? Here are some questions of the kind most often encountered in ethics.

When we asked above what the driver ought to do, what was meant by "ought"? When we asked about the right action for the physician, and what the good man would do in politics, what was meant by "right" and "good"? What, indeed, do people ordinarily mean by such terms as these when they in-

[1] "What Would You Do?" *Life*, XXXI, No. 11 (Sept. 10, 1951).

quire whether or not certain actions are right or good or ought to be done, or when they assert that other actions are, or are not, right or good?   Does "right" refer to obedience to a rule or to realization of an end?   Is what we ought to do determined by divine command, enlightened self-interest, the common good, or something else?   Does "good" mean generally approved or acceptable to conscience, or is there an objective standard by which good is to be determined?   Here are some questions, also frequently encountered in ethics, of a more basic kind than those mentioned in the preceding paragraph.   Answers to questions of this second variety are much more likely simply to be taken for granted than are those to the first.

In a general way we are all aware that ethics, which includes a wide range of questions of the two varieties indicated, inquires concerning standards of conduct.   But let us now try to be more specific.   When we speak of *conduct* we refer to chosen actions, not to such involuntary responses as heartbeats and knee jerks, but to such voluntary activity as working at a job, investing money, marrying, buying a house, and discussing politics.   To be sure, other disciplines than ethics—biology, sociology, and psychology, for example—also inquire concerning conduct; but these nonethical inquiries into conduct are mainly concerned with description and causal connections. Ethics, on the other hand, is primarily concerned with the rightness, goodness, and obligatory character, or "oughtness," of conduct.   Although the sciences of conduct other than ethics sometimes indirectly consider even the rightness and goodness of human activity, what they inquire about in this connection is what is *believed* to be right or good, and why.   Ethics directly asks what kinds of acts *are* right or wrong, good or bad, or ought or ought not to be done, and what the terms involved mean. We may accordingly say that ethics is *inquiry concerning the rightness, goodness, and "oughtness" of voluntary activity.*

THE PRINCIPAL DIVISIONS OF ETHICS

Looking back now to the questions with which we began we recall that these were of two different varieties.   These varieties represent two basic divisions of ethics, practical ethics and ethical theory. The questions included in the first paragraph belong to practical ethics. They concern various *kinds of actions,* such as killing a child, deceiving a patient, doing a political favor, and following one's inclinations. They inquire concerning such kinds of actions, whether or not actions of these kinds are right or good or ought to be done, and so to inquire is essentially what the questions of practical ethics nearly always do.

The number of kinds of actions about whose rightness or goodness such questions may inquire is, of course, virtually infinite if kinds of actions are spelled out in detail. But the number of the terms whose applicability to these kinds of actions our questions seek to determine is fairly small: "right," "wrong," "good," "bad," "ought," "ought not," and a few other terms closely related to these, but not many more. These terms may properly be referred to as moral or ethical terms. Accordingly, we may characterize practical ethics as the branch of ethics that inquires *whether or not the distinctive ethical terms properly apply to various kinds of acts;* for example, whether or not lying, or stealing, or paying debts, or keeping promises, or other more specific kinds of action are right or wrong, or good or bad, or ought or ought not to be done. Typical findings of practical ethics are to the effect that lying is wrong, that kindness is good, that such and such just actions ought to be done, and so on.

The questions included in the second of our initial paragraphs concern, not the kinds of actions that are right or good or ought to be done, but what is meant by "right," "good," and "ought" when we apply these terms to kinds of action. With other similar questions, these make up the theoretical division of ethics, which is commonly referred to as moral philosophy or ethical theory. When we inquire concerning the meaning of a moral term, we are not asking merely how the English word is used; different words in French, German, Russian, and Chinese may convey essentially the same meaning. Rather, we are inquiring about what is common to all the words in all languages that carry essentially the same meaning. We wish to know what is involved in the concept intended when we use the term, regardless of the particular language. The meaning that we seek is also not adequately given when we have pointed out examples of the application of the term, however useful that process may be. To give the meaning of a moral term as applied to an act is basically to point out those characteristics (if any) of the act by virtue of which the term is, according to accepted usage, properly applied to the act. But even to point out the characteristics of an act because of which, according to common usage, a moral term correctly applies to it, is still not quite enough: common usage itself is often vague and inconsistent, and fails to achieve as coherent an interpretation of man's moral experience as is possible. Further clarification through reflective analysis and constructive thought is often required. We may accordingly characterize ethical theory as the branch of ethics that *seeks so to bring to light and refine the meanings of moral terms as to afford the most coherent interpretation of man's moral experience.*

Questions of practical ethics are encountered in every significant aspect of our lives and are often extremely urgent. Such problems appear upon almost every page of the essay, drama, poetry, fiction, oratory, and even history; and the social sciences, though professing intellectual purity, really tend to build from first to last upon practical ethical assumptions. Problems of practical ethics also confront us outside of books—in business, in school, in the home, and in professional and community activities every day of our lives, whether we will or no. Moreover, upon our answers to these questions depend in considerable part our health, our fortunes, our human fellowships, our happiness, and perhaps, as becomes increasingly apparent, the very existence of our civilization.

The urgency of the problems of ethical theory is not so great as that of those of practical ethics nor is the frequency of their occurrence so evident, but in some respects they are in the end even more significant. Without concepts there is no human culture; and so much of the wisdom of the ages is embraced in the terms that man has chosen as basic to his morality that drastic changes in the uses of those terms might alter the course of civilization more deeply than substantial changes in specific moral rules.   Moreover, from a more practical point of view, although a rough understanding of moral terms enables us to solve simple moral problems, we can no more say with precision what kinds of acts are right or good without being clear about what "right" and "good" mean than we can say what figures are pentagons without being clear about what "pentagon" means.   Each of us makes certain personal assumptions about the meanings of "right," "good," and "ought"; but, because these assumptions are likely to involve inconsistent elements, both our own practical moral inquiries and our conversations about morals often break down hopelessly.   How, for example, can two people converse intelligently about whether or not "medical lies" are ever right when all the while one takes "right" to mean obedience to absolute moral law and the other takes it to mean conduciveness to human welfare?   Even when we have cleared away the ambiguities in our own and our neighbors' personal assumptions about moral meanings, we may still be caught in a net of confusion about what kinds of acts are right, unless we approach even generally accepted meanings of moral terms with critical caution, for these also may involve less coherence than we think.

THE DATA OF ETHICS AND THEIR DEVELOPMENT

Although ethics is not strictly or solely a science in the narrow sense of the term, it is a rational discipline and, like every other such discipline, must begin with, and be held accountable to, data or given facts.   The data of physics are observed motions; with these it starts, and to these—no matter how elaborate its intermediate constructions—it must be kept responsible.   What, then, are the data of ethics?   Generally speaking, they embrace the whole moral experience of man.   Such experience must be broadly construed.   It includes all man's feelings, thoughts, beliefs, and judgments concerning what is right, wrong, good, bad, and ought or ought not to be done, regardless of whether or not these responses are correct. It also presumably involves such mental or physical events as tend to support or exclude, or to confirm or disconfirm, these beliefs and judgments, although the extent to which such events are involved may, for reasons presently to be seen, vary according to the ethical theory adopted. Thus, for example, the data of ethics include my feelings of opposition to Communism, and my convictions that lying and stealing are wrong. They also involve, though not so directly, the disagreeable experiences with Communists that have led to my feelings about Communism, and the experiences of being lied to, or stolen from, that help me to see why lying, or stealing, is wrong. They include people's approval of kindness and of veracity, and also those experiences of the effects of these modes of action that sustain this approval. All such data as these, however much they may be in need of sifting and refining, are relevant to the answers to ethical inquiries, and by them all ethical theories and practical judgments must in the end be measured. No moralist is entitled to fashion his judgments out of whole cloth, and those ethical judgments that do not answer to the data of man's expanding moral experience are essentially worthless.

Man's moral experience did not, of course, suddenly appear in its present form; it has undergone a long and interesting development. Anyone who wishes to grasp the import of even the current data of ethics must see them in the larger perspective of this development. We cannot, of course, attempt to recount the whole story here. Those who are especially interested should refer to such authors as Edward Westermarck, L. T. Hobhouse, Ruth Benedict, Bronislaw Malinowski, W. E. H. Lecky, and other anthropologists and historians of morality. Most readers will already be acquainted with at least some parts of the growth of morality, and for the rest we must be content to call attention to a few significant phases of the process.

The earliest phase of man's moral experience—if, indeed, this early experience could as yet be called moral—lasted for hundreds of thousands of years, many times longer than the whole of recorded history, and may perhaps best be referred to as a *morality of tribal custom*. Man's behavior in this era, far from being that of the free and noble savage of some idealized pictures of primitive times, was dominated by rigid patterns of behavior defined by ancient tribal custom. Men did about as their fathers had done and as their fellows required, and such concepts as right and good, though perhaps dimly felt, seem never to have come to clear expression. The customs and taboos of the tribe were supported by spirits of ancestors, tribal totems, and the mysterious mana that pervaded all and gave power to magic and might to the shaman. Serious offenses against custom, which were indeed rare, were regarded not so much wrong as dangerous; and offenders were shut out from the fellowship and protection of the tribe, rather than punished as responsible agents. The range of this custom morality was very limited, being for the most part confined in each case to a single tribe, beyond which moral obligations and immunities ceased to hold. The demands of custom morality were largely for outward conformity; motives were regarded as unimportant if they were noticed at all. Many tribal customs, including, for example, certain cooperative procedures in hunting and in harvesting, were socially useful. Others, including multitudes of taboos concerning foods, shadows, shamans, and all manner of fertility rites, were essentially useless. Still others, including trials by ordeal, human sacrifice, and the punishment of the innocent for the misdeeds of members of their families were, by our standards, unjust and cruel.

The morality of tribal custom did not, of course, come to a sudden end, but continued long after the time of its ascendancy, and indeed projects itself, as we shall see, into our own age. Nevertheless, partly as a result of efforts to reinforce or to improve customs, and partly as a result of the demand for leadership in tribal wars, there gradually emerged a new phase of morality in which obedience to the decrees and laws of rulers and councils took its place beside, and sometimes above, the requirements of established custom. Since in this phase of morality the group within which moral demands were considered binding was larger than that of the previous phase (it often included many local tribes), the morality of this period may, if we use the word "nation" somewhat loosely, be referred to as the *morality of national allegiance*. The traditions, beliefs, and objectives of the collected tribes or nation, as represented by its rulers, were now considered sacred. Decrees and codes of law were often thought to emanate directly from the national deity, who was likely to be considered superior to all other deities, though not as yet the sole ruler of the universe. Offenders were not only unclean and unfit for fellowship but also guilty of disloyalty, sinners against the people and against their deity. The requirements of morality still for the most part concerned external conduct, but glimpses of the significance of motives began to appear. Evidences of this emerging inwardness may be seen, for example, in early Biblical provisions for cities of refuge in which the accidental killer remained safe from the avenging kinsmen of the deceased. Relations of cause and effect between actions and their results were now also much more clearly seen, and the demands of morality came to be more practical and more rational.

The conflicts that developed in this period, between established customs and new laws and between the customs of competing tribes and nations, constituted a peculiarly powerful challenge for moral growth. By bringing previously isolated patterns of behavior into touch with one another such conflicts tended to call elements of each competing pattern into question and to set in motion a quest for new standards, such as the will of a supreme God of all the earth, or the conscience of humanity, or even an abstract principle, that could transcend all of the older ones. This quest was naturally accompanied by a sharpening of the basic concepts involved; and it seems to have been in this process that the concept of a distinctively moral *right,* which was at most only implicitly present in the notions of customary and national morality, first came clearly to focus. The manner in which this distinctively moral concept emerged is suggested in the records of the early phases of a variety of cultures. It is indicated, for example, in the cry of the ancient

Egyptian farmers against their overlords for justice,[2] in the demands of the Hebrew prophets for righteousness, and in the protests of the Greek dramatists and moralists against tyranny in the name of integrity.

Like the morality of tribal custom, that of national allegiance continued alongside other types long after the period of its maximum ascendancy. In fact, it has remained active to the present day in such attitudes as reverence for law, the spirit of patriotism, and the current demand for strict conformity to national traditions and interests. Nevertheless, when, in the conflict between custom and national allegiance, appeal was made from either side to a higher standard, a new stage of ethical evolution had already dawned; and this stage as it was further developed became the *morality of universal ways of life*. This stage of moral growth was reached in different places at different times by a variety of routes. It emerged early in ancient Egypt in the great reform attempt of Ikhnaton, in India in the thought and life of Buddha and in some phases of Brahmanism. It appeared in ancient Israel in the work of the great prophets of the eighth and seventh centuries B.C., in China in the sayings of Confucius, in Greece in the great philosophers of the fifth and fourth centuries B.C., and in Arabia in the reforms of Mohammed.

The morality of this latest phase of man's ethical experience applies to all men and to the whole man. Its standard is neither tribal custom nor allegiance to ruler or council, but a right and good beyond them both. Its spirit remains essentially one of reverence; but its deity, when it rests upon deity, is neither the many gods of tribes, nor the superior gods of a nation, but the one God of all the universe. When its ultimate foundations are other than theistic, its basic moral reality, whether general principle, cosmic order, or human nature, is still essentially the same for all men. It is not satisfied with outward conformity to limited rules but demands inward and outward devotion to a way of life in which motives are as important as deeds. The focus of responsibility and value is no

2 See J. H. Breasted, *The Dawn of Conscience* (New York: Scribner, 1934).

longer the group or family but the individual, who must answer for his own deeds and whose conscience must make its
own final decision, even when divine revelation is accepted as
a guide. The welfare of each human individual is now much
more respected than in the earlier stages of morality, and the
causal relations on which it depends are much better known.
Only in the period of universal ways of life does the concept of
a moral *ought,* independent of tribal custom or ruler's command, come clearly to light, first perhaps as a command of the
one God and then in its own right. Similarly, only in this
period of an inward morality could the concept of the morally
good, which hinges upon purity of motive, fully emerge.

In the main, although significant features of earlier stages of
morality have remained alongside it, and occasional tendencies
to revert altogether to them have now and then appeared, the
morality of universal ways of life remains that of the contemporary world. But this morality has had many diverse manifestations and some new developments have taken place within
it. In order to illustrate both the earlier phases of certain important manifestations of this morality and some later developments within these manifestations we shall sketch briefly the
growth of two significant moral traditions.

The ethical concepts and beliefs of Western civilization have
for the most part been shaped by two major branches of the
ethics of universal ways of life, one Greek and the other Hebrew-Christian. The rationalistic ethics of classical Greece,
which emerged from traditionalism and nationalism in the age
of great dramatic poets of the fifth century B.C., reached its
culmination in the philosophy of Socrates and his successors.
Every man, Socrates taught, pursues his own best interests as he
sees them. This self-interest is not, as some would suppose,
perverse, but as it should be, for one's interest is his good. Unfortunately most people allow themselves to remain in ignorance of what their real interests are or of how to fulfill them,
and so they live in near animal stupor. The only way out is
through knowledge, particularly of one's self. Hence, virtue
is knowledge and vice is ignorance. But a man's true good

consists, not, as the many think, in wealth, power, and reputation, but in enlightenment and justice. "The unexamined life is not worth living." [3] "To do is worse than to suffer injustice." [4] Although much remained for the successors of Socrates to work out—and upon their systems we shall subsequently have more to say—Socrates' central emphasis upon a rational self-development that involves justice as a basic requirement runs, like a guiding thread, through the ethics of the Western world.

The Hebrew-Christian religious ethics emerged from traditionalism and nationalism in the prophets of the eighth and seventh centuries B.C. and culminated in the teachings of Jesus of Nazareth. Unlike Socrates, Jesus was not a moral philosopher and made no attempt to define ethical concepts. But the practical ethics that he presented has, more than any other, inspired the moral aspirations of the Western world and indirectly exercised no little influence upon the character of its basic moral concepts as well. Man, Jesus taught, is ordinarily not only ignorant but partially perverse as well, and deeply in need, not alone of enlightenment, but also of repentance. So far short of the perfection required of him does man fall that it becomes him best to stand before God and his fellows less in the pride of the virtuous knower than in the humility of the forgiven learner. Nevertheless, every human being, however low he may have sunk, is of inestimable value. The evildoer is like a lost sheep for whom the shepherd leaves the ninety and nine to search. The objective of the good man's conduct must never be either mere obedience to an external code or solely his own interest, however enlightened. Rather, it must include the good of every one of the children of God. Hence the supreme virtue and the supreme moral law are not to know but to love. "Whatsoever things ye would that men should do to you, do ye even so to them." The whole of the moral law is summed up in this command, "Thou shalt love thy neighbor

---

[3] Plato, "Apology," *The Dialogues of Plato,* tr. by Benjamin Jowett (New York: Random House, 1937), Vol. I, p. 420.
[4] *Ibid.,* p. 531.

as thyself." And one's neighbor is, as the good Samaritan found, every human being in need of help. This supremacy of love does not mean that there is no place for knowledge or for enlightened self-interest; for love, far from being mere sentimentality, is the intelligent endeavor to promote the genuine interest of all including one's self. Nor does it mean that there is no need of what is required in justice and law. What it does mean at this point is that love fulfills all that righteous law and justice require—and more: if anyone seeks the real good of others, he not only refrains from murder, falsehood, and adultery but seeks constructively to sustain life, speak truth, and respect personality.

In the Middle Ages the Greek and Hebrew-Christian streams of ethics, having at first struggled against one another, intermingled with one another to produce a durable compromise. The Greek way of life, as interpreted by Aristotle and St. Thomas, came to constitute the ethics of the level of man's natural everyday affairs, while more distinctively Christian virtues were required at the level of his spiritual life.

Although the Greek and Hebrew-Christian ethical traditions have remained the major molders of modern ethics, significant new factors have also entered the picture. Geographical discovery, far-reaching and vigorous trade, and the growth of capitalism have tended to ascribe new values to the virtues of thrift, industry, and commercial shrewdness. At the same time, modern science has fostered a quickened concern with quantitative fact and objective truth. The rise of the great modern nations has revived restricted loyalties and political sovereignties. The work of moral philosophers, which began with the Greeks and continued through the Middle Ages, has also been revitalized in the modern era and has exerted a considerable influence of its own upon contemporary ethics. Although modern moralists, like their predecessors, have been more interested in the interpretation of existing moral experiences than in the creation of new ones, their interpretations have themselves helped to increase the range and rationality of subsequent moral experiences. Generally speaking, though abandoning the Greek notion that contemplation is the highest good, they have adhered to the doctrine that reason is requisite to the gaining of the good; and, though often rejecting the special theology of Christianity, they have, for the most part, adopted and built upon its universalistic ethics of regard for the worth of every human individual.

From this welter of varied influences two types of modern morality may be said, perhaps with pardonable oversimplification, to have emerged. One is the Christian-democratic way of life, which retains the universalistic and individualistic tendencies of earlier universal ideals, finds ample room for tolerance, and discovers workable methods of combining constructive co-operation with agreement to differ. The other is the Marxist way of life, which, while retaining a kind of universalism, for all proletarians at any rate, abandons the inwardness and tendency toward individualism in most universal ways of life and reverts to ruthless suppression of all who refuse to conform. Deviants from these two broad patterns include, among others, the rampant "Super man" individualism of Nietzsche and the irresponsible "statism" of Fascism, but on the whole the great moral as well as military struggle of the present era is between the two broad patterns of Christian democracy and Marxism.

The end of the growth of moral experience is not yet, and each man's action and thought help to determine the still unpredictable directions that this experience will take. Thus, the data of ethics stretch out across a long and wide past and into an unknown future.

All man's past moral experiences are potentially significant data of ethics and many of them require investigation; but those of the distant past are not nearly so readily available as those of the present, and these latter are significant far beyond their relative quantity. The reason for this special significance of present data lies in the tendency of present moral experience to embrace the experience of the past. So deeply is every community concerned with the morals of its citizens, that it seeks to instill the best of ethical traditions into the character of its children from their earliest years. Hence, when we examine the moral responses of our fellows, we see in them not only what these individuals think and feel but some reflection of the moral experience of the race.   Indeed any well-trained person may, by looking carefully at his own moral responses and making due allowances for personal idiosyncrasies and special cultural influences, sense in himself much of the moral experience of mankind.   In this way we become, as Socrates reminded us, our own moral witnesses, although, of course, no court should confine itself to a single witness, and no philosophical inquiry should stop with any small group of them.

THE METHODS OF ETHICS AND OUR SUBSEQUENT STUDIES

If it be granted that the data of ethics are moral experiences, what are the principal methods by which ethical inquiry proceeds?   By the very nature of the differing purposes of ethical theory and practical ethics, the methods of these two branches of ethics can scarcely be quite the same.

Since ethical theory inquires into the meanings of such moral terms as "right" and "good," the part of moral experience that will most concern ethical theory will be the judgments and beliefs in which these terms occur.   What interests ethical theory concerning such judgments is not mainly why they are made or whether or not they are true, but what is meant by the moral terms used in them.   Its method will consist in the main of such psychological and logical inquiries into the intent and implications of ordinary judgments as have long been employed by philosophers to determine the basic meanings of any terms whatever, together with some more recent refinements of this method.

Any one or all of several ways of inquiring into psychological and logical aspects of usage can help to reveal intended meaning.   Such procedures seem obvious enough but are all too rarely applied with care.   One of the most useful of these is simply to observe and analyze the contexts in which we and others use moral terms, in such fashion as to disclose what interpretations are possible and probably meant, and what excluded. For example, if a man argues that giving to a charitable cause is right because it will make people happy, what he means by "right," or at least a part of it, is very likely conduciveness to human happiness; but if he argues that lies are always wrong because they involve inconsistencies, he presumably has some other interpretation of "right" and "wrong" in mind. A second useful procedure is to ask others and ourselves directly just what characteristics we intend to attribute to actions in calling them "right" or "good" or "obligatory." One may ask, for instance, "Is what you intend to say about an act of kindness in calling it 'right' that it fulfills personality, or that it is in accord with inflexible moral laws; or, just what do you intend? But since people are not always clear about what they intend when they use moral terms, a third procedure consisting of further probing may be needed. One form of such probing is to cite examples of suggested meanings and inquire whether or not the terms in question properly apply to these examples. This method was a favorite of Socrates; for instance, when he was told that justice was paying one's debts, he inquired whether it would be just to return the weapons of a friend who had meanwhile become menacingly insane.[5] Another form of probing into a proposed meaning is to examine the implications of the proposal to ascertain whether or not the proposer is willing to adhere to all that is involved in his proposal. For example, if someone says that "morally good" means pleasure, he may well be asked whether or not he is prepared to hold that pleasure in cruelty is morally good, as his theory would imply.

The use of such methods as these will reveal some clear patterns and much moral wisdom in people's intentions in using moral terms. It will also show that these intentions often involve a variety of possible meanings, and that some systems of terms render moral experience more intelligible than others. Accordingly, the moral philosopher must, while faithfully interpreting moral terms as he finds them, also suggest such selections among the systems of meaning involved as on the whole

[5] *Ibid.*, p. 596.

make most sense of man's total moral experience. In performing this task the moral philosopher must be guided by the
principles of logic and should never wander far from accepted
usage lest his suggestions become irrelevant and vain. But
when usage remains vague or ambiguous, and its logic indefinite or confused, he may, and should, propose such patterns
of meanings as seem to hang together most coherently and best
to illuminate his data in their entirety.

Since practical ethics inquires what kinds of acts are right or
good or ought to be done, the character of its methods and even
the selection of its data will depend upon the meanings that
are assigned to "right," "good," and "ought," that is to say,
upon the moral theory adopted or assumed. Thus, for example,
if "right" means approved the relevant data will be people's
actual feelings and judgments about the rightness of various
kinds of acts, and the method will be that of psychological and
sociological inquiry into what their feelings and judgments are.
But, if "right" means conduciveness to the general happiness,
the relevant data will not be feelings or judgments about the
rightness of acts but observed causal connections between acts
and their effects in terms of happiness or misery.

In the light of the foregoing considerations the following
will be the procedure for our further study. Although in fact
practical ethics and ethical theory have grown and continue to
grow together, ethical theory is, as we have seen, the logically
prior member of the couple. Moreover, for most people it is
the neglected member. Accordingly, despite the more immediate urgency of practical ethics, we shall not only begin with
ethical theory but concentrate somewhat the larger part of our
attention upon it.

Our study of ethical theory could of course begin with a
direct effort to solve its problems in the light of its data. But
many great minds have addressed themselves to these same
problems; and, if we ignore what they have said, we shall unduly narrow the range of suggested solutions, project unrecognized biases into the data, wander needlessly into blind alleys,
and at best get little farther than the first inquirers in the field.

Hence, in order to approach the subject with all possible breadth and to stand as it were upon the shoulders of those who have gone before us, in Part One we shall examine critically the work of the best available representatives, regardless of when they lived, of each of the major types of ethical theory. For convenience, the classification of theories is built solely upon interpretations of the single moral term "right," but accounts of other moral terms are also considered. Each type is evaluated in line with the methods of ethical theory outlined above, with reference to the points at which the type of theory does or does not correctly represent what people really mean by moral terms and contribute to intelligible interpretation of man's moral experience.

Fortified against narrowness, bias, and needless pitfalls by these studies of types, in Part Two, we shall approach the problems of ethical theory more directly. Using methods previously outlined, we shall inquire systematically what people really mean by each of the major moral terms, and what ordering of the disclosed meanings renders man's moral experiences most intelligible. No doubt we shall fall considerably short of ideal results, but in the light of the best insights of others and of our own candid inquiry we should at least be able to arrive at a working theory that will conform in the main to the intent of man's moral judgments and serve as a basis for our practical ethics.

In Part Three we shall turn to practical ethics itself, not indeed in any effort to exhaust or even to survey the whole field, but rather in the attempt to illustrate the operations of ethical theory in the realm of fact and with the hope of throwing some light on a few practical problems. After a discussion of the methods and general principles of practical ethics, we shall consider some problems of personal ethics and of the ethics of economics, politics, and international relations.

READINGS

G. H. Clark and T. V. Smith, *Readings in Ethics* (2nd ed., New York: Appleton-Century-Crofts, 1935), pp. 25–37; *or*

A. I. Melden, *Ethical Theories* (2nd ed., New York: Prentice-Hall, 1955), pp. 20–38; *or*

Benjamin Rand, *The Classical Moralists* (Boston: Houghton Mifflin, 1937), pp. 20–37; *or*

Wilfred Sellars and John Hospers, *Readings in Ethical Theory* (New York: Appleton-Century-Crofts, 1952), pp. 1–17.

QUESTIONS

1. What other subjects are most closely akin to ethics? What distinguishes ethics from these other subjects? Do you think that the findings of these other subjects help one to answer ethical questions? Why so or why not?

2. In what ways is conduct to be regarded as more than mere motions of an organism? Is one's activity while under the influence of alcohol conduct? Explain. What is the difference between ethical inquiry and sociological inquiry into the conduct of a person who has deliberately betrayed a confidence?

3. Which of the following statements belong to ethics and which to related sciences? (a) "Generosity is good." (b) "Kindness is an attitude of mind." (c) "Crime is caused by frustration of desire." (d) "Stealing is wrong." (e) "Conduct is motivated by interests." (f) "Right means conformity to custom."

4. In what specific ways can ethics be expected to throw light on other subjects—literature, for example? What bearing does ethics have on everyday problems? What special importance, if any, attaches to ethics in our era? What do you expect to get out of the study of ethics?

5. What is meant by "ethical terms" and what are the principal examples of terms of this kind? What, precisely, is the difference between ethical theory and practical ethics?

6. Which of the following statements belong to ethical theory and which to applied ethics? (a) "Lying is wrong." (b) " 'Wrong' means hurtful." (c) " 'Good' signifies pleasing to someone." (d) "Pain is a bad thing." (e) "Hitler's manner of dealing with the people of other races was vicious." .

7. Of what value is ethical theory? Don't people already know what "right" and "good" mean? What, precisely, do you think they mean? Ask your best friend what he thinks. What do you suppose most of our national leaders mean by these terms? How about

the men in the Kremlin? What are the practical effects of differences involved here? What sort of inquiry, if any, would help to resolve the differences?

8. How are the data of ethics like those of physics, and how do they differ? What aspects of human experience is ethics concerned with and why? Why should ethical theory be especially concerned with the way people commonly use language?

9. In what phase of moral development would you say most of our moral ideas are rooted? Would you say that the Greek or the Hebrew-Christian tradition has played the more dominant role in the shaping of our moral ideas? What is essential in each, and what evidences of each do you find in American political ideals and institutions?

10. Just what does ethical theory try to accomplish? Why is mere description of the way ethical terms are used not always sufficient for the purposes of ethical theory? In what ways are people's explanations of their own meanings sometimes inadequate? Explain and illustrate two ways of probing for the meanings of ethical terms.

11. In what ways do the answers to the questions of practical ethics depend upon the assumptions one makes in ethical theory? In what ways would you suppose one's attitudes toward practical issues would help to shape his ethical theory? Of what use is inquiry into other people's ethical theories in the attempt to arrive at one's own theory?

REFERENCES

Aristotle, *Nicomachean Ethics,* in Ross, W. D. (ed.), *The Student's Oxford Aristotle* (New York: Oxford University Press, 1942), Bk. I, Chs. 1–2; Bk. III, Chs. 1–8.

Benedict, Ruth, *Patterns of Culture* (New York: New American Library, 1953).

Breasted, J. H., *The Dawn of Conscience* (New York: Scribner, 1934).

Dewey, John, and Tufts, J. H., *Ethics* (rev. ed., New York: Holt, 1932), Ch. 1.

Drake, Durant, *Problems of Conduct* (2nd rev. ed., Boston: Houghton, Mifflin, 1935), Ch. 1.

Garvin, Lucius, *A Modern Introduction to Ethics* (Boston: Houghton, Mifflin, 1953), Ch. 1.

Green, T. H., *Prolegomena to Ethics* (5th ed., Oxford: The Clarendon Press, 1907), Introduction.

Hare, R. M., *The Language of Morals* (Oxford: The Clarendon Press, 1952), Chs. 1–4.

Hartmann, Nicolai, *Ethics,* tr. by Stanton Coit (New York: Macmillan, 1932), Vol. I, sec. 1.

Hill, T. E., *Contemporary Ethical Theories* (New York: Macmillan, 1950), Ch. 1.

Hobhouse, L. T., *Morals in Evolution* (5th ed. rev., New York: Holt, 1915).

Lecky, W. E. H., *History of European Morals* (1894 ed., New York: D. Appleton, 1929).

Malinowski, Bronislaw, *Magic, Science and Religion* (New York: Doubleday, 1948).

Moore, G. E., *Principia Ethica* (Cambridge: Cambridge University Press, 1903), Ch. 1.

Plato, "Meno," and "The Republic," Bks. I and II, *The Dialogues of Plato,* tr. by Benjamin Jowett (New York: Random House, 1937).

Pratt, J. B., *Reason in the Art of Living* (New York: Macmillan, 1949), Ch. 1.

Sidgwick, Henry, and Widgery, A. G., *Outlines of the History of Ethics* (London: Macmillan, 1939), Ch. 1.

Sharp, F. C., *Ethics* (New York: D. Appleton, 1928), Chs. 1–3.

Spencer, Herbert, *Principles of Ethics* (New York: D. Appleton, 1892), Vol. I, Ch. 1.

Titus, H. H., *Ethics for Today* (2nd ed. rev., New York: American Book, 1954), Chs. 1–3.

Toulmin, Stephen, *An Examination of the Place of Reason in Ethics* (Cambridge: Cambridge University Press, 1950), Ch. 1.

Tsanoff, R. A., *The Moral Ideals of Our Civilization* (New York: Dutton, 1942), Pt. I.

Urban, W. M., *Fundamentals of Ethics* (New York: Holt, 1930), Ch. 1.

Westermarck, Edward, *The Origin and Development of the Moral Ideas* (New York: Macmillan, 1906–08).

Wheelwright, Philip, *A Critical Introduction to Ethics* (rev. ed., New York: Odyssey Press, 1949), Ch. 1.

PART ONE

Ethical Theories

2

Emotive and Social Approval Theories

WHEN ANYONE JUDGES an act to be right, he approves the act, but he seems also to attribute to it an objective characteristic represented by the word "right." In this dual aspect of moral judgments is found the basis of a Great Divide in ethical theory. Those theories, on the one hand, that find the meaning of moral terms solely in the attitudes of someone judging the act are called subjective, or approval, theories, and those, on the other hand, that find the meaning of moral terms in an objective characteristic of the act being judged, regardless of whether or not the act is approved, are called objective theories. In this and the next chapter we are mainly concerned with subjective or approval theories. But before proceeding to consider such theories we must pause to look at an approach to ethical theory that, though resembling approval theories, rejects both these and all other constructive theories and stands as a challenge, which must be met, to the very existence of moral philosophy.

THE EMOTIVE THEORY, A. J. AYER

The emotive theory is like approval theories in holding that "right" is concerned with attitudes of one who judges rather than with characteristics of an act judged. But the emotive theory differs from approval theories in contending that "right," instead of meaning approved, only *expresses* or *seeks to elicit* an *emotion* and has no meaning at all. According to this theory, to say that lying or murder is wrong is not to say anything about lying or murder (even that they are disapproved) but is simply equivalent to pronouncing the word "lying" or the word "stealing" with rasping voice or wry face. Similarly to say that generosity and loyalty are right is equivalent to saying these words with a pleasant tone or a smile. In the one case, voice and gesture either *express* or *tend to call forth* disagreeable emotions; and, in the other, they express or tend to call forth agreeable emotions. This is all that is involved either in "right" or "wrong" or in any other moral term.

Such a theory as this is rather sophisticated and is rarely expressed or assumed by ordinary people, though echoes of it can perhaps be caught in the comments of cynical people, whose characteristic remarks concerning other people's moral judgments are likely to run somewhat as follows. "Well, now I know what his feelings are." "He will never change my attitude by that kind of talk." Or, "What an interesting display of temperament." In philosophy also this theory has been only rarely encountered, at least until recently. When some of the Sophists of ancient Greece, who were disillusioned concerning moral codes, suggested that justice was the interest of the stronger, they seem to have suggested that the strong in using such words as "just" are really trying to get others to do as they wish. Similarly, when other Sophists affirmed justice to be the interest of the weak, they may well have meant that the weak, in commending something as just, were only trying to get others to approve it. In the modern period some suggestions of an emotive theory are found in the writings of David Hume, who deeply distrusted reason and suggested reliance upon feeling and instinct both in morals and elsewhere. But it is in a group of contemporary writers, frequently referred to as logical positivists or logical empiricists, that the theory has been most boldly expressed. Although these writers have presented the theory with varying degrees of moderation, in order to feel its full impact we direct our attention to an unequivocal statement of it, in A. J. Ayer's book, *Language, Truth, and Logic.*

Professor Ayer's book is essentially a study of the limits of meaningful statements of fact. Its central thesis is that no statement of any matter of fact can have cognitive, or intelligible, meaning unless it is verifiable, at least in principle, by observation.[1] Although there are some meaningful statements that are not of this empirical kind, they are empty truths of logic and not statements of facts, and no matter how complex they become, they are mere tautologies, such as "A = A," or "5 + 7 = 12," or "every occulist is an eye doctor." [2] They yield no information about the world and are "consistent with any assumption whatsoever concerning . . . future experience." [3] Thus all meaningful statements either are verifiable by observation or are tautologies. All other apparent statements are mere "pseudo-propositions." [4]

In his attempt to establish this thesis Professor Ayer is undisturbed by the statements of ethical theory, for he finds these, as disclosures of meaning, to be mere matters of logic or tautologies. But the statements of practical ethics, which are the primary data of ethical theory, do disturb him because they seem to attribute to certain kinds of acts a rightness or goodness that cannot be observed. He suggests several possible ways of avoiding this unwelcome result. One may seek the meanings of ethical terms, as all subjective theories do, in the attitudes of someone judging the act. Or one may seek them, as some objective theories do, in pleasurable effects produced by the actions being judged. In either case the assigned meaning is in a psychological attitude asserted by judgment and testable by a kind of observation. Yet neither of these solutions accords with what people really mean in using ethical terms, for it is perfectly possible to say without self-contradiction that an act is either approved or tends to produce maximum happiness and yet is not right or good. The usual alternative, which is, of course, incompatible with the verifiability theory of meaning, is that moral terms are nonobservable qualities apprehended

---

[1] A. J. Ayer, *Language, Truth and Logic* (London: Gollancz, 1950), pp. 35 ff.
[2] *Ibid.*, p. 85.
[3] *Ibid.*
[4] *Ibid.*, p. 35.

by intuition; but this must be rejected on the ground that
people's alleged moral intuitions often contradict one another.

The only plausible remaining alternative is to recognize that
moral terms are really only emotive expressions having no intelligible meaning at all.   That is to say, instead of describing any
actual or imagined situation, moral terms merely either "express" feeling, or are intended to "arouse feeling," or both.[5]
Thus, to write "Stealing money is wrong" is really no more than
to write, "Stealing money!!"—the exclamation marks indicating
a moral feeling expressed and perhaps also sought in others.[6]
Similarly, "It is your duty to tell the truth" may be regarded
both as the expression of a certain sort of ethical feeling about
truthfulness and as an implied command, "Tell the truth." [7]
Even when a moral judgment contains a factual aspect, the
ethical aspect contributes nothing, and the ethical term remains
a mere expression of emotion.   Thus, "if I say to someone,
'You acted wrongly in stealing that money,' I am not stating
anything more than if I had simply said, 'You stole that money.'
In adding that this action is wrong I am not making any further
statement about it.   I am simply evincing my moral disapproval
of it.   It is as if I had said, 'You stole that money,' in a peculiar
tone of horror." [8]

As expressions of feeling, ethical judgments obviously cannot
be either true or false in the objective sense of being correct
if the acts judged really have the characteristics intended by the
moral terms attributed to them and of being incorrect if they
do not.   Even so, if a moral judgment at least affirmed the existence of a feeling toward the act judged, as approval theories
say it does, it could still be true in the subjective sense that it
would be correct in case one really had the feelings in question
toward the act.   Thus if "Thrift is good" meant "I approve
thrift," the judgment would be true if I really did approve
thrift.   But since moral judgments do not affirm the existence
of feelings toward acts but only express such feelings, moral

5 *Ibid.*, p. 108.
6 See *ibid.*, p. 107.
7 *Ibid.*, p. 108.
8 *Ibid.*, p. 107.

judgments cannot be true even in this subjective sense. While an affirmation of the presence of a feeling can be true or false, a mere expression of one never can be. One can never argue with such an expression for it states nothing. One can neither validate nor refute it, give reasons for it or reasons against it, for it does not say anything. It only *seems* to be a statement at all and does not really belong to intelligible discourse.

CRITICAL EVALUATION OF THE EMOTIVE THEORY

What now shall we say of this bold theory that denies cognitive meaning to all genuinely ethical statements and rejects all constructive ethical theories? For some incidental aspects of the emotive theory we should no doubt be deeply grateful. This view has put the problem of ethical theory squarely before us as that of the interpretation of ethical terms. It has properly pointed out the need for caution in such interpretation and challenged all moralists to clarify the meanings of moral terms before going on to other matters. Its initial refusal to be satisfied with interpretations that are at variance with people's actual intentions in using ethical terms is also fully in accord with the demands of sound procedure in moral philosophy. In addition to these methodological merits the emotive theory correctly calls attention to the fact that nearly all moral judgments are at any rate *accompanied by* emotional factors and that these factors often tend to dominate alleged moral judgments to an extent not commonly recognized.

The really crucial question is, however, whether or not the central argument of Ayer and other emotivists [9] against the supposed cognitive meaningfulness of moral statements can be sustained. Ayer's argument, as outlined above, includes three parts. The first is the general claim that all cognitively mean-

[9] In criticizing each of the types of theory studied in this book we are ultimately more concerned about the validity of the type of theory than about that of the thought of any one of the advocates of the particular type of theory. However, in order that our critical remarks should be reasonably definite, we shall orient them to a considerable extent to the thought of the selected representative of the type, even though not all that is said is equally applicable to the thought of other advocates of this type of theory.

ingful, or intelligible, statements are either tautologies or statements capable of observational verification. The second is the
contention that no plausible account of ethical statements can
place ethical statements in either of the two classes of meaningful statements. The third is the conclusion that ethical statements are in fact mere expressions of emotion without cognitive
significance, and neither true nor false.

Although the first part of this argument lies in the main
outside of the scope of ethics, a few remarks concerning it
should be sufficient to suggest its doubtful character. The
division of all cognitively meaningful statements into tautologies and observationally verifiable statements has never by any
means been generally accepted by all schools of philosophy, and
in recent years there has appeared an increasing tendency even
among those groups of philosophers that formerly did accept
this division to regard it as no longer significant or useful.[10]
Some philosophers go much further, insisting that verifiability
is irrelevant to meaningfulness, and few at the present time will
in any case attempt to lay down specific criteria of meaningfulness in terms of observational verifiability. Many apparently
quite unobjectionable statements in such fields as art, religion,
common-sense discourse, and even perhaps science have at any
rate every appearance of being meaningful without being verifiable in any but a very loose sense; and so clearly meaningful
do most of the statements of ethics seem to be that to set up a
criterion of the meaningful that excludes these statements would
seem just because of that exclusion, if for no other reason, to be
arbitrary and incorrect.

The validity of the second part of Ayer's argument, to the
effect that no plausible interpretation of moral statements can
bring them within the scope of the criteria of the meaningful,
depends, of course, upon whether or not Ayer's criteria are accepted and how rigidly they are construed. Even if these
doubtful criteria are accepted, unless they are construed so
narrowly as to be highly implausible and indeed more rigidly

---

[10] See especially W. V. Quine, "Two Dogmas of Empiricism," *From a Logical
Point of View* (Cambridge: Harvard University Press, 1953), pp. 20–46.

than Ayer himself intends, the meaninglessness of moral statements does not follow from these criteria. Ayer's way of deducing the meaninglessness of ethical statements from his criteria is to say that while subjectivist and pleasure theories do
indeed meet the demands of the criteria, these theories do not
indicate what people really mean by moral statements, and that
intuitionist theories lead to contradictory results and so fall
short of the demands of the criteria. But this line of argument
will not do. In the first place, the alternatives proposed by no
means exhaust the possibilities. Again, whether or not subjectivist and pleasure theories correctly represent what people
mean by moral statements, these theories are at any rate much
closer to what people mean than Ayer's own outright denial
that people mean anything intelligible at all by moral statements. Finally, even an intuitionist theory involves, as we
shall see, observational elements to which Ayer fails to do justice, and forms of intuitionist theories have been developed that
involve no such contradictions as those to which Ayer refers.
As a matter of fact, neither Ayer nor any other advocate of an
emotive theory has even seriously attempted the sort of thorough
examination of constructive ethical theories that should precede
a categorical rejection of all such theories.

The third part of Ayer's argument, to the effect that moral
terms are merely emotive, without cognitive meaning, and
neither true nor false, depends, in Ayer's presentation of it,
upon the first two parts of the argument, so that if, as we have
suggested, these first two parts must be rejected, the last loses
most of its force. However, if this concluding part of the
argument is tested independently, by those grammatical, psychological, and logical indications of people's actual intentions
in using moral terms by which, as we have seen, moral theories
ought to be tested, the implausibility of the emotive theory
becomes more apparent than ever. Whatever emotions may
accompany moral judgments, no one is ever, save for purposes
of a special theory, likely to see in what he takes to be a moral
judgment a *mere* expression of an emotion or *simply* an attempt
to induce an emotion in others; and if anyone comes to feel that

a statement is no more than an attempt to express or to induce emotion, he ceases to regard the statement as a moral judgment. Grammatically, we constantly use moral terms in ways that parallel the ways in which we use other meaningful terms. For example, we say "Temperance is right" or "Generosity is good" in pretty much the same way as we say "Grass is green" or "The moon is round." Again, we say, "Just acts ought to be done" very much as we say "Kind acts can be done." Psychologically, while we are often at a loss to know whether our moral judgments are true or false, it scarcely even occurs to us to doubt that they are either one or the other, and we find the suggestion that they are neither very odd indeed. We should surely find it paradoxical to say, with the emotivists, that "Murder is wrong" is not true or that "Unprovoked cruelty is right" is not false; and to add that these statements are also not false and not true, respectively, does not resolve the paradox. We also find widely at variance with our actual intentions in moral judgments the implications of Ayer's theory to the effect that all our thought about moral meanings and all the efforts of moral philosophers to clarify these meanings are sheer folly, that the whole effort of man to apply intelligence to the moral sphere is useless, and that the moral judgment of the sage can contain no more truth than that of the fool. We proceed in courts, legislatures, business affairs, the social sciences, and personal life as though some actions were in fact better than others. And we regulate not only our thoughts but also our actions and the rewards and punishments that we mete out, in the light of this conviction. Finally, from the point of view of logic, we find ethical propositions, however different in origin from other propositions, treated as implying and implied by other propositions, and entering into all of the usual logical relations.

We may conclude that on the whole the evidence for the meaningfulness of moral terms is so much stronger than any evidence that can be brought against it that we need have no serious misgivings about embarking upon the quest of moral philosophy, the search for meanings of moral terms. Better proof of the meaningfulness of these terms will, of course, be at hand when we can specifically identify the meanings in question. To try to do this is the task before us.

THE SOCIAL APPROVAL THEORY,
EDWARD WESTERMARCK

After the foregoing excursion into a skeptical approach to ethics that, although resembling approval theories, rejected these along with all others, we come now to the consideration of approval theories themselves. These theories include a number of varieties depending upon whose approval is taken to constitute the meaning of moral terms. Three main types will be considered here. The one to be considered in this chapter identifies the meaning of moral terms with the approval of the social group, and the other two find such meaning respectively in the approval of the human individual and in that of God.

The *social approval* theory takes "right" to mean approved by the group, contends that all and only such actions as are approved by the group are right, and holds these actions to be right simply and solely for this reason. It treats other moral terms similarly.

Some such theory as this was already implicit in the first stage of human morality, in which men acted as the custom was and asked no further grounds for their actions than that they were in line with the approved ways of their fellows. Similar assumptions seem to be involved in the attitudes of children, who feel that they should do as they are told and, when asked why an act is right, can only reply that their parents approve. More mature people often make their major moral appeal to prevailing approvals, giving, for example, as a reason for declining to do a certain act that they were just not brought up that way or that this sort of thing just isn't done. In all such instances a social approval theory is at best only assumed rather than expressed; but when intelligent people come to ask explicitly what it means to say that any act is right, many will be disposed to

reply that the statement can scarcely mean anything other than
that the group approves the act.

Although most moralists have accepted the sociological thesis
that social approval has actually helped to shape moral ideals,
comparatively few have cared deliberately to advocate the philosophical theory that social approval alone properly determines
moral development or that "good" and "right" really mean no
more than socially approved. However, since this view is
widely held or implied outside of philosophical circles, it is
well worth while to pause to examine at least one rational philosophical formulation of the theory. Such a formulation is to
be found in the introductory theoretical chapters of Edward
Westermarck's famous work on the history of morals, *The Origin and Development of the Moral Ideas,* originally published
in 1906.[11] To this exposition we now turn in the effort to see
the social approval theory at its best.

The roots of all moral concepts, Westermarck holds, lie not
in characteristics of actions but in one or the other of two kinds
of human emotions. These two kinds of emotions are alike
in that both are retributive; that is, they are emotions that
make us want to pay someone back for something that he has
done.[12] One kind is hostility toward, or desire to harm, anyone
who has caused another person pain. The other is friendliness
toward anyone who has caused another person pleasure.

These two feelings would not, however, be moral if they remained merely untutored, interested, and partial feelings.
Actually, they begin very early to be molded so as to operate
in favor of all that society accepts and against all that it rejects,
regardless of whether one's personal interests are involved or not
and without respect of persons. Such disinterestedness and
impartiality are achieved partly by natural sympathy, which
produces pleasures and pains in one upon the appearance of
these in others. But even more important is one's tendency to

11 Westermarck's more recent book, *Ethical Relativity* (New York: Harcourt,
Brace, 1932), develops the same thoughts concerning ethical theory in almost the
same words.

12 Edward Westermarck, *The Origin and Development of the Moral Ideas* (New
York: Macmillan, 1906), Vol. I, pp. 21 ff.

copy the signs of retributive emotions in others.   For example, when a man becomes angry upon discovering that a stranger has lied to him, his son is likely to become angry also on seeing the signs of anger on his father's face, even if the lie does not hurt him personally.   When this is often repeated in the family or in society, retributive emotion against lying comes to be a group habit, regardless of who in the group lies or is lied to. Only when, in such ways as these, retributive emotions have come to be disinterested and impartial expressions of the feelings of the group, do they become genuinely *moral* emotions.

Moral concepts are, as it were, crystallizations of moral emotions, and moral judgments attribute these crystallized emotional responses to actions.   Thus, to say that an action is right or good is to say that our group-conditioned moral emotions are applicable to it or, in effect, that it is group-approved.   If the action in question really is group-approved in this sense, the judgment is true; otherwise it is not.   Precisely what defines a group, Westermarck does not say; but he strenuously insists that even the individual who claims a moral right to reject the ways of his group can do so only in the light of the approvals of some group to which he adheres.

CRITICAL EVALUATION OF THE SOCIAL APPROVAL THEORY

Regardless of the question of the general adequacy of its interpretation of moral terms, the social approval theory significantly and accurately calls attention to at least two important aspects of moral experience.   For one thing, it properly reminds us that most of our moral convictions, and our moral concepts themselves, have emerged in a social context and are for the most part taken over from our fellows.   For another thing, it soundly suggests that since the experience of society is more comprehensive than our own and in any case creates an order that avoids much needless friction among persons, we shall be on the whole wiser to follow the moral requirements of society than to obey only our own inclinations.

Nevertheless, the essential question remains, whether or not the social approval theory represents people's actual intentions in using moral terms sufficiently accurately to be seriously considered as a basis for an adequate moral philosophy. A rather decisive answer seems to be indicated by the following considerations.

First, if "right" means socially approved and the definitive approval is taken to be that of the group to which the doer of the act being judged belongs, then the odd consequences follow that he who acts in accord with the approval of his group can do no wrong and, in fact, that the rightness of his act cannot even be sensibly questioned, since to ask such a question would be to imply some other sense of right.[13] But plainly we do not intend the term "right" in such a way that the witch burnings of Salem, or the Jew baitings of the Nazis, or the slaying of Socrates in Athens could not, in their own times, have been wrong or even sensibly questioned. On the contrary, we intend so to use moral terms that the questioning of some socially approved acts and the recognition of wrong in some of them may be seen to be among the chief signs of moral progress.

Second, if "right" means socially approved and the definitive approval is that of *any* group then either "right" has a different meaning for each group or else the same act, being approved in one group and disapproved in another, may be both right and not right. But, concerning the first alternative, what we really intend in using moral terms is surely not so systematically ambiguous as to shift with every change of group; and, even when members of widely divergent groups debate their moral differences, they rarely ever doubt that they may have basic moral concepts in common or even that a standard beyond them both might serve as a basis of judgment between them. And, concerning the second alternative, we intend even less so to use moral terms as to imply such self-contradictions as that the same act, in the same sense, at the same time, is both right and not right.

[13] See G. E. Moore, *Ethics* (New York: Oxford University Press, 1912; Reset 1947), p. 65.

Third, if, on the one hand, social approval involves only feeling and no thought element, it is much more arbitrary than our moral judgments are meant to be; but, if, on the other hand, social approval does involve a thought element, this part of its meaning implies a senseless regress, for, in this case, that society approves an act means that the members of the society think the act right, and the term "right" in the defining phrase must be defined in the same way, and so on forever in a way that no one seriously intends.[14]

Hence, until and unless other theories can be shown to be at least equally at variance with what people seem to mean in using moral terms, we must regard the social approval theory as on the whole far too much at variance with ordinary meanings to merit further consideration in our present quest for a satisfactory interpretation of moral terms.

READINGS

Sellars and Hospers, *Readings in Ethical Theory,* pp. 393–402; *and* Melden, *Ethical Theories,* pp. 247–50, 275–86.

QUESTIONS

1. What do you think the Sophists meant by saying that man is the measure of all things?   To what extent is he?   What parts are played in moral judgments by intellect, on the one hand, and emotion, on the other?

2. Is morality more or less difficult than other areas of human interest, such as science and art, to formulate intellectually?   Why? Do you agree with some of the Sophists that one could defend either side of most moral questions equally well?   Why or why not?   What about the view that justice is the interest of the stronger?

3. What grounds does Ayer give for saying that genuine ethical judgments merely *express* emotion?   What further evidence could you add?

4. If ethical judgments are emotive, does it follow that they are neither true nor false?   Why or why not?

5. What is the difference between a persuasive and an expressive

14 See *ibid.,* pp. 66 ff.

moral judgment? As you examine your own moral judgments and those of others, do any of them seem to be of these kinds? Are all of them? What else do you find in them besides expressions of and attempts to elicit emotion?

6. How do you think Ayer would propose to resolve the current moral differences between East and West? What role would reason play in this? How about oratory? Is Ayer's type of solution for these problems satisfactory? Explain.

7. How in Westermarck's view are moral emotions distinguished from others? What is the difference between impartiality and disinterestedness, and how, according to Westermarck, is each secured?

8. How can moral judgments, interpreted in Westermarck's way, be true or false when, interpreted in Ayer's way, they can't? Is Westermarck's account of the truth of moral judgments in accord with what is commonly meant by the truth of such judgments? What does the truth of such judgments mean?

9. How does one ordinarily acquire his moral ideals? What does your answer imply with reference to moral tolerance? Is the fact that something is customary ever a good reason for doing it? A sufficient reason?

10. How did you come to believe that lying is wrong? Do you still believe this? If so, is the reason the same as when you first accepted this belief? If not, why was the initial reason insufficient?

11. Sir James Frazer relates that in the Kingdom of Eyeo it had long been customary for the king to kill himself when his subjects brought him a present of parrot eggs but that in about the year 1774 a certain king refused to follow the usual procedure and thereby, after a stiff fight, broke the back of the custom.[14] What would the social approval theory say about the king's action? How, according to the social approval theory, can such customs be rightly broken?

12. The present Russian leaders apparently believe that the extraction of a "confession" from an accused person by the use of strong-arm methods, or even drugs, is legitimate provided it serves the ends of the state. Most of us reject this view. Who is right? Is this merely an American prejudice of yours? Is the "cold war" merely a conflict of prejudices? If not, why not?

[14] See J. G. Frazer, *The Golden Bough* (abridged ed., New York: Macmillan, 1940), Vol. I, pp. 273 ff.

REFERENCES

The Emotive Theory

Ayer, A. J., *Language, Truth and Logic* (London: Gollancz, 1950), Ch. 10.

Carnap, Rudolf, *Philosophy and Logical Syntax* (London: Kegan Paul, 1935).

Ewing, A. C., *The Definition of Good* (New York: Macmillan, 1947), Ch. 1.

Feigl, Herbert, "Logical Empiricism," in *Twentieth Century Philosophy* (New York: Philosophical Library, 1943).

Hill, T. E., *Contemporary Ethical Theories* (New York: Macmillan, 1950), Chs. 2–3.

Pap, Arthur, *Elements of Analytic Philosophy* (New York: Macmillan, 1949), Ch. 2.

Plato, "The Republic," Bks. I and II, and "Gorgias," *The Dialogues of Plato,* tr. by Benjamin Jowett (New York: Random House, 1937), Vol. I.

Pratt, J. B., *Reason in the Art of Living* (New York: Macmillan, 1949), Ch. 6.

Russell, Bertrand, *A History of Western Philosophy* (New York: Simon and Schuster, 1945), Chs. 10, 31.

Sidgwick, Henry, and Widgery, A. G., *Outlines of the History of Ethics* (London: Macmillan, 1939), pp. 17–22.

Stevenson, C. L., *Ethics and Language* (New Haven: Yale University Press, 1946).

Wheelwright, Philip, *A Critical Introduction to Ethics* (rev. ed., New York: Odyssey Press, 1949), pp. 36–52.

The Social Approval Theory

Broad, C. D., *Five Types of Ethical Theory* (New York: Harcourt, Brace, 1930), Ch. 4.

Durkheim, Emil, *The Elementary Forms of Religious Life,* tr. by J. W. Swain (London: Allen & Unwin, 1915), Ch. 7.

Hill, T. E., *Contemporary Ethical Theories* (New York: Macmillan, 1950), Chs. 4, 6, 9.

Levy-Bruhl, Lucien, *Ethics and Moral Science* (London: Constable, 1905).

Mannheim, Karl, *Ideology and Utopia,* tr. by Louis Wirth and E. Shils (New York: Harcourt, Brace, 1936), Ch. 2.

Moore, G. E., *Ethics* (New York: Oxford University Press, 1912; Reset 1947), Chs. 3–4.

Pratt, J. B., *Reason in the Art of Living* (New York: Macmillan, 1949), Ch. 8.

Sidgwick, Henry, and Widgery, A. G., *Outlines of the History of Ethics* (London: Macmillan, 1939), pp. 295–98.

Sumner, W. G., *Folkways* (Boston: Ginn, 1911), Chs. 1–2.

Tsanoff, R. A., *The Moral Ideals of Our Civilization* (New York: Dutton, 1942), Ch. 30; pp. 521–24, 574–76.

Westermarck, Edward, *Ethical Relativity* (New York: Harcourt, Brace, 1932).

—— *The Origin and Development of the Moral Ideas* (New York: Macmillan, 1906), Vol. I, pp. 21–22, Chs. 4–6.

3

Reflective and
Theological Approval Theories

ALTHOUGH THE APPROVAL of the group is likely to be greater
in duration and often broader in perspective than that of the
individual, the latter may be more incisive and sometimes even
more comprehensive in outlook. Hence many who have seen
the folly of either relegating morality to the emotive realm or
accepting social approvals at face value have looked to individual conscience as the touchstone of morality.

THE REFLECTIVE APPROVAL THEORY,
JOSEPH BUTLER

The grounding of morality in conscience has a long history
in philosophical thought. It is prominent in Socrates, who preferred the reflective assent of one thoughtful witness to the vote
of the many and replied to an offer of escape from prison by saying that he was "one of those natures who must be guided by
reason."[1] Similar confidence in individual approval was dis-
played among the Stoics, who are credited with giving to the
term "conscience" its modern meaning. Even in Medieval
thought, where the authority of the Church was dominant, reliance upon conscience played a significant part in the system of

[1] Plato, "Crito," *The Dialogues of Plato,* tr. by Benjamin Jowett (New York:
Random House, 1937), Vol. I, p. 430.

St. Thomas and became the very heart of that of Abelard, where motive rather than action almost wholly determined moral value. In the eighteenth century a notable group of writers, protesting against Thomas Hobbes' reduction of morality to calculation of selfish interest, turned to individual conscience as the basis of their reply. Anthony Ashley Cooper, the third Earl of Shaftesbury (1671–1713), proclaimed the notion that man has both social and nonsocial affections and that right is obtained by harmonizing them through an affection toward affections. Francis Hutcheson (1694–1747) of Glasgow University developed this view further, giving the name *moral sense* to the guiding affection. David Hume (1711–76), the the famous Edinburgh philosopher and historian, undertook to explain the approving or disapproving faculty in man in terms of sympathy, while Adam Smith (1723–90), the celebrated author of the *Wealth of Nations,* accounted for it in somewhat more intellectual terms, as an "impartial spectator" within the breast of man.

Reliance on the validity of individual conscience has also played an extremely important role in human life outside of philosophy proper. St. Paul, for example, undertakes to vindicate his conduct by saying that he has a "conscience void of offense toward God and men"; and appeal to conscience was a chief support of the early Christians against a hostile world. A similar confidence, as expressed in the doctrine of the priesthood of all believers, was a principal bulwark of the leaders of the Protestant Reformation. The American Declaration of Independence is grounded in the individual's rational insight, and, together with the Constitution, it undertakes to sustain liberty of conscience for every citizen. Present laws in many nations recognize, even in time of war, a right of "conscientious objection." Moreover, the rise of totalitarian powers, although having sometimes tempted democracies to adopt authoritarian practices, has often brought about a more acute awareness of the essential importance of a free conscience in every individual.

What we are principally concerned with here, however, is

somewhat more specific than general reliance upon conscience as the touchstone of morality. Such reliance may or may not be accompanied by an identification of conscience with the meaning of right, and it is with this identification—as suggested, for example, in expressions to the effect that an act *must* be right if approved by conscience and wrong if disapproved—that we are primarily concerned here. Moreover, we are mainly interested in one particular interpretation of conscience itself. Conscience is sometimes taken to be a special feeling of approval or disapproval, but the account of it upon which we concentrate here is one in which it appears as a kind of reflective insight that takes all factors into account and seeks the most reasonable solution possible in the circumstances.

We may therefore define the theory primarily to be discussed in this section as one that holds that *"right" means reflectively approved by the individual,* such and only such acts being right as are so approved, and for that reason.

Now it is doubtful if any moral philosopher has ever held just such a theory as this, but the tendency to assume such a theory is often encountered both in popular thought and in philosophy. Such a theory seems, moreover, to represent the most plausible type of identification of conscience with the meaning of right. Accordingly, in order to see a little more specifically what may be involved in such a theory, we shall indicate here some leading features of that part of the work of one significant moral philosopher which leans most toward the kind of reflective individual approval theory we have in mind.

Joseph Butler (1692–1752), whose work resembles in some respects that of the eighteenth century writers referred to above, was one of the most fair-minded and balanced of all moral philosophers. Accordingly, he was never quite able to confine himself to a single ethical theory but found room in his thought for several. Rather prominent among these is a significant, though by no means exclusive, tendency to equate the right with the reflectively approved, and it is this aspect of Butler's thought that concerns us here.

Since morality has to be practiced by man, Butler quite

reasonably assumed that moral philosophy should be rooted
in understanding of human nature. And, because he felt that
Hobbes' egoism represented a distorted view of human nature,
he undertook in his famous *Sermons Preached at the Rolls
Chapel* and later in his *Of the Nature of Virtue* to present what
he considered a sounder analysis of man's nature, in which he
endeavored to demonstrate the folly of Hobbes' then fashionable
egoistic view. As a background for Butler's interpretation of
right we must now glance at this analysis, which, in broad outline at least, remains tenable.

At the lowest level in man's nature are certain "affections,"
"appetites," or "passions," on the harmonious fulfillment of
which man's happiness ultimately depends. Some of these appetites, like hunger and thirst, tend more directly toward
private good; others, like "desire of esteem from others" and
"indignation against successful vice," tend more especially to
public good.[2] But each type serves both ends. None of these
appetites is either selfish or unselfish, for they all seek their
objectives directly without regard to the pleasure or pain that
results from them. They are necessarily prior to all thought
of pleasure or pain; for, if we had no initial affinity for the
objects that they seek, we should have no pleasure in obtaining
these objects.

On a second and higher level in human nature appear two
broader, more comprehensive principles. The first is self-love,
a deliberate pursuit of our own private welfare or happiness,
which requires a sane ordering of our various appetites. The
second is benevolence, a reasonable attempt to promote the welfare of others, which is something more than blind affection for
them. These two are not, as they might at first seem, fundamentally opposed to one another. On the one hand, one cannot win the happiness that he seeks in self-love without seeking
the happiness of others because one's happiness depends on the
satisfying of his natural affections toward other people. On
the other hand, one cannot promote the welfare of other people

---

[2] Joseph Butler, "Sermons Preached at the Rolls Chapel," in Benjamin Rand,
The Classical Moralists (Boston: Houghton Mifflin, 1937), pp. 371-72.

without preserving and developing himself, for one's capacity to serve others depends on what he is.[3]

Above the level of self-love and benevolence is yet a third level at which is encountered the broadest and most deliberate of all the aspects of human nature, the "reflective principle" in man that surveys the whole of his actions and either approves or disapproves them. This principle is also sometimes called "conscience," "moral reason," "moral sense," and "divine reason." It is both rational and affective, being both "a sentiment of the understanding" and "a perception of the heart." [4]

The keystone of morality is to be found, Butler believes, in that part of human nature which is most truly representative of the whole, that which is most comprehensive and characteristic of man. Certainly that element cannot be the particular affections because they are human nature at its narrowest, least inclusive level, each affection having before it only its immediate object.

Self-love apparently comes closer to containing the distinctive essence of human nature, for it surveys all the particular affections and chooses among them according to the manner in which they tend to promote private happiness. It is so far superior to the particular affections that to violate its demands in favor of these affections is "utterly disproportionate to the nature of man." [5] Indeed, Butler goes so far as to say on one occasion that "though virtue or moral rectitude does indeed consist in affection to and pursuit of what is right and good, as such, we can neither justify to ourselves this or any pursuit, till we are convinced that it will be for our happiness, or at least not contrary to it." [6] Nevertheless, as even the above passage suggests, self-love does not contain the *meaning* of right. It involves no desire to do right. It fails adequately to represent the whole nature of man. Its judgments are frequently biased;

[3] Butler, "Sermons," *The Whole Works of Joseph Butler* (London: William Tegg, 1852), p. 143.

[4] Joseph Butler, "Of the Nature of Virtue," *Analogy of Religion* (Everyman ed., New York: Dutton, 1936), p. 264.

[5] Butler, "Sermons," in G. H. Clark and T. V. Smith, *Readings in Ethics* (2nd ed., New York: Appleton-Century-Crofts, 1935), p. 241.

[6] Butler, "Sermons," *The Whole Works,* p. 128.

its demands, and those of benevolence, however similar in most
instances, are in some instances, and especially in some types of
persons, quite different.[7]   Moreover, cultivated in excess, self-
love may cause serious anxiety or "disappoint itself and even contradict its own end, private good." [8]

Benevolence seems to some to be a closer approximation of
the keystone of morality than self-love.   It aims directly at the
happiness of all.   It encourages those social affections that
bring happiness not only when their aims are achieved but
merely by their presence.   It is the best antidote against bias
in favor of one's self.   It is not self-defeating.   It promotes
one's own and society's welfare simultaneously.   Nevertheless,
even benevolence is not itself the keystone of morality.   Its
scope is less than comprehensive, and although its demands
generally lead in the direction of moral duty, they are at times
at variance with duty.   For example, punishing an innocent
man or taking the property of one man and giving it to another
might sometimes seem to tend most to the common good, but
such acts would scarcely be one's duty.[9]

Thus, the principle in man that alone is comprehensive
enough to sit in judgment upon the claims of others and that
is characteristically representative of the whole man is the reflective principle, or conscience.   The very nature of conscience
is to rule.   Its breadth of vision gives it an authority out of
proportion to its strength and "had it strength, as it has right;
had it power, as it has manifest authority, it would absolutely
govern the world." [10]

If, indeed, human beings were wise and good enough, they
might discover the path of duty by enlightened search for happiness, but in actual fact they must rely upon conscience, for
the Creator has made men to attend to virtue and to leave their
happiness to Him.[11]   To debate with, or to delay one's obedience to, conscience on grounds of other claims is only to risk

---

[7] See Butler, "Sermons," in Clark and Smith, *op. cit.,* pp. 250 ff.
[8] Butler, "Sermons," *The Whole Works,* p. 119.
[9] Butler, "Of the Nature of Virtue," *loc. cit.,* p. 277.
[10] Butler, "Sermons," in Clark and Smith, *op. cit.,* p. 244.
[11] Butler, "Of the Nature of Virtue," *loc. cit.,* pp. 270–71.

deceiving one's self and failing to do the duty that one plainly sees.

Precisely what kinds of acts conscience approves, Butler does not state in detail.   He does assert that there is a "universally acknowledged standard."   He further indicates the general nature of the content of this standard in terms of what he takes to be the commonly accepted morality: "It is that which the primary and fundamental laws of all civil constitutions over the face of the earth, make it their business and endeavor to enforce the practice of upon mankind, namely, justice, veracity, and the common good." [12]   However, one does not need, he thinks, to know in detail in advance what conscience would approve, for the reflective principle is essentially adequate to any circumstances: "Let any plain honest man, before he engages in any course of action, ask himself, Is this I am going about right, or is it wrong?   Is it good or evil?   I do not doubt in the least, but that this question would be answered agreeably to truth and virtue, by almost any fair man in almost any circumstances." [13]

Butler's account of morality as thus far developed contains, of course, no specific statement of what "right" means, and one could find here grounds for identifying this meaning with either the will of God, the claims of human nature, enlightened happiness, or a unique quality that conscience discloses.   But, since the criterion for moral decision seems always to be conscience and no account is given of a property disclosed by conscience, the suggestion becomes plausible that in the parts of his work referred to here Butler was inclined to identify the meaning of "right" with approval by the reflective principle or conscience. An account of "right" similar to Butler's views so interpreted represents, at any rate, a view toward which the ordinary man's emphasis upon conscience sometimes gravitates, and this view requires careful critical examination.   The critical remarks that follow are therefore primarily concerned with this sort of assumption rather than with Butler's moral philosophy as a whole.

---

[12] *Ibid.*, p. 272.
[13] Butler, "Sermons," in Clark and Smith, *op. cit.*, p. 247.

CRITICAL EVALUATION OF THE REFLECTIVE
APPROVAL THEORY

The view that right means reflectively approved by the individual is oriented to a more advanced level of man's moral evolution than is the social approval theory, and accordingly it may be expected to yield at some points a more refined account of moral experience. Indeed, at two important points, at least, the reflective approval or conscience theory under consideration not only advances beyond the social approval theory but describes moral experience in ways that are very illuminating and quite unexceptionable. First, although many of our moral ideas are shaped by our social settings, we nevertheless, as the conscience theory insists, now and again come to see moral truths for ourselves, and the insights of moral pioneers sometimes forge far ahead of the approvals of their social groups. Thus, for example, a child, having long refrained from stealing because he was told to do so, may, on an occasion of being stolen from, recognize for himself why stealing is wrong; and a saint in a slave economy may see the wickedness of the ways of his world no matter how outnumbered he may be. Second, not only does conscience sometimes in fact see moral truths for itself, but such insight is, as the theory before us suggests, the final court of appeal in moral matters and there is presumably never a time when one ought to disobey his conscience in the sense under consideration. Not that conscience is itself the ultimate moral standard or is infallible, for the court is not the law and courts may err in their application of the law; but, even so, no authority beyond conscience can be found to take over the responsibility of conscience. The approvals of society, and perhaps of God, must often be taken into account, but in the final analysis, it is the reflecting individual who must decide what is to be done and bear the responsibility of his decision.

Nevertheless, if we seek in the reflective conscience theory, a sufficient interpretation of moral terms, we encounter, in only slightly different forms, the same difficulties that render the social approval theory impossible.   (1) If the approval of the *individual* who does the act is taken to be definitive, then no one who acts in accord with his conscience can possibly do a wrong act.   But, in fact, while we do not blame people who do wrong conscientiously in quite the same way as we blame others, and while we may even call their acts right in a certain subjective sense, we certainly do not say that consistently conscientious people *always* do right in the usual sense.   Indeed it would appear that many of the worst wrongs ever done in history have been those done by conscientious fanatics.   (2) No matter how much more incisive reflective individual approval may be than social approval, it does not always yield the same results in different individuals.   Hence, if the definitive approval be taken to be that of *any* individual the same act will sometimes turn out paradoxically to be both right and not right.   Moreover, this impossible logical contradiction will be encountered, not only in comparing the approvals of members of different groups, but even in comparing those of closely related individuals, for there are hardly any two individuals anywhere who do not disagree on the rightness of at least some actions.   (3) The definition of "right" as reflective approval is caught in the same senseless regress as appeared in the definition of "right" as social approval.   To approve anything reflectively in the moral sense can scarcely mean anything but to approve it reflectively as right; but to the question concerning what the "right" implied in the defining term means, the reflective approval theory can only repeat the same answer, and so on endlessly.   In terms of practical judgments, as well as in theory, this regress is fatal; for, while it is well enough, in asking whether or not an act is right, to be told to reflect, one must, if he is to make any progress, also be informed concerning what he is to reflect on, or what reflection is to look for.[14]

[14] See G. E. Moore, *Ethics* (New York: Oxford University Press, 1912; Reset 1947), pp. 76 ff.

THE THEOLOGICAL APPROVAL THEORY,
EMIL BRUNNER

While the conflicting approvals among social groups and among individuals involve each of the corresponding theories in impossible paradoxes, the approval of God presumably rises above these conflicts, and, to this extent at least, may afford the basis for a more promising type of approval theory.   The moral theory that results from such an appeal to God holds that right means God's approval, and wrong, His disapproval.   This kind of view has played a considerable role in the history of morals. Its essential assumptions supported the declarations of the Hebrew prophets and in a measure undergirded the custom morality of early Greece.   With the decay of the rationalism of classical Greece it came, through Christianity (although it by no means represents the whole of Christian moral thought), to play a prominent part in the ethical thought of Medieval civilization. At the present time, in the crisis of modern rationalism, it is enjoying a notable resurgence, although its future in the modern world is, as yet, undetermined.

Moderate expressions of the theological approval theory are to be found in certain parts of the thought of the Apostle Paul, St. Augustine, some Medieval theologians, Martin Luther, and John Calvin.   More decisive expressions are to be found in the works of an influential group of contemporary theologians, all of whom have followed to some extent the Danish philosopher-theologian Sören Kierkegaard.   This group includes such writers as Karl Barth and Emil Brunner in Switzerland, Karl Heim in Germany, and Reinhold Niebuhr and Paul Tillich in America.   Although these writers are theologians rather than philosophers, they command considerable respect in the modern philosophical world because they are conversant with philosophical methods and aware, as theologians have not always been, of the latest findings both of scientific inquiry in general and of Biblical criticism in particular.   Hence we look to a book of one of the members of this group for the clearest and most convincing expression of the theological approval theory, and the book that best serves this purpose is Emil Brunner's *The Divine Imperative*.

Brunner believes that virtually all nontheological, or natural, moral systems can be reduced to two classes, which he calls eudaemonistic systems and legalistic systems. The eudaemonistic systems, on the one hand, explain morality in terms of human happiness or well-being. These systems properly recognize that the vital impulses of man and the ends for which he strives must have a place in ethics, but they fail to acknowledge anything beyond what *man* wants, and in reality they do not provide such essential distinctions as would lift the morality of man above the instinctive behavior of the animal world. The legalistic systems, on the other hand, interpret morality in terms of rigid moral laws. These systems sometimes rise to the expression of lofty principles, but in doing so they lose sight of the importance of life and impulse. Moreover, when they attempt to rediscover the lost perspective they merely indicate in refined ways how *man* may get what *he* wants. Thus, all natural ethical systems leave humanity in the midst of hopeless conflict and confusion. "The picture presented by natural ethics is that of a heap of ruins. The original truth of God has been split up into a thousand fragments, and each of these fragments, by its isolation from the whole, is itself 'twisted,' distorted into a caricature of the original." [15]

The basic reason for the fragmentariness and inner conflict of natural morality is man's sinfulness, a fact that moralists are prone to ignore. Man has rebelled against God and tried to make a god of himself. Instead of simply obeying God man tries to work out his own moral theories. But these theories are idols, and man's assumption that he can be moral in his own strength is rebellion. Indeed "in the last resort it is precisely morality which is evil." [16] Hence, man-made moral codes are necessarily futile and hopelessly conflicting.

[15] Emil Brunner, *The Divine Imperative, A Study in Christian Ethics,* tr. by Olive Wyon (Philadelphia: Westminster Press, 1947), p. 67.
[16] *Ibid.*, p. 71.

If natural morality is too sinfully self-centered to be sound, what kind of morality is sound? Only such morality as begins with God rather than with man. Religious morality, even at the lowest level, has important advantages over secular morality; for "every form of religion, even the most superstitious, represents the right of the holy and divine basis and sanction of the moral." [17] Religious morality at a higher level has far greater advantages. But an ethics that is really free from the internal conflicts that vex natural morality is to be discovered only in terms of a supernatural revelation of which God is the source and end.

The true basis of right is simply and solely the will of God, which we can know only in part. The very idea of anything's being good in itself is sinful. That which is good or right is so because God wills it. There is no essence or purpose behind God's will to which God looks for the meaning of right; for all essences are products of God's will,[18] and there is no purpose beyond God's purpose. "God's will controls absolutely everything." [19] "What God does and wills is good; all that opposes the will of God is bad." [20] If happiness is a proper end for man it is only because *"He* wills it, and He wills it in such a way that no one else knows what His will is." [21]

Some moralists suppose that, having discovered right to mean the approval of God, they may go on to conclude that God has approved some principle that one may therefore follow in the assurance that in doing so he is doing right. Butler, for example, in some phases of his work, seems to have thought that God had willed us to follow conscience and that therefore in following conscience we were obeying God and doing the right thing. Along similar lines many Christians have thought of love as the central principle of Christian morality. But, according to Brunner, such dependence upon principle is all wrong; it is to fall back into the old sin of rebelling against God

17 *Ibid.,* p. 63.
18 *Ibid.,* p. 598.
19 *Ibid.,* p. 119.
20 *Ibid.,* p. 53.
21 *Ibid.,* p. 120.

by relying on human concepts instead of depending on God. Even Christian love is no satisfactory general principle of morality: "The Good is simply what *God* wills that we should do, not that which we would do on the basis of a principle of love." [22] The will of God, which determines right and good, is beyond all general principles. It is, moreover, a will that, for men, bears only on particular decisions of particular moments.[23] Men can never know anything to be right or wrong except what God approves or disapproves for a given individual at a given time and place.

This is not, however, to be taken to mean that we are left without any general guidance whatever in morals. Christians are always aware, at least, of the fact that God is Creator and Redeemer, and therefore they know concerning His will that "He cannot command anything but the obedient imitation of His activity as Creator and Redeemer." [24] Man should, therefore, endeavor to conserve God's creation and remold it along the lines that he sees in God's own Word and work, giving to each part a care proportional to that which God gives. This requirement demands both negative and positive activity. For example, with respect to the patterns of society the right approach is "a watchful, aggressive, determined attitude of hostility to all that is contrary to the will of God within human life; but this critical and reforming temper must always be based upon a grateful acceptance of human life, coupled with a readiness to serve wherever we may be." [25] Moreover, the Bible, including the Commandments, is a special witness to the revelation of God, although it is never to be slavishly followed in a cold isolation from the living testimony of the Holy Spirit. Upon the basis of these considerations, despite his rejection of universal principles, Brunner sets forth an outline of a Christian system of practical ethics, which he develops in some detail through nearly three hundred pages.

22 *Ibid.*, p. 117.
23 *Ibid.*, p. 83.
24 *Ibid.*, p. 122.
25 *Ibid.*, p. 338.

CRITICAL EVALUATION OF THE THEOLOGICAL
APPROVAL THEORY

In certain respects the identification of moral meanings with God's approval is somewhat closer to our actual intentions in using moral terms than is the identification of these meanings with either social or the reflective individual approval. Since God belongs to no group or individual but is judge of all, if right means God's approval, the man who obeys his own group or his own conscience may not only not be right but be radically wrong. And, since God is wholly rational, and never contradicts himself, if right means his approval, the same act can never be both right and not right. Hence neither of the first two paradoxes that vitiated the other approval theories applies to the theological one. Moreover, if a righteous God reveals his will to man, in the doing of this will man will surely be right; and, even if man's ideas of the will of a righteous God are only his own inventions, these ideas are still likely to be his best and least biased moral ideas.

Nevertheless, the theological approval theory falters in face of the third of the difficulties encountered by the other two types of approval theories, even if the initial postulate of the independent existence of God is fully granted. If God's will be taken to rest upon his thought, then the right becomes what God thinks right and we shall still need to know what it is that he thinks when he thinks something to be right. If, as Brunner seems to prefer, the will of God be taken to be a completely inscrutable will, then morality takes on an arbitrariness and irrationality that we surely do not, and should not, intend in calling anything right or good. Logically God could then make hatred and cruelty instead of love and kindness right by willing them to be so, but we cannot really think that any act of any will could bring about such a result. If an attempt is made to remove this difficulty by insisting, as no doubt one should, that God would not be God if he were not a righteous God, we have on our hands again the problem of defining the "right" in "righteous." Indeed God cannot intelligibly be called a righteous God at all unless some independent meaning be found for "righteous." A further, equally fatal, difficulty arises from the fact that if "right" meant God's approval, atheists could not mean by "right" what others mean, whereas in practice they do seem to mean much the same thing.[26] A less striking but more frequently encountered kind of illustration of this sort of difficulty may be seen in the fact that most of us seem to be a good deal surer of the right than we are of the will of God, as we should not be if the theory were true. For such reasons as these we cannot but conclude that although the will of a righteous God is always right and he who succeeds in following it is also right, even the approval of God cannot be quite what "right" means.

CONCLUDING REMARKS CONCERNING APPROVAL THEORIES

With the disclosure of the failure of these three forms of approval theory we seem, despite the discovery of significant insights in each type of approval theory, to be fairly safe in assuming that no kind of approval theory can satisfactorily interpret our moral experience.[27] As a matter of fact, we might have seen from the beginning that moral terms are fundamentally intended to refer not to attitudes of the one judging but to acts judged, though it seemed worth our while to look at these theories to see if we might not be wrong and to gain such help as we could from them. We are now free to turn to the more natural of the two broad types of theories sketched in the beginning of the preceding chapter, the objective ones which find the meaning of right not in approval but in characteristics of the act.

READINGS

Melden, *Ethical Theories*, pp. 215–46; *or*
Clark and Smith, *Readings in Ethics*, pp. 234–52; *or*
Rand, *The Classical Moralists*, pp. 378–93.

[26] See Moore, *op. cit.*, pp. 94 ff.
[27] For detailed development of the kind of objections to approval theories indicated in this and the preceding chapters, see Moore, *op. cit.*, Chs. 3 and 4.

QUESTIONS

1. On what grounds did Butler reject the view that all men are by nature altogether selfish? Do you consider his reasoning sound at this point? Do the demands of self-love and benevolence really coincide, as Butler thought, most of the time? All of the time?

2. What levels in human nature did Butler distinguish? On what basis did he claim that one was "higher" than another? Why did conscience have the right to rule?

3. A youth believes that he can contribute most to his own happiness and that of others by going to college and on to medical school, but repeated reflection nevertheless convinces him that it would not be right for him to leave his aging parents. What, according to Butler, should he do? Is there for Butler any further test? Is Butler correct on this point?

4. Can you think of any occasions on which your conscience was wrong? Do you think, then, that you should have disobeyed it? What would be the effect on character of repeatedly disobeying conscience? Does one have a duty to endeavor to educate his conscience?

5. In some parts of the world cannibalism still seems to receive the approval of people's consciences. Among us it is rejected with disgust. How can a conscience theory of right reconcile such facts as these? What sort of test do you think conscience ought to apply? What would this imply about the meaning of right?

6. Why does Brunner object to all human ethical systems? Why does he oppose even the conception of an ultimate *principle* of Christian ethics? What, according to him, is the true standard? How does one go about applying it? What do you think would be the practical results of a widespread acceptance of this view?

7. An ecclesiastical court is endeavoring to make an important decision. One of its members, in advocating one course of action, declares, "This course must certainly be right for it alone will produce the greatest good for the greatest number." Another recommends a different action, saying, "No, this is the right choice because it is good in itself and God is good." A third takes his stand upon the Bible, saying that the Scripture approves a third type of action. A fourth argues that while all these lines of reasoning, legitimate as they may be as channels of knowledge of right, are insufficient and that the task of the court is simply to search here and now for the living word of the living God. With which would Brunner be most likely to agree? Why?

8. In what way does the theological approval theory avoid the paradox involved in the other approval theories?   If God is perfectly righteous and wise, is his will an infallible guide to right?

9. Would it be possible to define right in terms of the will of God without using or assuming the term to be defined?   Is it possible intelligibly to ascribe righteousness to God without having some independent definition of righteousness?   Explain.   In what sense is the conviction that it is always right to obey God reconcilable with a rejection of the belief that the will of God is not, as such, what right means?

10. What is the basic weakness of all the approval theories?   Can you see any way in which an approval theory could overcome this fault and still remain purely an approval theory?

REFERENCES

Conscience

Broad, C. D., *Five Types of Ethical Theory* (New York: Harcourt, Brace, 1930), Chs. 3–4.

Butler, Joseph, "On the Nature of Virtue," *Analogy of Religion* (Everyman ed., New York: Dutton, 1936).

Martineau, James, *Types of Ethical Theory* (Oxford: The Clarendon Press, 1885), especially Chs. 1, 5, 6.

Moore, G. E., *Ethics* (New York: Oxford University Press, 1912; Reset 1947), Ch. 3.

Pratt, J. B., *Reason in the Art of Living* (New York: Macmillan, 1949), Ch. 7.

Rand, Benjamin, *The Classical Moralists* (Boston: Houghton Mifflin, 1937), Chs. 22, 25, 26, 29, 33, 34.

Rogers, A. K., *The Theory of Ethics* (New York: Macmillan, 1922), Chs. 1–4.[28]

Sharp, F. C., *Ethics* (New York: D. Appleton, 1928), Chs. 5–7.[28]

Theological

Barth, Karl, "The Problem of Ethics Today," *The Word of God and the Word of Man,* tr. by Douglas Horton (London: The Pilgrim Press, 1928).

Brunner, Emil, *The Divine Imperative, A Study in Christian Ethics,*

[28] The books of Rogers and Sharp represent modern approximations of the conscience theory that stress the emotional aspect of moral responses.

tr. by Olive Wyon (Philadelphia: Westminster Press, 1947), Chs. 3–14.

Calvin, John, *The Institutes of Religion,* tr. by John Allen (Philadelphia: Presbyterian Board of Publication, 1813), Bk. II, Ch. 8; Bk. III, Chs. 6–10.

Hill, T. E., *Contemporary Ethical Theories* (New York: Macmillan, 1950), Ch. 7.

Moore, G. E., *Ethics* (New York: Oxford University Press, 1912; Reset 1947), Ch. 4.

—— *Principia Ethica* (Cambridge: Cambridge University Press, 1903), Ch. 4.

Niebuhr, Reinhold, *An Interpretation of Christian Ethics* (New York: Harper, 1935), Chs. 1–5.

Pratt, J. B., *Reason in the Art of Living* (New York: Macmillan, 1949), Ch. 3.

4

Formal Theories: Rational Consistency, Kant

IF THE MEANINGS OF "right" and other moral terms are not to be found in anyone's approval of the acts to which these terms are applied, they must presumably be found in some one or more characteristics of the acts themselves. Hence, we turn from subjective, or approval, theories to objective ones. Among accounts of the meanings of moral terms as characteristics of acts, two possible varieties are encountered representing the two major divisions of objective theories. The meanings of moral terms may be found mainly in the form of the act, or they may be found primarily in the end or goal of the act. Theories of the first variety are called "formal theories"; those of the second, "teleological theories."

The suggestion that the meanings of moral terms are to be found in forms of action may perhaps be made clearer by reference to the analogy of beauty. What do some natural scenes, persons, paintings, poems, symphonies, and statues have in common that makes them beautiful despite their differences? One answer that readily suggests itself is that some form, perhaps not easy to single out, is always present when an object is properly called "beautiful." The situation may be similar with reference to moral actions; acts as well as artistic creations have forms. For example, an act of charity has the form of sharing one's property with another, a just act has the form of giving another his

57

due, and telling the truth has the form of correspondence between thought and word.   Perhaps there is something common
to all these forms that is always present whenever an act is properly called "right" and that constitutes the meaning of right.

If this suggestion is correct the question of course remains,
What kind of form constitutes the meaning of "right" and makes
right those acts that have it?   Different answers to this question
are offered by two varieties of formal theories, which we shall call
the "rational consistency theory" and the "moral suitability
theory."   We are now to consider the first of these two varieties,
which sets forth a single clearly definable formal characteristic
as the distinguishing mark of the right.   This characteristic, in
terms of which the rightness of an act is defined, is consistency,
or freedom from self-contradiction, in the principle of the act,
and such consistency is for the view in question the first requirement of reason in ethics.

Such a theory was suggested by Socrates, the father of many
ethical theories, when he declared with reference to the proposal that he escape from prison, "Now that this chance has be-
fallen me, I cannot repudiate my own words: the principles
which I have hitherto honoured and revered, I still honour." [1]
A different aspect of the same approach is suggested by the
Golden Rule of Jesus, "Whatsoever ye would that men should
do unto you, even so do ye also unto them." [2]   In the modern
era the more purely rational aspect of the theory is affirmed in
Great Britain in the thought of William Wollaston (1660–1724),
who held that deeds as well as words could contain contradictions
of truth (as when a man denies the true ownership of a horse
by stealing it), and that right consisted in so behaving "as by no
act to contradict truth." [3]   In contemporary ethical thought examples of views approximating the consistency theory may be
seen in such diverse moral systems as those of Warner Fite, who
held that "the moral man is the man who, so far as he is moral,

[1] Plato, "The Republic," *The Dialogues of Plato,* tr. by Benjamin Jowett (New
York: Random House, 1937), Vol. I, p. 430.

[2] Matthew 7:12.

[3] William Wollaston, "The Religion of Nature Delineated," in Benjamin Rand,
The Classical Moralists (Boston: Houghton Mifflin, 1937), p. 363.

knows what he is about," [4] and Irving Babbitt, who took reason and restraint to be the essential core of morality.   However, the incomparable philosophical representative of the consistency theory is Immanuel Kant (1724–1804).

Kant had been trained in a philosophy that considered knowledge to consist of ideas innate in the mind and unfolded in the course of life.   When Kant saw that this view was discredited by the fact that much of our knowledge is dependent on sense experience, he concluded, in his famous *Critique of Pure Reason,* that the universal and necessary element in our knowledge of facts was found neither in originally implanted ideas nor in passing sense experiences but in the structure of rational human minds, which was prior to all ideas and all experiences.   When he came to account for moral knowledge, it was natural that he should proceed along similar lines.   Such knowledge could not be said to be insight into a realm of eternal ideas, for men have no direct means of access to such a realm; nor could it be sense experience, for that is far too variable to yield the universal knowledge that morality requires.   Moral knowledge was, rather, rooted in the structure of rational mind as applied to practice, and the basic requirement of rationality was universal applicability or consistency.   Kant attempted in his *Fundamental Principles of the Metaphysic of Morals* to establish and explain this conclusion, first, in a comparatively simple account of the meaning of our ordinary moral experience and, then, in a more philosophical analysis.   In the sections that follow we consider these two in that order.

GOOD WILL

Any honest appraisal of the facts concerning the moral experience that is common to all rational beings would, Kant believed, call attention to one central fact.   Kant puts it thus in the famous opening words of his *Metaphysic of Morals:* "Nothing can possibly be conceived in the world, or even out of it,

[4] Warner Fite, *Moral Philosophy* (New York: Lincoln MacVeagh, The Dial Press, 1925), p. 3.

which can be called good without qualification, except a Good Will." [5]   Power, riches, honor, and health may only lead to pride.   Even wisdom, courage, and temperance may be vicious when employed in a bad cause.   The happiness of an evil character can never be pleasing to "an impartial rational spectator." The only thing that can in all circumstances receive unqualified approval is sincere practical purpose, or "the summoning of all means in our power," to do our duty.   The attainment of this good will is the end for which "reason is properly intended." Even if such good will "should lack the power to accomplish its purpose, . . . like a jewel it would still shine by its own light, as a thing which has its whole value in itself." [6]

But what is involved in this fundamental fact of the common moral consciousness?   It requires, to begin with, that in order to have moral worth an act must be done not only in accord with duty but *from* duty.   That is, one must not only do his duty but do it from a sense of duty; he must act, if his act is to have intrinsic worth, not only *"as duty requires"* but *"because duty requires."*   For example, seeking to preserve one's own life has no moral value when, as is usually the case, it is prompted by impulse; but if an unfortunate man "wishes for death . . . yet preserves his life . . . from duty—then his maxim has moral worth." [7]   Similarly, there is normally no moral worth in seeking one's own happiness; but when the pursuit of one's happiness is prompted by a sense of duty that sets aside pressing inclinations, it may be morally valuable.

If good will cannot be in any sense dependent on inclination but prompts us to act wholly from duty, its action must be action purely from principle or "respect for law."   In other words, if good will cannot be prompted by any inclination or purpose outside itself, it cannot be prompted by anything other than

---

[5] Immanuel Kant, "Fundamental Principles of the Metaphysic of Morals," *Kant's Critique of Practical Reason and Other Works on the Theory of Ethics,* tr. by T. K. Abbott (London: Longmans, Green, 1879), p. 11.

[6] *Ibid.,* p. 13.

[7] *Ibid.,* p. 18.   By *maxim* is meant the rule that is expressed by his action—in this case, that one should preserve his own life.

"the universal conformity of its actions to law in general." Accordingly, "I am never to act otherwise than so *that I could also will that my maxim should become universal law.*" [8]

This principle expresses the underlying meaning of the moral consciousness. It excludes, as moral consciousness does, such evils as the making of lying promises. If "I be content that my maxim (to extricate myself from difficulty by a false promise) should hold good as a universal law, both for myself and others [and that] everyone may make a deceitful promise when he finds himself in a difficulty from which he cannot otherwise extricate himself, . . . there would be no promises at all, since it would be vain to allege my intention in regard to my future actions to those who would not believe this allegation, or if they over-hastily did so would pay me back in my own coin. Hence my maxim, as soon as it should be made a universal law, would necessarily destroy itself." [9] Indeed the principle of suitability to become universal law holds the key not only to the prohibition of lying promises but to all moral duties. "Inexperienced in the course of the world, incapable of being prepared for all its contingencies, I only ask myself: 'Canst thou also will that thy maxim should be a universal law?' " [10] This is the consistency that we ordinarily demand of ourselves and others. It is the principle on which the common man—in so far as he is moral—seeks to act, and in the light of it "we do not need science and philosophy to know what we should do to be honest and good, yea even wise and virtuous." [11]

Nevertheless, the wants and inclinations of man's nature press in upon his reason with such force that they sometimes persuade even reason to argue in their favor against duty. Hence, although basically the application of the fundamental principle of good will is enough to guide him, he needs a more philosophical analysis of morality to counteract the seductions of desire. To Kant's account of such an analysis we now turn.

8 *Ibid.*, p. 25.
9 *Ibid.*, pp. 26–27.
10 *Ibid.*, p. 27.
11 *Ibid.*, p. 28.

THE CATEGORICAL IMPERATIVE

Although the necessity for supplementing the popular account of moral experience with a more profoundly philosophical one in Kant's view rests principally on the danger that conscience may be misled by selfishly prejudiced moralizing, it is also grounded in the nature of moral insight, which is prior to experience and therefore unlikely to be altogether adequately treated in popular discussion. This priority of morality to all experience is evident to the careful inquirer in every phase of morality and must never be lost sight of. Moral principles are not mere generalizations derived from particular cases; rather, full insight into cases depends upon the previous application of rational principles. Although no one is ever completely good, one may nevertheless know what goodness is, for his knowledge of goodness is independent of his having attained goodness. One would not know that God was good if he did not already know what goodness was. Certainly, morality could by no means apply, as it must, to all rational creatures if it were not rooted in a rationality that is logically prior to human experience.

In order to discover the precise nature and demands of the moral faculty, or practical reason, that precedes particular experience, it is necessary to trace this practical reason through other stages until one arrives at the point at which duty in the proper sense "springs from it." Practical reason in general is the same as will, which is the ability to act "according *to the conception* of laws." [12] To have the ability to act in this way when one does not always want to do so is to have an *obligation*. An *imperative* expresses an obligation, or says to a will that does not always do a thing because it is good, "that something would be good to do or to forbear."

Imperatives are basically of two kinds. A hypothetical imperative says that something would be good to do as a means; that is, it commands one to do something *if* he wishes something else. A categorical imperative says that something would be

12 *Ibid.,* pp. 41–42.

good to do in *itself,* or that one ought to do it unconditionally —without any *if.* Hypothetical imperatives may be divided into two subtypes, those of skill and those of prudence. Imperatives of skill, on the one hand, say that one must do a certain thing if he wishes a certain result, whether or not he does actually desire that result. For example, such an imperative might say that if a person is to poison another effectively he must use this or that drug. The question whether or not this effect is desired is irrelevant as far as skill is concerned. Imperatives of prudence, on the other hand, refer to ends that one does actually desire, such as happiness, which is universally sought. Such an imperative might say, for example, that if one wishes to be happy he must preserve his health. A categorical imperative, however, differs from both of these kinds of hypothetical imperatives in that any end result whatever, whether actually desired or not, is irrelevant to it. It commands unconditionally. Hypothetical imperatives have their own technical or pragmatic uses, but only the categorical imperative is a moral imperative.

But what does a categorical imperative say? The answer, in order to be as it should be purely rational, must be found in the bare conception of a categorical imperative. Since the categorical imperative cannot by definition contain anything relating to impulses or desires, it can contain nothing but "the general principle that one's maxim should conform to a universal law." Hence the very idea of an unconditional command yields the following, which is the first form of the categorical imperative: *"Act as if the maxim of thy action were to become by thy will a Universal Law of Nature."* [13] In this manner Kant's philosophical analysis of morality brings him around to the same command that he discovered through his more popular analysis of the meaning of the moral consciousness.

The applicability of this form of the categorical imperative and the manner in which it expresses the sense of duty of mankind may readily be seen in a variety of areas of the moral life.

[13] *Ibid.,* p. 55.

Suppose, in the realm of duty to one's self, a man weary of life wanted to kill himself. His maxim would be: "From self-love I adopt it as a principle to shorten my life when its longer duration is likely to bring more evil than satisfaction." [14] But if he should ask whether or not this "principle of self-love could become a universal law," he would be obliged to answer in the negative, for in such a case the very principle that prompts one to maintain life would be contradicting itself. Such a contradiction is unthinkable. Again, suppose a man in financial distress were prompted to act on such a maxim as the following: "When I think myself in want of money, I will borrow and promise to repay it, although I know I can never do so." [15] If he asked himself whether or not he could will this principle as a universal law, he would realize that in a situation in which all men acted upon such a maxim, "the promise itself would become impossible, as well as the end that one might have in view in it, since no one would consider that anything was promised to him, but would ridicule all such statements as vain pretenses." [16]

To take a case of a somewhat different sort, one might conceive of a society in which all men acted on the principle of neglect of their natural gifts; but he could not will that such a maxim become a universal law; for, "as a rational being, he necessarily wills that his faculties be developed." The situation is similar with respect to the duty of benevolence. One who sees others suffering in wretched poverty might be inclined to say to himself coldly: "Let every one be as happy as heaven pleases or as he can make himself; I will take nothing from him nor even envy him, only I do not wish to contribute anything either to his welfare or to his assistance in distress!" [17] To be sure, a world in which such an attitude prevailed would be thinkable, and indeed in some ways it might be better than the actual one where injustice is prevalent; but it could not be consistently willed for the reason that "many cases might occur

[14] *Ibid.*, p. 56.
[15] *Ibid.*, p. 57.
[16] *Ibid.*
[17] *Ibid.*, p. 58.

in which one would have need of the love and sympathy of others." [18]

When, as in the first two instances named, the maxim of the act cannot without contradiction be even thought of as a universal law, the duty that forbids the action is strict or rigorous. When, as in the last two named, the maxim can be consistently thought of as a universal law but cannot be willed in this way, the duty is laxer. In either case the rightness of an act lies in the fact that it can be consistently willed as a universal law and the wrongness of an act in that it cannot. In this sense, the meaning of right or wrong, for Kant, lies in the consistency or the inconsistency of the principle involved in the performance of the act.

OTHER ASPECTS OF KANT'S MORAL THEORY

The part of Kant's moral system that we have thus far traced includes the essential elements of his ethics in so far as it is an expression of the consistency type of formal theory. However, we should also at least note in passing two other less formal features of his system, not only for their historical interest but also for the light that they throw upon the relation between the formal theory and certain other theories presently to be considered. The first of these features consists of certain other formulations of the categorical imperative, which Kant, perhaps mistakenly, takes to be simply variations of the one already given; the second consists of the famous "postulates of the practical reason," or those assumptions regarding the nature of reality that Kant thinks morality demands.

Variant Forms of the Categorical Imperative

As the previous discussion reveals, a categorical imperative is a command indicating that something would be good to do or ought to be done unconditionally. For a categorical imperative to exist, therefore, there must be some end that has absolute or unconditional worth. Kant believes that such an

[18] *Ibid.*, p. 59.

end is found in man himself: "man and generally any rational being *exists* as an end in himself, not merely as a *means* to be arbitrarily used by this or that will." [19]   This being true, the categorical imperative may be reformulated as follows: *"So act as to treat humanity, whether in thine own person or in that of any other, in every case as an end withal, never as a means only."* [20]

The validity and applicability of this way of putting the basic moral principle may readily be seen in particular cases.   For example, suicide would imply treating one's self, a rational being, as a means to "a tolerable condition up to the end of life"; and therefore it would not be permissible.   Lying promises would be using another person as a means to one's own ends, as would attacks on the freedom or property of another. Even stinginess would fail to harmonize positively with the end of rational creatures and so would be wrong, at least in the laxer or less rigid sense of the word.

One more formulation of the categorical imperative now emerges from the fact that duty is unconditional and independent of all interests.   The only assurance that the universal law to which the will is subject is not relative to some particular interest is that it is given by the rational will itself.   If it were given in any other way, some special and therefore relative attraction would be needed; but if it is given by the will, its command is clearly independent of such relative attractions.   The nature of duty then requires the assumption that every rational will should legislate for itself, that its laws should be *those of its own giving.*   The same principle, which Kant calls the *autonomy of the will,* is indicated by the *dignity* of a rational being, which is violated by obedience to any law other than one "which he himself gives."   Thus the third formulation of the categorical imperative requires us "so to act *that the will could at the same time regard itself as giving in its maxims universal laws."* [21]

19 *Ibid.*, p. 65.
20 *Ibid.*, p. 67.
21 *Ibid.*, p. 75.

The principle of the autonomy of the will does not mean, of course, that one may command himself to do as he pleases; rather, it binds him to the rigid law of practical reason that forbids all that could not be willed universally. But at the same time it forbids his accepting anything as a final sanction of his duty save his own moral reason. Human nature, happiness, even the perfect will of God, yield only commands from the outside and are therefore binding only as they can take hold in one's own rational will.

Postulates of Practical Reason

The second of the less formal features of Kant's ethical system is his discussion of the assumptions that must be made if the demands of moral consciousness are to be meaningful. The special importance of this phase of the system consists for Kant in the fact that he believes that it offers us a glimpse of that which lies beyond anything man can know through theoretical reason. Theoretical reason is always limited by the colored spectacles of space, time, and the forms of thought through which it must view the world, but practical reason enables us to go beyond this limited perspective in that it implies certain assumptions about ultimate reality—hence, the "primacy of the practical reason." Duty is quite as real as anything we know, and the assumptions that it requires of us give us a reflected hint of the nature of "things-in-themselves." These assumptions are the postulates of the practical reason.

The first of these postulates is that of the freedom of the will. It is implied in morality in this manner. If there is a duty or a categorical imperative that is binding upon every rational creature, then every rational creature must be free to do his duty or to obey the imperative. *Ought* implies *can.* To be sure, man as a part of nature is not free; but man's rational will must be free, else morality would be meaningless.

The second postulate is that of immortality, which is implied in morality in a similar manner. The moral law commands perfection, but perfection is not attainable within man's limited span of years. Hence, there must be a life beyond this present life if the command of morality is to have a meaning.

The third postulate is that of the existence of God. It, too, is necessarily implied in the fact of duty. Although duty is never to be determined by happiness, man's sense of duty does require him to believe that happiness should be proportional to moral goodness. But no such proportion exists in this world, for often the just suffer and the wicked prosper. Hence, if this demand of moral reason is to have meaning, men are obliged to assume that there exists a being who guarantees the ultimate establishment of the required relation between happiness and morality. The law of morality "must postulate *the existence of God.*" [22]

CRITICISM OF THE RATIONAL
CONSISTENCY THEORY

Quite apart from the success or failure of Kant's formal theory as such, the ethical thought of Kant contains numerous insights and emphases for which moral philosophy will always be in his debt. Kant has correctly, even if sometimes to excess, insisted upon the fact that the moral life is a life of reason, and that no mere sensing of values and obligations can serve as a satisfactory substitute for clear perception of its fundamental rational principles. His essentially sound, even if somewhat exaggerated, declaration concerning the moral value of good will likewise remains a permanent part of the heritage of ethical thought. Again, Kant's stress on the worth and dignity of a rational creature and his strictures against the treatment of any human being as a mere means are significant contributions to the progress of humanitarianism and democracy. His high-minded insistence upon dutifulness regardless of personal consequences is also a faithful reflection of certain aspects of the best in moral experience. Kant's principle of the autonomy of the will is at the same time a significant insight into the nature of responsibility, an illuminating recognition of what we have previously

[22] Immanuel Kant, "Critique of Practical Reason," *Kant's Critique* . . . , p. 321.

referred to as the subjective sense of right, and a foundation for the self-realization theory, which we shall presently consider. Finally, Kant's moral postulates, although scarcely satisfactory as they stand, involve both acknowledgment of distinguishable aspects of moral experience and a suggestive stimulus to an important type of inquiry into the nature of ultimate reality.

As an interpretation of the meaning of right in formal terms, Kant's theory is essentially sound up to a certain point. It surpasses all of the approval theories in recognizing that the rightness of an act hinges not on attitudes of an observer but on characteristics of the act itself. Again, the theory is correct in calling attention to the fact that appropriate form is among the essential characteristics that a right act must have, for, whatever else a right act may require, no definition of it can be complete, as we shall presently see, without indicating the form suitable to it. Finally, the form that Kant himself proposes seems clearly to be at least a minimum requirement of the right. When a rational creature stops to consider the matter, he can scarcely think that he ought to do what he would forbid others in similar circumstances to do, or fail to do what he would demand of others in like situations. Conduct in accord with this observation is close to the very core of reason's demands in the practical sphere, for the first requirement of reason is consistency and such conduct is nothing but consistency in practice.

Nevertheless, the fact that right involves form does not imply that the whole meaning of right can be interpreted in formal terms; nor, more particularly, does the fact that rational consistency is a minimum requirement of right imply that it is the sole requirement. What one could not will to become a universal law is at least subjectively wrong; but not all that one could so will is objectively right. Much depends on what one could so will, and this in turn depends not only upon rational consistency but also upon the character of one's desires and valuations. When one's purposes become abnormal, what he could will as a universal law is no reliable criterion of right; and when they become extremely distorted, Kant's principle is of virtually no use at all. Indeed, as one critic of Kant has put

it, one can consistently will almost anything provided he does
not care what happens. This dependence of the validity of
Kant's demand for universal applicability upon desires and
valuations may be amply illustrated in terms of the examples
used by Kant himself, in each of which the practical conclusion
at which he arrives is in the end contingent upon the existence
of sound purposes. Consider, for instance, the matter of lying
promises. It is true, of course, that so long as one is concerned
about the significant use of promises he cannot will that everyone should make lying promises; but, provided he does not care
about the failure of his own promises or the chaos that would
result from everyone's making lying promises, there is no
inconsistency in his making such a promise. Again, consider
the problem of suicide. Evidently, if the world of living human
beings is valued, the maxim of seeking relief from discomfort
by taking one's own life cannot be universalized; but then, if
one does not so value living persons, there is nothing inconsistent in the act of suicide.

Fortunately, few people are unconcerned about the use of
promises or the existence of the human race, and Kant would
undoubtedly say that those that are, are not rational. In this
he would be correct if the word rational is used in a broad sense;
but the point is that in order to say that one is rational in this
broad sense, or to render Kant's principle significant, it is necessary to assume that one *is concerned* about these matters, that
is to say, that he *has* certain *desires* and *valuations* as well as
the capacity for formal reasoning. Pure reason is in part the
guide, and in part the servant, of desires and valuations; but,
apart from them, it loses its significance, and, when they become distorted, it is employed for distorted ends, however
formally correct it may remain. This insufficiency of pure
reason unmistakably suggests that perhaps both formal rational
consistency and all other purely formal factors are insufficient by
themselves to represent either the criterion or the meaning of
right, and that a satisfactory theory will have to add to such
formal factors some reference to desires and values. However,

on this point, we must reserve final judgment until we have considered another very different kind of formal theory.

READINGS

Melden, *Ethical Theories,* pp. 292–340; *or*
Clark and Smith, *Readings in Ethics,* pp. 257–78; *or*
Rand, *The Classical Moralists,* pp. 539–58.

QUESTIONS

1. Define each of the following terms as Kant uses it: *good will, imperative, hypothetical imperative, categorical imperative, maxim.*

2. Do you agree with Kant that good will is the only thing unconditionally good? If so, why? If not, how would you answer his arguments on this point? What is the difference between acting in accord with duty and acting from duty? Do you agree that only the latter has moral value? Support your contention.

3. Trace the processes by which Kant passes from the unconditional worth of good will to the requirement of action in accord with law and from the rationality of morality to the categorical imperative. Does the reasoning appear sound in each case?

4. Would the first form of the categorical imperative effectively rule out the following: (a) cheating on a quiz, (b) betraying a secret, (c) Gestapo police methods? Why, or why not, in each case? What would be the bearing of this principle on the problem of government use of "strike injunctions," of manufacture of nuclear weapons?

5. Indicate two current industrial practices that tend to violate Kant's second form of the categorical imperative, two labor union practices, two types of political practices. Do you think the application of this principle of Kant's could solve most current moral problems? Explain.

6. What did Kant mean by the primacy of the "practical reason"? In what sense, if any, do you think "moral experience" affords insights into the nature of ultimate reality? Do you think there are ever instances in which one ought to do what he cannot do? How so? Or if not, why not?

7. Can you think of any case in which one ought to violate the first form of the categorical imperative? Do you think that obeying it

would require people to act rightly in most cases? In all cases? In what kind of cases?

8. In the closing months of World War II Hitler sought to persuade his generals to fight on to death. Apparently he was willing to accept for himself and his people the destruction entailed. Did he violate the first form of the categorical imperative? Did he act rightly? What of the case of the assassin who is willing to be shot down if only he can kill his victim? Or of the jailed criminal who would be glad for all criminals to escape if only he could, too?

REFERENCES

Adler, Felix, *An Ethical Philosophy of Life* (New York: D. Appleton, 1929), Bk. II.

Bradley, F. H., *Ethical Studies* (Oxford: The Clarendon Press, 1927), Essay IV.

Broad, C. D., *Five Types of Ethical Theory* (New York: Harcourt, Brace, 1930), Ch. 5.

Carritt, E. F., *The Theory of Morals* (London: Oxford University Press, 1928), Ch. 9.

Dewey, John, and Tufts, J. H., *Ethics* (rev. ed., New York: Holt, 1932), pp. 238–45.

Ewing, A. C., "The Paradoxes of Kant's Ethics," *Philosophy*, XIII (1938), pp. 40–56.

Hartmann, Nicolai, *Ethics*, tr. by Stanton Coit (New York: Macmillan, 1932), Vol. I, sec. 4.

Kant, Immanuel, *Kant's Critique of Practical Reason and Other Works on the Theory of Ethics*, tr. by T. K. Abbott (London: Longmans, Green, 1879), especially pp. 11–93.

Leys, W. A. R., *Ethics and Social Policy* (New York: Prentice-Hall, 1941), pp. 135–41.

Moore, G. E., *Ethics* (New York: Oxford University Press, 1912; Reset 1947), Ch. 5.

Pratt, J. B., *Reason in the Art of Living* (New York: Macmillan, 1949), Chs. 4–5.

Rashdall, Hastings, *Theory of Good and Evil* (London: Oxford University Press, 1924), Vol. I, Ch. 5.

Roberts, W. H., *The Problem of Choice* (Boston: Ginn, 1941).

Rogers, A. K., *Morals in Review* (New York: Macmillan, 1927), Ch. 16.

—— *The Theory of Ethics* (New York: Macmillan, 1922), Ch. 3.

Schilpp, P. A., *Kant's Pre-critical Ethics* (Evanston, Ill.: Northwestern University, 1938).

Sidgwick, Henry, and Widgery, A. G., *Outlines of the History of Ethics* (London: Macmillan, 1939), pp. 271–77.

Titus, H. H., *Ethics for Today* (2nd ed. rev., New York: American Book, 1954), Ch. 9.

Urban, W. M., *Fundamentals of Ethics* (New York: Holt, 1930), Ch. 3.

5

Formal Theories:
Moral Suitability, Ross

THE WRITERS WHOM WE ARE now to consider agree with Kant that the rightness of an act lies in its formal character. Instead of making the determining factor a purely rational property that can be defined without specific reference to circumstances, however, they find the meaning of "right" in the relation of the act to its circumstances. More precisely, they see the meaning of "right" in a unique kind of fitness of an act to its situation, which they commonly refer to as moral suitability.

A few illustrations drawn from other fields should help to clarify the central point. In tennis, when one's opponent is far to the left, the competitively suitable placement is far to the right. In painting a touch of color that blends with the surrounding shades and highlights an important part of the whole picture is aesthetically suitable. In a play a saying that expresses the situation in a single striking phrase is dramatically suitable. Similarly, in practical life certain acts that fit their circumstances may be morally suitable; thus, for example, to keep one's promise is the act suitable to circumstances in which one has bound himself by a promise, and to pay a debt is suitable to circumstances in which such payment has become due.

Among the earliest philosophical suggestions of this view are some of the sayings of Plato, who held that the soul has immediate insight into ideal patterns in terms of which actions are rightly related to their settings.   Early in the modern era the so-called Cambridge Platonists, following this lead, held that it is possible to perceive immutable laws of morality. They, in turn, were supported by the Scottish Common Sense School of which Thomas Reid, who taught that common sense immediately recognizes the self-evidence of basic moral principles, was the chief exponent.   Some aspects of Butler's thought are quite in line with this approach to ethics.   Indeed, many of those who insist upon the central role of conscience in all moral matters—if they avoid confusing the discerning process of conscience with the thing that conscience discerns—really believe that the rightness perceived by conscience is moral suitability.   Thus, many a plain man basically believes that in discovering the right his conscience is simply recognizing a special kind of fitness.   In the contemporary period an extremely influential group of British philosophers, frequently referred to as the New Intuitionists, have undertaken to give philosophical expression to this belief.   These writers differ somewhat from the older champions of moral suitability in that, instead of trying to defend particular moral principles as always fitting, they insist upon a distinctness in moral situations that prohibits any attempt to lay down absolute moral laws in advance and requires moral suitability, in the last analysis, to be directly recognized afresh in every new situation.   The chief representatives of this school include H. A. Prichard, E. F. Carritt, C. D. Broad, and W. D. Ross.

On the whole, the most satisfactory presentation of the moral suitability theory appears in Ross's *Foundations of Ethics*.[1] This book has the merit not only of stressing specific suitability, which is insisted on by the latest and most plausible version of the theory, but also of giving due consideration to such moral principles as the older versions stressed.

---

[1] Ross's earlier work, *The Right and the Good* (Oxford: The Clarendon Press, 1930), is a less comprehensive statement of the same views.

RIGHT AS A UNIQUE KIND OF SUITABILITY

The rightness of right acts cannot, Ross thinks, consist in mere approval, since in judging an act to be right one says something about the act and not simply about someone's attitude. Nor can it be pleasantness, for no one really means *pleasant* when he says *right*. Moreover, it cannot be solely the production of the greatest possible good, no matter how good is defined, for such right acts as telling the truth or promoting a just *distribution* of happiness do not necessarily produce the greatest possible good.

In truth, it is impossible to state precisely what moral right is because such right is unique. There are no precise parallels or other terms to which it may be reduced. Right is right, and to try to make anything else of it is to lose it. It is simply itself and nothing else. It is therefore indefinable in the sense in which a certain color sensation as such is indefinable. No one can know about it until he sees it. No words can adequately describe it.

However, moral rightness has a certain kinship with other kinds of rightness that suggest its meaning by analogy. A "right road," or a "right key," for example, is a road or key that is fitting to a "particular situation in which some one is placed." [2] That is, the right road leads where one wants to go, and the right key opens the door that one wants to open. Similarly, an act that fits the whole situation in a certain manner is morally right. Thus "moral suitability" is what right means. To be more precise, an act is right if it has "the greatest amount of suitability possible under the circumstances." [3]

But just what is the *certain manner* in which an act must be suitable to be right, or what is it that distinguishes moral suitability from any other kind of suitability? According to Ross it is just this aspect of right that is indefinable and altogether unique. There is nothing else quite like the peculiarly moral aspect of moral suitability; it may be recognized but not de-

[2] W. D. Ross, *Foundations of Ethics* (Oxford: The Clarendon Press, 1939), p. 51.
[3] *Ibid.*, p. 53.

scribed or explained.   Perhaps Ross's meaning may be made clearer by an analogy.   One can define an order as a regular arrangement of things or events.   He can also define time as a certain kind of order, and he can readily recognize the kind of order that he means.   But he cannot quite put into words the peculiar quality of the order that he calls "time," for there is nothing comparable to it, and if any man is unable to see it for himself further words will not help him.   The distinctively moral element in moral suitability is similar to time in its uniqueness, and right is an indefinable sort of suitability to circumstances.

THE KINDS OF ACTS THAT TEND TO BE
MORALLY SUITABLE

Although the peculiarly moral element in moral suitability cannot be defined, it can be illustrated by reference to some of the varieties of acts that always tend to have it.   If a description of these acts does not disclose what right means, it at least points out the kinds of things that are likely to be right.   Such acts are more restricted forms of the right of which moral suitability is the general form.

One impressive variety of the acts that tend to be morally suitable consists in doing the most good [4] possible under the circumstances, for clearly if one has no other urgent duties the most fitting thing that he can do in any circumstances is to try to bring about as much of that which is desirable as he possibly can, and it is indeed doubtful whether there is any act that is right that produces no good at all.   At the same time acts that result in the production of maximum good constitute only one of several kinds of acts that tend to be morally suitable.   Others include types of action often referred to as "special obligations," such as the repayment of benefits, the keeping of promises, and

---

[4] Ross devotes considerable attention to the question of the general meaning of good, which he takes to be worthiness of approval, as well as to that of the meaning of moral good, which he finds dependent on motives.   But since neither of these topics belongs to the strictly formal part of Ross's theory, we pass them by here.

restitution for injuries, because favors done to us, promises made by us, and injuries inflicted by us are all circumstances that call for special responses. Moreover, special obligations are quite independent of, capable of conflict with, and may at times take precedence over, the obligation to promote the most possible good. For example, a person who has promised to pay a sum of money to another at a certain time has no right to defer payment on the ground that somewhat more good might be done by giving the money to a charitable cause; nor has one who has received special benefits from another the right to bestow his own favors on the single principle of doing the most good, without any regard for the benefits he has received. Any one of the special obligations is also capable of conflicting with any other. For example, one's promised payment of a debt may interfere with his compensating for an injury or this latter effort may tend to prevent his fulfillment of the proper claims of those who have been especially kind to him.

TOTAL RIGHT

Although Ross finds the basic forms to which right acts must conform in the kinds of obligations we have just indicated, he is altogether too sensible to insist, with some ethical theorists and many nonphilosophical moralists, that these patterns of action are never to be violated under any circumstances or that the sort of act involved in any one of them is always right. He is fully aware, for example, that the evil involved in the repayment of a debt or the telling of the truth to a dangerous criminal who is likely to use the payment or the truth to destroy others may be sufficient to override the obligation to pay the debt or to tell the truth. Similarly, it is perfectly clear to him that the duty to repay a benefit or to make restitution for a wrong may sometimes properly require failure to fulfill the obligation to pay a debt promptly when it is due. Moral situations are complex, and Ross warns that an act may be right in some respects and wrong in others. It is for this reason that all of the forms of

conduct discussed above are, for him, only *prima facie* obligations, that is, acts that are at first sight right, or tend to be right.[5]

Total rightness is moral suitability when all the *prima facie*
obligations involved in it are taken into consideration; that is,
when all the obligations to all the persons concerned are given
their proper weight, when all the respects in which it is right or
wrong are duly recognized.   It is only this totally right act that
actually ought to be done.   *Prima facie* obligations are simply
factors that should be seriously considered.   Thus the form in
which rightness consists is its total suitability to its situation, including all of the obligations involved in its various aspects.   If,
for example, I want to know what I ought to do with a certain
sum of money, I must consider not only the good that can be
done with it but also my debts, my duties to my benefactors, my
responsibilities to those whom I may have injured, my promises
and any other *prima facie* obligations that may be involved in
my present situation.   Only that which is right in the light of
all such pertinent factors is really right, however insistent any
one obligation may seem to be by itself.

How should one proceed toward a practical solution of a problem involving conflicting *prima facie* obligations?   Ross answers
that just as knowledge of such obligations was originally arrived
at by generalizing from direct moral insights into particular
situations, so the solution of a complex moral problem must also
depend ultimately on direct moral insight into the particular
situation.   In such a situation I may and should weigh the
various obligations involved and sum up as far as possible the
various goods.   Nevertheless, the final moral judgment must
depend upon an immediate comprehensive intuition.   I shall
in the end either see the correct answer or not see it; I cannot
deduce it.   Thus, for example, in deciding how I use limited
funds that seem to be required equally by my duties to my
benefactors and by the needs of other people, I must compare
the good results that could be achieved by various uses of the
funds and measure the various obligations, and all this will help

[5] Ross, *Foundations of Ethics*, pp. 84 ff.

to illuminate the problem, but the final judgment will be a direct recognition of the act that involves the maximum moral suitability on the whole.

CRITICAL EVALUATION OF THE MORAL SUITABILITY THEORY

The moral suitability theory shares with the consistency theory a correct recognition that rightness involves a formal element, for, as we have said, rightness can scarcely be intelligibly identified without reference to form of action.   At the same time the formal factor of suitability to circumstances is much more specifically applicable to the particular actions whose rightness or wrongness must be judged than is the consistency upon which Kant relied.   Indeed suitability to circumstances seems clearly, in the light of everyone's intentions in using moral terms, to be at least one requirement of any act that is right.   It may be also affirmed, on the basis of the intentions commonly involved in the critical use of moral terms, that what Ross calls *prima facie* obligations really are such forms as tend to be applicable to acts that are right.   Moreover, recognition of both the general requirement of suitability and the tendency of Ross's *prima facie* obligations to be right is entirely compatible with the moral truths that we have discovered from other theories.   Suitability in general, and the promotion of good, the paying of debts, the keeping of promises, and compensating for injuries in particular are all clearly approvable alike by society, by enlightened conscience, and by God; they can also be willed consistently.   Nor indeed is any moral theory subsequently to be discussed likely to offer plausible grounds for contradicting them.   Moral theorists may not agree concerning what suitability means or even whether or not it means by itself anything definite enough to distinguish right from wrong, and different writers may hold various opinions concerning why the keeping of promises and the fulfillment of other special obligations are right; but virtually no moralist would question the fact that a moral act is a suitable one or that the paying of debts, the keeping of promises, and the like tend to be morally obligatory. To this extent the basic intentions of common sense and the analyses of moral theories are agreed, and both are indebted to such moralists as Ross for giving clear expression to these aspects of morality.

However, this theory, so well begun in insisting upon the requirement of suitability and the tendency of special obligations to be right, remains inadequate at the point of distinguishing moral suitability from other kinds of suitability and reconciling its special obligations with one another.   To be told in answer to inquiry about the meaning of right that the right act is the one that is morally suitable to its circumstances seems significant, but to be told in answer to further inquiry concerning the distinguishing mark of *moral* suitability that although there are certain kinds of acts that tend to be morally suitable, such suitability is really a unique factor that must be directly intuited is to be disappointed at the crucial point.   No additional information is furnished about the characteristic in which rightness consists and in one respect we are left even more bewildered than before: we are now confronted with conflicting *prima facie* obligations for the reconciliation of which with one another we are given no guiding principle.   At this point, although the moral suitability theory avoids the theoretical paradoxes involved in the conscience theory by placing rightness in the act rather than in someone's judgment, it is *practically* no more illuminating than the conscience theory, for both require reliance solely upon the individual's immediate insight without in any way indicating what property this insight is to look for.   Both, in effect, are like a geometry that, in answer to the question of what a circle is, instead of replying that a circle is a closed figure having each point on its circumference equidistant from a given point, simply says that a circle is what you perceive a circle to be, thereby helping to locate the judge of circularity but saying nothing about its character.

The difficulty in question, of which Ross and other advocates of the moral suitability theory are of course aware, is not, however, simply a practical one.   It represents, rather, a more fundamental refusal to undertake the full responsibility of moral

philosophy, namely, to set forth as clear and coherent an interpretation as possible of the real intentions involved in people's
actual use of moral terms.   Careful examination of the use of
the term right readily reveals that the intent behind this use is
not such that no reasons can be given for the rightness of a thing.
To be sure, we do sometimes speak of the rightness of an act as
though the fact that it was seen settled the matter.   But, then,
in cases of conflict we always demand, or expect to give, reasons.
Moreover, even when no conflict is involved, we believe, when
we say that an act is right, that we are saying something that can
be supported with reasons and that we should be ready upon
demand to give reason for the moral faith that is in us.   Nor
is this reference to reasons, as the suitability theorists are inclined to suppose, ultimately paradoxical or misleading.   Although genuine distinguishing characteristics of right and wrong
do not lie immediately upon the surface, they are clearly implicit in moral judgments and they can be consistently stated,
provided values as well as formal factors are taken into consideration.   More than one moral theory has, as we shall see, closely
approximated them, and at least one has apparently furnished a
fairly accurate account of them.   Accordingly, at any rate pending the careful consideration of these theories, we must reject the
effort of the moral suitability theory to restrict moral philosophy
to limits that seem clearly to be narrower than the intentions of
ordinary moral judgments, and we must persevere—despite this
theory—in our efforts to discover a distinguishing characteristic
of right that is both practically usable and theoretically accurate.

CONCLUSIONS CONCERNING FORMAL THEORIES

Before we resume our quest a further remark or two on formal
theories in general may prove suggestive.   These theories correctly insist that the meaning of right involves reference to forms,
and rational consistency, suitability to circumstances, and even
some of the *prima facie* duties do tend to be requisites of right
actions.   But neither consistency nor suitability nor any other

formal factor seems to be sufficient in itself to distinguish right from wrong in any such way as actual moral judgments intend to do, and therefore no formal factor appears to represent an adequate account of the meaning of right. Moreover, the inadequacy of the two major formal principles that we have considered seems to be rooted in the fact that they fail to take sufficient account of value considerations. This conclusion suggests that perhaps the criterion of right for which we are searching is to be found in terms of some method in which values or ends, as well as forms, are fully considered. To such theories we now turn.

READINGS

Sellars and Hospers, *Readings in Ethical Theory,* pp. 163–197.

QUESTIONS

1. What do the administration of justice according to laws and the playing of a game according to the rules have in common with doing the morally right act?

2. Is suitability to its circumstances a characteristic of every right action? Does this mean that if an act is suitable it is right? Would Ross say so? If so, why? If not, what more would he require of a right act?

3. Is it always right to keep one's promises, pay one's debts, and make restitution for injuries? (Consider all sorts of cases.) Does each always tend to be right? Will each always be right provided there are no conflicting obligations? Do you think such duties need special emphasis or are they sufficiently covered by the duty to do the most possible good? Explain.

4. A high government official has solemnly promised on behalf of his government to make a payment on a debt on a certain date, but meanwhile monetary values have altered and his nation has become impoverished, so that to pay would be a great hardship for his people and little help to their creditors. He now has it in his power to pay or not to pay. A young man has promised to meet a friend promptly at eight o'clock and he knows she is counting upon him and

will be embarrassed if he does not appear, but shortly before the appointed hour his mother who lives alone with him becomes ill and there is no way to inform the young lady. How would Ross say one should go about resolving such problems as these? What answers do you think he would arrive at?

5. In a few places in the world head-hunting seems still to be regarded not only as a right but as a duty, whereas to most of us such a custom seems barbarous. Many people strongly believe that any sort of deception that serves the ends of a constituted government is legitimate or even commendable patriotism; others are equally certain that such deception is wrong. How do you think Ross would undertake to meet the sort of difficulty involved in these conflicts?

6. Are Ross' suggestions about comparing obligations and relying on intuitions helpful in the kinds of cases suggested in the two preceding groups of questions? Are they sufficient? Does common sense moral reasoning stop with them? Do you think critical moral inquiry must stop with them?

REFERENCES

Historical

Rand, Benjamin, *The Classical Moralists* (Boston: Houghton Mifflin, 1937), Chs. 2, 15, 16, 21, 24, 33, 34.

Contemporary

Bergson, Henri, *The Two Sources of Morality and Religion,* tr. by R. A. Audra and Cloudesley Brereton (New York: Holt, 1935).

Broad, C. D., *Five Types of Ethical Theory* (New York: Harcourt, Brace, 1930), especially Chs. 6–7.

Carritt, E. F., *The Theory of Morals* (London: Oxford University Press, 1928), especially Chs. 8, 9, 16.

Ewing, A. C., *The Definition of Good* (New York: Macmillan, 1947), especially Chs. 4–6.

Hill, T. E., *Contemporary Ethical Theories* (New York: Macmillan, 1950), Ch. 19.

Pratt, J. B., *Reason in the Art of Living* (New York: Macmillan, 1949), Ch. 2.

Pritchard, H. A., "Does Moral Philosophy Rest on a Mistake?" *Mind*, XXI (1912).

—— *Duty and Interest* (Oxford: The Clarendon Press, 1928).

Ross, W. D., *Foundations of Ethics* (Oxford: The Clarendon Press, 1939), especially Chs. 1, 3, 4, 11, 12.

—— *The Right and the Good* (Oxford: The Clarendon Press, 1930).

Wheelwright, Philip, *A Critical Introduction to Ethics* (rev. ed., New York: Odyssey Press, 1949), Ch. 5.

6

Universal Nature Theories:
Stoicism

IF THE MEANINGS OF moral terms are not to be found either in anyone's approval or in forms of the act, then presumably they are to be sought mainly in the ends or goals of the act. Hence all of the theories remaining to be considered here belong to the second, or teleological, division of objective ethical theories. They all find the meanings of moral terms primarily in the ends or goals sought by the actions to which these terms are attributed.

Before entering specifically upon the study of teleological theories, however, we must pause to clarify certain distinctions that have thus far been allowed to remain somewhat blurred. Our discussion of the moral terms "right" and "good" has, for the most part, proceeded almost as though what could be said of the meaning of one of these terms could be said of the meaning of the other also. This procedure has not been quite correct, even regarding the theories considered, for, in almost any theory, each term involves aspects not intended in the other. Since both terms have been taken in their moral senses, no serious confusion has so far resulted. But, when we come to the teleological theories, a sense of "good" begins to come to the fore that is not strictly moral, and this general sense of "good" must be clearly distinguished from the moral sense before either can be properly related to "right." The term "good" in its *moral* sense refers to actions that are believed to be right and are done from praiseworthy motives. However, we often use the term "good" in a broader sense to refer to that which is valuable, desirable, or worth having without regard to its rightness or to the motives involved. What is said to be good in this sense may or may not be done from good motives, but, in calling it good, one is concerned only with the fact that it is valuable and not with the motives as such. Most morally good acts are also instances of the good in this general sense, but by no means all that is good in this general sense is necessarily morally good. Thus, for example, an act of kindness, or one of self-denial in the interest of fairness, is both good and morally good, but a pleasant conversation, a delightful meal, or a mystical experience may be good without being morally good.

Obviously the good in this general sense will not correspond nearly so closely with the right as will the good in the moral sense, but the general sense of "good" may nevertheless turn out to be more useful in defining "right" than the moral sense. Since the right, in teleological theories, consists in achieving ends, and the good, in the general sense, refers to the valuable, or to ends worth seeking, the right will be related to the generally good as that which tends to achieve it most fully. Accordingly, although the term "good" has previously been used mainly in the moral sense, it is with "good" in the more general sense that we shall from now on be primarily concerned. We shall need, as a rule, to determine what a teleological theory means by "good" before we can indicate its definition of "right."

Among the most comprehensive of possible ends is that suggested by the order of nature, and some writers have taken this to be the end aimed at in right action. Thus, rightness comes to be identified with *naturalness* or conformity to the ends of nature. Those who have sought the meaning of right in this manner have interpreted naturalness in at least two significantly different ways. One way has been to regard nature as a whole as setting the norms of morals and therefore to interpret right as conformity to nature in its comprehensiveness. The other way has been to focus attention more specifically upon the moving developing process in nature commonly called "evolution," and to define right in terms of conformity to the ends of this process. We shall refer to the first as the "universal nature theory" and to the second as the "evolutionary theory." In the present chapter we are concerned only with the first.

Moralists who adopt this first type of nature theory hold that all men are integral parts of a universal nature, which they take to be a single whole that is rational throughout. They believe that rightness consists in conformity to universal nature through submissive acceptance of and active obedience to the demands of this nature as revealed in natural events and in the character of the rational natures with which universal nature has endowed men.

This type of theory has been extremely influential in political and in moral thought. On the political side, it has played a considerable part in molding the ideas out of which modern democratic institutions, including those of the United States, have emerged; for example, our Declaration of Independence demands for our people "the separate and equal status to which the laws of nature, and of nature's God, entitle them." As a moral theory, it has had numerous philosophical advocates both in the ancient and in the modern world. However, its fountain-head and its best expressions are to be found in the classical Stoic philosophy, which shaped the thought and life of many of the noblest characters during the periods of the decline of Greece, the ascendency of Rome, and some later periods as well.

Stoicism is not a unified system of thought or the product of any one writer. However, it does tend to revolve about a central core of thought and in attempting to illustrate the universal nature theory in terms of it we shall, without attempting to distinguish its separate branches, simply draw such material as is representative of the aspect of Stoicism that concerns us from the three most notable Stoic philosophers. The first of these is Zeno, the retired merchant founder of the school, who came to live in Athens in the early part of the third century B.C. The second is the liberated slave Epictetus, who taught in Rome in the first century B.C. The third is the celebrated Roman Emperor, Marcus Aurelius, who ruled Rome in the second century B.C.

THE GOOD AS NATURE'S ORDER

In the early half of the fourth century B.C., when a measure of political freedom still existed in Greece, Plato could speak of the good as an ideal form to be realized in the State and in the individual, for there was yet ground for hope that such an ideal might be realized. However, by the close of that century freedom and hope had diminished in Greece to such an extent that, to the people of Zeno's generation, any ideal that could not be shown to be the actual objective of some process more tangible and forceful than the philosopher's thought would have appeared an impossible dream. In the circumstances, the Epicureans, chief opponents of the Stoics, found the good in pleasure, which was clearly the objective of the actual efforts of many men, including some very clearheaded ones. Such a goal, however, seemed to the Stoics unworthy of human beings and in any case impossible of attainment. Accordingly they turned in their search for the meaning of good to the objectives of a process that was far more fundamental than the pathetic search of selfish men for pleasure, to those of nature herself. Thus, good came to mean for them that which nature seeks. The good was the natural, and the things for which nature strove were the things that were good. Moreover, the good for the universe and the good for man were the same. Thus Zeno reminded his followers that the end and chief good of their lives was "life in agreement with nature." [1] Marcus Aurelius, in like manner, advised his disciples, "Accept everything that happens, even if it seems disagreeable, because it leads to this, the health of the universe." [2]

To be sure, such a conception of good could scarcely be held without certain rather definite assumptions about nature. If, for example, nature were—as the Epicureans and some nineteenth-century scientists have claimed—merely a vast purpose-

---

[1] Diogenes Laertius, *Lives and Opinions of Eminent Philosophers,* tr. by R. D. Hicks (Cambridge: Harvard University Press, 1938), vii, 87.
[2] Marcus Aurelius Antoninus, *The Meditations of the Emperor Marcus Aurelius Antoninus,* tr. by George Long (New York: A. L. Burt, 1864), v, 8.

less machine, one could not assert that good referred to the ends
of nature, for nature would have no ends.   Unless the universe
has rational order, one cannot define good in terms of its ends.
The Stoics definitely adopted the view that nature is a rational
purposive order.   Although it is a material order, its matter is
penetrated at every point by an active intelligent principle.
Every part depends on every other part and the whole is rational, never doing anything without a purpose.   The material
part can be thought of as the body of God and the rational part
as God himself.   Moreover, God is a God of providence, who
orders all things for the best for His creatures, bestowing the
favors of mind and of the possibility of virtue upon them and
blessing them with discipline and opportunity for moral victory
even in the hardships of life.   One must not be deceived into
thinking that nature is evil or indifferent because it brings
floods, earthquakes, and disease upon man, for these things cannot be evil if nature sends them.   One must recognize that the
things that are good for man are not comfort and security and
pleasure but such wisdom and virtue as are found in nature.

RIGHT AS CONFORMITY TO NATURE

Like most of the philosophers of the ancient world, the Stoics
do not make extensive use of the word "right"; but they do speak
of virtue and of what men should do in ways that are sufficiently
close to the usage of "right" to show us what their idea of what
we call "right" is.   Since they think of the good in terms of the
ends of nature, we might well expect them to define "right"
in terms of the realization of these ends, and this is very close
to what they do.   We would, Epictetus declares, "help on nature" if it were possible to peer into the future to see where nature was going next, but since that is impossible, "it is appropriate
that we should hold fast to the things that are by nature fit to be
chosen; for indeed we are born for this." [3]   The right, for the
Stoic, is the nearest possible approach to a definite effort to fore-

[3] Epictetus, *Discourses and Manual*, tr. by P. E. Matheson (New York: Oxford
University Press, 1916), ii, 10.

see and advance the purposes of nature. It is conformity to the present requirements of nature as far as we can see them.

The Stoic philosophers never tire of reminding men on all sorts of occasions to follow nature. Diogenes, the Cynic, affirms that our task is "to act with good reason in the selection of what is natural." [4] Epictetus exhorts his followers to adopt "a way of life in harmony with nature." [5] He further contends that since men differ as to the application of their ideas of holiness and justice, their special need is to learn to apply these conceptions "to particular occasions in accordance with nature." [6] To this end it is of no avail to understand what the great teachers have said *about* the will of nature; rather, one must "understand the will of Nature." [7] Marcus Aurelius is equally zealous to have his followers keep in tune with nature. Fear of nature is foolish; for "if any one is afraid of an operation of nature he is a child," [8] and "nothing is evil which is according to nature." [9] "Judge every word and deed which is according to nature to be fit for thee. . . . Go straight on, following thy own nature and the common nature." "Do not look around thee to discover other men's ruling principles, but look straight to this, to what nature leads thee." [10]

SPECIFIC REQUIREMENTS OF CONFORMITY
TO NATURE

Conformity to nature is, after all, a rather general requirement. Just what does one do to conform to nature? The Stoics put their answer in terms of a number of definite demands, which, although not entirely distinct from one another, emphasize somewhat different requirements of cooperation with the universe.

[4] Diogenes Laertius, *op. cit.*, vii, 88.
[5] Epictetus, *op. cit.*, i, 6.
[6] *Ibid.*, 22.
[7] *Ibid.*, 17.
[8] Marcus Aurelius Antoninus, *op. cit.*, ii, 11.
[9] *Ibid.*, 17.
[10] *Ibid.*, v, 2, and vii, 55.

Cheerful Acceptance of Misfortune

The most conspicuous of these requirements is that men submit to the decrees of nature—that they willingly, or even cheerfully, accept whatever destiny may have in store for them. If virtue is doing nature's bidding, the least that one can do is to accept her decrees without rebellion or gloom. Thus the Stoic philosopher repeatedly exhorts his followers to receive graciously whatever takes place. Each must "be pleased and content with what happens and with the thread which is spun for him." [11] Nature is a whole and we are but parts of it. It behooves the part to yield to the whole. No matter what apparent losses may be involved for us we must not give way to selfish grief. Is it loss of fortune? This is a part of our natural destiny. Is it the decline of health and vitality? This is the way of the universe. We must learn to be ready to give up easily even our children and friends, whispering to ourselves as we tenderly kiss our children, "Tomorrow you will die," and as we greet our friends, "Tomorrow you or I shall go away and we shall see one another no more." [12] Death is according to nature and is no more a cause for weeping than the harvesting of ears of corn. How else could there be room for new generations if the older ones did not pass away? Nature gives and nature takes away. We must rejoice in what she gives rather than weep over what she takes away. We must put ourselves in tune with all that she does: "Everything harmonizes with me, which is harmonious to thee, O Universe. Nothing for me is too early nor too late, which is in due time for thee. Everything is fruit to me which thy seasons bring, O Nature; from thee are all things, in thee are all things, to thee all things return." [13] Submission to nature is to the Stoic what submission to the will of God is to the Christian; indeed the Stoic sometimes uses the same language as the Christian in this

11 *Ibid.*, iii, 16.
12 Epictetus, *op. cit.*, iii, 24.
13 Marcus Aurelius Antoninus, *op. cit.*, iv, 23.

connection.   Asked what he means by nature, Epictetus replies, "I mean God's will."   When one keeps in mind this characteristic tendency of Stoicism to identify God and nature, the fundamental obligation to submit to nature becomes a matter of piety, any murmuring against the course of events being a rebellion of man's spirit against God.   Accordingly, "the good man" is one who "has submitted his mind to Him that orders the universe, as good citizens submit to the law of the city."[14]   He makes no complaint if he is crippled lest he foolishly "arraign the universe for one wretched leg."   Rather he will "joyfully yield it up to Him who gave it."[15]   He does not pray, "How shall I not lose my little son?"; but, rather, "How shall I not be afraid to lose him?"[16]   Epictetus advises, "Ask not that events should happen as you will, but let your will be that events should happen as they do, and you shall have peace."[17]   Marcus Aurelius is unwilling to question Providence; "the gods have determined about me and about the things that must happen to me and they have determined well."[18]   The favorite lines of Epictetus are these: "Lead me, O Zeus, and lead me, Destiny, Whither ordained is by your decree."   This servant of Zeus is ready both to go and to remain where God sends him.   When circumstances become difficult, he will not rashly desert through suicide the post given him by his commander, although when he is led into circumstances in which he can no longer continue to live honorably, he will regard this as the signal for his departure.

Conformity to Human Nature

A second requirement involved in conformity to nature is conformity to that part of nature which is our own.   To be true to nature as a whole we must be true to our nature as human beings, for this nature also belongs to the whole of nature.   Hence

---

14 *Ibid.,* i, 12.
15 *Ibid.,* 22.
16 *Ibid.,* ix, 40.
17 Epictetus, *op. cit.,* "Manual," 8.
18 Marcus Aurelius Antoninus, *op. cit.,* vi, 44.

Marcus Aurelius warns his followers to "turn not away from anything that belongs to an intelligent animal" [19] and "to do what is according to the nature of the rational and social animal." Epictetus in like manner admonishes men, "Look to it then that you do nothing like a wild beast, else you destroy the Man in you and fail to fulfil his promise." [20]

By way of interpreting the idea of following human nature, the Stoic brings to light a number of interesting thoughts, two of which are to be noted here. For one thing the Stoic seems to have a fairly clear idea of what we generally call conscience. He describes it as "the intelligence that guides to the things which appear suitable," [21] and insists that if one is to be truly human he must live by it. Then again, the Stoic holds that man's nature is social. Indeed, in his view, "we are made for co-operation, like feet, like hands, like eyelids, like the rows of upper and lower teeth." "To act against one another is then contrary to nature." [22] Every man is a son of Zeus who "has so created the nature of the rational animal, that he can attain nothing good for himself, unless he contributes some service to the community." [23] Being a son of Zeus a man must also remember that he is a brother to every man. He is also a citizen not of Athens or of Rome but of the universe. His role is therefore that of a brother and fellow-citizen of all. These broad ties should not make him unmindful of the bonds of family and friendship, which bind him to the extent that natural affection indicates, but they should prevent his being so much absorbed in the interests of those closest to him that he forgets his larger obligations.

Concentration upon What Is in One's Power

A third requirement involved in conformity to nature, which follows from the ideas of submission to universal nature and

---

[19] *Ibid.*, iii, 7.
[20] Epictetus, *op. cit.*, iii, 9.
[21] Marcus Aurelius Antoninus, *op. cit.*, iii, 16.
[22] Diogenes Laertius, *op. cit.*, iii, 16.
[23] Epictetus, *op. cit.*, i, 19.

conformity to man's nature, is the demand that one concentrate upon what is within his own power and learn simply to accept what is not in his power.

Universal nature in her providential wisdom has placed certain things—namely, our thoughts and our feelings—within our control. These things are, accordingly, the essential elements in our human nature and our only real concern in life. The same nature has placed certain other things—including "body, property, reputation, office"—beyond our control and outside the capacities of our natures. Therefore, if we are to follow nature and human nature, we must focus our attention upon what is in our control and not concern ourselves about what is not. Indeed we must so direct our thoughts and feelings as to make ourselves indifferent to things beyond our reach. These things seem good or bad only because men think them so, and if we discipline ourselves to see that they are no affairs of ours, we shall be completely secure amid all the changes of fortune. No external evil can ever hurt a good man, for his good resides within the realm of his own thought and feeling which cannot be shaken by misfortune, imprisonment, or death.

Wisdom

A fourth requirement of conformity to nature is, like the third, dependent upon the idea of obedience both to universal nature and to human nature, which universal nature has formed. It is the demand that one live a life of reason or wisdom. Nature herself is rational through and through, and to conform to her is to act as far as possible with a wisdom like hers. The place of our own human souls among other kinds of souls is clear evidence of nature's purpose for us in this regard. Nature has given vegetable souls to the plants and animal souls to the beasts; but to man she has given a rational soul, and this imposes upon man a peculiarly compelling obligation to be reasonable in the conduct of his life. This obligation is fundamental to the Stoic, almost as much so as the idea of conformity to nature itself. His good man is, like Socrates, always a sage and philosopher under all circumstances, remembering that true philosophy and wisdom are both practical and theoretical and that the rational life is reason in practice.[24]

Virtue

This brings us to a final demand of conformity to nature. Nature requires of us—and the Stoics are zealous in reinforcing the requirement—that we live strictly in accord with the demands of virtue. This requirement demands in practice achievement of the traditional Greek virtues of justice, temperance and courage, all of which the Stoics interpreted in a lofty and uncompromising manner. Virtue was not to the Stoic a means to an end; it was itself, as the way of nature, the supreme end of man. It was the only good and this fact was the bulwark of the security of the good man; for although one may take away the possessions or even the life of a virtuous man, no one can take away his virtue.[25]

CRITICAL EVALUATION OF THE UNIVERSAL NATURE THEORY

Apart from its structure as a universal nature theory, Stoicism has made several notable and important contributions to moral thought and life. For example, its insistence upon the necessity of reason in the moral life, the high place that it accords to virtue among the values, and its emphasis upon a man's social nature and the brotherhood of all men have all entered the stream of moral thought and become a part of the best moral practice. Moreover, the Stoic formula of concentration upon what is in our power is a notable contribution to the recipe for happiness; for although we may wish to remind the Stoic that property, health, and reputation are not altogether beyond our control, we must agree with him that worry about them beyond the point

---

[24] *Ibid.*, "Manual," 52.

[25] It should be noted that in many respects reason and "virtue for virtue's sake" are as fundamental principles in the loosely knit structure of stoic ethics as is conformity to nature.

at which our control over them ceases only leads to needless suffering and hurtful rebellion.

However, it is as a universal nature theory that Stoicism particularly interests us at the moment. We have seen that formal theories fail to connect morality sufficiently closely with life by ignoring ends and values and defining right only in terms of forms. From this point of view the chief merit of Stoicism, as a universal nature theory, lies in the fact that while retaining a formal element (conformity to nature), it insists that right has a reference to the ends (the ends of nature). One who searches for the solution of moral problems now has something more than contentless patterns to guide him. Whatever his remaining difficulties, an actual process that he can observe and follow has been pointed out to him as the place in which he is to look for moral guidance. Moreover, the right is for the Stoic not merely a severe command that furnishes no reason for obedience but the service of the values entailed in ends in accordance with which all creation seems to move. Finally, the natural process by reference to which Stoicism finds the meaning of morality has, upon any account of the matter, a significant relation to morality. Man lives his life as a part of an order vastly greater than himself. He never attains a satisfactory understanding of himself or of his ends until he becomes aware of his place in the whole of things. He certainly is incapable of knowing *how to obtain* his ends apart from knowledge of the facts of nature. Hence, whether or not harmony with nature is the meaning of "right," everyone who wants to do the right will surely have to consult nature at every step, and the Stoic has performed a useful service in calling attention to this fact.

Nevertheless, conformity to nature cannot be the whole meaning of right. Universal nature is an extremely broad term. Taken at face value it involves everything that is, and thus includes much that common sense could never call right. It includes earthquake, flood, volcanic eruption, disease, and drouth, as well as lovely landscape, warm sunshine, refreshing shower, ripening harvest, and glowing health. It includes envy, deceit, theft, adultery, murder, hate, and violence, as well as justice and

love. It encompasses the good and the bad alike without distinguishing them; and this difficulty remains, as we shall see,
even when one emphasizes *man's* nature. If the basis of a
satisfactory distinction between right and wrong lies in the conception of nature, moralists have been unable to point it out.
To be sure, the Stoics themselves do distinguish between right
and wrong, and often very nobly, but this distinction they
achieve not by actually analyzing nature but, rather, by attaching
to it ideals originally arrived at by altogether different methods.
Universal nature itself, being all-comprehensive, can yield no
criterion of right, unless there is no such concept as wrong, in
which case the concept of right also is without significance.

READINGS

Melden, *Ethical Theories,* pp. 150–63; *or*
Clark and Smith, *Readings in Ethics,* pp. 101–12; *or*
Rand, *The Classical Moralists,* pp. 92–112.

QUESTIONS

1. Why did the Stoics withdraw from convention to nature in
their search for a moral guide?   In what sense is natural morality
better than conventional?

2. On what view of nature did the Stoics build their morality?
To what extent is this view supported by the findings of physics and
chemistry and the character of the evolutionary process?

3. What, according to the Stoics, is under our control and what is
not?   To what extent is this classification correct?   Do you agree
with the Stoics concerning the manner in which we should meet what
we cannot help?

4. What, according to the Stoics, was the chief reward of virtue?
Is virtue really valuable in itself?   Is it then sufficient to itself in the
sense that the man who has it needs nothing more and that a good
man cannot be hurt by an evil one?

5. Would it be possible for a person of even the noblest intentions
to act rightly without a knowledge of such elemental natural facts
as the tendency of unsupported objects to fall or the dependence of

the body upon food and drink? Would more knowledge of nature help us to act rightly more often? In what sense?

6. Do you consider the practical morality of the Stoics essentially sound? What is its chief defect? Which of its practical requirements is most applicable to the current world situation? Can one deduce such a practical ethics from nature?

7. A cholera epidemic breaks out in a Chinese city. A young scientist volunteers to join a mission to help stem the tide of infection. A fellow scientist remonstrates that he is not only foolish but wrong since this is only nature's way of regulating population. Who is right? Would it make a difference if the town involved were the one in which you and your family live?

8. Revenge seems to be more natural than forgiveness; is it therefore more apt to be right? Artificial limbs are only in a somewhat strained sense natural; is the rightness of using them therefore doubtful? What would the Stoics say about these matters? What would you say? Do you think any further test is needed?

REFERENCES

Antoninus, Marcus Aurelius, *The Meditations of the Emperor Marcus Aurelius Antoninus,* tr. by George Long (New York: A. L. Burt Company, 1864).

Bevan, E. R., *Stoics and Skeptics* (New York: Oxford University Press, 1913).

Cicero, *De Officiis,* tr. by G. B. Gardiner (London: Methuen, 1899).

—— *De Finibus Bonarus et Malorum,* tr. by Harris Rackham (New York: Macmillan, 1914), especially Bks. I and III.

Deshumbert, Marius, *An Ethical System Based on the Laws of Nature* (La Salle, Ill.: Open Court Publishing Company, 1917).

Diogenes Laertius, *Lives and Opinions of Eminent Philosophers,* tr. by R. D. Hicks (Cambridge: Harvard University Press, 1938), Bk. VII.

Epictetus, *Discourses and Manual,* tr. by P. E. Matheson (New York: Oxford University Press, 1916).

Hicks, R. D., *Stoic and Epicurean* (New York: Scribner, 1910).

Hyde, W. D., *The Five Great Philosophies of Life* (New York: Macmillan, 1932), Ch. 2.

Murray, Gilbert, *The Stoic Philosophy* (New York: Putnam, 1915).

Rand, Benjamin, *The Classical Moralists* (Boston: Houghton Mifflin, 1937), Chs. 4, 7, 8.

Schweitzer, Albert, *Civilization and Ethics,* tr. by J. Naish (London: A. S. C. Block, 1923).

Wenley, R. M., *Stoicism and Its Influence* (Boston: Longmans, Green, 1927).

Zeller, Eduard, *The Stoics, Epicureans, and Skeptics,* tr. by Oswald Reichel (rev. ed., London: Longmans, Green, 1892).

7

Nature Theories:
Evolution

IF THE MEANINGS OF moral terms, however illuminated by universal nature, are not specifically revealed by it, perhaps they can still be found by reference to the evolutionary process involved in nature. Such an approach to ethics can be both more restricted and more distinctively teleological than that of the Stoics. The good will be identified with the ends toward which evolution moves, and *"right" will mean conformity to the demands of these ends.*

Although in ancient Greece sporadic hints of an idea of evolution appeared from time to time, these seem never to have worked their way into Greek ethics. In the Medieval period the idea of natural development was largely lost sight of in face of an overwhelming emphasis on eternal principles. However, with the coming of the modern period a new interest in natural development emerged and this time it carried over into moral theory. Giordano Bruno (1548–1600) thought of the universe in terms of an infinite dynamic reality. Gottfried Wilhelm Leibniz (1646–1716), although holding that the order of things was fixed by God, nevertheless believed that this order unfolded itself in temporal development. Hegel regarded human history and advancing thought as supreme revelations of Absolute Mind. His contemporary, Schelling, saw a developing process in nature itself.

New and tremendous impetus to the evolutionary theory came from the side of science. Such men as Pierre Laplace, Georges Buffon, Erasmus Darwin, Jean de Lamarck, Robert Malthus, and Charles Lyell called attention to specific evidences for such a view in observed and carefully recorded facts concerning the heavenly bodies, the earth's surface, and the development of living organisms. Then, in the middle of the nineteenth century, Charles Darwin (1809–82) set forth a theory of organic evolution so clearly and convincingly as to give it a foremost place among the scientific hypotheses of our time. Basing his conclusions upon an enormous amount of specific biological data, Darwin contended that the whole panorama of life-forms could be accounted for in terms of minute variations among the offspring of the same parents, the tendency of these variations to be transmitted, and the natural selection of organisms of certain types in the struggle for existence.

Darwin himself undertook, on a limited scale, the reinterpretation of moral theory in terms of the evolutionary hypothesis. His position was that the keen capacity for sympathy and the retention of past experience that evolution had produced in men caused them to be just and considerate of one another and thereby served the evolutionary end of morality, which was the production and preservation of as many healthy members of the species as possible. After Darwin numerous systems of evolutionary ethics appeared. In England Sir Leslie Stephen (1832–1904), in an extensive treatise, *The Science of Ethics,* developed the thesis that the health of society was the objective of evolution and therefore the core of the meaning of morality, and W. K. Clifford (1845–79) presented the view that the aim of evolution was not a mere individual self but a sort of tribal self. In France Jean Marie Guyau (1854–88) advocated a somewhat more spiritualized version of evolutionary morality. In America John Fiske (1842–1901) undertook to vindicate the ethical end of evolution by showing how moral sense had been developed through the prolonged infancy of human beings. Many other writers including Thomas H. Huxley, Benjamin Kidd, Alexander Shand, Alexander Sutherland, Peter Kropotkin, and

Samuel Alexander made substantial contributions. Contemporary advocates of an evolutionary theory of morals include C. H. Waddington, Olaf Stapledon, Arthur Lynch, and Julian Huxley, among others.

A reasonably satisfactory conception of what evolutionary moralists are driving at may be obtained by noting the views of two important and very different writers. The first is Herbert Spencer (1820–1903), who began his work on evolutionary ethics even before Darwin, and who more than any other writer has endeavored to make the evolutionary theory the basis of a whole system of philosophy. The second is Friedrich Nietzsche (1844–1900), who, although he never developed a systematic philosophy, was far more courageous than most writers in bringing to light some of the implications of an evolutionary theory of ethics.

SPENCER'S EVOLVED SOCIETY

Herbert Spencer, for a time the most influential of British philosophers, is still the best spokesman for those who are confident that the world is inevitably getting better and better. In youth he declined the customary university education to begin his career as an engineer. Later, he undertook an editorship for a few years, and then at forty abandoned all other enterprises for the writing of his ambitious *Synthetic Philosophy*, which was intended to gather and systematize the general principles of all the knowledge attained by the separate sciences. Early in life he had become interested in the concept of evolution, and when he came to write his *Synthetic Philosophy* he made it the keystone of his whole system. It became for him, as for Darwin, the explanation of the variety among the species of living organisms; and in this connection he added to the Darwinian formula the suggestive concept of the "survival of the fittest." But he was unwilling to limit the conception of evolution to the sphere of living things; he also saw in it the cause of the development of the heavenly bodies and of the earth, the appearance of mind, the unfolding of the inner life of the individual, and the growth of social relations.

Spencer's general concept of evolution involved a number of relatively distinct factors. These included, first, a growing coherence or consolidation of matter in which the parts increasingly become not only closer together but also more dependent upon one another; second, increasingly greater differences between wholes and their environments and among the various parts of wholes; third, increasing definiteness and order; and, finally, changes in motion parallel to those in matter. Putting these features of the evolutionary process together, Spencer arrived at the following definition: *"Evolution is an integration of matter and concomitant dissipation of motion; during which the matter passes from an indefinite, incoherent homogeneity to a definite coherent heterogeneity; and during which the retained motion undergoes a parallel transformation."* [1] This definition at first sight appears formidable and hopelessly involved. However, for our purposes it simply means that the progress of evolution is an increasing complexity and organization like the progress from the amoeba to man or from a savage tribe to a civilized world.

On the basis of this general account of evolution, which indeed was worked out in part for the special purposes of moral philosophy,[2] Spencer proceeds to build his theory of ethics.[3] The central claim of this theory is that the moral, or right, is the *evolved.* Conduct necessarily involves "adjustment of acts to ends," is at every stage a product of evolution, and must be tested at every stage by the extent to which it embodies "those traits which his [man's] conduct assumes on reaching its limit of evolution." [4]

The truth of this contention that right and evolved conduct are one and the same, may be seen in the fact that the conduct men actually do approve corresponds at every point with the

1 Herbert Spencer, *First Principles* (6th ed., New York: D. Appleton, 1899), p. 367.

2 See Herbert Spencer, *The Data of Ethics* (New York: A. L. Burt, 1897), pp. iii ff.

3 Spencer also develops a pleasure theory of morals that parallels and in some respects underlies his evolutionary theory. However, since both theories are said to yield essentially the same results and since it is only from the evolutionary view that Spencer believes a satisfactory scientific deduction of moral principles is possible, only the evolutionary theory need concern us here.

4 Spencer, *The Data of Ethics*, p. 332.

conduct that is most evolved. In general, the ends of evolution include the following: (1) that "life is the greatest, both in length and breadth"; (2) that "the needful number of young are preserved to maturity"; and (3) that "life may be complete in each and his offspring, not only without preventing completion of it in others, but with furtherance of it in others." [5]   When one compares these evolutionary ends—self-preservation, preservation of offspring, and human cooperation—with what men actually approve in conduct, the following results may be observed. With respect to the first, "approving and disapproving utterances make the tacit assertion that, other things equal, conduct is right or wrong according as its special acts, well or ill adjusted to special ends, do or do not further the general end of self-preservation." [6] With respect to the second, "the expressions good nursing and bad nursing . . . recognize as special ends which ought to be fulfilled, the furthering of the vital functions with a view to the general end of continued life and growth"; and "goodness or badness is affirmed" of *education* "according as its methods are so adapted to physical and psychical requirements, as to further the children's lives." [7]   With respect to the third, "the words good and bad have come to be specially associated with acts which further the complete living of others and acts which obstruct their complete living." [8]   In other words, the conduct that is commonly approved as right is that which "simultaneously achieves the greatest totality of life in self, in offspring, and in fellowman." [9]   Thus the conclusion cannot be escaped "that the conduct to which we apply the name good [that is, morally good or right] is the relatively more evolved conduct; and that bad is the name we apply to conduct which is relatively less evolved." [10]

What, more specifically, is the evolved conduct in which rightness consists?   Spencer considers this from four distinct standpoints: the physical, the biological, the psychological, and the

---

[5] *Ibid.*, p. 28.
[6] *Ibid.*, p. 26.
[7] *Ibid.*
[8] *Ibid.*, p. 27.
[9] *Ibid.*, p. 28.
[10] *Ibid.*, pp. 27–28.

sociological.   Looked at from a purely physical (or, as one would
say today, behavioristic) standpoint, evolved conduct has all of
the characteristics toward which the evolutionary process itself
moves.   Thus it is *coherent,* as may be seen in the dependability
of the responses of the moral man; it is *definite,* as may be seen
in the just man's precision in the performance of contracts; and it
is *heterogeneous* or diversified, as may be seen in the variety of
community and domestic relations to which a moral man is
responsive.   Looked at from the standpoint of biology, evolved
conduct is that in which "the functions of all kinds are duly fulfilled," [11] for the functions of the human organism represent its
needs.   Evolved conduct is also both "immediately pleasurable,"
and "conducive to future happiness," [12] for pleasure, being a
means of drawing us toward the objects with which it is associated,
must necessarily be associated with useful activities in the types
of organisms that survive in the evolutionary struggle.   Observed from a psychological standpoint, evolved conduct is that
which is more complex or more remote from mere reflex action
and sensation.   Finally, seen from the sociological point of view,
evolved conduct is that which is "fitted to the associated state,
in such wise that the lives of each and all may be the greatest possible, alike in length and breadth." [13]   In a word, then, evolved
conduct is complex and highly organized conduct.

Evolved conduct is not purely altruistic conduct.   Especially
during the earlier phases of man's life egoism had to take precedence over altruism.   Even afterward one's concern must be
somewhat more for himself than for others else there would
be no value in doing things for others.   Equality ought to be
equality of opportunity rather than equality of material things
or of happiness.   The welfare of individuals is always the goal
and the state should intervene as little as possible.   Nevertheless,
it must be remembered, as shown through the sociological approach, that the greatest totality of life aimed at by evolution
cannot be achieved without a genuine altruism that includes not

11 *Ibid.,* p. 88.
12 *Ibid.,* p. 117.
13 *Ibid.,* p. 158.

only noninterference with the life of others but also positive furtherance of it. As society evolves progressively from the low level of military civilization to a higher industrial level, mutual aid will tend to replace contention, and even competition will come to be a rivalry in kindness. The ultimate goal of evolution may then best be thought of as a "social equilibrium" in which each finds his own satisfaction in seeking the welfare of society and the welfare of society is promoted by the efforts of each for his own good.

How precisely is the standard of an evolved social equilibrium to be applied to the problems of our obviously unevolved society? In this connection two quite distinct phases of ethics must be recognized, which may be called absolute ethics and relative ethics. Absolute ethics consists of the rules of conduct, deduced from the nature of evolution, that would belong to the life of a perfectly good man in a perfectly good, or completely evolved, society. It can be achieved only when both men and societies are fully developed, for the perfect man could neither appear nor survive apart from the perfect society.[14] Since neither men nor societies are now perfect, and since neither will be for a long time to come, it is necessary that absolute ethics give way in practice to relative ethics, which consists of those rules of conduct that are appropriate to the stage on the way to the evolved society that has been achieved at any given time.

Absolute ethics is logically prior to relative ethics in the sense that it indicates the ultimate nature of right by reference to which all relative right must be measured. Just as in geometry or astronomy, perfect figures must first be studied and their implications worked out in order that by indicating the deviations from them we may indicate the nature of actual planetary motions and mundane figures, so in ethics absolute or fully evolved conduct must first be studied before the conduct proper to actual situations becomes clear. But relative ethics actually supplies us with the standards by which we must live. Once absolute ethics has done its work and we know what the conduct of the perfect man in the perfect society would be, relative ethics under-

14 *Ibid.,* p. 330.

takes to show just what deviations from absolute ethics are justifiable at the present stage or what conduct at this stage would be most conducive to the ultimate emergence of the evolved society.

In the practical working out of relative ethics we must remember the survival mechanism by which evolution moves forward as well as the social equilibrium at which it aims. This means that we should, to a considerable extent, let the natural consequences of acts have their way, not interfering unduly with nature either by education or by law. Government charities, for example, can scarcely be said to be legitimate, for they interrupt nature's elimination of the unfit, although private charities are natural and therefore proper. The economic order requires no regulation, and state activity beyond the protection of the citizens from dangers without and within is to be discouraged. Political, religious, and social sanctions serve a useful role, but they, with the sense of moral compulsion that accompanies them, must be allowed to wither away as moral insight into the consequences of acts replaces them. Thus the sense of duty will one day be outgrown. Moral intuitions have their place as products of the moral experience of the race; but they are not in themselves final. Progress must be steadily from a military order of nature with its severer, more egoistic virtues to an industrial order with its gentler, more altruistic virtues. The particular deviations from absolute right that are allowable and desirable at the present stage are of course many and varied. They may not be known with complete precision although they may be estimated with sufficient accuracy for practical purposes. The detailed discussion of them in which Spencer indulges at great length in the latter books of his *Principles of Ethics* belong mainly to applied ethics and cannot be treated here.

CRITICAL EVALUATION OF SPENCER'S VERSION OF EVOLUTIONARY ETHICS

Spencer's description of the ethical end as an equilibrium in which each in seeking his own good seeks the good of others, and in seeking the good of others seeks his own, is sound as far as it goes, for while other ends than this may also be desirable, this seems to be not only desirable itself but also indispensable to the fullest realization of the others. Further, when Spencer points out the impracticability of living as though this end were already realized and the necessity of recognizing the imperfections of the present stage on the way to the realization of it, his thought is in sane accord with the facts of our kind of world. Beyond these sound major emphases Spencer has contributed to ethical thought in a number of other ways. His reaffirmation of the basic biological connection between pleasure and healthy functioning of the organism, his insistence upon the necessity of considering natural processes in all manner of moral calculations, his recognition of the interdependence of the good man and the good society, and his insights concerning the educative role of political, religious, and social sanctions in the development of morality are all suggestive and essentially justifiable.

Quite apart, however, from these significant insights into important phases of ethics the question of whether or not his evolutionary theory represents on the whole a sound interpretation of moral concepts hinges upon whether or not Spencer is correct in equating right with an inevitably increasing complexity and integration that scientific inquiry discovers in natural evolution. The answer must for two basic reasons be an emphatic negative.

The first of these reasons is that scientific observation of natural development fails to disclose such an inevitably increasing complexity and integration as Spencer thinks it does. To be sure, the evolution of the species may be said to have followed fairly regular patterns, although even here the process of evolution has entailed many more dead ends and periods of degeneration than Spencer imagined, not to speak of the disintegrating force of struggle itself. But, whatever the regularity of organic development, when intelligence and social organization enter the scene, the picture is seriously altered. Progress can continue, but its certainty rapidly diminishes, and dangerous forces of incalculable power are released. Intelligence may be used to destroy as well as to create, and society may integrate only to make the disintegration of wars the more devastating. Integra-

tion far beyond that of purely organic processes becomes possible
but for this very reason it ceases to be inevitable.   What becomes of human societies depends on what human beings do,
and the outcome can be a hell as well as a heaven.   Spencer lived
near the close of a long era of relative peace.   A generation that
has lived through two colossal world wars and seems to be girding
for a third in which even the horrible devastation of the first
two would be dwarfed by comparison is no longer impressed
by the myth of inevitable natural progress.   But, if Spencer can
no longer claim that his idea of increasing complexity and integration is supported by nature, either he must in holding on to
his integrative ideal admit that it does not represent at all the
scientific natural ethics he thought it did, or else in adhering to
nature wherever it may lead he must accept the possibility of a
monstrous ethics of violence; either way his theory loses its claim
to plausibility.

   The other reason that Spencer's attempt to identify right with
the natural integrative complexity of his evolutionary principle
fails is that even if such integrative complexity were naturally
inevitable it would not be coextensive either with what people
intend by right or with what they legitimately think in the light
of such intentions to be right.   To begin with, people reserve
the privilege of judging rightness or wrongness in the evolutionary process itself, which suggests that the evolutionary process can scarcely be the meaning of right.   But apart from this,
when we analyze our intentions in using ethical terms, we are
unable to see, in the mere fact that an act is evolved, any reason
why it should be right or wrong, unless perhaps evolution itself
is in some sense a fulfillment of rational or human purposes that
would give to right a nonevolutionary meaning.   Indeed, when
we inquire further concerning the integrative complexity that
Spencer intends by "evolved," we cannot but think that some
aspects of it not only do not represent the meaning of right but
are not right at all or are even definitely wrong.   For example,
would not even Spencer have to admit that, with regard to some
such virtues as honesty and benevolence, simplicity is better than

complexity, and is not complexity in many moral matters the same as duplicity? At any rate, in numerous instances of this kind one cannot make the complexity of acts correspond with their rightness without interpreting them in extremely artificial ways. Similarly, what shall one say of the stout resistance to public education and public charities involved in Spencer's own account of integrative complexity or of his championship of ruthless economic individualism against even the most moderate government intervention in the name of humanity? Such consequences are clearly in direct opposition to important claims implicit in critical moral judgments, and accordingly a theory that leads to them is scarcely in line with what people really mean by "right." Finally, even the splendid social equilibrium that Spencer envisions as the far off goal of ethics fails to encompass much to which the critical use of the term "right" would seem to have reference, for while the right requires harmonious human relations it also involves many other values of which Spencer seems unaware.

NIETZSCHE'S SUPERMAN

While Spencer left out of account much of the seamy side of the evolutionary process and some significant values in his attempt to found a largely traditional moral code upon an evolutionary basis, a younger German contemporary of his, who has the reputation of being one of the fathers of modern Fascism, made the most of this severer aspect of evolution in an attempt to disclose new values and indeed to create a new kind of morality.

Friedrich Nietzsche felt that virtually all moralists had stopped far short of their true task. They had attempted only to discover a basis for the prevailing morality of their own societies, whereas they ought to have gone on to analyze—and call in question—not only that morality but all morality. "The problem of morality itself has been *omitted*." [15] Such an analysis would

[15] Friedrich Nietzsche, "Beyond Good and Evil," tr. by H. Zimmern, *The Philosophy of Nietzsche* (New York: Random House, 1937), p. 95.

have led them to reject both the old foundations and the old morality and to adopt a new code as well as a new theory.

The foundation on which Nietzsche seeks to build his radically new morality is, as in the thought of Spencer, an evolving nature. But nature, for him, is not nature as it has generally been thought of by others. Certainly it is not the reasonable providential nature of the Stoics, for it is "boundlessly extravagant, boundlessly indifferent, without purpose or consideration, without pity or justice, at once fruitful and barren and uncertain." [16]   Nor is it the law-abiding nature of physics, for the whole concept of "Nature's conformity to law" is nothing but "a naïvely humanitarian adjustment" by which the physicists "make abundant concessions to the democratic instincts of the human soul."   It is not even Darwin's evolving nature of mechanical adaptations through variation and selection, for possible adaptation is the very antithesis of life and nature.   Finally it is not Spencer's orderly progress toward coherence, for nature is often wildly incoherent and moves toward no certain end.   Nature is in fact a thoroughly irrational dynamic surge.   It is "the tyrannically inconsiderate and relentless enforcement of the claims of power." [17]   It is ever the expression of unconditional "Will to Power."

A morality dependent on such a thoroughly dynamic evolving nature is a changing morality with no fixed standard of reference in terms of such a goal as Spencer visualizes.   The good is always relative to its own age.   The good of one age is the bad of another, and the bad of one generation the good of another.   "All good things were once bad things; from every original sin has grown an original virtue." [18]   Marriage, for example, once regarded as a depriving of the community of its rights, came later to be respected as an essential moral institution.   Similarly the humility needed to offset the overweening selfishness of the fifteenth century came to be out of place in subsequent centuries of weakness of will.

16 *Ibid.,* p. 8.
17 *Ibid.,* p. 25.
18 Friedrich Nietzsche, "The Genealogy of Morals," tr. by H. B. Samuel, *The Philosophy of Nietzsche,* p. 116.

Nevertheless the vast battle of the Will to Power yields at least some general clues to the nature of a higher morality.   As one looks at the past, he sees such a clue in the superiority of the virtues of masterful men to the virtues of slaves.   Looking to the future, one may carry this clue a step further by considering the prospect of the appearance of a higher type of man.   Putting these clues together one may discover the meaning of morality in the emergence of the Superman, to which the relentless Will to Power in all life presses man onward.   To produce this Superman of the future is the goal of all life, and the moral life—insofar as Nietzsche recognizes such a life—is the life that is conducive to the production of such a man.

The function of today's men of higher morality, or free spirits, accordingly is essentially that of bridges over which the Superman may arrive.   Nietzsche's prophet Zarathustra states it thus to such men: "Ye are only bridges: may higher ones pass over upon you. . . . Out of your seed there may one day arise for me a genuine son and perfect heir: but the time is distant." [19]

But what does it mean to be a bridge for the arrival of the Superman?   In general it means so to live by strength, courage, and cleverness that the weak will be crushed down and in time the relentless order of heredity will bring about the appearance of the stronger higher man.   To live in this manner would, of course, involve a radical rearrangement of the prevailing moral ideals. It would demand what Nietzsche calls a "transvaluation of all values."   We must then learn to regard as good all that is now thought to be bad, and as bad all that is now thought to be good. In our civilization, Nietzsche contends, the morality of the Jews, an inferior morality with such an emphasis on humility and kindness as slaves value, has been dominant for many centuries.   It was fastened upon us by the slave revolution of early Christianity. It is supported by the fact that there are so many more of those who can obey than of those who can command.   But it must be ruthlessly uprooted.   In its place, at least for free spirits, there must be re-established a morality of masters that exalts pride,

[19] Friedrich Nietzsche, "Thus Spake Zarathustra," tr. by Thomas Common, *The Philosophy of Nietzsche*, p. 282.

courage, egotism, cleverness, and even cruelty.   Only by such a
code has true nobility emerged in the past.   Only as free spirits
live by it today shall we advance through elimination of the
weak toward the Superman.

The necessary transvaluation leaves none of our cherished
values untouched.   Men have been accustomed to give at least
lip service to truth above all else.   But truth is only one value
among others, and who knows that it is worth more than falsehood?   In any case it is always relative, and the right standard
lies elsewhere.   "The falseness of an opinion is not for us an
objection to it. . . . The question is, how far an opinion is life-
preserving, species-preserving, perhaps species-rearing." [20]   Indeed we must *"recognize untruth as a condition of life."* [21]   Men
have also thought well of pity.   But pity is the very antithesis of
good.   We must learn with the brave Zarathustra to strike the
whimpering weakling and thus show up his hypocrisy.   Again,
men have highly praised selflessness, but egotism is natural to
man and essential to his nobility.   The advance toward the
Superman is impossible without it.   Many have thought the
moral goal a common or community good; but how can there be
any common good?   Goods are the goods of individual men who
must ruthlessly struggle for their attainment.   So deeply is
cruelty ingrained in man's nature that when a man is unable to
be cruel to others his cruelty turns inward, in the pangs of conscience, upon himself.   Cooperation and kindness are not natural to the strong, not even in the service of race.   (In this rejection of radical racism Nietzsche is of course not a forerunner of
the Nazis, but in his advocacy of ruthlessness as well as in his
strictures against Jewish culture he is.)

Democracy with its insistence upon equality is the favored
political trend of the time.   But equality is preposterous.   It
is utterly opposed to nature, where power and rank prevail.
It pretends to be just, but its barbarous leveling is utterly
unjust to the privileged and the superior.   "It is *immoral* to

---

[20] Nietzsche, "Beyond Good and Evil," *loc. cit.*, p. 4.
[21] *Ibid.*

say that 'what is right for one is proper for another.' " [22]   Men
glibly assert that man is at heart capable of the prevailing virtues;
but this is all a sham, and the new standards must recognize man
as he is: "They are beautiful, glistening, jingling, festive words:
honesty, love of truth, love of wisdom, sacrifice for knowledge,
heroism of the truthful. . . . [But] this worthy parade of verbi-
age also belongs to the old false adornment, frippery, and gold
dust of unconscious human vanity, and . . . even under such
flattering colour and repainting, the terrible original text *homo
natura* must again be recognized." [23]

CRITICAL EVALUATION OF NIETZSCHE'S VERSION OF EVOLUTIONARY ETHICS

Nietzsche's version of evolutionary ethics improves at two significant points, at least, over that of Spencer.   For one thing it
is more honest in reckoning with the seamy and disorderly side
of the evolutionary process, which Spencer's version on the whole
ignored.   Whatever else may be said of Nietzsche's account of
evolution it has all the roughness in it that the evolutionary
process actually involves, and whatever may be wrong with
Nietzsche's ethics it does not depend upon idealized natural development.   In the second place, Nietzsche is aware—as Spencer
is not—of the vast potentialities for the realization of positive
new values in the process of evolutionary development and of the
obligation of the man of today to the man of tomorrow.   For
Spencer the end of evolution and the values inherent in it are
apparent almost from the beginning; for Nietzsche evolution involves genuine emergence of that which is really new, and there
is no plotting out in advance of the precise character of the values
that may be discovered in the process.   Nietzsche properly sees
not only that morality is a system of positive personal values but
also that moral philosophy must forever be on the alert for the
discovery of such values as have never before been experienced

22 *Ibid.,* p. 160.
23 *Ibid.*

and indeed that the concepts of value and right themselves have
far more implicit in them than any ethical theory has hitherto
revealed.

But has Nietzsche's theory disclosed or even suggested the
essential meanings of the moral terms?   Although the practical
ethics is very different, the basic theoretical difficulties are much
the same as those of Spencer's theory.   Since the requisite meanings are sought in the alleged facts of evolution, we must begin
by asking whether or not the facts of evolution seem really in the
main to be as they are here presented.

1. Impartial observation of the progress of nature does not,
as we have seen, sustain Spencer's smoothly integrative evolution
toward social equilibrium; but neither does it lend much support to Nietzsche's opposing chaotic disintegrative evolution of
the ruthless Superman.   If Spencer has erred in overlooking the
harshness of nature, Nietzsche has gone astray in exaggerating it.
From the very beginning evolution proceeds as much by cooperation as by conflict, and, as progress is achieved, united effort
becomes increasingly the condition of further advance.   The
capacities that enable one to survive are as likely to be those that
draw him to his fellows as they are to be those that set him against
them.   The evolutionary process itself seems to be relatively
indifferent to the creation of notably superior individuals, and
to be much more devoted, if it is devoted to anything, to the
development of groups that can survive.   Geniuses seem rather
to be its sports, who live in strength but die without passing on
their talents, than to be its primary ends.   Evolution reveals, to
be sure, some trends but it discloses no such distinctive purposes
as Spencer from one side and Nietzsche from another presuppose.
We may make of it what we can, but it declares to us no unmis-
takable objectives.   Accordingly, while Nietzsche might have
defended his morality on other than evolutionary grounds, or
adopted another morality to accord with evolutionary facts, he
could scarcely defend his own ethics on the basis of evolutionary
facts.

2. Even if Nietzsche's account of evolution were in full ac-

cord with the facts and his account of ethics entirely in line with his view of evolution, this consistency would have no tendency to show that moral terms meant evolved in his sense, or in any other. Most of us, as has been previously indicated, reserve the right to pass moral judgment upon at least some trends in social evolution, and this we could scarcely do apart from some assumptions, other than evolutionary ones, about the meanings of moral terms. In saying, for example, that evolution toward superior personality is good, we can scarcely mean simply that such evolution is in accord with evolution. But not only do we so use moral terms as to be able to judge evolutionary trends, we often judge such trends to be evil or wrong, and we may even properly think the whole evolutionary drift contrary to ethics, as the evolutionist T. H. Huxley himself did. Such judgments would, of course, be not only false but sheerest nonsense if the meaning of right or good were found in evolution.

3. The special difficulty of Nietzsche's particular version of evolutionary ethics is not merely that the modes of conduct commended by Nietzsche are sometimes out of line with traditional standards. That may in some instances even be a merit in his view, for tradition is not always right. The difficulty is, rather, that the modes of conduct that he recommends are often so antithetical to what is intended by such terms as "morally good" and "right" that whatever commendatory terms may correctly apply to these modes of conduct cannot possibly mean the same as "morally good" or "right."

The meaning of "right," whatever it is, is scarcely such as to commend either general indifference to truth or the ruthless suppression of the weak by the strong. Nietzsche's Superman is at best an inhuman self-defeating monster who, having crushed his victims, is in the end frustrated: and the terms in which he is praised are not only not those of ethical discourse, but are also at many points plainly incompatible with ethical discourse. Some of our applications of moral concepts no doubt need radical reappraisal, but what Nietzsche has done is not merely to alter the applications but to abandon moral concepts for others of his own choosing. This substitution, of course, he was entitled to make if he chose, but, in making it, he could scarcely expect his results to be accepted as satisfactory moral philosophy.

CONCLUSIONS CONCERNING NATURE THEORIES

In insisting that any adequate quest for moral meanings must be comprehensive rather than merely conventional in its scope and in revealing the relevance of knowledge of nature to the discovery of particular duties the nature theories are thoroughly sound. To try to determine moral meanings solely within the framework of one's own mores or to confine one's ethical outlook to his own temporal perspective is unduly to limit the validity of one's findings. One must be ever alert to discover not only new values but also wider and deeper meanings implicit in the concepts of good and right themselves. In moral practice one can never know whether or not a given type of action is right without knowing what the operation of natural laws will do with it; and if one is to act intelligently in the long run, he needs to know the relation of his action to the broad trends implicit in natural development.

Nevertheless, the meanings suggested by the nature theories are far too broad to correspond with such coherent intentions as are discoverable in people's use of moral terms or to furnish intelligible distinctions between right and wrong. Everything that happens is in the usual sense of the term natural and almost all that people do really represents evolved conduct. The practical ethical codes presented by the Stoics and Spencer are of course more restricted than nature, and, on the whole, they are essentially sound, but they are clearly not deducible from nature or evolution as such. In every case the nature theorists have grafted their own moral systems upon the stock of nature rather than gathering, as they have supposed, the moral fruit of nature. Their failure to derive moral theories from nature as such serves to emphasize a fundamental principle, which careful ethical analysis inevitably reveals, and the nature theorists have ignored, namely, that facts and values are not the same in meaning and often do not correspond in extent. The fact that nature has or is about to acquire certain characteristics has no tendency to prove that these characteristics are good or right; and although an act must be natural in order to be right, much that is natural is not right. The conclusion seems to be suggested that the major role of knowledge of nature, with reference to morality, is not that of determining what right means or even of determining by itself what is right but rather that of indicating those means or methods that will most effectively promote the human end values that right action supports. Nature cannot tell man what is good; it can only help him discover how the good may be effectively obtained.

READINGS

Rand, *The Classical Moralists,* pp. 687–702.

QUESTIONS

1. On the basis of what you have learned about biology what general trends can you see in the evolution of the species? From what you know of history and the social sciences what basic trends can you discern in the development of humanity? To what extent do these trends seem to you to harmonize with Spencer's account of evolution?

2. Do Spencer's objectives of the preservation of life and healthy function and of the transition from military to industrial organization seem to you morally sound? Why, and to what extent?

3. In what respects are Spencer's account of the social equilibrium and Butler's account of the relation between self-love and benevolence alike? In what do they differ? Do you consider the achievement of a social equilibrium a desirable objective? What sort of changes would such an equilibrium require in the organization of society? In the attitudes of individuals? Do you think the natural evolution of society likely to attain it?

4. What does Spencer mean by absolute ethics? Of what use is such ethics? Why is it necessary also to be concerned with what Spencer calls relative ethics?

5. If public education and public charities interfere with nature,

as Spencer thought, are they therefore wrong?   What about population control and public health regulations?

6. If Spencer is overoptimistic, would you say that Nietzsche is
pessimistic?   If not, why not?   If so, in what senses?

7. Would you agree with Nietzsche that new values are discovered
in the course of man's development?   What are some that seem to
have come to light within the past four hundred years?   Does the
emergence of new values necessarily require the relinquishing of old
ones?   Illustrate.

8. Consider carefully some of the new values that Nietzsche intro-
duces.   Do you think they deserve a prominent place among human
values?   What about the values he rejects?   Have you ever observed
evidences of the slave-morality that Nietzsche despises?   Do you
think Nietzsche's criticisms of traditional Christianity and Judaism
merit consideration?   Does he seem properly to have apprehended
the essential spirit of the ethics of these religions?   Why or why not?

9. Do you think that people now living have an obligation to
generations yet unborn?   Why?   Do you think these generations can
best be served as Nietzsche supposes?   If not, how can they best be
served?

10. In what respects does impartial study of nature support
Nietzsche's contentions?   In what does it tend to require denial of
them?   In what ways does critical analysis of moral insights support
or undermine Nietzsche's views?

11. If knowledge of nature fails to disclose the meanings of moral
terms, is it of any use in ethics?   If so, what?   What sort of moral
theory is suggested by the fact that nature theories prove to be too
broad?

REFERENCES

General

Carritt, E. F., *The Theory of Morals* (London: Oxford University
     Press, 1928), Ch. 3.

Darwin, Charles, *The Descent of Man* (New York: Frederick Warne,
     1930), Chs. 4–6, 21.

Deshumbert, Marius, *An Ethical System Based on the Laws of Nature*
     (La Salle, Ill.: Open Court Publishing Company, 1917).

Fiske, John, *Outlines of Cosmic Philosophy, Based on the Doctrine
     of Evolutionary Naturalism* (Boston: Houghton Mifflin, 1902).

Guyau, J. M., *A Sketch of Morality Independent of Obligation or*

Sanction, tr. by Gertrude Kapteyn (London: Watts & Co., 1898).

Hill, T. E., *Contemporary Ethical Theories* (New York: Macmillan, 1950), Ch. 8.

Huxley, J. S., *Evolutionary Ethics* (London: Oxford University Press, 1943).

Huxley, T. H., *Evolution and Ethics and Other Essays* (New York: D. Appleton, 1902).

Kropotkin, Peter, *Ethics, Origin and Development,* tr. by T. S. Friedland and J. R. Piroshnihoff (New York: The Dial Press, 1924).

Lynch, Arthur, *Ethics, An Exposition of Principles* (London: Cassell and Company, 1922).

Moore, G. E., *Principia Ethica* (Cambridge: Cambridge University Press, 1903), Ch. 2.

Rashdall, Hastings, *Theory of Good and Evil* (London: Oxford University Press, 1936), Vol. II, Bk. III, Ch. 4.

Robinson, D. S., *The Principles of Conduct* (New York: Appleton-Century-Crofts, 1948), Ch. 19.

Stapledon, Olaf, *A Modern Theory of Ethics* (London: Methuen, 1929).

Stephen, Leslie, *The Science of Ethics* (New York: Putnam, 1907).

Urban, W. M., *Fundamentals of Ethics* (New York: Holt, 1930), Ch. 6.

Waddington, C. H., *Science and Ethics* (London: Allen and Unwin, 1942).

Nietzsche

Kaufmann, W. A., *Nietzsche: Philosopher, Psychologist, Antichrist* (Princeton: Princeton University Press, 1950).

Knight, A. H. J., *Some Aspects of the Life and Work of Nietzsche* (New York: Macmillan, 1933).

Morgan, G. A., *What Nietzsche Means* (Cambridge: Harvard University Press, 1941).

Nietzsche, Friedrich, "Beyond Good and Evil," tr. by H. Zimmern, *The Philosophy of Nietzsche* (New York: Random House, 1937).

——— "The Genealogy of Morals," tr. by H. B. Samuel, *The Philosophy of Nietzsche* (New York: Random House, 1937).

——— "Thus Spake Zarathustra," tr. by Thomas Common, *The Philosophy of Nietzsche* (New York: Random House, 1937).

——— *Will to Power,* tr. by Anthony Ludovici (London: Allen & Unwin, 1909).

Reyburn, H. A., *Nietzsche: The Story of a Human Philosopher* (New York: Macmillan, 1948).

Sidgwick, Henry, and Widgery, A. G., *Outlines of the History of Ethics* (London: Macmillan, 1939), pp. 291–92.

Tsanoff, R. A., *The Moral Ideals of Our Civilization* (New York: Dutton, 1942), pp. 517–20.

Spencer

Asirvatham, E., *Herbert Spencer's Theory of Social Justice* (New York: Stechert, 1936).

Collins, F. H., *An Epitome of the Synthetic Philosophy* (5th ed., New York: D. Appleton, 1905).

Sidgwick, Henry, and Widgery, A. G., *Outlines of the History of Ethics* (London: Macmillan, 1939), pp. 293–95.

Spencer, Herbert, *First Principles* (6th ed., New York: D. Appleton, 1899).

——— *The Man versus the State* (Caldwell: Caxton Printers, 1940).

——— *The Principles of Ethics* (New York: D. Appleton, 1892–93).

——— *Principles of Sociology* (New York: D. Appleton, 1896).

——— *Social Statics* (rev. ed., New York: D. Appleton, 1892).

Tsanoff, R. A., *The Moral Ideals of Our Civilization* (New York: Dutton, 1942), pp. 505–12.

8

Human Nature Theories:
Human Excellence, Aristotle

THE PRINCIPAL WEAKNESS OF the nature theories consists, as we have seen, in the fact that nature, in whose ends these theories have grounded morality, is too broad to yield a real distinction between right and wrong. Accordingly it is not surprising to find that an important type of ethical theory has, without losing sight of the fact that morality has a significant connection with nature, focused attention, not upon the whole of nature or even upon its evolutionary process, but rather upon a much more restricted aspect of it. Being unable to find man's goals and duties in the general nature that produced him, supporters of this kind of theory seek such goals and duties in man's own nature, that is, in what man is and can become. Such moralists hold that *"right" means conformity to human nature and "wrong" the opposite of this.*

Advocates of this view, however, approach the problem in two rather different ways, which suggest two distinguishable theories. On the one hand, some of them think of men as a part of the natural world and as having an observable and clearly describable nature within this world. They believe that the right consists in the excellent functioning of man's nature. On the other hand, others think of man as essentially above and distinct from the natural world and as being not merely a knowable nature but also a knowing subject that cannot itself be fully

known.   Right conduct, they believe, requires *the realization
of the as yet unknown possibilities of the self.*   The view held
by the first group, which concerns us in the present chapter, will
be referred to as the "human excellence theory"; the second,
which will occupy our attention in Chapter 9, will be referred
to as the "self-realization theory."

The view that right consists in the excellent functioning of
man's nature seems to be rather definitely rooted in the thought
of Socrates, who was eager above all else to know himself as a
representative of humanity and saw in injustice something contrary to the soul of man.   This theory is also prominent in the
thought of Plato, who worked out his practical morality in terms
of harmony of the human soul.   Through the centuries this
theory has claimed the allegiance of many great minds.   It is of
special interest at the present time because of the re-emphasis
upon it by the neo-Thomist philosophers of the twentieth century and because it is a basis of the official moral philosophy
of the Roman Catholic Church.   The classical expression of the
theory in antiquity is the *Nicomachean Ethics* of Aristotle; and
its best expression within the framework of Christianity is the
reformulation of the Aristotelian statement in the works of
Thomas Aquinas.   Other statements of the theory have been
numerous and interesting, but have on the whole added little.
We shall accordingly treat Aristotle's moral philosophy as presented principally in his *Nicomachean Ethics* as our major example of the human excellence theory.

THE ARISTOTELIAN VIEW OF THE
WORLD AND MAN

Although Aristotle was very careful to keep his ethical thought
closely in touch with everyday moral experience, his world view
was always present at least in the background of his ethical
thought, which cannot be understood without some appreciation
of this world view.   Aristotle held that all real things consisted
of two distinct although inseparable principles, which he described in a variety of more or less parallel ways.   Things con-

sist, to begin with, of *matter* and *form*. Matter is the indefinite, essentially passive factor upon which form does its work; form is the definite dynamic factor in things that makes them what they are and causes them to do what they do. In a bronze triangle, for example, the bronze is the matter and the triangularity the form. Something like the same relation is described by the words *actuality* and *potentiality,* the latter being that from which a thing comes and the former what it becomes. For example, the seed is the potentiality of the oak and the oak the actuality of the seed. A similar account of things is suggested by the words *essence* and *substrate*. The latter is the underlying stuff of which a thing is made; the former is what it is as distinguished from other things.

This duality is always *in things*. Neither of its two sides exists alone apart from the other; and only real things *are,* have *being,* or are *substances* in the full sense of that term. However, the factors of form and matter are relative in that what is from one standpoint matter can be from another standpoint form. Thus, for example, bronze is matter from the standpoint of the bronze triangle; but it is form from the standpoint of the elements of which bronze is compounded. Similarly the bronze triangle, which is form from the standpoint of the bronze, may be matter when taken as a part of a total decorative pattern. As one in this manner ascends the scale of matter and form, matter as such becomes more and more idealized until at last one reaches the level of pure form in which the resistance of matter is completely overcome. This pure form is also the first cause, the end of all things. It is, in fact, Deity in whom all things are known immediately and in whom perfect happiness abides.

The two-in-oneness implied in the relations of form and matter is the central explanatory principle of everything in nature. Matter is the colorless substratum of all objects and form is the cause of their shapes and activities. Motion is a response to form. Plants and animals consist in part of matter and could not exist without bodies, yet their shapes and functions and the shapes and functions of their respective organs are determined by forms, which remain fixed for each species. The nature or essence of any particular thing is not necessarily revealed in the present condition of that thing. It depends also on the form that is hidden within the matter of the thing. It must include the potentiality as well as the present actuality of the thing. Thus the real nature of an embryo is not fully revealed until the potentiality of the embryo is actualized in the mature animal.

Man is no exception to the dual structure of things. Although he is in a sense the end at which the biological world aims, he consists both of form and matter. The formal, or soul, element within him involves a vegetable soul, which shares with the plants the functions of nutrition and growth, an animal soul, which shares with the lower animals the functions of perception and feeling, and a rational soul, which is distinctively human and has the capacity for conceptual thought. However, only the rational part of man—that is, his rational soul together with that in his animal soul which responds to reason—constitutes the distinctive essence, or nature, of man, who may accordingly be described as a rational animal.

The significance of such an account of the world and man for ethics is plain enough. The objective or good of man must be that the form in him mold the matter, that the potential manhood in the child or the undeveloped man be actualized in mature rational activity, that man's essential or rational nature be expressed in his thought and life. Similarly the right must be that which produces such development in man; and the wrong that which hinders it. But Aristotle works this out much more fully in his specifically ethical writings than in his general metaphysical ones.

HAPPINESS OR ACTIVE HUMAN EXCELLENCE AS THE END OF MAN

In writing on ethics proper, Aristotle finds his way toward the kind of conclusion noted above through a very different and more distinctively moral approach. He begins his *Nicomachean Ethics* with a specific discussion of ends or goods. "Every art and every investigation, and likewise every practical pursuit or undertaking seems to aim at some good." [1] "Good is that at which all things aim"; [2] and the end "which we wish for its own sake" is the "one ultimate End" or "the Good, and indeed the Supreme Good." [3] It is with reference to this one supreme good that a satisfactory ethics is to be developed. The first task of ethical inquiry is accordingly to discover what this supreme good at which man ultimately aims in all things is.

Concerning the broad character of the supreme good, there seems, Aristotle thinks, to be almost unanimous agreement, "for both the multitude and persons of refinement speak of it as Happiness, and conceive 'the good life' or 'doing well' to be the same thing as 'being happy.'" [4] This generally accepted opinion that happiness is the supreme good is borne out by the observation that happiness is in reality "the end of all things done by human action," that "we always choose it for its own sake and never as a means to something else." [5] Further evidence for the supremacy of happiness is that happiness is beyond praise, for we do not praise "the standards to which everything else is referred"; [6] rather, we consider them "higher and more divine than things we praise." [7]

When it is agreed, however, that happiness is the supreme good, the precise nature of the supreme good remains vague until the nature of happiness is determined. At this point a wide variety of opinion exists. Some think that happiness is wealth or honor; others that it is pleasure; others that it is "the Life of Money-making"; and still others, such as Plato, that it is life in accord with the Universal Good. But all these ideas of happiness are clearly mistaken, the first three because they refer only to means to happiness, and the last because it does not denote any single quality that can be known or attained. Other similar conceptions of happiness are no more promising.

1 *Aristotle, The Nicomachean Ethics,* tr. by Harris Rackham (Cambridge: Harvard University Press, 1934), I, i, 1.
2 *Ibid.,* 2.
3 *Ibid.,* ii, 2.
4 *Ibid.,* iv, 2.
5 *Ibid.,* vi, 1 and 3.
6 *Ibid.,* xii, 5.
7 *Ibid.,* 4.

Thus one must inquire again what the supreme good of man is. Since the good of a flute player is performing the function of flute playing well, and that of a carpenter building well, the good of man would seem to consist in performing the function of a man well. Surely, if flute players, carpenters, and the like have functions, man must have a function, too, and if so his good can scarcely be anything other than performing that function well.

But what, specifically, are the function and the good of man as man? The function of man cannot be "the mere act of living," for this is "shared even by plants, whereas we are looking for the function peculiar to man." Nor can it be mere "sentient life," for this is "shared by horses, oxen, and animals generally." There remains the possibility that the distinctive function of man is "the practical life of the rational part of man," and such indeed is man's function. The function of man is "the exercise of the soul's faculties and activities in association with rational principle." [8] Accordingly the function of the *good* man is "to perform these activities well and rightly" or to perform them in accordance with their own "proper excellence." If this is the function of man the definition of his good follows from it: "the Good of man is the active exercise of his soul's faculties in conformity with excellence or virtue." [9]

Such an account of the supreme good reveals the nature of happiness, for if happiness and the excellent performance of man's functions as man are both in the same sense the Supreme Good of man, they are themselves one and the same thing. Happiness is thus no merely passive state of enjoyment; it is an active exercise of rational excellence. One should, however, note that Aristotle, unlike the Stoics, thinks that good fortune and bad fortune have a bearing upon happiness.

The account of the supreme good as the exercise of the human soul in its proper excellence not only shows what Aristotle takes happiness to be but also reveals the view of other moral concepts that is implied or expressed in his thought. The right be-

[8] *Ibid.,* vii, 14.
[9] *Ibid.,* 15.

comes what is in line with or promotes the true nature or proper excellence of man. *Virtue* is, as Aristotle himself insists, this excellence itself, and *the virtues* are particular excellences that properly belong to man. Just what these particular excellences are we are now to see.

VIRTUE AND THE MORAL AND INTELLECTUAL VALUES

Since virtue is excellence in the functioning of rational creatures, its divisions depend upon the divisions of their souls. Since the vegetable soul of man, which is most active in sleep, does not participate in reason, it has no human excellence. The animal soul in man, however, responds to reason, and the rational soul is by definition rational. It is to these two rational parts of the soul of man that the basic divisions of virtue correspond. The moral virtues are the excellences natural to the rational phase of man's animal soul, and the intellectual virtues are the excellences of the rational soul itself. The moral virtues free the individual for the exercise of the superior intellectual virtues and seem at the same time of some value on their own account. The rational virtues are supremely valuable in their own right.

Moral virtue consists neither of emotion nor of native capacities as such but of dispositions or habits. It is made up of such dispositions as represent the proper excellence of man, or prompt him to seek his supreme Good. It is acquired not by chance or by instruction but primarily by practice. Oddly enough, in arriving at a detailed account of its requirements, Aristotle does not attempt, as his principles would seem to suggest, to deduce the virtues from the functions of man. Instead he undertakes to discover and formulate clearly the kinds of dispositions that are generally considered virtuous, especially by prudent men. Apparently he assumes that what such men consider virtuous accords with the functions of man. This assumption discloses, of course, a limited resemblance between Aristotle's theory and the social approval theory.

However, Aristotle is not content to leave his readers without a general principle concerning the character of moral virtue. He suggests and attempts to show in detail that virtue is a mean between two extremes of vice.   What is meant by a mean may readily be seen by reference to simple arithmetic.   If 10 is taken as the more and 2 as the less, the mean between the more and the less is 6.   In similar fashion a moral virtue is a mean in conduct between a more and a less, but both the more and the less are vices, the one being an excess and the other a deficiency of that which is present in the virtue in proper proportion.

The particular character of the moral mean may be noted by examining such accepted virtues as courage, temperance, and liberality.   Thus, in the matter of "fear and confidence," the extreme of excess is rashness, and the extreme of deficiency is cowardice; courage avoids both extremes and is a virtuous mean between them.   With respect to "pleasures and pains," the excess is profligacy, and the deficiency is insensibility; the virtue of temperance is a proper mean between the two.   Similarly, with regard to "giving and getting money," the excess is prodigality, and the deficiency meanness, while the virtuous mean is liberality.

The principle of the mean is not, however, in itself a complete statement of the proper excellence of human nature in the practical field.   It needs to be supplemented in several ways.   One of its shortcomings is the failure of the virtuous mean to fall in all cases, precisely halfway between the vicious extremes, for the mean is often nearer one extreme than the other.   Thus in order to use the principle of the mean discreetly, certain qualifying rules must be kept in mind.   The first is "to avoid that extreme which is more opposed to the mean." [10]   The second is "to notice what are the errors to which we are ourselves most prone . . . and . . . drag ourselves away in the opposite direction." [11]   The third is to be "on guard against what is pleasant

[10] *Ibid.,* II, ix, 3.
[11] *Ibid.,* 4 and 5.

and against pleasure." For the rest Aristotle bids us follow the tastes and example of the prudent.

A second shortcoming of the idea of the mean is its apparent failure to cover such virtues as justice. Hence Aristotle presents a separate discussion of this virtue, without benefit of the principle of the mean,[12] although not without dependence on the general mathematical conception of proportion. Justice, Aristotle thinks, is essentially fairness or equality. It includes distributive justice, which is the proper apportionment of honor and wealth, and corrective justice, which includes the readjustment of irregularities in buying and selling as well as the punishment of crime. Such equality as is involved in justice is always proportional in the sense that while treating equals equally it also makes due allowance for differences in status among unequals. It does not, for example, attribute the same rights to slaves, women, and children as to citizens. It accords rights and privileges to people in proportion to their qualities and stations in life.

In contrast to the moral virtues, the intellectual virtues depend upon pure intellect. They include, Aristotle thinks, a more practical virtue and a more speculative virtue. The more practical virtue is prudence. Prudence is concerned not with first principles or deductions from absolute and unchanging axioms but with the moving, changing affairs of daily life. It is the exercise of sound deliberation in practical concerns and accordingly is the faculty of mind that discovers the proper mean with respect to moral virtues.[13] "Prudence is a truth-attaining quality in relation to the things that are good for human beings." [14] It is very much the same as Butler's "reflective principle" or conscience.

The more speculative intellectual virtue is wisdom, which consists of a "consummated knowledge of the most exalted objects." [15] In the exercise of this virtue in the contemplation of

12 See *ibid.*, p. xviii.
13 See *ibid.*
14 *Ibid.*, VI, v, 6.
15 *Ibid.*, vii, 3.

eternal truths, man most fully achieves his true function and realizes his fullest happiness. Such contemplation is the expression of his highest part, the most self-sufficient, the most human, and the most divine of all his activities.

CRITICAL EVALUATION OF THE HUMAN EXCELLENCE THEORY

The Aristotelian ethics of human excellence is at several points significantly sounder than the nature theories of Spencer and others. By restricting the meaning of right to the sphere of rational—or, at any rate, conscious—beings it makes such meanings much more definite. It also concentrates upon an appropriate area, for, when we scan the whole scope of possible moral meanings, we are unable to see how anything can in the end be morally significant apart from some reasonably close relation to conscious beings. At the same time Aristotle's theory avoids the dangerous illusion by which both Spencer and Nietzsche were misled that the heartless struggle that is so conspicuous in the lower levels of organic evolution must also play a prominent part in the moral conduct of rational creatures. Aristotelianism is also right in stressing the significance for ethics of precise knowledge of human nature, for, while sound practical moral judgments also require knowledge of external nature, they are peculiarly dependent upon those insights into the nature of man that reveal the kinds of experiences that are likely to be produced by various possible deeds. In the light of all this, whereas it may be said with some significance that in order to be right an act must be natural, it may be stated with much more definite meaning that in order to be right an act must be human.

However, that in order to be right an act must in the sense indicated above be human does not mean that if an act is human in this sense it is right. The human excellence theory, like the nature theories, turns out upon inspection to remain far too broad. Certainly accord with human nature cannot be strictly *what we mean* by "right" for we reserve the privilege of judging human nature as well as nature. But human nature is also not even a sufficiently restricted *criterion* of what we intend by "right," for all that human beings do is really human. The undiscriminating character of the appeal to human nature is somewhat obscured by Aristotle's insistence on that *excellence* which he took to be natural to man, but the obscurity is soon overcome when we analyze this concept. Human excellence is really an ambiguous notion. On the one hand, it sometimes suggests that which is most *characteristically human*. In this sense it certainly will not do as a test of the morally good or right, for moral evil is as characteristically human as moral good and the trouble with many of us is not that we are not human enough but that we are "all too human." On the other hand, human excellence sometimes suggests that which is *best in human beings*. But, while this may of course be a moral criterion, it is no longer, as Aristotle intends, a test in terms of human nature but rather one in terms of a *best* that has a partially independent meaning. This difficulty may be made clearer if, in inquiry concerning moral good, we ask the Aristotelian who it is that exemplifies the nature or excellence of man. Surely he cannot reply that it is the average man, for even the Aristotelian would freely confess that the average man is full of flaws. But then, if he replies that it is the *best* man, we shall have to ask him what the *good* is of which this *best* is the superlative, and this only brings him back to the point from which he started.

Human nature is both worse and better than Aristotle's appeal to it presupposes. There is virtually no experimental or rational evidence for the claim that man naturally tends to become just the kind of creature that Aristotle describes or for that matter any other single kind of creature that is precisely describable in advance. Rather, within man are vast unexplored and all too little known possibilities for all manner either of good or of evil. It is because of these varied possibilities in man that Aristotle is unable to make more than a bare beginning of deducing his practical code of morals from human nature as such and that he is obliged instead to refer back for the most part in this matter to recognized social approvals. It is also because of Aristotle's failure fully to appreciate these varied possibilities in man that such practical moral judgments as he does attempt to deduce from human nature, fine as they are in many respects, are seriously defective in others.   The attempt to make virtue at its best a mere mean instead of a supreme achievement rests upon too low a view of that of which man is capable.   The interpretation of justice as an unequal proportion takes man too much in terms of his limited known attainments and too little in terms of those immeasurable potentialities in him which forbid basic inequalities.   Finally Aristotle's effort to ground duties of consideration for others solely in man's natural altruism shows an insufficient appreciation both of the narrowness of man's actual selfishness and of the sweep of his potential unselfishness.

READINGS

Melden, *Ethical Theories,* pp. 89–128; *or*
Clark and Smith, *Readings in Ethics,* pp. 59–82; *or*
Rand, *The Classical Moralists,* pp. 53–79.

QUESTIONS

1. What does Aristotle mean by good?   By supreme good?   What, according to him, is the supreme good?   Do you agree?   Why?
2. What is Aristotle's conception of happiness?   How does it differ from the common conception of happiness?   How is it related to pleasure?   Do you think it is really a definition of happiness or an account of the way in which happiness is achieved?   Explain.
3. In what sense is action according to the *mean* for Aristotle natural to man and a means to happiness?   Illustrate the principle of the mean in terms of two of Aristotle's own examples.   In terms of the virtue of industriousness.   How would Aristotle's rules for the application of the mean apply in the case of the last-named virtue?
4. A common laborer brings a justifiable suit against a citizen of wealth and high position for payment on account of injuries received.   According to Aristotle should the settlement be the same as if the situation were reversed?   What would you think about the matter and why?
5. Aristotle seemed to believe that one should get things done in order to be free to think.   We in America are more apt to believe that one should think in order to get things done.   Who is right?   Is contemplation really the supreme good?   If not, is it then valuable

only for its results or is it worth at least something in itself?   Explain.

6. If you knew more about what kinds of actions produce pleasures and pains both at the time they are committed and in the long run and about what kinds help to create courage, temperance, and kindness, would this knowledge be of any significant use in helping you to act rightly?   If so, how?   Would this kind of knowledge help you to see what right or good means?

7. Of two identical twins one became a leading citizen and a "great soul" and the other became a despicable rogue.   Which acted according to his nature?   According to what did the other act?   Was one more human than the other?   If so, in what sense?   If the first was doing something more than "actualizing" his nature, what additional kind of end was he achieving?

REFERENCES

Adler, M. J., *A Dialectic of Morals* (Notre Dame, Ind.: University of Notre Dame Press, 1941).

Aquinas, Thomas, *Summa Contra Gentiles,* tr. by Dominican Fathers (London: Burns, Oates and Washbourne, 1923–29), Bk. III, Chs. 1–63.

———— *Summa Theologica,* in *The Great Books of the Western World* (Chicago: Encyclopedia Britannica Press, 1952), Vol. 20, First Part of Second Part, QQ. 49–114, pp. 1–379.

Aristotle, *Nicomachean Ethics,* in Ross, W. D. (ed.), *The Student's Oxford Aristotle* (New York: Oxford University Press, 1942), especially Bks. I and II.

Gomperz, Theodor, *Greek Thinkers,* tr. by G. G. Berry (London: J. Murray, 1914), Vol. IV.

Hyde, W. D., *The Five Great Philosophies of Life* (New York: Macmillan, 1932), Ch. 4.

Maritain, Jacques, *The Rights of Man and Natural Law* (New York: Scribner, 1943).

———— *Science and Wisdom* (New York: Scribner, 1940).

Mure, G. R. G., *Aristotle* (New York: Oxford University Press, 1932).

Ross, W. D., *Aristotle* (3rd ed., London: Methuen, 1937), Ch. 7.

Sidgwick, Henry, and Widgery, A. G., *Outlines of the History of Ethics* (London: Macmillan, 1939).

Taylor, A. E., *Aristotle* (New York: Thomas Nelson, 1943).

Tsanoff, R. A., *The Moral Ideals of Our Civilization* (New York: Dutton, 1942), pp. 15–21.

9

Human Nature Theories:
Self-Realization, Green

As we have seen, one of the weaknesses of the human excellence version of the human nature theory is that it tends to limit man to a fixed and unchangeable nature. The self-realization version of the human nature theory, which we are now to examine, overcomes this weakness by insisting that man is not so much a known object as a knowing self who has virtually infinite possibilities. It contends that man is not really a part of nature at all but a being that knows nature and transcends it. *"Right"* in this theory *means that which aids in realizing the vast unknown possibilities of man as a conscious self.*

The sources of the self-realization theory are in part the same as those of the human excellence theory. They include from the classical period the work of Socrates and Plato and especially that of Aristotle. However, the modern fathers and chief advocates of the self-realization theory are mostly nineteenth century philosophers who, while preserving the essential Aristotelian idea of the exercise of the full capacities of a man, based their ethical theories more directly upon the idealism implicit in the thought of Kant and especially upon Kant's conception of the spiritual freedom of man. Among the notable advocates of the theory were Hegel and his followers in Germany; F. H. Bradley, W. R. Sorley, J. H. Muirhead, and J. S. Mackenzie in England; and Josiah Royce, B. P. Bowne, W. E. Hocking, W. M. Urban, and

M. W. Calkins in America. A very large number of other writers have supported more popular versions of the theory in many countries, stressing a variety of aspects of self-realization, such as the full expression of one's powers, the concept of the all-round man, and the energizing of all one's capacities. However, the most influential statement of the claims of the theory is probably that of one of its English founders, T. H. Green (1836–82), whose *Prolegomena to Ethics* may still be regarded as the representative formulation.

THE ETERNAL CONSCIOUSNESS AND THE HUMAN SELF

Living as he did in an era when people were more and more inclined to think of the universe as a vast machine that produced everything, including man, with no purpose or aim, Green felt that there must be a new view of man and the universe, placing man over against the whole natural world, before there could be any satisfactory account of morality. He insisted that if we human beings are merely products of purposeless evolution, "our assertions of moral obligation are merely the expression of an ineffectual wish to be better off than we are, or are due to the survival of habits originally enforced by physical fear, but of which the origin is forgotten," [1] and that in this event the idea of what ought to be done as distinct from what is done is only a "serviceable illusion." But Green was sure that such could not be the case, for even the staunchest advocates of evolution "are as forward as any to propound rules of living, to which . . . man *ought* to conform." [2] Hence he contended that it was of utmost importance to look more deeply into the problem of the nature of the universe and of man. The required insight could best be achieved by re-examining the presuppositions on which our knowledge of the world rested.

Such a re-examination should begin, Green thought, with the

---

[1] T. H. Green, *Prolegomena to Ethics* (5th ed., Oxford: The Clarendon Press, 1907), p. 11.
[2] *Ibid.*, p. 10.

question of the difference between knowledge and illusion. On what basis can one say that some things are so and that others, such as the apparent motion of the sun around the earth, only seem to be so but are not? Any satisfactory answer must show that things are really related as we feel or think them to be related. But we cannot even ask intelligently whether things are related as we think they are unless we assume "a single and unalterable order of relations." Without such an order there would be nothing with which our impressions could be compared. The awareness of such an unalterable order, however, could never come to us from nature, for nature, consisting as it does of a disjointed series of events, could not possibly give rise to a concept of an unalterable system. Hence the concept of a permanent unalterable order of nature, without which the very idea of an objective nature as distinct from mere appearance could never emerge, must have its origin outside nature in an eternal consciousness.

A second question concerning the presuppositions of our knowledge of the world and also requiring re-examination is that of our basic apprehension of nature. How do we know or experience nature at all? An adequate answer must recognize that nature as experienced requires "a principle which renders all relations possible and is itself determined by none of them." Nature as experienced demands a unity in diversity. It contains a multitude of events that, unless they are somehow held together in a single manifold, are not nature at all but chaos and confusion. The necessary unity in diversity can be achieved, however, only by a consciousness that distinguishes itself from nature. Events that follow upon one another could never be brought within that unity which the succession of nature implies, nor could spread-out events ever be brought into the spatial order found in nature, were it not for an eternal consciousness that is outside of time and space.[3] "Nature in its reality, or in order to be what it is, implies a principle which is not natural." [4]

[3] See *ibid.*, p. 59.
[4] *Ibid.*, p. 61.

Hence through this second inquiry as through the first we are led to the idea of an eternal consciousness as the ground of knowledge.

The relation of man to the eternal consciousness that is presupposed in knowledge is that of man's participation on one side of his being in the eternal consciousness itself. Man belongs to two worlds. On the one side, he is a series of events among events, a creature of nature. This side of man evolves with the material process of evolution and grows with the growth of the individual. But, on the other side, man shares in the eternal consciousness that transcends not only particular events but the whole of nature. Thus Green writes of man: "While on the one hand his consciousness is throughout empirically conditioned,—in the sense that it would not be what at any time it is but for a series of events, sensible or related to sensibility, . . . —on the other hand his consciousness would not be what it is *as knowing,* or as a subject of intelligent experience, but for the self-realization or reproduction in it of an eternal consciousness, not existing in time but the condition of there being an order of time, not an object of experience but the condition of there being an intelligent experience, and in this sense not empirical but 'intelligible.' " [5] We must now see what kind of a meaning Green attributes to moral terms in the light of this account of man and the universe.

"GOOD," "MORALLY GOOD," AND "RIGHT"

Green's definition of "good" in its most general sense is similar to Aristotle's definition of "good" in this sense. Thus Green defines "the good generically as that which satisfies desire." [6] Desire is of course rooted in natural instinct and belongs in part to the natural order, but desire always also includes, for Green, consciousness of objects, which in turn involves consciousness of self. Moreover, basic human desires

5 *Ibid.,* p. 85.
6 *Ibid.,* p. 195.

are primarily not desires for pleasure, for the pleasantness of anything depends upon its goodness and not the other way around.

The morally good is accordingly to be distinguished from the generically good, not as that which produces pleasure in a certain way, but as "that which satisfies the desire of a moral agent, or that in which a moral agent can find the satisfaction of himself which he necessarily seeks, . . . [that] in which the effort of a moral agent can really find rest." [7] To be capable of desire at all is already to be a self sharing in eternal consciousness; to be a moral agent is to be capable of consciousness of an ideal self; and to satisfy the desire of a moral agent is to fulfill all that is implicit in such an ideal self. Thus "morally good" refers to the realization of a self participating to the fullest extent possible in eternal consciousness. Its end is a state in which "man, having become all that he is capable of becoming—all that, according to the divine plan of the world, he is destined to become—would find rest for his soul." [8]

"Right" for Green seems to mean essentially the same thing as "morally good." That is, an act is right if it furthers the realization of the human self not only as natural creature but also as manifestation of the eternal consciousness; and an act is wrong if it hinders such self-realization.

The significance of these definitions becomes somewhat clearer when one discovers more fully what Green means by a self. To begin with, a self is always a personality, an individual being that is "consciously an object to itself." [9] A self is never a nation or a community, for "national spirit and will" do not exist save "as the spirit and will of individuals." Hence the good can never be, as totalitarian governments pretend, the good of the state in which the good of the individuals is unimportant. In addition, a self is a being with a variety of capacities, such as those for intellectual apprehension, active endeavor, aesthetic appreciation, and religious worship. Since

[7] *Ibid.*, pp. 195–96.
[8] *Ibid.*, p. 196.
[9] *Ibid.*, p. 208.

all of these capacities belong to the self, none of them should be neglected. The man who develops only a part of himself at the expense of the rest is not fully a man. Self-realization is the realization of all one's capacities. One must be allowed and encouraged to become all he is capable of becoming. Finally, a self, in being conscious, is also a part of one all-embracing Eternal Consciousness, in which the capacities that are yet to be realized in its individual life are already realized. Our search for the better implies the existence of a best that is altogether desirable and in which we share. The fully realized ideal self exists "not merely *for,* but *in* God, and gives us ground for hope for its realization in ourselves. There must be eternally such a subject which is all that the self-conscious subject, as developed in time, has the possibility of becoming; in which the idea of the human spirit, or all that it has in itself to become, is completely realized. This consideration may suggest the true notion of the spiritual relation in which we stand to God; that He is not merely a Being who has made us, in the sense that we exist as an object of the divine consciousness in the same way in which we must suppose the system of nature so to exist, but that He is a being in whom we exist; with whom we are in principle one; with whom the human spirit is identical, in the sense that He *is* all which the human spirit is capable of becoming." [10]

On the basis of this account of the self it may be said that moral good and right consist, for Green, in the actual realization of all those capacities of an individual self that are already implicitly realized in the eternal consciousness within him. However, this statement remains rather general, and it does not immediately permit one to see what particular ideals he should aspire to or what duties he ought to perform. To Green's answer to this difficulty we now turn.

MORAL IDEALS

Green is well aware that the deduction of definite ideals and duties from a general definition of right in terms of self-realiza-

10 *Ibid.,* pp. 215–16.

tion is not easy, but he does not think the problem insoluble. Accordingly he proceeds to point out a number of ways in which the goal of self-realization may show the path of particular duties.

At the outset, Green is confident that the awareness of an ideal self to the realization of which our particular acts contribute, in itself, yields practical moral guidance. It is impossible, he thinks, for anyone to hold the idea of such a self before his mind without being led by it onward and upward. This idea is the source of all moral progress in the past and the promise of any that is to come. It indicates the general lines of our positive duties, and at the same time it points out paths that should not be followed, blind alleys into which the spirit of man might be tempted to stray. It indicates, for example, that the life of the voluptuary is self-defeating because it seeks its satisfaction in that in which a being who shares the divine consciousness cannot by his very nature find satisfaction.[11] It shows, further, that no individual is ever justified in making an exception to the command to do that which would contribute to the self-realization of any spiritual being, either for the sake of his own pursuit of pleasure or for anything else that would be incompatible with such an end.

The self-realization principle can, however, furnish still more definite moral guidance. Since the consciousness of men partakes of an eternal consciousness, and since awareness of the fact of a perfect moral ideal has been the root of all moral progress up to now, the customs, institutions, and moral ideals that man has developed represent in general the moral demands of the eternal consciousness in us for the present stage of our development. The prevailing laws and ideals of our era represent for the most part our contemporary duties. Since in order to live for the realization of the eternal consciousness we must live for it in some definite time and place, "each has primarily to fulfil the duties of his station." [12] Thus to live the practical moral life is in the main to do the thing that the laws of one's country

11 See *ibid.*, pp. 199–200.
12 *Ibid.*, p. 209.

and the prevailing code demand within the particular situation in which one has been placed. Departure from the duties of custom and station is never warranted save as loyalty to the ideal of a perfect self may demand it.

This relation of prevailing customs and ideal self means that most specific moral ideals are relative and not absolute. Times and circumstances change and specific moral ideals must change with them. But this is no objection to moral ideals as such. Indeed there would be ground for objection if they did not vary, for progress toward the realization of the one changeless ideal of the realization of the eternal consciousness in us is not possible except as more detailed requirements are changed to meet changing conditions.

In addition to the moral guidance afforded by the particular customs and codes that indicate our present duties, rational analysis of the customs and codes that the eternal consciousness has produced through the centuries indicates three broad principles. Although these principles are discovered by study of the past, they may properly be projected into our decisions for the future.

The first principle is that the moral good is a common good, not of course in the sense that it is a good distinct from the good of individuals but in the sense that each must share the good with others in order to have good for himself. Every man is so much a part of society that his own good can never be realized apart from the good of others. Although this interdependence is in part due to the fact that each is endowed with an animal sympathy that causes him pleasure or pain in the pleasure or pain of his fellows, it is more significantly rooted in the fact that men share alike in an eternal consciousness. No man can fully realize the demands of the eternal consciousness of which he is a part without seeking to realize it in others who are also parts of it. Every man represents an end to be realized; and every man must also stand in a "relation to some group of persons whose well-being he takes to be his own, and in whom he is interested in being interested in himself." [13] After all, "reasonable Self-

13 *Ibid.*, p. 233.

Love and Benevolence" are not only coordinate but identical. In fact, "the distinction of good for self and good for others has never entered into the idea of a true good on which moral judgments are founded." [14]   To serve ourselves we must serve others and in serving others we also serve ourselves.

The second principle revealed by analysis of the manifestations of the eternal consciousness in the moral development of man is that the common good must logically come to include all men.   This principle has been disclosed through the progressive expansion of the idea of the common good to include larger and larger numbers of persons.   In primitive society man applied his conception of the common good to a very limited group, his family or his tribe.   He was likely to be altogether inconsiderate and ruthless in his attitudes toward persons outside this group.   However, as his contacts became broader, he gradually came to include more and more persons in the group to which he felt a responsibility, until at last the terms of affection by which he formerly referred to the narrower group came to be applied to man generally, as when one speaks of "a human family, of a fraternity of all men, of the common fatherhood of God . . . or . . . the Humanity for which Christ died." [15]   Those who scoff at this notion as hypocritical usually do so to cover their own selfishness.   The fact is "it is almost an axiom of popular Ethics that there is a duty of every man to every man—a duty which becomes actual so soon as one comes to have dealings with the other." [16]   That this extension of the scope of the moral ideal should have come about as it has is in considerable measure due to Christianity, which has enlarged the compass of every one of the ancient Greek virtues and given them a wider context. Yet basically the cause of the expansion is the nature of the moral ideal, which, being the good of a conscious self that includes among its ends the good of other conscious selves as ends in themselves, cannot ultimately stop short of the inclusion of every self-conscious individual.

14 *Ibid.*, p. 238.
15 *Ibid.*
16 *Ibid.*

Thus extended, the idea of a common good has yielded a conception of justice in which "no one should seek to gain by another's loss, gain and loss being estimated on the same principle for each." [17] It has produced a conviction that "Every human person has an absolute value; that humanity in the person of every one is always to be treated as an end, never as a means; that in the estimate of well-being which forms the true good every one is to count for one, no one for more than one; that every one has a 'suum' which every one else is bound to render him." [18] In practice we recognize this ideal to the extent of according equal rights to all but, unfortunately, not to the extent of seeking for all the opportunity of a decent living.

The third principle discovered by analysis of the development of moral and social institutions is that, since men have come progressively to regard good will as the supreme good, good will must indeed be such a good.   In the earliest times the common good was sought in terms of bodily goods, although even these were pursued with an unrecognized reference to the fulfillment of a spiritual self.   Later the goods of the soul were more distinctly recognized, as, for example, when men came to distinguish the deserving of prosperity from prosperity itself.   At this time courage, temperance, and like virtues began to be valued on their own account.   Finally, after many centuries, the content of the self to be realized in ourselves and others was seen to be conscientiousness or good will.   Nothing other than this can possibly be the supreme good.   Indeed it is only when good will is supreme that good can ever be common good, for all other goods involve conflict in the sense that one person's gain in them is another's loss in them.   Good will itself is not, however, an empty form but a will for all those goods that the divine consciousness, working through the institutions of society, has taught us to cherish.

Specific moral ideals are thus to be discovered in the main by keeping in mind the particular demands of the society in which one lives in the light of the community, inclusiveness, and in-

17 *Ibid.*, p. 254.
18 *Ibid.*, p. 253.

wardness of good. At the same time, since society is made up of creatures who have animal as well as spiritual natures and so may err, one must stand ready to see and correct the mistakes of society by holding before himself always the idea of a self already realized in the eternal consciousness. The same devotion to the idea of a perfect self-realization that keeps the saint loyal to accepted duties guides the prophet in the discovery of new ones. Just as a geometrical principle applied to new patterns yields new rules, so devotion to the idea of a perfect self applied to new moral situations supplies new ideals.

CRITICAL EVALUATION OF THE
SELF-REALIZATION THEORY

The self-realization theory has done moral philosophy a significant service in focusing attention more than any other view upon the essential place of personality in moral matters. Far more than upon how anyone feels about an act, or the bare form of the act, or the conformity of the act to nature or even to human nature, the rightness of an act depends upon its effect upon living, growing personalities. Green sees this relationship much more clearly than does even Aristotle, and his stress upon the vast unrealized potentialities in human selves is more in line with both psychological evidences and the intentions of critical moral statements. Because of Green's broader vision at this point he is able to see, as Aristotle, who sanctions slavery and inequality, is not, the inestimable worth of every human being and the demand implicit in that worth for equality in the administration of justice and in the distribution of opportunity. Personality is the principal seat of all the values. In conscious experience alone is good realized, and personality is the chief abode of such experience. Thus it may be said with at least approximate accuracy that every right act is one that in some measure helps and enhances personality and every wrong act is one that hinders or undermines personality. In this sense self-realization is at least an important aspect of the meaning of right.

The question, however, still remains whether or not self-realization is always right and whether, even if it is, it constitutes the sole meaning of "right." The answer must be in the negative, and the main reason is similar to one noted in the case of the human excellence theory. When Green identifies right with the realization of self, he seems really to assume both that the self in its true nature is fully in line with what is good and that the real self represents the very meaning of good in its moral sense. However, if the first of these assumptions involves any more than the tautology that the *moral* self is moral, it appears to be plainly false; and, if so, the plausibility of the second one is largely undermined. There is nothing about a self as such that guarantees that it will have the qualities ordinarily meant by goodness. A bad self can be quite as real as a good one. As even Plato long ago admitted, although evil is the enemy of the soul, evil does not itself destroy the soul. An evil self may realize itself in evil as well as a good one in good. Everything depends upon the *kind* of self that is realized and in *what* it is realized. Nor does appeal to an eternal consciousness, to social institutions, to the capacities of man, or to well-roundedness help to clear away this difficulty, for institutions, capacities, and well-roundedness can all have evil bents, and even the idea of an eternal consciousness as such contains nothing to assure its goodness. To be sure, if one follows the phase of Green's thought that makes the self at the outset a good or *moral* self, one of course escapes this side of the difficulty; but, in such a case, one at the same time assumes the concept to be defined in the definition and shifts from the ground of actual experience to that of extremely unrealistic suppositions. Indeed, this ambiguity is the chief root of the confusion all along. Green seems really to be thinking most of the time of a *good* self, of a *good* consciousness, of *good* institutions. Accordingly, for those who already know and intend to be guided by such goods, self-realization is an admirable ethical end. But for those who do not already know what good is, the idea of self-realization is of little use. In moral philosophy one must ask what good itself means, and a satisfactory ethical theory must express rather than merely assume the principal phases of the answer.   When one takes for granted, rather than endeavoring specifically to point out, the good that the self is to realize, one produces not only theoretical difficulties but also practical ones as well.   Sooner or later those whose assumptions about good are not so sound as Green's own and whose selves, unlike his good self, are bad will make use of the theory, as they have often done, to justify the realizing of the evil ends of their evil selves; and, unless some further account of good is given, there is nothing in the self-realization principle as such to say that their acts are wrong.

Because the self-realization theory lacks a sufficiently specific definition of the good that is attained in the individual's self-realization, its account of the good and the right that are involved in relations among different persons is likewise seriously deficient.   Granted that Green says some very fine things about our duties to others, about the community of good, and about the universal scope of self-realization, the difficulty remains that none of these things really follows from the conception of realizing one's self, unless either the self happens to be much more generous than most of our selves actually seem to be or the self is in circular and arbitrary fashion identified with the good self.   To be sure, the concept of men's joint participation in a single eternal consciousness may be evoked at this point but this concept depends at best upon a whole system of somewhat doubtful metaphysical constructions.   One may also appeal to the universal character of good, which seems to be independent of *mine* and *thine*, but this universality apparently has nothing directly to do with the nature of the self.   In any case there are kinds of selves that seem to be realized in conflict.   It is *good* selves that are realized in cooperation, and the problem is to define the good.   Moreover, even if this objection to grounding the right that pertains to human relations in self-realization alone were ignored, another serious one would remain.   It would be nonsense, according to the self-realization theory, to say that any individual ever could, or should, sacrifice his good for the good of others, for in serving others he quite properly would act in the end for his own good.   But actually we do sometimes *say* with apparent meaning that individuals can and should make such sacrifices, and there seem to be sufficient reasons also for *believing* that people can and should make them.

CONCLUSIONS CONCERNING HUMAN NATURE THEORIES

In the light of the foregoing considerations, our conclusions about human nature theories must be somewhat as follows. These theories have vastly improved upon nature theories by pointing out a much more restricted area in which moral meanings are successfully to be sought out and values realized. Values are attainable only in conscious experience, and, as the self-realization theory has properly shown, the possibilities in each person are so vast that the opportunities of none should be neglected. Accordingly, right acts are human and conducive to self-realization. But acts that have these properties are none the less not necessarily right, for human selves may be bad as well as good. Human nature theories, like nature ones, are too broad to express adequately the real intentions of critical moral judgments. What is needed is some more specific criterion that designates more precisely that among the varied experiences attainable by human beings which is good for man and is the end of right action. To some theories that endeavor in more definite terms to point out such a criterion we now turn.

READINGS

Clark and Smith, *Readings in Ethics,* pp. 314–34; *or*
Rand, *The Classical Moralists,* pp. 740–59; *or*
Melden, *Ethical Theories,* pp. 393–424.

QUESTIONS

1. Recently an enormously expensive military airplane was found to be nearly out of fuel over the eastern Atlantic. The pilot could either land on the ocean and probably save the personnel aboard but lose the plane or try to reach land and save the plane at much greater

risk to the personnel.   Without hesitation he chose the former course.
Did he act rightly?   Why or why not?   What do you think about the
priority of personal rights over property rights?   How do the courts
seem to you to treat this matter as a rule?   How would Green treat
it?

2. Some educational systems seem to take it to be their duty to set
forth fully the type of knowledge and character they want to establish in their students and then to try to mold their students in precisely these patterns.   Would Green agree?   If he would protest,
why?   Why and how would you want to improve upon such educational procedure?

3. Granted that prevailing moral customs do not represent the
whole meaning of morality, of what moral value are they according to
Green?   If you disagree with Green concerning the particular purpose they serve, what role would you assign them in the moral life?

4. Is it possible for a self to attain the greatest good for itself
without bestowing good on others?   Can one properly set limits to
the circle of those who should receive consideration?   Explain.   Is
this expansiveness in morality rooted altogether in the nature of the
self or does it rest also partly on the character of a good that may be
attained by, but is not necessarily inherent in, the self?

5. Do you think that Stalin realized himself less than Franklin
Roosevelt realized himself?   If so, in what sense?   What is the
difference between realizing one's self and attaining the best that one
is capable of attaining?   Is the latter definable in terms of the former?
Why or why not?

6. During World War II a group of soldiers were trapped in a
foxhole in enemy territory.   One of them, having quickly sized up
the situation, deliberately dashed out of the foxhole in the direction
of the enemy in order, in drawing their fire upon himself, to allow
his buddies to escape.   Was he simply realizing himself or was he
making a genuine sacrifice?   Explain.   Is it possible for an act to
have more moral good than self-realization in it?   How so, or why
not?

REFERENCES

Bradley, F. H., *Ethical Studies* (2nd ed. rev., New York: Oxford Uni-
    versity Press, 1927), Ch. 5.
Calkins, M. W., *The Good Man and the Good* (New York: Macmillan,
    1928).

Carritt, E. F., *The Theory of Morals* (London: Oxford University Press, 1928), Chs. 5–6.

Everett, W. G., *Moral Values* (New York: Holt, 1918), Chs. 4–5.

Ewing, A. C., *The Definition of Good* (New York: Macmillan, 1947), Ch. 3.

Green, T. H., *Prolegomena to Ethics* (5th ed., Oxford: The Clarendon Press, 1907).

Hegel, G. W. F., *The Philosophy of Right,* tr. by S. W. Dyde (London: G. Bell, 1896).

Hill, T. E., *Contemporary Ethical Theories* (New York: Macmillan, 1950), Ch. 16.

Hocking, W. E., *Human Nature and Its Remaking* (New Haven: Yale University Press, 1923).

Mackenzie, J. S., *Manual of Ethics* (London: University Tutorial Press, 1910).

Muirhead, J. H., *Elements of Ethics* (New York: Scribner, 1932).

Paton, H. J., *The Good Will* (New York: Macmillan, 1927).

Rashdall, Hastings, *Theory of Good and Evil* (London: Oxford University Press, 1924), Vol. II, Bk. II, Ch. 3.

Rogers, A. K., *Morals in Review* (New York: Macmillan, 1927), Chs. 17–18.

Seth, James, *A Study of Ethical Principles* (17th ed., New York: Scribner, 1926).

Titus, H. H., *Ethics for Today* (2nd ed. rev., New York: American Book, 1954), Ch. 12.

Tsanoff, R. A., *The Moral Ideals of Our Civilization* (New York: Dutton, 1942), Ch. 35.

Urban, W. M., *Fundamentals of Ethics* (New York: Holt, 1930).

Wright, W. K., *General Introduction to Ethics* (New York: Macmillan, 1929).

10

Specific Value Theories: Pleasure Theories

OUR SEARCH FOR THE MEANING OF right has so far suggested that the nature and human nature theories are correct in seeking such meaning in ends rather than either in attitudes or in forms of action as such, that of these two theories the latter focuses attention more sharply than the former upon the general area in which the meaning of morality is to be found, and that of the two versions of the human nature theory the self-realization one properly concentrates upon personal consciousness. At the same time, we have noticed that the human nature theory, even in its more convincing self-realization version, fails to identify the character of that within experience which is valuable sufficiently specifically to support the kind of distinction that is commonly intended between the right and the wrong.

The writers whose theories we are now to consider attempt to remedy this defect by bringing to light the precise property attaching to such human experiences as are valuable that makes them valuable. That is, these writers define "good" not simply in terms of human nature or selfhood but in terms of something more definite that makes a self or its experiences good. For these writers, as for advocates of other teleological theories, the right depends on the good and consists in the production of good, but the good is more specific than in other teleological theories. Thus for the writers in question "good" comes to refer to *some definite relation or quality of experience toward which effort ought to be directed* and "right" means *the production of as much of this good as possible.* Because of the character of the account that is here given to the term "good" we shall call the theories of the philosophers under consideration "specific value theories."

Obviously, a considerable variety can exist within the general formula of the specific value theories, for the specific kinds of ends that good is taken to refer to may differ widely. For our purposes, however, only three basic forms of specific value theory are important. The first of these equates the good with the *pleasant.* The second identifies it with the desired. The third, unable to reduce the good to pleasure, to the desired, or to anything else, regards good as a *unique quality.* We shall refer to these three theories in the order indicated as the "pleasure theory," the "desire theory," and the "unique good theory." Although each differs from the others as to the meaning of "good," they all agree that "right" means the production of the most possible of whatever is good.

The type of specific value theory that has been most prominent in the history of ethical thought is the one equating the good with the pleasant and hence the right with the production of maximum pleasure. This type of theory is commonly known as *hedonism* from the Greek *hedone,* meaning pleasure.

Hedonistic or pleasure theories are divided into a number of subtypes according to whose pleasures and what pleasures are emphasized and how the pleasure principle (that pleasure alone is good) is verified and applied. Theories that define right in terms primarily of the agent's own pleasures are commonly called "egoistic," those that define it in terms of the pleasures of all are often called "universalistic." All of the non-egoistic theories to be considered here are universalistic, and all of these theories are to be referred to, in accord with customary usage, as forms of "utilitarianism." *Egoistic hedonism* interprets the rightness of an act in terms of conduciveness to the pleasure of doer of the act. *Universalistic hedonism* interprets such rightness in terms of conduciveness to the pleasure of all human beings. Universalistic hedonism has been presented in a variety of forms, and in all its forms is commonly referred to as "utilitarianism." *Quantitative utilitarianism* determines the right in terms of the amount of pleasure produced regardless of the kind of pleasure. *Qualitative utilitarianism* emphasizes kinds or qualities of pleasure. *Intuitional utilitarianism* supports and supplements the pleasure principle by reference to certain axioms said to be given by immediate insight or intuition.

EGOISTIC HEDONISM, EPICURUS

The foremost representative of egoistic hedonism is Epicurus (340–270 B.C.), the genial sage of Athens whose name is often attached to all forms of pleasure theories. In the popular conception Epicurus is often represented as advocating a heedless pursuit of the pleasures of unrestrained eating, drinking and making merry, but in actual fact what he favored was a much saner and more moderate quest for more durable pleasures.

Epicurus was uncompromising in his expression of the conviction that pleasure is the only good. "I know not," he writes, "how I can conceive the good, if I withdraw the pleasures of taste, and withdraw the pleasures of love, and withdraw the pleasures of hearing, and withdraw the pleasurable emotions caused to sight by beautiful form." [1] Again, he declares: "We call pleasure the beginning and end of the blessed life. For we recognize pleasure as the first good innate in us." [2] He is quite willing to accept all the consequences of this doctrine. Thus, "every pleasure because of its natural kinship to us is good even as every pain also is an evil"; [3] and the obverse is equally true: "no pleasure is a bad thing in itself," [4] and no

[1] Epicurus, "Fragments," *Epicurus, The Extant Remains,* tr. by Cyril Bailey (Oxford: The Clarendon Press, 1926), p. 123.
[2] Epicurus, "Letter to Menoeceus," *Epicurus, The Extant Remains,* p. 87.
[3] *Ibid.,* p. 89.
[4] Epicurus, "Principal Doctrines," *Epicurus, The Extant Remains,* p. 97.

pain is good in itself.   The only thing that is evil about an ill-chosen pleasure is the pain that may follow it.   Even the grossest injustice would involve no evil if one could escape the penalty of it, although in fact one can never altogether do so. "Injustice is not an evil in itself, but only in consequence of the fear which attaches to the apprehension of being unable to escape those appointed to punish such actions." [5]   No relation or activity in life can be said to be good or valuable except as it yields to personal pleasure; even friendship is rooted in the uses that a friend may serve in promoting one's pleasures.   The same thing may be said of virtue and knowledge and everything else that goes to make up one's life.

If pleasure is for Epicurus the only good, the production of the maximum pleasure of the individual is for him the only right.   To be sure, Epicurus, like all the rest of the Greek moralists, makes no extensive use of the words "right" and "duty," but, quite clearly, it is the production of one's greatest pleasure that fills the role of that to which modern terminology applies the word "right."   The production or attainment of one's maximum pleasure is the ethical end, or that which one ought to endeavor to achieve.   This view implies a rejection of some pleasures and even an acceptance of some pains in the interest of the greatest total of personal pleasure.   Hence Epicurus holds that "not every pleasure is to be chosen," and "not all [pains] are always of a nature to be avoided." [6]   We are to remember that "sometimes we pass over many pleasures, when greater discomfort accrues to us as a result of them: and similarly we think many pains better than pleasures, since a greater pleasure comes to us when we have endured pains for a long time." [7]

Epicurus seeks to base his doctrine that pleasure is the only good and that right consists in seeking the most pleasure on the belief that men do in fact seek always pleasure and avoid pain for themselves.   Asserting the naturalness and inevitability of pursuit of the one and flight from the other, Epicurus de-

5 *Ibid.*, p. 103.
6 Epicurus, "Letter to Menoeceus," p. 89.
7 *Ibid.*

clares: "All living creatures as soon as they are born take delight
in pleasure, but resist pain by a natural impulse apart from
reason"; [8] and "from pleasure we begin every act of choice and
avoidance, and to pleasure we return again." [9] The only
sane moral inference from the fact that men do always seek
their own pleasure is, Epicurus thinks, that men always should
seek their own pleasure as intelligently as possible, and to the
following of this quest he repeatedly exhorts his disciples.
Men are so constituted that they must seek pleasure and avoid
pain; accordingly, the wise course for them is to do both as
effectively as they can. The doctrine that men always *do* in
fact seek their own pleasure is commonly referred to as *psychological* hedonism to distinguish it from the kindred but different
doctrine of *ethical* hedonism, that men *should* seek pleasure.
Thus Epicurus may be said to have based his ethical hedonism
upon psychological hedonism, and in this procedure, as we
shall see, most hedonists, until comparatively recent years,
have followed him.

If right consists in winning as much pleasure and avoiding as
much pain as possible for one's self, one needs to be able to
ascertain the amounts of pleasure or pain involved in or promised by the various experiences that life offers. As Epicurus
puts it, "by a scale of comparison and by consideration of
advantages and disadvantages we must form our judgments on
all these matters." [10] Although Epicurus furnishes no such
precise scale as would seem to be required, he does make some
interesting suggestions about the measurement of pleasure.
The pleasures of the mind are to be preferred to those of the
body. The more passive pleasures, consisting primarily in the
absence of pain, are better on the whole than the more active
ones. Indeed the complete absence of pain seems to be a sort of
a limit of pleasure, being itself a pleasure to which neither
greater intensity nor duration can add anything. Pleasure appears to be in large part removal of pain and to have no degrees

---

8 Diogenes Laertius, "Life of Epicurus," *Epicurus, The Extant Remains*, p. 171.
9 Epicurus, "Letter to Menoeceus," p. 87.
10 *Ibid.*, p. 89.

of more or less. Writes Epicurus: "That which creates joy insuperable is complete removal of a great evil. And this is the nature of good, if one can grasp it rightly, and then hold by it, and not walk about babbling idly about the good." [11] Again, he says, "Infinite time contains no greater pleasure than limited time, if one measures by reason the limits of pleasure." [12] Concerning the measurement of pain Epicurus has little to say, but he reminds his readers that most intense pains are of short duration and that since a life reasonably free from pain is all that is required, man can well attain his goal.

By what means is the pleasurable life to be attained once its objective is understood? Epicurus answers this question in terms of two more or less distinct procedures that remind one somewhat of the moral and intellectual virtues of Aristotle. One concerns conduct directly; the other concerns thought. Beginning with the more practical of the two, Epicurus commends the accepted virtues as means to the life of pleasure. To be sure, the exercise of such virtues must be kept in its place as only instrumental to an end, for "virtue is preferred for the sake of pleasure and not for its own sake, just as a doctor's art is employed for the sake of health." [13] Nevertheless, the virtues are indispensable to pleasure, for "the virtues are by nature bound up with the pleasant life, and the pleasant life is inseparable from them." [14]

The virtues that Epicurus believes to be necessary means to pleasure include all the traditional Greek virtues. One cannot hope to be happy unless he is willing to practice temperance, courage, and justice, for the consequences of failure to practice these virtues are nearly always unpleasant. However, for Epicurus, the supreme virtue is prudence, which selects the kinds of activities producing the most pleasure and commends the other virtues to us. Prudence bids us choose the milder pleasures in preference to the more exciting ones. It bids us elect the simple diet in order that we may not be in want and

11 Epicurus, "Fragments," p. 135.
12 Epicurus, "Principal Doctrines," p. 99.
13 Diogenes Laertius, *op. cit.*
14 Epicurus, "Letter to Menoeceus," p. 91.

that we may be the more ready to enjoy a feast when it is offered. It bids us set strict limits to, or to refrain altogether from, sexual indulgence, and to avoid domestic and political responsibilities. Prudence is the very touchstone of morality. From its standpoint "it is better to be unfortunate in reasonable action than to prosper in unreason." [15] Nevertheless, like all the other virtues, prudence is only a means to the attainment of pleasure; and its worth depends in the end solely on the pleasure that it enables one to find.

The second of Epicurus's procedures for securing pleasure, reminiscent of Aristotle's intellectual virtue, is a proper regulation of thought. Such regulation consists in part in directing the mind toward pleasant rather than unpleasant objects. Epicurus sets a notable example of this sort of discipline by writing to a friend shortly before his own death: "On this truly happy day of my life, as I am at the point of death, I write this to you. The disease[s] in my bladder and stomach are pursuing their course, lacking nothing of their natural severity: but against all this is the joy in my heart at the recollection of my conversations with you." [16]

However, the chief part of the intellectual means to pleasure recommended by Epicurus is the attainment of a view of the world in keeping with the end of peace of mind. In contrast to Aristotle, Epicurus was not interested in truth as such, but he felt that superstitious fears of the supernatural and of death were serious hindrances to happiness and that the only cure for these ills was a materialistic philosophy that explained the world without reference to the gods or to an afterlife. Such a philosophy he found in the work of the earlier materialist, Democritus. Following this thinker, he set forth a world view somewhat as follows. The universe consists of atoms endowed with spontaneous motion and proceeding endlessly and generally downward through infinite empty space. The gods exist but, being completely happy themselves, they are altogether uncon-

15 *Ibid.,* p. 99.
16 Epicurus, "Fragments," pp. 127, 129.

cerned about the world or men. What men call the soul is only a collection of fine and smooth atoms, which, although it has a freedom of choice that enables it to select its pleasures well or ill, disintegrates with the body. Because the gods neither care nor do anything about man, men need not fear them; and because death is not yet before it comes to one, and one is no more when it has come, men need not fear death either.

QUANTITATIVE UTILITARIANISM, JEREMY BENTHAM

Epicurus's hedonism could scarcely have been expected to survive in the atmosphere of Catholic theology that dominated Western thought during the Medieval period; nor could the prevailingly egoistic tone of his theory be expected to reassert itself in any Christian era. Nevertheless, after a near eclipse in the Middle Ages, hedonism did reassert itself in new and different forms and has ever since continued to play an influential role in moral philosophy. It reappeared first on the European continent in the thought of Pierre Gassendi and then in England in some phases of the thought of Thomas Hobbes. Beginning with John Locke, it took a theological and somewhat more benevolent turn, which involved the belief that a good God made use of each man's desire for his own happiness to prompt men, by appropriate rewards and punishments, to seek the happiness of mankind. The idea of a general happiness of mankind as the end of morality was placed in a secular framework by Jeremy Bentham (1748–1832). In working out this idea in his *Principles of Morals and Legislation* with reference to its application to the legislative problems of his own age, Bentham gave to hedonism what is in many respects its characteristic modern expression.

Like Epicurus, Bentham is a confirmed psychological hedonist; that is, he believes that men always seek their own pleasure. He begins his book by declaring, "Nature has placed mankind under the governance of two sovereign masters, pain and pleasure. . . . They govern us in all we do, in all we say, in all we think." [17] Again like Epicurus, Bentham bases a hedonistic definition of good upon his psychological hedonism. "Now, Pleasure is in *itself* a good—nay even, setting aside immunity from pain, the only good; pain is in itself an evil—and, indeed without exception, the only evil; or else the words good and evil have no meaning." [18] Once more Bentham quite agrees with Epicurus that the ethical or the right is that which produces the most pleasure. Thus in the psychological foundations of their systems and in their basic definitions the two writers are alike.

Beyond these underlying areas of agreement, however, Bentham parts company with his ancient predecessor. Whose pleasure is it that is to be promoted in right action? Epicurus, while occasionally recognizing the value of service, had answered, fundamentally, "one's own pleasure"; but Bentham, while not neglecting the pleasure of the agent, answers, essentially, "the pleasure of the community." The word that Bentham uses to define the principle of right is "utility," of which he gives the following account: "An action may be said to be conformable to the principle of utility . . . when the tendency it has to augment the happiness of the community is greater than any it has to diminish it." [19] This principle of utility, or of the promotion of a balance of pleasure over pain for all concerned, represents the only meaning that "right" and "duty" can possibly have. "When thus interpreted, the words *ought*, and *right* and *wrong*, and others of that stamp, have a meaning when otherwise, they have none." [20] Accordingly, in Bentham's thought right action is always the promotion not simply of one's own pleasure but of that of the community of all persons affected by one's act. It is in view of this social outlook that the type of universalistic hedonism advocated by Bentham is to

---

[17] Jeremy Bentham, *An Introduction to the Principles of Morals and Legislation* (Oxford: The Clarendon Press, 1907), p. 1.
[18] *Ibid.*, p. 102.
[19] *Ibid.*, p. 3.
[20] *Ibid.*, p. 4.

be distinguished from the narrower egoistic hedonism of Epicurus.

What is the community whose happiness is to be promoted and how is happiness to be distributed among its members? The community, Bentham informs us, is simply "the individual persons" who are affected by an action; and its happiness consists of the happiness or the pleasures of the persons who make it up.   Happiness is to be distributed along equalitarian democratic lines.   No one's happiness is to be thought of as being any more important than that of anyone else.   As Bentham puts it: "everybody to count for one, and nobody for more than one."   Thus, the moral end can be put in a phrase that Benthamism has borrowed from a moralist of another school, namely, "the greatest happiness of the greatest number."

Concerning the question of how pleasure is to be measured in order to insure the greatest amount of it for all, Bentham is again at variance with Epicurus.   Pleasure, he thinks, does not reach its limit in the absence of pain, nor is it unaffected by intensity and duration.   On the contrary, it is a positive factor that may exist in a wide variety of degrees.   Bentham undertakes to set forth a scale for its precise measurement. Such a scale must, he thinks, be purely quantitative.   Pleasures can differ as pleasures only in amount, not in kind, and happiness is only a sum of pleasures, not, as Aristotle thought, something above and beyond them.   One activity is as good as another if the resulting pleasures are the same: "Pushpin is as good as poetry."   Factors involved in a satisfactory quantitative scale include: *intensity, duration, certainty,* or *uncertainty,* and *propinquity* or *remoteness.*   In considering acts that directly yield pleasure or pain, one should also consider the *fecundity* of the pleasure, that is "the chance it has of being followed by sensations of the same kind"; and its *purity,* or "the chance it has of being followed by sensations of the opposite kind." [21]   Moreover, in considering the totality of the pleasure produced by a given act, one must also consider its

[21] *Ibid.,* p. 30.

extent or "the number of persons to whom it *extends*." When all these factors are duly considered, the following procedure will determine the total pleasure that any act may be expected to produce, and hence the rightness or wrongness of the act. Add the pleasures that seem to be involved for the individual and then add the pains and note the balance. Repeat the process with respect to all individuals whose interests are concerned. Add the numbers representing the degrees of pleasurableness for those for whom the results of the act are pleasurable on the whole. Do the same for those for whom its results are painful on the whole. Take the balance. If the balance is on the side of pleasure, the act is right; if the balance is on the side of pain, it is wrong. To be sure, the whole process does not need to be repeated in detail in the case of each act, for estimates can often be rapidly made in the light of past experience; but the full procedure should always be kept in mind as the basic standard to which appeal can be made in difficult cases.

Since Bentham bases his pleasure ethics on the claim that men desire only their own pleasures while holding that right requires the promotion of the pleasure of the community, he is confronted, as Epicurus was not, with the problem of showing why the individual should seek the pleasure of the community. This problem had been solved by the earlier theological hedonists through the contention that God so meted out rewards and punishments, especially in the future life, that the individual in the long run derived most pleasure for himself by promoting that of the community. Although Bentham does not specifically deny this answer, he gives it a relatively small role, calling attention to man's ignorance of the nature of the future life. His solution of the problem is mainly in terms of four sanctions or forces, that tend to make it certain that the individual shall not attain his own maximum happiness without seeking to promote that of the community. These are *physical, political, moral,* and *religious* sanctions. The first consists of that in the physical world, including the physical constitution of man, which punishes antisocial conduct and rewards socially useful conduct. The second consists of legal penalties and rewards; the third, of public opinion; and the fourth, of fear of divine retribution or hope of supernatural reward.   All of the other sanctions depend in the end for their effectiveness upon the first.   But, from the practical standpoint, by far the most important is the second, for through suitable laws the legislator can purposefully employ all of the sanctions to guarantee that the individual finds his own greatest pleasure and least pain in that which also promotes the general happiness.   Indeed, in this respect, Bentham assigns the legislator very much the same purpose as theological hedonism assigns to the divine being.

THE ATTEMPT OF QUALITATIVE UTILITARIANISM TO CORRECT THE MISTAKES OF QUANTITATIVE UTILITARIANISM, J. S. MILL

Although Bentham formulated the universalistic pleasure theory with remarkable clarity and consistency, his version of this theory involves, apart from the central pleasure principle, at least four points at which serious difficulties, alike for common sense and for other utilitarians, are likely to arise.   The first of these is the transition from the psychological hedonism to ethical hedonism, for it is by no means self-evident that because men do seek pleasure they ought to do so.   The second is the transition from one's own pleasure to that of the community, for it is not at all clear that because one does, or even should, seek his own happiness one does or should seek the happiness of everybody.   The third is the claim that pleasures differ only in amount and are all alike in kind, for some pleasures seem to most people to be better than others even when they are not so great.   The fourth is the implication that virtue is, as it was for Epicurus, only a means to an end outside itself, for to most men virtue has value in its own right.

Since a theory that failed to meet these difficulties could not be accepted by common sense and tended to bring down upon itself a storm of criticism, later champions of universalistic hedonism naturally tried to formulate their utilitarianism in ways that avoided these difficulties. We must glance at the thought of some of the later utilitarians and see how they undertook to meet the difficulties under consideration and to what extent they succeeded. One of the foremost of the later utilitarians was John Stuart Mill, an English philosopher of the third quarter of the nineteenth century whose father was a friend and follower of Bentham. To his thought we now turn.

Concerning the central formula of utilitarianism John Stuart Mill (1806–73) was almost entirely in agreement with Bentham, in whose philosophy he had been carefully drilled from earliest youth. Like Bentham, Mill defined right in terms of the promotion of maximum happiness: "Actions are right in proportion as they tend to promote happiness." [22] Also like Bentham, he defined happiness as "pleasure, and the absence of pain," [23] and held that the happiness involved was not simply that of the agent but the general happiness.[24]

The initial phase of Mill's effort to bolster up Benthamism concerns the first two difficulties noted above, namely, the transition from one's desire for his own pleasure to the duty to promote pleasure for himself and thence to his duty to promote it for all men. At this point, at least at first, Mill fully agreed with Bentham that universalistic ethical hedonism must be based on and derived from egoistic psychological hedonism. However, not content to *assume* with Bentham that the former followed from the latter, Mill undertook to reveal and even in a sense to "prove" the connection. The core of Mill's statement of the inference is as follows: "The sole evidence . . . that anything is desirable is that people do actually desire it. . . . No reason can be given why the general happiness is desirable except that each person . . . desires his own happiness. . . . This, however, being a fact, we have . . . all the proof . . . which it is possible to require, that happiness is a good: that each person's happiness is a good to that person, and the

[22] J. S. Mill, "Utilitarianism," in E. A. Burtt (ed.), *The English Philosophers from Bacon to Mill* (New York: Random House, 1939), p. 900.
[23] *Ibid.*
[24] *Ibid.*, p. 908.

general happiness, therefore, a good to the aggregate of all persons." [25]

Unfortunately, however, instead of proving the connections in question, Mill's argument only reveals certain logical and linguistic confusions that had all the while served illegitimately to support utilitarianism, and thus in effect it really weakens rather than sustains Bentham's theory.   While Mill apparently did not notice any difficulty here, one has only to look carefully at what he has said to observe two fairly obvious mistakes.[26] For one thing, when Mill informs us that happiness is desirable he is evidently using the term desirable in the sense of *able to be desired*.   But when he proceeds, as he presently does, on the assumption that good and desirable are the same, his assumption implies the sense of desirable in which it means *worthy to be desired,* which is of course very different from *able to be desired.*   Hence, the fact that happiness and good are both desir- able really affords no ground for the claim that happiness and good are the same, since the two are desirable only in very different senses.   The second mistake consists in drawing from the fact that each desires his own happiness the inference that everybody's happiness is a good to all.   Actually all that follows from the fact that each desires his own happiness, even if happi- ness in Mill's sense is the good, is that each person's happiness is a good to somebody (that is, himself), not certainly that the happiness of each, or of all, is a good to all.   To assume that because each desires his own happiness the happiness of all is a good to all is like saying that because each child in a family wants a stick of candy for himself, all of them want all the others to have one.   Any observant parent knows that this is not so.

In addition to stating the inference from psychological hedon- ism to ethical hedonism in his *Utilitarianism* in such a way as unintentionally to reveal basic confusions involved in this tran-

25 *Ibid.,* p. 923.
26 See Sidgwick's analysis of Mill's inference of ethical hedonism from psy- chological hedonism in Henry Sidgwick, *The Methods of Ethics* (7th ed., London: Macmillan, 1907), pp. 387 ff.

sition, Mill, in his *Autobiography,* also makes other concessions
relative to the basis of the pleasure theory that in effect call in
question the truth of psychological hedonism itself. Here
Mill confesses that, whereas he had in early life believed with
Bentham that one could successfully seek his own happiness
through serving others, he has now become convinced through
a profound emotional experience that one could only be happy
as he surrendered the search for his own happiness in the endeavor to promote the welfare and happiness of others. He
expresses this conviction as follows: "Those only are happy
who have their minds fixed on some object other than their
own happiness. . . . Ask yourself whether you are happy, and
you cease to be so. . . . Treat not happiness, but some end
external to it, as the purpose of life. . . . Let your self-con-
sciousness, your scrutiny, your self-interrogation exhaust themselves on that; and if otherwise fortunately circumstanced you
will inhale happiness with the air you breathe." [27]   This conviction that happiness can be successfully achieved only by aim-
ing at something other than happiness, commonly referred to
as the paradox of hedonism, seems clearly to be in line with
experience, but it does not accord very well, to say the least, with
the psychological hedonism on which the hedonists had always
depended or, for that matter, with ethical hedonism itself.
Thus, the first phase of Mill's revision of utilitarianism, although exceedingly illuminating, is really rather damaging to
the theory.

The second phase of Mill's revision of utilitarianism concerns
the failure in other formulations of the theory to recognize different kinds of pleasures. Bentham's claim that no pleasure
was any better than any other, save in its pleasantness and in
that of its consequences, had evoked widespread criticism to
the effect that utilitarianism was a "pig philosophy" since a
pig's pleasures would, in terms of it, be as good as a man's pleasures. To this Mill replies, as Bentham might have done, that
hedonists have always recognized that the exercise of higher

[27] J. S. Mill, "Autobiography," in *The Harvard Classics* (New York: P. F. Collier & Son, 1909), Vol. XXV, p. 94.

capacities is better than that of lower ones in that the pleasures yielded by the former are more lasting and less costly than those produced by the latter. But, also conceding to the critics of hedonism that a distinction among *qualities* of pleasure is needed, Mill goes on to assert that the pleasures produced by the exercise of higher faculties are not only greater in amount but different in kind from those given by the exercise of lower ones.[28] To such an extent is this true, he holds, that some distinctively human pleasures are far better even than an unbroken succession of animal pleasures. If it be asked precisely which of two kinds of pleasure is higher, Mill is ready with the answer that the judgment of the person who knows both kinds is sufficient. Thus he states his claim as follows: "It is better to be a human being dissatisfied than a pig satisfied; better to be Socrates dissatisfied than a fool satisfied. And if the fool, or the pig, are of a different opinion, it is because they know only their own side of the question." [29]

Again Mill seems to be quite correct in his insight, but again he has compromised the pleasure theory, which cannot afford this kind of defense. If it is impossible to rest satisfied with Bentham's claim that all pleasures are alike save for their quantities and aftereffects, it is equally impossible to be a good hedonist and still admit that some pleasures are higher than others; for, in doing this, one is judging goodness by something other than pleasantness, that is, by the preferences of educated people or some other such criterion. In introducing *qualities* of pleasure Mill was inadvertently surrendering the position that pleasure is the only good.

The third and final phase of Mill's revision of Benthamism is his attempt to show that utilitarianism, despite appearances, can do justice to the idea, which seems to be implicit in our use of moral terms, that virtue is not merely a means to good but good in itself. In reply to objections to hedonism on this point, Mill suggests that at least the hedonists "place virtue at the very head of the things that are good as means to the ultimate

28 Mill, "Utilitarianism," p. 901.
29 *Ibid.*, p. 902.

end." [30]　He also goes on to claim that, although not originally a part of the desired ends of man, virtue often becomes a part of these ends through "strong association" with other parts that we tend to achieve through it. Thus, just as money, originally desired only for the sake of the desired things it will buy, comes ultimately to be desired by the miser for its own sake, so virtue, at first desired only for the sake of the other pleasures it produces, comes in the end to be desired for its own sake.

Now, if hedonism holds only that "good" refers to something that is pleasant, the problem is readily solved by Mill's method. Virtue, though not at first a pleasant thing, may become one. Hence virtue itself may become a good.　But if hedonism holds, as it often does, that the good is pleasure itself, and not merely something that is pleasant, the difficulty comes more sharply than ever to focus.　Virtue not only does not start out as pleasure; it never becomes pleasure.　At very best it only becomes "strongly associated" with pleasure.　Hence virtue is never really good in itself, and those who suppose it is deceive themselves, much as misers deceive themselves in supposing that money is good in itself.

INTUITIONAL UTILITARIANISM AND ITS CRITICISM OF EARLIER FORMS OF UTILITARIANISM, HENRY SIDGWICK

Although all of Mill's modifications of Benthamism seem to be in sound accord with moral experience, they all tend to weaken utilitarianism and to suggest that perhaps after all a universalistic hedonism that accords with the actual intentions of people's critical moral judgments cannot be formulated. There is, however, one other writer, the most discriminating of all of the hedonists, who undertakes to restore utilitarianism to its original purity and at the same time so to state its principles as to avoid the usual criticisms launched against it.　We must

[30] *Ibid.,* p. 924.

now see how this writer, Henry Sidgwick (1838–1900), goes about this task.

In his *Methods of Ethics* Sidgwick undertook to analyze all of the more promising types of answers to the fundamental moral questions. The result of his investigation is a universalistic hedonism similar to that of Bentham and Mill but founded on an entirely different basis, and giving a larger role to the rules of common sense in guidance of practical activity. Like Bentham and Mill, Sidgwick unequivocally defines the moral end in terms of the most good for all concerned. Like them he believes the notion of utility to be identical with that of moral rightness. He refers to his theory as Universalistic Hedonism, or Utilitarianism, defining it as "the ethical theory, that the conduct which, under any given circumstances, is objectively right, is that which will produce the greatest amount of happiness on the whole; that is, taking into account all whose happiness is affected by the conduct." [31] Happiness consists, for Sidgwick as for Bentham and Mill, of pleasures. Pleasure is "desirable feeling, apprehended as desirable by the sentient individual at the time of feeling it." [32] "Good" does not quite *mean* pleasant, as it seems to do for Bentham, but pleasure remains the only thing that is in fact good.

In order to defend the utilitarian formula successfully Sidgwick thinks it necessary to reject Mill's distinction among different kinds or qualities of pleasure and to return in the main at this point to Bentham's quantitative measurement of pleasure. "Consistency requires," he declares, "that pleasures should be sought in proportion to their pleasantness; and therefore the less pleasant consciousness must not be preferred to the more pleasant, on the ground of any other qualities that it may possess." [33] If one prefers the less pleasant on grounds of qualitative distinctions, he is "clearly introducing a non-hedonistic ground of preference." [34]

[31] Sidgwick, *op. cit.*, p. 411.
[32] *Ibid.*, p. 129.
[33] *Ibid.*, p. 121.
[34] *Ibid.*, p. 95.

However, with reference to the basis of the hedonistic claim that pleasure alone is good, Sidgwick feels that it is essential to depart from Bentham as well as Mill. He not only exposes Mill's fallacious arguments [35] but rejects the whole idea that ethical hedonism can be inferred from psychological hedonism. His grounds for this radical departure from the line of proof upon which the hedonistic tradition had always depended are two. In the first place, he rejects psychological hedonism, or the doctrine that men always seek their own greatest happiness. Concerning his own experience he declares: "throughout the whole scale of my impulses, sensual, emotional, and intellectual alike, I can distinguish desires of which the object is something other than my own pleasure." [36] With Butler and other notable moralists as well as most modern psychologists, he believes that particular objects are more likely to be the original objects of one's desires than is the attainment of pleasure and that the prior existence of desires for objects is generally a condition of one's getting pleasure from them—that, for example, if one had no prior impulse for food he would not enjoy eating it. However, apart from the claim that psychological hedonism can be shown to be false, Sidgwick holds, for reasons that we have already suggested in connection with Mill's argument on this point, that ethical hedonism can not be proved from psychological hedonism. Ethics is ethics and psychology is psychology. What one desires for one's self proves nothing about what he ought to desire even for himself, not to speak of what he does or should desire for others. In a word, Sidgwick holds that psychological hedonism is not true and that even if it were it would afford no proof of ethical hedonism.

Having thus decisively rejected the traditional basis of hedonism, on what basis could he found a properly qualified hedonism? Sidgwick believed that a correct answer could be discovered by careful analysis of common sense morality. Examination of the commonly accepted rules of morality shows that many of them are not quite true and that others of them are logically

[35] *Ibid.*, pp. 387 ff.
[36] *Ibid.*, p. 45.

circular. However, it also shows that a few general principles of morality, when properly stated, are as certain as the axioms of mathematics, so self-evident indeed that anyone who can understand them must accept them. To furnish a proper foundation of morality is to sift out and accurately formulate these principles.

The first of these self-evident general principles is that of Justice, which declares "that whatever action any of us judges to be right he implicitly judges to be right for all similar persons in similar circumstances. . . ." [37] This principle has been widely recognized in a less precise form in the "Golden Rule." It bids us make no claim for ourselves that we would not acknowledge for others. The second moral axiom is that of Prudence, which states that "one ought to aim at one's own good . . . on the whole." [38] It reminds us that "a smaller present good is not to be preferred to a greater future good (allowing for difference of certainty)." [39] It bids us restrain present desires for the sake of our own greatest total good. The third moral axiom is that of Rational Benevolence, which tells us that "each one is morally bound to regard the good of any other individual as much as his own." [40] It calls attention to the need of promoting the good of others as well as avoiding injuries to them. It demands that in the pursuit of good we put ourselves on the same plane with others, so that one ought never "to seek his own happiness on any occasion if it involved a certain sacrifice of the greater happiness of some other human being." [41]

It will readily be seen that these three axioms when taken together in a certain order constitute a demand that a person do as much good and avoid as much evil as he can for all persons affected by his actions. Except for the absence of the principle that pleasure alone is ultimately good, this is approximately what the other utilitarian theories have required. Upon these

37 *Ibid.*, p. 379.
38 *Ibid.*, p. 381.
39 *Ibid.*
40 *Ibid.*, p. 382.
41 *Ibid.*

three axioms, then, Sidgwick bases the nonhedonistic part of his utilitarianism.   He then proceeds to round out his universalistic hedonism by a hedonistic intuition that regards " 'Universal Good' as 'Universal Happiness,' " or universal pleasure.   Universal good, he says, can be neither virtue nor any organic state, nor consciousness as such, for one should not wish these to exist alone.   When one examines himself candidly it is only "Desirable Consciousness which we must regard as ultimate Good"; [42] and desirable consciousness is for Sidgwick precisely what pleasure is.

Thus, instead of founding his utilitarianism upon an alleged desire of each for his own pleasure, Sidgwick has based it upon what he takes to be the intuitions of all men as to the necessity of impartiality with respect to one's own claims and those of others, one's present and future goods, and one's own good and that of others, and as to the universal goodness of pleasure. In applying this utilitarian system to practical problems, Sidgwick goes beyond Bentham and Mill in insisting on the advisability of relying on the rules of the generally accepted morality as fairly satisfactory statements of the kinds of conduct that are likely to yield the greatest happiness for all; but, with reference to difficult cases and new problems, he agrees with them that one must still fall back on calculation of the pleasures of all.

However, Sidgwick freely acknowledges that when firmly based on an intuitional basis, with ample aid from common sense, utilitarianism involves a serious difficulty.   The axioms of Prudence and Rational Benevolence may stand in conflict with one another.   Despite the fact that service to others normally leads to one's own happiness, there are instances in which a selfish act seems plainly to lead to more happiness for the individual than does an unselfish act.   This unreliability of rewards of virtue does not seem to be as it should be; but it does seem to be a fact as far as the world of nature is concerned. Apparently the only way in which this kind of conflict between the happiness of the community and that of the individual can be resolved is through belief in a divine being, or a moral order

42 *Ibid.*

of the universe, which assures happiness to the unselfish. Such a belief is of course beyond the sphere of ethics, but the need for coherence in man's thought and life as a whole may require it.

GENERAL CRITICISM OF PLEASURE THEORIES

The history of hedonism contains within itself most of the essentials of an appropriate criticism of that theory, for each succeeding form of hedonism has pointed out important errors in the preceding ones. Hence our task at this point is already for the most part performed by hedonists themselves.

As the English utilitarians all saw, the egoistic hedonism of Epicurus can scarcely be considered a plausible interpretation of moral concepts. When a man whose action will deeply affect others as well as himself makes his choices with a view solely to his own pleasures, his actions are scarcely likely to be called either right or morally good. And when most men do call an act right or morally good, they do not intend to say merely that it produces maximum pleasure for the agent. Philosophers who defend egoistic moral theories are likely to do so, either directly or indirectly, on the ground that as each person seeks his own good the common good is best promoted. For the rest, therefore, the kind of hedonism with which our critical remarks will be concerned is that universalistic hedonism, or utilitarianism, which defines the right in terms of the good of all.

The major contribution of the universalistic hedonists—and an important contribution it is—is their development of what we shall call the utilitarian method. This method consists in regarding goodness as a fairly specific characteristic of experiences and treating the right as the promotion of as much good as possible for all, regardless of how in particular the good is defined. Some such method has seemed increasingly to be indicated by the kind of criticisms we were obliged to make of previous types of ethical theory, and the utilitarians have furnished a form of it that, save for the need for relatively minor revisions, appears essentially sound. Goodness, we have seen, can scarcely con-

sist in any such broad patterns as are suggested by the concepts
of nature and human nature, but must be found in some more
specific character of experience. Similarly, the right, as we
have observed, cannot be identified either with the approved
or with a form of action, or with conformity to nature or human
nature, but must consist in conduciveness to some more specific
good. Bentham's formula of balance of good over evil is not
quite adequate as it stands. Nor is Mill's demand for promotion of the common good precise enough. But Sidgwick's
idea of conduciveness to the greatest amount of good for all who
are affected by the act would seem, when interpreted in the
light of Bentham's "each one to count for one" and Sidgwick's
axioms of justice and benevolence, to be very near to the formula that critical interpretation of moral concepts requires.
Some reasons for accepting such a view have already been suggested and others will subsequently be developed.

The crucial question concerning the adequacy of universalistic hedonism is, however, that of the correctness of its attempt
to equate the good and the pleasurable. This attempt may be
made in any one of three ways, and the evaluation of each must
be somewhat different.

1. One way of equating the good and the pleasurable—indeed
the only one in which hedonism constitutes an ethical theory
in the strictest sense—consists in saying that "good" *means* pleasant. This procedure seems to be suggested in the views of
Epicurus and Bentham and possibly at times in that of Mill.
But it will hardly do. When anyone says that something is
good he does not ordinarily seem to mean at all that it is pleasant, however pleasant in fact it may ordinarily be. This is
properly suggested by G. E. Moore's "open question" argument,[43] in the following manner:

Whereas we can always sensibly ask of anything pleasant whether or
not it is good, we could not sensibly ask such a question if "good"
meant pleasant, for in that case we should be in effect asking, "Is this
pleasant thing pleasant?" or "Is this good thing good?"

[43] G. E. Moore, *Principia Ethica* (Cambridge: Cambridge University Press, 1903),
pp. 15–16.

The objection may, of course, be raised that we can also inquire with some sense concerning the application of a term
when identity of meaning is involved, as when we ask whether
or not a three-sided plane figure is at triangle. But whereas we
ask this sort of question only when we do not understand the
terms involved, we inquire concerning the goodness of pleasant
things when the meanings of the terms are well understood.
Moreover, the open question appropriately reminds us that inquiries concerning the pleasantness of anything and those concerning its value seem to be on quite different levels, in that
the one inquires about a psychological state and the other about
being valuable or worth while. Thus, a thing's being pleasant
and its being good are two different facts, even if all pleasant
thing are good and all good things pleasant.[44]

2. A second way of attempting to equate the good and the
pleasurable is to say that, although "good" does not *mean* pleasant, still the good *is in fact* pleasure. In other words, nothing is
good but pleasure and all pleasure is good. Although this version of hedonism has the merit of distinguishing between what
"good" means and what the good is, it is, when taken at face
value, quite as implausible as the first version, though for a different reason. The reason is suggested in what was said earlier
concerning Mill's defense of the goodness of virtue. While virtue may involve pleasure in close association with itself, virtue
is not itself pleasure either at the beginning or later on. The
situation is similar concerning experiences of eating, drinking,
talking, walking, reading, and seeing beautiful pictures. Each
such experience involves pleasure in close association with other
ingredients, but none is itself simply or wholly pleasure. If
pleasure alone were good, none of these experiences as such
could properly be called good. Only the ingredient of pleasure in them would be correctly so spoken of. But, in fact, we
do not so restrict the use of the word "good"; rather, we quite
deliberately attribute goodness to all manner of experiences
containing but not *being* pleasure.

[44] See R. M. Hare, *The Language of Morals* (Oxford: The Clarendon Press,
1952), pp. 82 ff.

3. The third way of equating the good and the pleasurable is to affirm that while "good" does not *mean* pleasant and the good is not *in fact* pleasure only, still *the good* is *the pleasant;* that is, only pleasant things are good, and all things are good in proportion as they are pleasant and vice versa.[45] This interpretation has the advantages both of avoiding confusing the *meaning* of "good" with what is good and of permitting us to say—as we certainly do—that experiences of virtue, eating, painting, and many other things, containing pleasure and therefore being pleasant but not being pleasure, are good. It also has the merit of recognizing what seems to be an indisputable fact that there is very considerable correlation between what we call pleasant and what we call good. For these reasons it is probably the most plausible of all attempts to equate the good and the pleasurable. Nevertheless, as Mill's own, all-too-honest account of qualities of pleasures indicates, things are not always good strictly in proportion to their pleasantness. Though the admission is fatal to hedonism, the pleasures of a man are indeed better than those of a pig, even when the man's pleasures are less; and those of a Socrates are better than those of a fool, even when those of the fool are greater. The enlightened appreciation of a great drama is found by those capable of both experiences to be better than the excitement of a televised wrestling match, though the pleasure may be less; and the joys of intelligent companionship, than the pleasures of the table's fancy foods, though the amount of pleasure be the same. The sufferings of a great man for his fellows are likewise found better, even apart from consequences, than the delights of the sadist in the agonies of his victims; and the joys of the creative artist, than the amusements of the mimicking child. Such disproportions as these not only exclude the view that makes good proportional to pleasure contained, but render less plausible than ever the theoretically more important claim that good means pleasant.

If the good is to correspond to any psychological state, pre-

[45] See G. E. Moore, *Ethics* (New York: Oxford University Press, 1912; Reset 1947), pp. 29, 47.

sumably that state will be one, such as satisfaction, capable of more refinement than is pleasure. But, whether or not good corresponds completely even with satisfaction remains to be seen. Meanwhile we must examine another type of specific value theory, one that equates the good with the desired.

READINGS

Epicurus and Bentham

Melden, *Ethical Theories*, pp. 143–49, 341–64; *or*
Clark and Smith, *Readings in Ethics*, pp. 87–95, 291–304; *or*
Rand, *The Classical Moralists*, pp. 110–16, 483–93.

Mill and Sigdwick

Melden, *Ethical Theories*, pp. 365–92; *or*
Clark and Smith, *Readings in Ethics*, pp. 304–10; 354–60; *or*
Rand, *The Classical Moralists*, pp. 669–76, 702–10.

QUESTIONS

1. In what sense is Epicurus' account of good more specific than Aristotle's? What does Epicurus mean by pleasure? What kinds of pleasure does he think preferable? What value does he attach to virtue? Of what use is philosophy in his thought?

2. A bank clerk was able by clever bookkeeping over a period of years to take ten thousand dollars without being caught. According to Epicurus' egoistic hedonism, did he act rightly? Explain.

3. The suggestion is thrown out by one of the characters in Plato's *Republic* that perhaps what one ought to do is to *seem* rather than to *be* just, that if a man had a ring like that of a certain Gyges, which would render him invisible at will, he would be under no obligation to be just. Do Epicurus' basic principles imply that if one could be sure of not being caught it would not be wrong to commit murder, theft, and adultery? Why or why not? Do you agree with what you take to be the implications of Epicureanism at this point? Why or why not?

4. What does Bentham mean by *utility*, by *right*, by *good*? On what does he base his definition of good?

5. Suppose a conscientious businessman is confronted with the

question of whether or not to adopt a new practice that is certain to pay but may or may not be right. By what steps, according to Bentham, should he proceed in attempting to determine his duty?

6. Despite the interdependence of human beings, some people insist on seeking their private pleasures in ways that are harmful to public happiness. How does Bentham propose to bring these devious quests for private pleasure into line with the interests of the public? How are his legislators to be brought to find their private pleasure in public welfare?

7. What is meant by the paradox of hedonism? What other expression of this principle have we previously encountered in our study of ethics? What is the bearing of this paradox on psychological hedonism? What are the principal arguments of Butler and Sidgwick against psychological hedonism?

8. Do you agree with Mill that some pleasures can be better than others without being more pleasant? If not, how do you account for the widespread conviction, for example, that the pleasures of good literature are better than those of Swiss cheese? If you do agree with Mill, what is it about the better pleasures that makes them better?

9. What did Sidgwick mean by a moral axiom? What were his first three moral axioms? Are they sound? What is their relation to universalistic hedonism?

10. In the notorious Dreyfus case the reputation of the French army was at first maintained by condemning an innocent subordinate instead of a guilty superior, but it is at least possible that Dreyfus' suffering was less than the uneasiness that later disturbed all of France when the case was reopened. If so, would it have been better, as a consistent hedonist would apparently have to say, to have let the case rest? Explain.

11. Does moral integrity have any value in its own right? Is the claim that moral integrity does have such value sustained by Mill's principle of association? How so, or why not? Would recognition of intrinsic value in moral integrity have any bearing on the solution of such a problem as that of the Dreyfus case?

REFERENCES

General

Carritt, E. F., *The Theory of Morals* (London: Oxford University Press, 1928), Ch. 2.

Dewey, John, and Tufts, J. H., *Ethics* (rev. ed., New York: Holt, 1932), Ch. 11.

Everett, W. G., *Moral Values* (New York: Holt, 1918), Ch. 3.

Ewing, A. C., *The Definition of Good* (New York: Macmillan, 1947), Ch. 2.

Hill, T. E., *Contemporary Ethical Theories* (New York: Macmillan, 1950), Ch. 12.

Patterson, C. H., *Moral Standards* (New York: Ronald, 1949).

Rashdall, Hastings, *Theory of Good and Evil* (London: Oxford University Press, 1924), Vol. I, Bk. I, Chs. 2, 3; Vol. II, Bk. II, Chs. 1, 2.

Robinson, D. S., *The Principles of Conduct* (New York: Appleton-Century-Crofts, 1948), Ch. 7.

Urban, W. M., *Fundamentals of Ethics* (New York: Holt, 1930), Ch. 4.

Epicureanism

Epicurus, *The Extant Remains,* tr. by Cyril Bailey (Oxford: The Clarendon Press, 1926).

Hicks, R. D., *Stoic and Epicurean* (New York: Scribner, 1910).

Hyde, W. D., *The Five Great Philosophies of Life* (New York: Macmillan, 1932), Ch. 1.

Pater, Walter, *Marius the Epicurean* (New York: Macmillan, 1909).

Taylor, A. E., *Epicurus* (New York: Dodge Publishing Company, 1910).

Zeller, Eduard, *The Stoics, Epicureans and Skeptics,* tr. by Oswald Reichel (rev. ed., London: Longmans, Green, 1892).

Utilitarianism

Albee, Ernest, *History of English Utilitarianism* (New York: Macmillan, 1902).

Bentham, Jeremy, *An Introduction to the Principles of Morals and Legislation* (New York: Doubleday, 1935), Chs. 1–12.

Bradley, F. H., *Ethical Studies* (2nd ed. rev., New York: Oxford University Press, 1927), Essay 3.

Broad, C. D., *Five Types of Ethical Theory* (New York: Harcourt, Brace, 1930), Ch. 5.

Green, T. H., *Prolegomena to Ethics* (5th ed., Oxford: The Clarendon Press, 1907), pp. 163–67, 226–40, 374–88.

Mill, J. S., *Utilitarianism* (Everyman ed., New York: Dutton, 1910).

Moore, G. E., *Ethics* (New York: Oxford University Press, 1912; Reset 1947), Chs. 1, 2, 7; pp. 96–105.

——— *Principia Ethica* (Cambridge: Cambridge University Press, 1903), Ch. 2 and especially Ch. 3.

Sidgwick, Henry, *The Methods of Ethics* (7th ed., London: Macmillan, 1907), especially Bk. I; Bk. II, Ch. 1; Bk. III, Chs. 1, 13, 14; Bk. IV.

Stace, W. T., *The Concept of Morals* (New York: Macmillan, 1937), Ch. 6.

Titus, H. H., *Ethics for Today* (2nd ed. rev., New York: American Book, 1954), Ch. 10.

11

Specific Value Theories:
Desire Theories

IMPLICIT IN THE THOUGHT OF all of the great hedonists, except
Sidgwick, was the belief that, in order to prove that anything
was good, one had first to prove that it was desired. But in so
believing, hedonists seem really to be assuming that the good is
at base equivalent to the desired. This apparent assumption,
which was, of course, not specifically pointed out by the hedonists
themselves, suggests another kind of ethical theory, which is
especially likely to be appreciated when it becomes necessary
to abandon the idea that pleasure alone is either desired or good.
Instead of narrowly insisting that pleasure alone is good because
it alone is desired, why not say more broadly that *whatever* is
desired is good and indeed that "good" means desired. This
is precisely what a great many thinkers have in one way or another said. Hence we are now to consider the view that "good"
means desired, and that the right consists in conduciveness to
a maximum of harmonious satisfaction of people's desires.

To the ancestry of the *desire theory* belong indirectly nearly
all of the earlier hedonistic writers. The more direct fore-
bears of the theory are those writers who have perceived the
connection between desire and good without making the mistake of supposing that pleasure was the only thing desired.
The desire element was prominent in the thought of Socrates,
who characteristically declared that "all men have a choice

between various courses, and choose and follow the one which they think most conducive to their advantage," [1] and who would have found it odd for anyone to think anything good which was not desired by someone.   Aristotle gave to desire a considerable place in his thought on the good, saying of the chief good that it is an end "which we wish for its own sake, while we wish others only for the sake of this." [2]   Thomas Aquinas' thought involved something of the same idea.   In the modern era nearly all moralists have in one way or another injected the idea of desire into their accounts of good.   Thus, for example, Spinoza grounded one type of ethical theory upon a definition of good as the desired saying that "we endeavor, wish, desire or long for nothing because we deem it good; but, on the other hand, we deem a thing good because we endeavor, wish for, or long for it." [3]   T. H. Green employed the notion that the good is the desired as a stage in the building of an entirely different kind of moral system.

Three writers may well be taken as representative of the desire theory itself.   They agree in holding that the meaning of good is *desired*, but they differ widely in other respects. The first, Thomas Hobbes, lived amid the turmoil of the Puritan Revolution in England at the beginning of the modern era, and developed a theory of a selfish man in a totalitarian state. The other two, R. B. Perry and John Dewey, have been witnesses to the turmoil of the contemporary scene and have developed theories of a social man in a democratic society.

THOMAS HOBBES'S SUBJECTIVE TOTALITARIAN DESIRE THEORY

The moral theory of Thomas Hobbes (1588–1679) is closely connected with his rather remarkable view of man and the

---

[1] Quoted in Xenophon, *Memorabilia,* tr. by E. C. Marchant (London: William Heinemann, 1923), III, ix, 4.

[2] *Aristotle, The Nicomachean Ethics,* tr. by Harris Rackham (Cambridge: Harvard University Press, 1934), I, ii, 1.

[3] Benedict Spinoza, *Ethics,* tr. by A. Boyle (Everyman ed., New York: Dutton, 1910), p. 92.

condition of humanity apart from the state.   Man, like the rest
of creation, is matter in motion.   What goes on in his mind is
in fact somewhat like the action of billiard balls.   His pleasures are motions from the head to the heart stimulating
vital activity.   His reasoning is an addition and subtraction of
"parcels" depending upon names.[4]   His desires are "small beginnings of motion, within the body of man, before they appear
in walking, striking and other visible actions . . . when they
are toward something that causes them."   His aversions are
opposite motions.   His deliberation is an alternation of desires
and aversions; and his will is only the latest and strongest of
his desires.   Man is also thoroughly selfish.   His every impulse
is directed toward his own self-gratification; for "of the voluntary acts of every man, the object is some *good to himself.*"[5]
Even a man's free gifts to others are "in hope to gain the reputation of charity, or magnanimity; or to deliver his mind from
the pain of compassion; or in the hope of reward in heaven"; [6]
and his pity "ariseth from the imagination that the like calamity
may befall himself."[7]   This doctrine that man is altogether
selfish is frequently referred to as psychological egoism.

Since man is completely selfish, and since "nature hath made
men so equal . . . as that . . . the difference between man and
man is not so considerable, as that one man can thereupon
claim to himself any benefit, to which another may not pretend
as well as he," [8] the "natural condition of mankind," that is, the
one in which he lives before there is any government, is one of
constant strife.   Every man, being ambitious, greedy, and envi-
ous as well as fearful for his safety, strikes out against his fellows
before they strike first at him.   Man's life becomes "such a
war as is of every man against every man."   In this condition
"every man has a right to everything, even to one another's
body"; and "the notions of right and wrong, justice and injus-

---

4 Thomas Hobbes, *Leviathan,* in E. A. Burtt (ed.), *The English Philosophers
from Bacon to Mill* (New York: Random House, 1939), p. 143.
5 *Ibid.,* p. 165.
6 *Ibid.*
7 *Ibid.,* p. 153.
8 *Ibid.*

tice, have there no place." Obviously such a condition is one of extreme misery for all. In it "there is no place for industry; . . . no culture of the earth, no navigation, nor use of the com: modities that may be imported by sea; no commodious building; . . . no arts; no letters; no society; and which is worst of all, continual fear, and danger of violent death; and the life of man, solitary, poor, nasty, brutish and short." [9]

It is because of this miserableness of the natural condition of man that ethics, as well as the politics that must be inseparably connected with it, emerges and maintains its hold. What then is the ethics to which men are driven by the misery of their natural state?

Since Hobbes regards man as altogether selfish, it is not surprising to find that he defines "good" in subjective terms. "*Good and evil,*" he informs us, "are names that signify our appetites and aversions." [10] But the appetites and aversions in question are not just anybody's. Rather they are only one's own appetites and aversions. Hobbes makes it clear that the speaker's own appetites are the one's intended when he says elsewhere that "whatsoever is the object of any man's appetite or desire, that is it which *he for his part* calleth good." [11] Thus what I desire is good to me and what you desire is good to you. There is no such thing as good in general. What you desire is not good at all from my standpoint, unless I happen to desire it; and what I desire is worthless from your standpoint, unless you happen to desire it. But from this subjectivist doctrine of good Hobbes proceeds to a much more objectivist view of right.

In general Hobbes's account of right represents what he takes to be the indispensable method of obtaining as much good as possible. Before men can be sure of attaining any good at all, it is necessary to find a way of escape from the intolerable state of perpetual warfare of each against every other. Hence the primary condition of the securing of any good, or the first law of reason or nature, is "*that every man ought to endeavor peace.*" [12]

[9] *Ibid.,* p. 162.
[10] *Ibid.,* p. 173.
[11] *Ibid.,* p. 149. Italics added.
[12] *Ibid.,* p. 163.

But since the root of the natural war of all against all is the claim of each man to unlimited rights, the first condition of peace, or the second law of reason or nature, is *"that a man be willing, when others are so too, as far forth as for peace and defense of himself he shall think it necessary, to lay down this right to all things; and be contented with so much liberty against other men, as he would allow other men against himself."* [13] Such an agreement, to be sure, restricts a man's rights and bids him restrain some of his desires, but in return it tends to assure him of a long enough life to have desires at all and of the opportunity to fulfill more of them than would otherwise be possible.

However, because men's agreements are not to be relied upon, this surrender of one's rights is ineffective unless it be a complete surrender of virtually all rights, save that of self-defense, to a sovereign who is given the power to enforce the performance of agreements, and who cannot be deprived of the rights bestowed upon him. Accordingly the social contract must be so constituted that the sovereign is unconditionally granted the surrendered rights in such a manner that his acts become those of the people and that for them ever to demand these rights back again would be a self-contradiction. To attempt to withdraw the contract is in any case to revert to the miserable state of nature; and those who refuse to participate in it, once it is made, have no ground for complaint if they are destroyed, for they are still in a state of nature.

It is only when this contract bestowing sovereignty upon a ruler has been established that right and wrong and justice and injustice come into being. Thus the meaning of right is found fundamentally in that fidelity to one's expressed or implied agreement to obey his sovereign which is the sole guarantee of his attainment of good.[14] The notion *"that every private man is judge of good and evil actions"* has no application where there is law, for here "it is manifest, that the measure of good and evil actions is the civil law, and the judge the legisla-

---

13 *Ibid.,* pp. 163–64.
14 See *ibid.,* p. 164.

tor, who is always representative of the commonwealth." [15]
For a man who lives under government "the law is the public
conscience." [16]

The primary duty incumbent upon all in such a system is
obedience to the government. What the government commands is right, and what it forbids is wrong. At the same time,
reason dictates certain other rules, obedience to which is required in order to secure peace even when the sovereign has
not commanded them. They include, for example, the performance of contracts, gratitude, respect for others, and fair
dealing. Their sum and substance is: *"Do not that to another,
which thou wouldst not have done to thyself."* [17] One should
note that although these rules are quite in line with accepted
morals, the reason for adhering to them in each case is not
concern for others, which is in fact impossible, but solely a
recognition of the necessity of obeying these rules in order to
preserve the peace on which one's security depends. One
should also remember in appealing to them as laws of God,
that of the laws of God "the principal is that we should not
violate our faith, that is a commandment to obey our civil
sovereign, which we constituted over us by our mutual pact
with one another." [18]

CRITICAL EVALUATION OF HOBBES'S THEORY

Whatever may be the merits or defects of Hobbes's chief
ethical contentions that "good" means desired and "right" means
agreement, his thought is clearly mistaken on four points at
least. The first is his insistence that man is altogether selfish.
The essential grounds for rejecting this position have already
been noted in connection with psychological hedonism. Man
often desires objects themselves without reference to the reflex
effect that obtaining them has upon his own welfare. Indeed, if

15 *Ibid.*, p. 205.
16 *Ibid.*, p. 206.
17 *Ibid.*, p. 172.
18 *Ibid.*, p. 222.

introspective analysis be permitted at all, man often desires objects for the sake of their favorable effects upon others. The second mistake, which grows out of the first, is that of defining "good" purely subjectively as a name one gives to what *he* desires. By this definition, either good has no single meaning; or, if it does, and if you desire a thing to which I have an aversion, the same thing is both good and not good. Either alternative is, as we have elsewhere seen, repugnant to our intentions in using the term "good." The third mistake of Hobbes's system depends on the other two, together with certain emotional reactions that the Puritan Revolution stirred in Hobbes himself. According to his theory the right is determined by a totalitarian state. However, if it is not possible to discover in man any more concern for his fellows than Hobbes does, no state at all is possible; and if it is possible to discover more, a totalitarian state is not necessary. In neither case would a totalitarian state be desirable, for in the first case it would thwart more of one's own desires than it could fulfill and in the second it would prevent fulfillment both of one's private interests and of the interests that he has in common with others in addition to his interest in peace. Peace is good, but it is hardly worth Hobbes's price of complete loss of liberty. Hobbes's fourth mistake is in not extending his state to world limits, for clearly whatever is sound in his argument for political agreement among men is quite as applicable to world order as it is to national order and it may well be that some world agreement is necessary if the life of man as a whole is not to be "poor, nasty, brutish and short."

RALPH BARTON PERRY'S GENERAL
INTEREST THEORY

Fortunately, the desire theory is not without defenders who, while preserving Hobbes's belief that the good is the desired and the right agreement, exclude from their moral systems Hobbes's objectionable egoism, subjectivism, totalitarianism, and nationalism. Consideration of the thought of a desire theorist of this sort should give us a clearer conception of the possibilities of the desire theory at its best.

R. B. Perry, Emeritus Professor of Philosophy at Harvard University, agrees in general with Hobbes that the good is the desired. However, he prefers to substitute for the term "desire" the somewhat broader term "interest," and he refuses to acknowledge either that the interests of man are always selfish or that the thing that interests anyone is good only to that person. Men may be interested in objects as such; and they may be, and often are, interested in the interests of others. Moreover, that a given individual is interested in something does not suggest simply that it is good *to him*. The suggestion is rather that the thing is good quite generally, to everybody, at least to the extent of any individual's interest in it. To be sure, the thing would be better if many people were interested in it than if only one were interested; but even if one individual were the sole interested party the thing would be universally good to that extent. Thus Perry declares that value as goodness "attaches promiscuously to all objects of all interest." [19] Value is then "any object of any interest." [20] It is "that special character of an object which consists in the fact that an interest is taken in it." [21]

In order to know precisely what good is we must then discover just what interest is. Although Perry does not share Hobbes's crude materialistic account of man, he does think that, in order to free ethics from the criticism that its data are internal and therefore unscientific, it is necessary to describe interest in terms of something definitely observable. For this purpose he chooses the idea of body sets. Interest involves two body sets. One of them is the general body set or "governing propensity" of the individual toward food, members of the opposite sex, beautiful objects, and the like. The other is a particular body set or "expectation" of the individual with reference

[19] R. B. Perry, *General Theory of Value* (New York: Longmans, Green, 1926), p. 21.
[20] *Ibid.*, p. 115.
[21] *Ibid.*, p. 124.

to some special object. When these two come together the individual is interested. When, for example, my general body set toward food is unfulfilled and I see a piece of well-prepared steak that I "expect" would satisfy it, I am said to be interested in or to desire that steak. Hence, defining good more precisely, Perry would say that a thing is good when an unfulfilled general body set and a particular body set converge upon it. In this manner the goodness of a thing is objective, not only in the sense that, if it is good at all it is good quite generally, but also in the sense that its goodness is observable by all, since theoretically anyone could observe anyone else's body set.

Like all specific value moralists, Perry holds that "right" refers in general to conduciveness to maximum good. However, since the attainment of good means for Perry the fulfillment of interest, the question of exactly what right means will depend on just how the interest and its fulfillment are to be measured.

One might, Perry thinks, undertake to measure first the correctness of the judgments on which an interest rests. Such correctness is very important since upon it depends in large measure the satisfaction of the interest and the contribution of activities on behalf of this interest to future satisfaction of this and other interests. But correctness is after all a standard for the judgment by which interest is mediated rather than for interest, and the reward of correctness in judgment measures the utility of the mediating judgment not the interest. Interest itself is to be measured by a threefold scale. To begin with, interest may be measured by *intensity*. Such a scale indicates the extent to which an interest in something "has acquired command over the body as a whole." Thus, if one's whole attention is absorbed in seeking, for example, a certain gem, his interest is of a 100 per cent intensity, but if the obtaining of the gem is only one objective among many, the interest is of 50 or 20 or 10 per cent intensity. A second scale is that of *preference*, by which is meant simply the individual's choice of the exercise of one interest over that of another regardless of the intensity of either at the moment. Thus, for example, one may prefer music to eating although he may enjoy eating as keenly as music. The third scale is that of *inclusiveness,* which measures the amount of interests of the individual and of all other individuals which is involved in a given course of action. When, for instance, one has had enough to eat already, serious reading may contribute to the fulfillment of more of his total interests than more eating would, or when he has money to spend, investment in public parks will probably fulfill more interests of more people than investment in a private estate.

In what order are these scales to be applied? If one begins with intensity, selecting first the object that most absorbs his attention at the moment, he will preclude the possibility of exercising his interests in other objects that he might have preferred had he compared his preferences first. Similarly, if one settles upon the interest of his preference before discovering whether or not it lies within the largest system of interests that he might further, he precludes the possibility of choosing an interest whose fulfillment would involve the fulfillment of more of his own and others' interests. Thus, in measuring interest one must always begin by asking how many of one's own and others' interests its exercise will further. If several alternatives remain open he should ask which of the alternatives he really prefers; and only then, if several things are preferred to the same extent, should he consider how intensely he desires each of them. The proper order of the scale of interest, and of good, is then inclusiveness, preference, and intensity. To use the scales of interest in any other order is almost certainly to fail to recognize or carry out the course of action that would fulfill the most interest.

The rule that in order to promote the greatest total good in the long run an interest must first of all be inclusive yields, when applied to conflicting interests, the key to the precise meaning of "right," for it is always at the point of conflicting interests that the question of moral right arises. Accordingly one must observe what inclusiveness of interest requires when conflicting interests are involved.

When conflicting interests occur in the life of an individual, the most promising way of including all interests is to discover a line of action that overcomes the conflict and fulfills both interests fully; and, barring that, the next most promising procedure is to find a course of action that, although it may subordinate one interest to another, is still acceptable to both interests. However, when one comes to the area of conflicts between the total interests of one individual and those of another, subordination is out of place. Indeed there is in this area no satisfactory method either for choosing between interests or for measuring one over against another. One cannot even be sure that the happiness of all the rest of the world would outweigh the suffering of one lost soul. Hence, the only assurance that we can have of fulfilling the greatest possible interest is through discovering some course of action upon which all parties can fully agree. Only if such agreement can be obtained is it clear that the interests of all are being duly considered despite the fact that it is impossible to compare the interests of different individuals. Moreover, since every action of any individual at least potentially involves the interests of others, the primary requirement of an action designed to satisfy the most possible interest is that it be one that can be agreed upon by all.

This first requirement of the satisfaction of the greatest interest supplies the essential feature of Perry's definition of "right." "Right" means for Perry, as for Hobbes, agreement with reference to the fulfillment of interests. If an act is agreed upon by all, it is right; otherwise, it is wrong. If no agreement can be obtained in a given matter, then no right can be discovered concerning it.

Such definitions of "good" and "right" may at first seem far removed from people's ordinary thought concerning the good and the right. But a little reflection reveals that the theory is not nearly so remote from common sense as it may seem. If the theory recognizes that even the objects of the interests of the drunkard have some value, it still condemns drunkenness as wrong because drunkenness thwarts both the other interests of the individual and those of other people, and is rarely, if ever, agreed to both by the individual and by others affected by his actions. Similarly, while the theory acknowledges that the interests of the criminal bestow some value even upon his acts of crime, it condemns these acts as wrong because they hamper the other interests of the criminal and thwart those of his victims, who by no means agree to what he does. As a matter of fact, this kind of theory demands temperance, honesty, and courage; and, as Perry himself emphatically insists, it makes love the supreme virtue, which above all others contributes to the fulfillment of the interests of all men.

It should, moreover, be noted that, although Perry agrees with Hobbes that good must be defined in terms of desire or interest, he does not by any means tie to this view such a political system as that of Hobbes. Rather, entertaining a more generous view of man's capacity for cooperation and a more objective view of his good, Perry is an ardent champion of democracy, alike on a national and on an international scale. He holds that, because every man's interest makes objects good and because men have many interests in common, the political system must be of a kind that engenders a cooperation in which each has an opportunity to make his interests felt. Each has a concern for the common interest and even for his fellows' interests, but each is also the best judge of his own interests. For similar reasons, Perry likewise contends that the agreements that make things right or wrong must not be static in being made once and for all, but must provide for progressive adaptation to changing situations and interests by being frequently renewed.

However, even though purged of the more obvious defects of Hobbes's version, Perry's type of desire theory retains the questionable feature of implying the goodness of objects of even the crudest and most base desires. It is in the attempt to meet difficulties of this kind, as well as for certain other reasons of their own, that a group of writers, of whom John Dewey was the most influential, have presented another version of the desire theory.

JOHN DEWEY'S REFLECTIVE DESIRE THEORY

The version of the desire theory presented by John Dewey (1859–1952) differs from that of Perry principally in insisting that it is not desire as such but reflective desire that makes a thing really good.

To be sure, there is, for Dewey, a primitive sense of the word "good" in which it may be applied simply to that which is desired, or which is an object of any interest. From this standpoint "good is that which satisfies want, craving, which fulfills or makes complete the need which stirs to action." [22] It refers to an object of *liking* or prizing.

But desire, interest, liking, prizing, and the like represent, Dewey thinks, only "a starting point" [23] in defining genuine value. To complete the definition one must include also a reflection that points out ways of resolving unsatisfactory situations. Objects of random desires may be apparently good, but only objects of reflective desires are truly good or valuable. Thus true good must be defined not as any object of any interest but as the object of a constructively thoughtful interest, or as the object of reflective desire. One may impulsively desire many things that would hurt him or others; but they are not therefore good. Otherwise the valuations of the burglar and the policeman would be the same.[24] Only those things that one still desires after careful constructive thought are really good. Good things are the objects of appraising rather than of prizing, of evaluation rather than of valuing as such. Only thus does good come "to have rightful authority in the direction of conduct." [25]

In defending this view Dewey relies upon a number of arguments. For one thing, he finds this view in accord with language and custom, which refuse to call just any desired thing

---

[22] John Dewey and J. H. Tufts, *Ethics* (rev. ed., New York: Holt, 1932), pp. 204–5.
[23] *Ibid.*, p. 17.
[24] See John Dewey, *Theory of Valuation* (Chicago: University of Chicago Press, 1939), p. 19.
[25] See John Dewey, *The Quest for Certainty* (London: Allen & Unwin, 1930).

good. Again, he finds this view in accord with the fact that desire takes place in actual concrete situations and that the value of its objects is related to these total situations. He contends that scientific facts have such direct bearing upon values as cannot be explained unless reflection is included in one's account of value. Again, Dewey undertakes to show that his view brings means and ends into more intimate connection and so offsets the prevailing preoccupation of moralists with ends to the neglect of the study of means.[26]   If one is to discover the good, he must not only weigh means for the sake of their contribution to the attainment of ends but he must also re-evaluate ends in terms of the means that are necessary for their attainment.[27]   If, in order to attain a given end, it is necessary to engage in harmful practices, there is something wrong with the end.   Recognition of this fact brings technical knowledge to bear upon valuation and bases value judgments upon "scientifically warranted empirical propositions [which are] capable of being tested by observation of results actually attained as compared with those intended."[28]

The right is, in a very general way, for Dewey, as for other specific value theorists, that which achieves the most good, which in this case would be that which satisfies the most of reflective desire.   Achievement of the right depends of course in large part, for Dewey as for Hobbes and Perry, upon agreement. However, since in Dewey's thought the good is more than the desired, as such, right has here a somewhat more thorough grounding in actual conditions of the social and physical world than in the other two desire theories.   Moreover, the right in part depends, Dewey tells us, upon the claims that individuals have upon one another in the kind of social situation in which they live.   "Right expresses the way in which the good of a number of persons, held together by intrinsic ties, becomes efficacious in the regulation of the members of a community."[29]

26 See Dewey, *Theory of Valuation*, Ch. 4.
27 See John Dewey, *Human Nature and Conduct* (New York: Holt, 1922), Pt. III, Ch. 4.
28 Dewey, *Theory of Valuation*, p. 24.
29 Dewey and Tufts, *op. cit.*, p. 249.

Agreement plays a basic role among these ties, but it must be supplemented by the particular social institutions and even physical ties that bind a community together before the precise nature of the right is apprehended.

CRITICISM OF DESIRE THEORIES

In making the object of any man's desires good merely for that man, Hobbes, as we have seen, so ties his version of the desire theory to subjectivism that, despite much suggestiveness and originality, his version of the desire theory can scarcely be tenable.   In making the object of any man's desires good, not merely for that man only, but simply good, Perry's theory is much more promisingly objective; and, in other ways as well, Perry's theory refines the cruder beginnings of Hobbes.   By introducing a cognitive element into the discernment of good, Dewey appears to bring the desire theory to closer approximation to actual moral experience.   But in making the desires that determine good reflective, Dewey has really refined the desire theory away, much as Mill did the pleasure theory when he introduced qualities of pleasure.   If objects are good to the extent to which they are objects of *reflective* desire, then the good is determined by something other than desire and is no longer either defined or measured simply in terms of desire.

Accordingly, if we are to evaluate the desire theory as such, we must for the most part bypass the crude beginnings of Hobbes and the damaging refinements of Dewey and concentrate upon Perry's enlightened, yet relatively unqualified, version.   Two questions are of cardinal importance here.   One concerns the attempt to equate the good and the desired, and the other, the effort to equate the right and agreement.

At the outset two nonessential points concerning the first of these issues must be noted in passing.   For one thing, Perry's attempt to interpret desire in behavioristic terms, although having some scientific advantages, tends to withdraw moral inquiry from the realm of actual moral experience, where it belongs, and at the same time to demand a knowledge of relations between desires and bodily attitudes that we neither have nor have any immediate prospect of acquiring. But, then, this behavioristic method is by no means essential to the main drift of Perry's theory, and, in any case, bodily attitudes can to some extent be taken at least as *signs* of genuine desires. Hence this difficulty need not disturb us unduly here. The other preliminary problem is Perry's introduction of *preference,* which is neither a desire nor a measure of quantity of desire, as a standard of value. Perry's reliance upon preference is, of course, in line with common sense, but, as in the case of Dewey's reliance upon *reflection,* Perry's reliance upon something other than desire seems to suggest that desire alone cannot determine the good. However, preference is at least akin to desire, and this difficulty also need not be pressed at this point.

Our first major question, then, is, whether or not, quite apart from qualifications in terms of reflection or preference, the good can be identified with the desired. Certainly "good" can scarcely literally *mean* desired, for no one ordinarily intends in calling anything good to say merely that it is desired. Spinoza's dictum that we call things good because we desire them, rather than desire them because they are good, has always seemed to common sense perverse. Indeed, upon reflection, not only does being desired not seem to be the ground for calling things good, but their being valuable or good seems to be the only reasonable ground for desiring them at all. Common sense may, of course, be somewhat confused; but it would seem to be at least a fairly good judge of its own intentions, and it is scarcely likely to read them precisely backward.

Actually, the desire theorists perhaps really want, not so much to *assert* that we mean desired when we speak of good, as to *propose* that, because of a complete correlation between the good and the desired, we should use the corresponding terms as equivalent. This modest proposal is much more plausible than the assertion of the identity of the meanings of "good" and "desired." There is, in fact, a rather natural and fairly high degree of correlation between what we call "good" and the objects of desire. Desire is, moreover, sometimes a better index of the good than is pleasure, as, for example, in the case of the mother who sometimes desires the unpleasant company of her complaining child more than the pleasant companionship of her cheerful friends, or in that of an artist who desires to paint even with pain more than to relax with pleasure.

But the alleged correlation of the desired and the good breaks down at certain important points, and is perhaps on the whole less complete than that of the pleasant and the good.   Pleasure is closer to satisfaction than is desire, and satisfaction is, as we have suggested, probably closer to the good than is pleasure. The attempt to correlate the desired with the good begins at the wrong end of the desire-satisfaction relation and is accordingly not infrequently led farther afield than the pleasure theory. Often we desire experiences, such as certain companionships, the reading of certain books, and the hearing of musical selections, and find, when we have them, that we fail to gain the expected satisfaction from them or are even annoyed by them. Again, we are not infrequently surprised by satisfactions for which we had no desire, as when a stranger speaks a kind word or a musical composition yields unanticipated joy.   In all such cases, it surely seems to be the satisfactions rather than the desires that afford the better indexes of good or evil.   It should, of course, be noted that, in some phases of his thought, Dewey stresses satisfaction rather than desire, and that when Perry writes of the attainment of value, he often forgets that he has defined value in terms of interest itself rather than of satisfaction of interest; but these considerations really lead to a different theory that we cannot consider here, though we shall come back later to the problem of the relation of good and satisfaction.

We turn now to the second important question concerning the desire theory, that of the soundness of the identification of right with agreement, adopted in full by Perry and with qualifications by Hobbes and Dewey.   Insofar as the desire theory is an account of who ought to be considered in determining the right, the emphasis upon agreement is entirely appropriate.   Enlightened experience generally takes its stand with

Perry's concern for every human being who is affected by an act, even to the one lost soul. Moral action must, as the agreement concept implies, be action grounded in consideration of all. Moreover, insofar as the desire theory suggests agreement as a process for the discovery of the right, it is also in the main sound. Whatever right is, it must be discerned by human minds. Since every human mind when it operates by itself is likely to be biased in its own favor, that which can be agreed upon by all is far more likely to represent the product of an impartial judgment, from which distorting biases have been eliminated, than is that on which the parties concerned remain violently at odds with one another. This point may be amply illustrated by considering current conflicts among classes and nations.

Nevertheless, there are other aspects of moral right that, without being in any sense inconsistent with these insights of advocates of the agreement principle, preclude the possibility of identifying right with agreement. To begin with, whatever the correspondence of right actions and actions that are agreed upon by all concerned, when people agree that an act is right they certainly do not ordinarily intend simply to agree that they agree. Rather they seem to unite in ascribing some other property to the act itself, which their agreement only recognizes. Hence "right" can scarcely literally *mean* agreement. Further, right actions and actions that are agreed upon by all concerned do not, by any means, always correspond. On the one hand, some actions seem plainly to be right upon which agreements cannot be reached. Few of the inmates of prisons agree that they should be there; but at least some of those who will not admit it are probably rightly there. Similarly in the current East-West dispute agreement seems to be virtually impossible, but this condition can scarcely be taken to mean that no right solutions of the present problems in question are possible. People often have to act where agreement cannot be obtained, and it is manifestly contrary to what they intend by "right" to say that nothing they can do can be right. Conversely, many actions on which agreement is obtained appear in the light of the most

critical judgment to be nevertheless wrong.   Socrates seems in
the sense required by Perry to have agreed to his condemnation.
The deluded "witch" of the New England witch-hunting orgies
not infrequently "confessed" and willingly accepted "punishment." Similarly, the victims of some recent trials in Russia
have accepted as just the verdicts of courts that condemned them
for crimes that they did not commit.   But none of these verdicts
is rendered right by having been agreed upon.   Implicit in
every genuine moral judgment is an appeal to some more
objective test, which agreement perhaps helps to verify and apply but does not by itself create.

READINGS

Hobbes

Melden, *Ethical Theories,* pp. 192–205; *or*
Clark and Smith, *Readings in Ethics,* pp. 180–93; *or*
Rand, *The Classical Moralists,* pp. 217–28.

Perry

Sellars and Hospers, *Readings in Ethical Theory,* pp. 292–309.

Dewey

Sellars and Hospers, *Readings in Ethical Theory,* pp. 272–91; *or*
Clark and Smith, *Readings in Ethics,* pp. 400–31.

QUESTIONS

1. In what sense is the desire theory already implicit in many
expressions of the pleasure theory?   In what ways does it improve
over the pleasure theory?   In what ways, if any, is it more questionable?

2. What is Hobbes' view of man?   What does he mean by the state
of nature and what is the state of nature like?   Why do Hobbes'
beliefs about these matters lead him to totalitarianism?   Do you
think that contemporary totalitarianism rests upon any of the same
foundations?   Discuss.

3. In 1776 the signers of the American Declaration of Independence proclaimed to the world: "We hold these truths to be self-evident, that all men are created equal, that they are endowed by their Creator with certain unalienable Rights. . . . That to secure these rights, Governments are instituted among Men, deriving their just powers from the consent of the governed,—That whenever any Form of Government becomes destructive of these ends, it is the Right of the People to alter or abolish it, and to institute new Government, laying its foundation on such principles and organizing its powers in such form, as to them shall seem most likely to effect their Safety and Happiness." Do you think the signers of this statement received any of their ideas, either directly or indirectly, through Hobbes? What in the foregoing statement would Hobbes have accepted and what rejected?

4. If I call that which I desire "good" to the extent that I desire it, why should I not call that which you desire "good" to the extent that you desire it? If right does not mean obedience to the state, is it nevertheless ever right to disobey the state? If not, why not? If so, when? On what does the obligation to obey the state at all seem to you to rest?

5. At what points does Perry's moral thought improve upon that of Hobbes?

6. How is it possible for Perry, while claiming that any object of any desire is good, at the same time to develop a code of practical ethics that corresponds largely to the prevailing common sense code? Explain in the cases, for example, of temperance and honesty.

7. A college student has to decide between going on to law school and accepting the job that is offered him immediately upon graduation. Indicate the steps by which Perry would apply his threefold standard of value to the solution of such a problem.

8. Compare the political thought of Perry and that of Hobbes, and show how they depend upon different assumptions concerning man and the meaning of "good."

9. What are the chief points at which Dewey's moral philosophy is critical of such a desire theory as Perry's? How would Dewey approach the problem of the student referred to in Question 7? Do you think the practical outcome would be very different? At what points in theory does Dewey desert the desirist hypothesis?

10. Examining your personal experiences carefully, point out at least one instance in which desire seems to correspond with good

and one in which it does not. Now consider what you have known of group decisions, indicating, if possible, one case in which a course of action agreed upon by all concerned seems to have been right and one in which such a course did not seem so. To what extent do you think the two cases of lack of correspondence can be explained away and to what extent do they appear to resist such explanation?

REFERENCES

Hobbes

Hobbes, Thomas, *Leviathan* (Oxford: J. Thornton, 1881).
—— *Leviathan,* selections in Burtt, E. A. (ed.), *The English Philosophers from Bacon to Mill* (New York: Random House, 1939).
Robinson, D. S., *The Principles of Conduct* (New York: Appleton-Century-Crofts, 1948), Ch. 9.
Rogers, A. K., *Morals in Review* (New York: Macmillan, 1927).
Sidgwick, Henry, and Widgery, A. G., *Outlines of the History of Ethics* (London: Macmillan, 1939), pp. 163–70.
Tsanoff, R. A., *The Moral Ideals of Our Civilization* (New York: Dutton, 1942), Ch. 8.

Perry

Hill, T. E., *Contemporary Ethical Theories* (New York: Macmillan, 1950), Ch. 14.
Perry, R. B., "The Definition of Value," *The Journal of Philosophy, Psychology and the Scientific Method,* XI (1914), pp. 141 ff.
—— *General Theory of Value* (New York: Longmans, Green, 1926), especially Chs. 1–7, 13, 20–22.
—— *The Moral Economy* (New York: Scribner, 1909), especially Chs. 1–4.
—— "The Question of Moral Obligation," *The International Journal of Ethics,* XXI (1911), pp. 282 ff.
Pratt, J. B., *Reason in the Art of Living* (New York: Macmillan, 1949), Ch. 21.

Dewey

Dewey, John, *Human Nature and Conduct* (New York: Holt, 1922), especially Pts. III, IV.

Dewey, John, "The Meaning of Value," *The Journal of Philosophy,* XXII (1925), pp. 126 ff.

————— "The Need for a Recovery of Philosophy," in Ratner, Joseph (ed.), *Creative Intelligence* (New York: Holt, 1917).

————— *The Quest for Certainty* (London: Allen & Unwin, 1930), especially Ch. 10.

————— *Theory of Valuation* (Chicago: University of Chicago Press, 1939), especially Chs. 3–8.

————— "Values, Liking and Thought," *The Journal of Philosophy,* XX (1925), pp. 617 ff.

————— and Tufts, J. H., *Ethics* (rev. ed., New York: Holt, 1932).

Hook, Sidney, *John Dewey* (New York: John Day, 1939).

Sidgwick, Henry, and Widgery, A. G., *Outlines of the History of Ethics* (London: Macmillan, 1939), pp. 323–25.

PART TWO

A Working Theory

12

The Meaning of "Good"

THROUGH THE FOREGOING EFFORTS to test a wide variety of proposed meanings of moral terms against the usage and apparent intent of such terms, we have presumably avoided a number of blind alleys and pitfalls in ethical theory and progressively approached the area in which the meanings of these terms may best be sought. At every stage in the process useful insights have been gained, but no definitive conclusions have been reached. The time has accordingly come when we must consider the problems of ethical theory more systematically and, in the light of what has been and can be discerned, endeavor to arrive at as tenable a working interpretation of moral terms as possible. This task must, of course, be undertaken with diffidence, for the problems are complex and final wisdom is not within our reach. Nevertheless, everyone must, as a working basis for his own practical decisions, make *some* assumptions about moral concepts. For this purpose, far better than to fall back on authority or instinct, is to endeavor with such aid as the successes and failures of our predecessors afford, rationally to examine the issues, no matter how imperfect the results must remain. Perhaps no two of us will arrive at exactly the same conclusions but it is hoped that the following may contain at least useful suggestions.

THE SENSES OF "GOOD"

Our previous inquiry has disclosed that the most promising ethical theories are neither subjective ones, which define moral

terms as approvals, nor formal ones, which define them as forms
of action, but teleological ones, which begin with ends considered good and define "right" as productive of maximum good.
Accordingly, since "right" is presumably to be defined by reference to the good, the best point at which to start our inquiry
is with the term "good."

Most terms that are as significant as "good" are used in a
variety of quite distinct senses. The term "man," for example, may be used in the senses of human being, male adult,
or exceptionally virile man; and, by way of illustrating at the
same time this ambiguity and a confusion of senses of another
term, the first sense of "man" may be said to be the one in
which man embraces woman; the second, the one in which he
wishes he could; and the third, the one in which she wishes he
would. The term "good" involves many more than three
senses, and failure to discriminate among them has been a major
cause of some of the difficulties we have encountered in the
ethical theories examined. If we are to avoid such difficulties,
we must, before undertaking to determine the meaning of
"good," observe carefully what the major senses of "good" are,
and determine the one of which we are trying to find the meaning.

One important distinction among senses of "good" has already
been noted, that between "good" in the general sense, in which
anything is good if it is valuable at all, and "good" in the moral
sense, in which anything is good if, and only if, it is done from
praiseworthy motives. Failure to keep this distinction clear
seems to have been involved, for example, in the Stoics' mistaken refusal to see the good in simple satisfactions that are expressions neither of virtue nor of vice; for, when one keeps in
mind that not all good is moral good, there is no longer any
reason for denying the goodness of such satisfactions as these.
On the other side, a similar mistake lies at the root of the hedonistic tendency to deny that virtue is good in itself; for, when
it is clear that all intrinsic value need not fall within a single
narrow pattern, there is no longer any reason why virtue cannot
be worth something in itself, quite apart from any pleasure that

may be found in its results. Indeed, anyone who fails to keep clearly in mind the distinction between the general and the moral senses of "good" is likely to be all too ready to praise morally evil acts because they involve *some* good or to condemn innocent satisfactions because they involve no special *moral* merit.

Cutting across the distinction between the general and the moral senses of "good" is another distinction that will turn out to be even more important for us. This is the distinction, initially suggested by Plato [1] and explicitly developed first by G. E. Moore and then in a different way by C. I. Lewis and others, between the intrinsic and extrinsic senses of "good." We have already encountered something very much like this in Aristotle's distinction between the good, which is that at which anything aims, and the supreme good, which is that for the sake of which all other things are aimed at.

"Good" in what we shall call its intrinsic sense refers to that which is good in itself, for its own sake, and apart from further consequences. In this sense, enjoyed experiences of eating steaks, talking with friends, watching plays, walking through fields, performing kind services, doing just acts, and multitudes of other kinds of conscious experiences can be good. Although the existence of all such experiences depends on other factors, the goodness of each experience, once the experience takes place, seems to be quite independent of anything else. The steak itself, the play, the walk itself, and other physical objects and events seem, however, not to be good in themselves, for the goodness of each seems to depend on the fact that it gives to someone a good experience. Conversely, an experience of nausea at sea or of suffering from a wound is intrinsically evil, but neither the sea nor the wound is itself intrinsically evil. Indeed, quite generally, it seems to be conscious experiences alone that are intrinsically either good or evil; for, whereas many experiences seem clearly to be good in themselves, for their own sakes, and apart from further consequences, physical

---

[1] See Plato, "The Republic," *The Dialogues of Plato,* tr. by Benjamin Jowett (New York: Random House, 1937), Vol. I, p. 621.

objects and events seem in the end to be good or evil only insofar as they have bearings upon the good or evil experiences of
conscious beings.

"Good" in what we shall call its extrinsic sense applies to
that which produces intrinsically good experiences. Thus, for
example, automobiles, beautiful paintings, carpenter's tools,
wholesome foods, physical exercise, gentle rains, and multitudes
of other physical objects and events are extrinsically good:
they all serve as means to the achievement of intrinsically good
experiences of human beings. Extrinsic goods are characteristically physical objects or events; for physical objects are the
obvious means of producing intrinsically good experiences.
But, presumably, mental events or states also can be extrinsically good, as, for example, painful processes of learning that
yield subsequent satisfactions, embarrassing discoveries about
one's self that serve to prevent later misfortunes or pleasant
thoughts that also prove to be enlightening. Even such in-
tangibles as ideals can be extrinsically good and may, indeed,
be among the most significant part of all that is in any sense
good. This is, for example, plainly true of such ideals as
justice and democracy that make possible the joys of free existence. States of affairs and patterns of human relations also
can be important extrinsic goods. A well-ordered society that
brings contentment to its members is surely an instance of good
in this sense, and so is the way of life of a happy family. Since
experiences, as well as objects, can be extrinsically good or bad,
as well as intrinsically so, it is possible for the same thing to be
good in both senses or bad in both senses, or good in one and
not in the other, or vice versa. For example, the enjoying of a
wholesome book is often both a genuine satisfaction in itself
and a source of subsequent good experiences, but the enjoyment of poisoned drink, though possibly momentarily satisfying, may entail disastrous results. The valid conception of
something's being good in one sense and not in another should
not, however, be confused with the self-contradictory notion,
implied in some ethical theories, of a thing's being both good
and not good in the same sense.

Failure to keep the distinction between the intrinsic and ex-trinsic senses of "good" clear led the approval theories mistak-enly to attribute goodness indiscriminately to things that are approved for their own sake and things that are approved for the sake of something else. It also lies at the root of the in-definiteness of the self-realization theories. Indeed, confusion of the intrinsic and extrinsic senses of good always leads to diffi-culties where ends and means are not clearly distinguished; for, however intimately related ends and means are in practice, they must be separated in principle if our objectives are not to become hopelessly muddled. Moreover, although the two senses of good involved here are quite distinct, common usage does not always keep them so but uses the term "intrinsically good" somewhat ambiguously to refer sometimes to that which is good only in independence of *some* further consequences and sometimes to that which is good independently of *any* further consequences. Thus, for example, a beautiful paint-ing, though requiring to be looked at to be good, is said to be intrinsically good in that its goodness is independent of further uses, as that of paint itself is not; but the *enjoyment* of the painting is said in a stricter sense to be intrinsically good in that its goodness is independent of any further consequences whatever. In order to avoid this sort of ambiguity we reserve the term "intrinsically good" to this latter strict sense and use the term "inherently good" to refer to the looser sense, which properly falls within what we have called the extrinsic sense of "good."

Within the extrinsic sense of good, we accordingly distin-guish, following C. I. Lewis,[2] two subsenses. One is the *in-herent* sense of "good," in which an object or event is said to be good if it requires only to be placed before the senses, or con-templated, in order to produce intrinsically good experiences. The other is the *instrumental* sense of "good," in which an object or event is good if it serves as a means or instrument for the promotion or creation of some inherently good thing.

[2] See C. I. Lewis, *An Analysis of Knowledge and Valuation* (La Salle, Ill.: Open Court Publishing Company, 1946), pp. 390 ff.

Thus, for example, a beautiful picture or rendering of a musical composition is inherently good, as needing only to be seen or heard to produce intrinsically good experiences; but the brushes of the painter or the violins and flutes of the musicians are only instrumentally good, as means to producing pictures and playing music. This distinction helps to keep clear the fact that, although goodness may be said, for example, to be in the picture in a sense in which it is not in the brushes, even the picture is good only for the sake of the experiences it yields and so is not intrinsically good.

Insofar as that which is good in the *moral* sense involves satisfying experience, even apart from further consequences, it is intrinsically good. But insofar as the morally good is a physical act having subsequent good consequences it is only extrinsically good.

In some of its relatively subordinate senses "good" is neither intrinsic nor extrinsic. Thus, for example, we sometimes speak, in what we may call an *exemplary* sense, of "a good snake" or "a good case of typhoid," meaning in each instance good of its kind. Again, in what we may call an *efficient* sense, we sometimes speak of "a good machine," meaning a machine capable of doing its job well whether the end result be good or evil. Generally speaking, people's interests in good examples and in efficient objects stem originally from the fact that these often serve, like extrinsic goods, to promote intrinsic goods; and indeed, the significance of such examples and objects for ethics consists solely in the fact that they do promote intrinsic goods. Hence, what is important for ethics in the exemplary and efficient senses of "good" may be included in the extrinsic sense, and the distinctive features of these two subordinate senses need not concern us further.

Actually, all of the senses of "good" that are significant for ethics fall within the intrinsic or extrinsic ones; and, since things that are good in the extrinsic sense are good only insofar as they contribute to intrinsic good, the sense of "good" with which our quest for the *meaning* of "good" is primarily concerned is the intrinsic one. Once this is clear, the meaning of "good" in its extrinsic sense can readily be inferred.

THE MEANING OF "GOOD" IN ITS INTRINSIC SENSE

Having now distinguished the basic intrinsic sense of "good" from all others, we must ask what "good" in this sense means or what it is that we intend to say about an experience in calling it good in this sense. When the crucial question about the meaning of "good" is thus clarified, the answer appears already to be implicitly given. In calling any experience good in the intrinsic sense we seem to be attributing to it a simple characteristic of being valuable or worth having, which we all recognize in some experiences and which need not, and perhaps cannot, be reduced to any other characteristic or characteristics.

Initial impressions can, of course, be misleading, and apparently simple characteristics can turn out to be complexes reducible to simple terms. It is partly for this reason that we undertook in the preceding chapters to examine the more significant theories that attempt to reduce "good," in somewhat less sharply distinguished senses, to simpler terms. As we have noticed, all of these theories proved to be inadequate; and if they were unable to reduce the less sharply distinguished senses of "good" with which they dealt to simpler terms, there is little likelihood that either these or other theories like them could reduce "good" in its basic intrinsic sense to simpler terms. Attempts to reduce "good" in this sense to approvals either rob it of any single meaning or lose its meaning in a vicious regress. Attempts to reduce it to nature or human nature are clearly far too broad, and pleasure neither can be fully correlated with the good nor is intended by the term "good." Not only so, but Moore's type of open question argument, as indicated in our criticism of the pleasure theory, would seem to preclude any type of attempt to reduce good to anything else. That is, we seem to be able to ask concerning any characteristic proposed as a meaning of good whether or not it is good, and to ask this in such a way as to indicate that the proposed reduction leaves out something important.

One further suggestion was, however, mentioned in passing in criticizing the pleasure theory, namely, that good might be more plausibly equated with satisfaction than with pleasure. We must now briefly consider this view. Satisfaction was never very far from what was meant by "good" in both desire and pleasure theories, and even in the self-realization ones. Moreover, in recent years many of those who, though unable quite to identify the good with either pleasure or the desired, still seek the meaning of good in a specific kind of experience have been increasingly disposed to find the meaning of good in satisfaction.[3] As a proposed equivalent of goodness, satisfaction has the advantage over pleasure of being far richer and more capable of embracing the wide variety of experiences found valuable in themselves. It has the advantage over the desired of being that aspect of the desire-satisfaction relation which nearly always comes most prominently into view in judgments of *intrinsic* value. The correspondence between the experiences that we call good and those in which we find satisfaction is in fact considerably greater than that between the good and either the pleasant or the desired. Indeed, if the right turns out, as it well may, to be that which produces the most good for all concerned, one could work out a very plausible and practicable theory of ethics as a whole—as Professor J. B. Pratt has in principle done [4]—in which a right act is taken to be one that brings to all who are affected by it the most possible of the experiences that they find satisfying.

Nevertheless, the correspondence between the good and satisfaction is not perfect. The term satisfaction suggests at least some previous desire, but previous desire need not have existed for the existence of good. Moreover, some of the best experiences seem to contain much more of dissatisfaction than the

---

[3] See J. B. Pratt, *Reason in the Art of Living* (New York: Macmillan, 1949), Chs. 16, 17; Lewis, *op. cit.*, Pt. III.

[4] See Pratt, *op. cit.*

satisfaction theory can allow. This lack of full correspondence between satisfaction and the good is not, however, the main difficulty with the interpretation of "good" in terms of satisfaction. One might by means of appropriate qualifications arrive at a description of a kind of experience that corresponded perfectly with the good and, even so, not yet have arrived at an adequate account of the meaning of "good." The major difficulty in a satisfaction theory of the meaning of "good" lies just here, in that, like pleasure and desire theories, a satisfaction theory attempts to identify the good with a psychological state as such and leaves out of account the distinctive valuation element in the good, what R. M. Hare calls "the prescriptive or commendatory element in value judgments." [5]

Thus we are brought back to the view that seemed most natural at the outset, that good in its intrinsic sense simply means valuable or worth experiencing for its own sake, the terms "valuable" or "worth experiencing" being here not formal definitions, but simply terms suggesting essentially the same characteristic as the term "good." This interpretation, first elaborated by G. E. Moore, seems to be essentially what is required by our actual intentions in using the term "good" and is to be presented here along lines for the most part suggested by Moore. Since the term "right" is subsequently to be defined through this interpretation of "good," we may now indicate that among the major types of ethical theory, the type toward which we are moving belongs to the *specific value type,* and that of three types of specific value theory mentioned at the beginning of Chapter 10, the theory being developed here belongs to the *unique good type* rather than to the pleasure type or the desire type.

In treating the meaning of "intrinsically good" as irreducible and the term as not adequately definable in other terms, we do not by any means put this term in a class by itself. Every language requires a number of terms such that their meaning can never be adequately put in other terms, and indeed through which other terms must be defined. Only when there are such

[5] R. M. Hare, *The Language of Morals* (Oxford: The Clarendon Press, 1952), p. 82.

terms, whose meanings cannot be revealed save by indicating the kind of experiences to which they refer, can the defining process get started at all.   As C. I. Lewis has pointed out in another connection, one could master all of the words in the dictionary in the sense of learning their verbal definitions without really knowing what a single word meant.   For this latter purpose, in order to connect the verbal system with experience, the *experiential* meaning of at least some key terms must be directly indicated; and we are suggesting that "good" in its intrinsic sense is such a key term.   But the fact that "good" is irreducible and basically indefinable does not mean that nothing can be said about its meaning.   At least the following six specific points, some of which have already been suggested, seem to be worth emphasizing.

1. Since "good" is an adjective, not a noun, the meaning intended by it must be sought, not in any kind of thing or experience as such, but in a *characteristic* of certain experiences.   To say that an experience is intrinsically good is to attribute to it the characteristic in question or to say that it *has* or *is qualified by* this characteristic.   The characteristic itself may appropriately be called "goodness" or "value," provided one is not misled by these terms into thinking that goodness or value is itself an independent thing or experience.

2. The characteristic meant in saying that anything is "good" in the intrinsic sense is not merely one of the independently variable characteristics that enter into the description of the experience that is good but a characteristic that results from all of the other characteristics of the experience.[6]   It is what Moore calls a *toti-resultant characteristic*.   Thus, for example, while squareness may be one of the descriptive characteristics in a perceptual experience of a box and redness another, and each may be varied independently, being intrinsically good is not merely one more such characteristic but a product of all of the other characteristics of the experience.   A complete factual description of the experience could be given without men-

---

[6] See G. E. Moore, "The Conception of Intrinsic Value," *Philosophical Studies* (New York: Harcourt, Brace, 1922), pp. 253–75.

tioning its intrinsic goodness, and a change in any one of the ordinary characteristics of the experience could conceivably be made without affecting any of the others. But, once the other characteristics of the experience are determined, the intrinsic value of the experience is also determined; and this value can be changed only by first changing some of the other characteristics. In this respect "good" resembles such terms as "pleasant" or "satisfying," rather than "rectangular" or "round," or "blue" or "green," for the pleasantness of an experience varies with all of its other qualities, whereas changes in its shape need have no effect upon its color or vice versa. But it should be noted that even pleasantness and satisfaction must, if present, be included in the total experience of which intrinsic goodness is a resultant, whereas the converse of this does not hold.

3. That characteristic of a total experience meant by "good" in its intrinsic sense is not, however, like some properties of things, a mere sum of the same characteristics in its ingredients. Rather, the goodness of any experience may be either more or less than the sum of the goodness of the parts. That is to say, a good experience is what Moore calls an "organic whole." [7] The length of a rod is exactly equal to the sum of the lengths of its parts, and the weight of a collection of rocks is exactly the same as the sum of the weights of the separate rocks. But the intrinsic goodness of an experience may deviate substantially from the sum of the goodness of its parts. For example, the value of weeping at a tragedy in the theatre may be far greater than the sum of the values of the understanding, bewilderment, joy, and sorrow that enter the experience, and that of uneasy pleasure in another person's discomfort may be less than the sum of the value in the ingredient knowledge, uneasiness, and pleasure. In this respect goodness is more like the intensity of a feeling than the quantity of a thing.

4. Intrinsic goodness, or the characteristic referred to in calling anything good in the intrinsic sense, is not a property of things but a quality of experiences. What is meant by this

[7] G. E. Moore, *Principia Ethica* (Cambridge: Cambridge University Press, 1903), pp. 30–36.

has already been in part suggested but must be further explained.

Many terms are used ambiguously to refer either to properties of objects or qualities of experiences, although these two are by no means the same. A property of a physical object is best spoken of as a capacity in the object to produce certain experiences in anyone who encounters the object. Such a property is not only in this sense public but may manifest itself in any one of several different ways at different times or even at the same time. Moreover, any given impression of a property in an object is subject to correction in terms of subsequent observations. A quality of an experience is, however, privately apprehended in the experience itself by the one who has the experience. It manifests itself immediately and uniquely, and this manifestation is not subject to change through subsequent experiences. Thus, for example, such a physical object as a necktie may be said to have the property of bright greenness in the sense of having a publicly verifiable capacity to produce a sensation of bright greenness in those who observe it in a normal light and, sensations of various other shades and colors as light conditions are changed. Any single observation of the shade and color of the tie is also subject to correction by later ones. But my consciously experienced image of the necktie at the present moment—whether I am looking at the tie or only imagining it—may be said to have the quality of greenness in the sense of being privately, uniquely, and finally apprehended by me as itself green; and this sensed greenness neither needs, nor is capable of, any other manifestation. The green image may be replaced by images of other colors, but the greenness of this image is simply given with the image itself. Clearly, though a single term "greenness" is used, two quite different senses of the term are involved here, and nothing but confusion can result from failure to distinguish them.

The terms "good" and "value" also occur ambiguously with reference to the property-of-object and quality-of-experience distinction. But the difference between these two usages is just as fundamental in the area of valuation as elsewhere; it is what some recent writers would call a "categorial" difference. Just as being red in the sensory way and being immediately pleasant are basically different from being red and being pleasant as properties of objects and, once distinguished from them, should never be confused with these properties because they are the sort of experiential qualities on the basis of which properties are attributed to objects at all, so being good or valuable in the quality-of-experience sense is basically different from being good as a property of an object and, once clearly distinguished, should never be confused with such a property because it is the experiential ground on which objects are said to have properties at all. Serious misdirection of thought nearly always occurs when one fails to keep this distinction clear. For example, if one tries to compare the goodness of things with reactions to them, he only succeeds in mixing capacities of things with experiences that reveal and measure them, in an impossible attempt to place alongside one another entities that belong to entirely different dimensions.

Although extrinsic goods can be good in the quality-of-experience usage as well as in the property-of-object one, we are proposing to confine the term "good" in the intrinsic sense to the quality-of-experience usage. This we do for two reasons. In the first place, it is only in the quality-of-experience way that anything is in the strictest sense good in itself, for its own sake, and apart from consequences. When we ask, concerning any object or property of an object, wherein its value really lies, or for what it is good, we must always in the end reply in terms of experiences. And, although some situations involving but not being experiences can, in a sense that blurs categorial distinctions in confusing fashion, be said to be good in themselves, their goodness will be found to reside ultimately and unambiguously only in the contained experiences, and the goodness associated with the remaining aspects of the situation will be seen to be rooted in reference to subsequent experiences. The other reason for confining good in the intrinsic sense to the quality-of-experience usage is that otherwise when we come to calculate the total intrinsic good resulting from an act we shall find ourselves seriously misled by counting the same values twice over, once as parts of situations loosely said to be good in themselves and once as experiential good subsequently produced by these parts. It is, we may note in passing, at the point of insisting upon confining the application of the term "good" in the intrinsic sense to experiences that the interpretation presented here differs chiefly from that of Professor Moore.

5. The meaning of "good" in its intrinsic sense is not a complex one that can be explained in terms of simpler meanings but, as previously indicated, one of those unique, simple meanings in terms of which more complex meanings must themselves be explained.[8] In this respect "good" is not like "square," "daily," "twenty," "solid," and "canine" but like "spatial," "single," "sensuous," "hard," and "red." "Square" can readily be explained in terms of spatial lines and areas, "daily" in terms of temporal intervals, "twenty" in terms of numerical units, "solid" in terms of structures and sensations, and "canine" in terms of a variety of colors, shapes, and activities. But "spatial," "temporal," "single," "sensuous," "hard," "red," and many similar terms cannot be explained unless the experiences they refer to are recognized; and, apart from these simpler terms and the experiences on which they depend, the more complex terms can hardly be explained either. In like manner, although "good" in its extrinsic sense can be explained in terms of conduciveness to the intrinsically good, unless one appreciates the goodness of good experiences and comes to understand the term "good" by hearing it in conjunction with such experiences, little can be done to explain the term "good" in its intrinsic sense to him. This uniqueness of "good" in the intrinsic sense is, as we have seen, evidenced in part by the failure of all efforts to reduce "good" in this sense to other terms, in part by the fact that we persist in asking concerning any proposed substitute whether or not it is good in this sense, in part by the fact that we explain whole ranges of other terms through this one, and more specifically by the fact now to be a little more fully developed of a special peculiarity of "good."

[8] Moore, *Principia Ethica*, pp. 5–21.

6. We now come to the core of the meaning of "good" in its intrinsic sense. The essential feature of this meaning is not its being a unique, toti-resultant, organic characteristic of certain experiences but its being a *valuational* or *commendatory* one. To attribute intrinsic goodness to any experience is not merely to attribute another factual characteristic, even though that characteristic be, as satisfaction seems to be, toti-resultant, organic, and unique; rather, it is also and especially to attribute a valuational characteristic. That an experience is intrinsically good means that the experience is worth experiencing for its own sake, apart from further consequences. That such an experience should be pleasant or satisfying or desired may contribute to its being intrinsically good; indeed, the degree of its goodness may correspond closely to the degree of the presence of these qualities; but its being intrinsically good *means* that it has the additional feature of being valuable. On the one hand, this characteristic, though often properly attributed to sense experiences, is not a sensory quality, and though most often found in experiences that are liked is not being liked. On the other hand, though not merely factual in the ordinary sense, it is neither mysterious nor other-worldly. Rather it is simply that unique characteristic of being worth having for its own sake often found in some experiences by those who have these experiences.

If, on the one hand, one protests that he is unable to locate the characteristic in question, in all likelihood he is not attending simply to whether or not his experience is worth experiencing for its own sake, apart from further consequences, but is looking for some publicly observable property like the *shape* of a table, or some descriptive character of an experience like the *redness* of an image, or even for some mysterious metaphysical entity like *being*. If, on the other hand, one objects that the account of the meaning of "good" as a unique characteristic of being valuable virtually amounts to saying that "good" means good, the fact should be kept in mind, in view of many misleading attempts to identify the meaning of "good" with other concepts, that the idea of the unique valuational character of good both rules out the irrelevant and prevents our so narrowing the quest for the good as to exclude much that people actually find good.[9]

THE APPREHENSION OF THE GOOD

In what has been said about the meaning of "good" the question of how we recognize good is already in principle answered. But it may be well to pause to be a little more explicit upon this point.

If intrinsic goodness could be equated with some other characteristic of an experience, such as its pleasantness or its satisfactoriness, the goodness of the experience might be *inferred,* from that other characteristic, from its pleasantness or from its satisfactoriness for example. Indeed, since pleasant and satisfying experiences do tend to be found intrinsically good, the pleasantness and satisfactoriness of an experience afford some evidence that it is also intrinsically good. But, since "good" can never be fully equated with "pleasant" or "satisfying," we can never strictly infer the goodness of an experience from its pleasantness or satisfactoriness; and, since "intrinsically good" does not *mean* the possession of these characteristics, we could not know that experiences that had them were intrinsically good at all if we could not apprehend the presence of this characteristic in some other way.

Actually, being a unique characteristic, not reducible to any other, goodness *cannot* be inferred at all and, being immediately found in certain experiences, it *does not need* to be inferred. As C. I. Lewis rightly puts the matter, "Experience wears its own intrinsic value-aspect on its face." [10] The goodness of any experience is given with the experience itself, and in having the experience we are already in a position to apprehend its goodness. All we have to do is to notice this aspect of what is already there with the experience itself.

Such immediate apprehension of good is not knowledge in the strict sense in which perception of physical objects or mem-

9 See Moore, *Principia Ethica*, p. 20.
10 C. I. Lewis, *Mind and the World Order* (New York: Scribner, 1929), p. 403.

ory of past experiences is knowledge, although the term knowledge may be loosely applied to it. In not being knowledge in the strictest sense it is like immediate sense experiences, which, being simply there for us in our experiences, are more likely to be said to be *given* than *known* but remain much more certain than things said to be known and constitute major sources of knowledge. Perhaps the kind of apprehension involved could be appropriately called intuition, provided we remember that "intuition" is not here used in any such comprehensive way as that in which the mystic, for example, uses the term but in the very elemental sense in which we are said to intuit our own sensations and feelings.

The fact that the intrinsic goodness of an experience is recognized intuitively if at all does not imply that an experience must necessarily be recognized to be good if it is good. Actually, even sense experiences have characteristics that are not noticed, for the simple reason, among others, that the characteristics in question have not been singled out or named. For example, the sensory field of the little child no doubt often involves circles as when he sees coins and similar objects, but these circles can scarcely be apprehended as circles until the concept of circularity has begun to be developed. Even after the needed distinctions are at hand many phases of a sense-datum are not noticed. To take a much-discussed case as an example, one's sensory image of a speckled hen includes a certain number of specks, but, though this number could presumably be ascertained if the image could be held long enough, one is scarcely likely to ascertain it. The situation is similar where goodness is concerned. Unless one learns to grasp the concept of goodness, he will not recognize his experience to be good when it is good; and even if the concept is available, he may often not notice that his experience is valuable when it is valuable, though presumably he could recognize that it is valuable if he attended sufficiently to it.

Not only does the intuitive character of our apprehension of goodness not imply that an experience cannot be good without being recognized to be so, it does not even imply, as might be supposed, that when we do seem to recognize intrinsic goodness in an experience, we cannot be mistaken. We are not following the conscience theories, which take "right" to mean approved by conscience. "Right" is not in question here at all, and "intrinsically good" is not here taken to *mean* intuited by value insight but only to refer to a characteristic that is in fact recognizable by such insight. Accordingly, no self-contradiction in principle is involved in the idea of a mistaken value-intuition, though such mistakes are actually very unlikely. But quite apart from the theoretical possibility of mistakes in value-intuitions, errors of other kinds can and do make their way into our judgments of intrinsic value. For example, one may not yet have gotten clearly in mind what intrinsic value is. Or he may fail, in any one of a number of ways, as we shall presently see, to notice carefully just what it is that he is valuing. Moreover, even if he makes no mistakes in these matters, difficulties almost inevitably arise when he tries to put his value-insights into words. Words, however useful, are quite incapable of conveying the precise or full import of experience; and for this reason, if for no other, intrinsic-value statements will always be inadequate and partly inaccurate.

The objection may, of course, be raised against the intuitive account of the apprehension of intrinsic good that such apprehension is socially conditioned, but this objection rests upon a misunderstanding. An experience that we evaluate certainly is often socially conditioned, and public approvals or disapprovals play a far larger role in determining the degree of satisfaction or dissatisfaction in it than we are likely to think. But it is the experience itself that is shaped by social conditioning; the intrinsic value of the experience is a unique valuational characteristic that results from all aspects of the experience, including those produced by social influences. Once the experience, with all it derives from social factors, is determined, its intrinsic value is determined; and, being a part of the experience itself, the awareness of approvals and disapprovals can scarcely perform the further function of determining also the intrinsic value of the experience. Those who are most impressed with the influence of society on values often wish to know what the intrinsic value of an experience would be apart from social conditioning, and to this end they carefully attempt to discount social biases. But, when all the discounting has been done, they can determine the intrinsic value of the purified experience only by asking directly what the experiencing of it is, or would be, worth in itself.

If we may now take the intrinsic goodness of an experience to be a unique value characteristic directly found in certain experiences, how, in practice, are we to determine the kinds of experiences that are good? When the experience in question is one that we are at the moment having, the problem is comparatively simple. Essentially what we have to do, if we are not already aware of the value of the experience, is simply to ask ourselves whether or not the experience is worth having apart from any further consequences. To be sure, the direction of special attention upon this aspect of the experience may alter the experience itself, but not, generally speaking, sufficiently to prevent our ascertaining its intrinsic goodness with a fair degree of reliability. Even when the question is about remembered experiences, the difficulties are not too great; for we can often remember the value of the experience as well as the experience itself, and, even if this cannot be done, it is often possible to recall the experience sufficiently vividly to evaluate it at the time of recollection. But, when the question is about the intrinsic value of possible experiences that are not being, and have not been, had, the problem is much more difficult. The best we can do is to recall the value of closely similar experiences in the past, or, if this is not possible, to project ourselves imaginatively into the experiences under consideration and see what value they seem, as imagined, to have. If the problem is that of estimating the value of other people's experiences, the difficulty is still greater. Strictly speaking, no man can fully apprehend the conscious experiences of another; and, although the analogy of our own experiences and those of others affords some insights we must be very cautious in the attempt to estimate other people's intrinsic values, and should remain much more ready to listen to others than to presume to judge for them.

"GOOD" AND "OUGHT"

That "intrinsically good" means having a certain unique characteristic does not imply that this meaning is unrelated to other characteristics. We have already pointed out that the intrinsic goodness of experience depends on all of the other characteristics of the experience, though whether or not the relation of the intrinsic goodness of the experience to these other characteristics is a constant one is a question that remains to be considered. In any case, the meanings of certain other terms that are derivative from that of "intrinsically good" are surely reliably related to that of this term. Thus *"intrinsic goodness," "intrinsic good,"* and *"intrinsic value"* represent the unique quality that intrinsically good experiences *have*. *"The intrinsically good"* and *"the intrinsically valuable"* refer to those experiences that are intrinsically good, together with those possible ones that would be intrinsically good if they existed. *"An intrinsic good"* and *"an intrinsic value"* refer to an experience that is intrinsically good or a possible one that would be intrinsically good if it existed. *"Extrinsically good"* and *"extrinsically valuable"* mean tending to produce the intrinsically valuable. *"Intrinsically evil"* means having, apart from further consequences, a valuational characteristic opposite to intrinsic goodness—that of being *intrinsically dis-valuable*. *"Intrinsic evil"* and *"dis-value"* refer to a distinctive characteristic of all those experiences that are intrinsically evil. *"An intrinsic evil"* and *"a dis-value"* refer to an experience that *has* intrinsic dis-value or is such as to be worth avoiding even apart from further consequences. "Extrinsically evil" means tending to produce the *intrinsically dis-valuable*.

In addition to having fairly obvious relations to valuational terms whose meanings are derivatives from its meaning, "good" in its intrinsic sense also stands in close, but less obvious, relations to the other major moral terms, "ought" and "right."

By examining the relation of "good" in its intrinsic sense to "ought," we shall perhaps be able not only to indicate an important connection between value as such and ethics but also to throw some further light upon the meaning of "intrinsically good." The relation of "good" in its intrinsic sense to "right" is reserved for discussion in a subsequent chapter.

"Ought" in the sense that is relevant to ethics evidently does not mean the same as "good"; its meaning involves an element of compulsion that is not explicitly involved in the meaning of "good." What sort of compulsion is this? Not physical compulsion, for we ought to do many things that we are not physically forced to do, and if we are forced to do anything, we would hardly appropriately say that we ought to do it. Nor is the compulsion in question that of desire, since we desire to do things that we ought not to do, and ought to do things that we do not desire to do. Is the compulsion in question then rational? This seems much closer to the required meaning, for one certainly ought in some sense to accept the conclusions that follow from his premises, and what one ought to do can be broadly identified with what a fully rational man would do. But even so, the "ought" of logical necessity is scarcely the same as that of morality, for we surely ought to do many things that cannot be logically *demonstrated* to be what we ought to do, and although logical necessity enters into moral reasoning, the conclusions of reasoning can involve no moral ought that was not already there in the premises. If I *ought* not to steal, I *ought* to accept the inference that I *ought* not to steal apples. But the moral "ought" in the conclusion depends on the one in the premise, and apart from the moral "ought" in the premise the connecting "ought" could produce no moral "ought" at all. About the best we can say, then, concerning the meaning of "ought" is that it refers to a kind of nonphysical compulsion that is akin to rational necessity but has its own unique character.

What, now, is the relation between this quasi-rational unique compulsion meant by "ought" in its moral sense and the unique quality of being valuable meant by "good" in its intrinsic sense? We seem to be able to see a connection such that if any kind of experience is good, those who can do so ought to try to bring it into existence. This formulation of the connection is, however, not quite accurate enough. Some things that are good are so related to others that one cannot say without qualifications that we ought to try to bring them into existence. For example, if I know that listening to a concert would be a good experience but that listening to a superior one at no extra cost would be better, or involve more intrinsic value, the good of listening to the first is surely not what I ought to seek. Similarly, if my carrying through a certain business transaction would yield some good, but, on the whole, far more evil to more people, the good resulting from the transaction is clearly not what I ought to strive for. Although the intrinsic value that would be produced by the poorer concert or the doubtful deal tend to create some obligation, this is decisively overbalanced by an obligation to bring a better experience into existence or to avoid bringing evil into existence. The relation of "intrinsic good" and "ought" is then best expressed, not by saying that every good experience ought to be brought into existence, but by saying that each type of experience tends to produce an obligation to bring it into existence that is proportional to its intrinsic goodness and accordingly that, all things considered, what ought to be done is presumably that which will bring about the most intrinsic good altogether.

READINGS

Melden, *Ethical Theories*, pp. 458–68; *or*
Clark and Smith, *Readings in Ethics*, pp. 371–96; *or*
Sellars and Hospers, *Readings in Ethical Theory*, pp. 63–91.

QUESTIONS

1. What's the good of distinguishing between intrinsic and extrinsic good? In what sense is good used the first time it appears in the preceding sentence? Why not discuss value in general regardless of whether it is intrinsic or extrinsic?

2. What are the distinguishing marks of intrinsic good? In what sense is a beautiful picture good? In what sense is your *enjoyment* of the picture good?

3. In what sense would good most likely be used of each of the following: (a) a novel, (b) a hammer, (c) enjoyment of a concert, (d) an act of generosity, (e) the motive prompting such an act, (f) a pleasant conversation, (g) a painting, (h) love, (i) the taste of an excellent steak?

4. High up in the Himalayas, in nooks that the boldest climbers rarely reach, lovely little flowers are said to bloom. If these flowers were never to be seen and if no one, not even God, were ever to think of them, would they be intrinsically valuable? How not? If they would, define carefully the sense in which they would. Just what is meant by saying that only experiences are intrinsically valuable?

5. Does the principle of the exclusively experiential character of the intrinsically good mean that a conscious experience is in all circumstances to be chosen in preference to a thing? Explain. What light does this principle throw upon the question of personal rights *versus* property rights?

6. Call to mind as fully as possible a recent intrinsically valuable experience of yours. Now isolate the principal parts of this experience and ask yourself what value each would have if it had itself been a complete experience. Does the whole experience seem to you to have had equal, or greater, or less, value than the parts would have had if experienced separately? What bearing does your answer have on the proof or disproof of a thesis suggested in the chapter?

7. When you say that your hour at the concert was a good experience, what do you mean? Could you do full justice to your intention by saying that the experience was natural, or human, or pleasant? In each case, why, or why not?

8. The experience of listening to *The Taming of the Shrew* is for the most part more pleasant than that of hearing *Hamlet*. Yet many people find the latter a *better* experience. Do you? If so, can one explain the apparent superiority of the one to the other in terms of any of the factors through which moralists most frequently attempt to reduce good to something other than good? How can one explain the apparent superiority of the one experience to the other?

9. Do you think it necessary to arrive ultimately at some elementary meanings in order to define anything adequately? Why, or why not? Suppose you try to explain to someone that good simply means good

and he replies, "So what?" What could you say in the effort to show that your claim was significant?

10. Does intuition seem to you to be requisite at any point to human knowledge? If so, why? If not, how is knowledge possible without it?

11. A locomotive builder wants to prove that his product is good. Would his inability to do so tend to discredit our view of apprehension of the intrinsically good? Explain.

12. How can the vast gaps separating the *mores* of primitive peoples and the moral ideals of highly cultured ones be reconciled with the intuitive theory of apprehension of intrinsic good?

13. A young man enjoys working with his hands and thinks with good reason that he would be fairly happy as a mechanic. Should he forthwith commit himself to a career as a mechanic or must other factors be taken into account? Explain. What light, if any, does your reply throw upon the problem of the relation of "good" and "ought"?

REFERENCES

Brentano, Franz, *The Origin of the Knowledge of Right and Wrong,* tr. by Cecil Hague (Westminster: Constable, 1902).

Clarke, M. E., *A Study in the Logic of Value* (London: University of London Press, 1929).

Dewey, John, *Theory of Valuation* (Chicago: University of Chicago Press, 1939).

——— and Tufts, J. H., *Ethics* (rev. ed., New York: Holt, 1932), Ch. 11.

Drake, Durant, *Problems of Conduct* (2nd rev. ed., Boston: Houghton Mifflin, 1935), Ch. 7.

Ewing, A. C., *The Definition of Good* (New York: Macmillan, 1947), especially Chs. 4–5.

Hare, R. M., *The Language of Morals* (Oxford: The Clarendon Press, 1952), Pt. II.

Hartmann, Nicolai, *Ethics,* tr. by Stanton Coit (New York: Macmillan, 1932).

Hall, E. W., *What Is Value?* (New York: Humanities Press, 1952).

Laird, John, *An Enquiry into Moral Notions* (New York: Columbia University Press, 1936), Pt. III.

——— *The Idea of Value* (Cambridge: Cambridge University Press, 1929).

Lewis, C. I., *An Analysis of Knowledge and Valuation* (La Salle, Ill.: Open Court Publishing Company, 1946), Chs. 12, 14.

—— *The Ground and Nature of the Right* (New York: Columbia University Press, 1955), Ch. 4.

—— *Mind and the World Order* (New York: Scribner, 1929), Appendix B.

Moore, G. E., "The Conception of Intrinsic Value," *Philosophical Studies* (New York: Harcourt, Brace, 1922).

—— *Ethics* (New York: Oxford University Press, 1912; Reset 1947).

—— *Principia Ethica* (Cambridge: Cambridge University Press, 1903).

Perry, R. B., *General Theory of Value* (New York: Longmans, Green, 1926).

—— *The Moral Economy* (New York: Scribner, 1909).

Pratt, J. B., *Reason in the Art of Living* (New York: Macmillan, 1949), Chs. 15–16.

Rashdall, Hastings, *Theory of Good and Evil* (London: Oxford University Press, 1936).

Ross, W. D., *Foundations of Ethics* (Oxford: The Clarendon Press, 1939), Ch. 9.

Schilpp, P. A., *The Philosophy of G. E. Moore* (Evanston, Ill.: Northwestern University, 1942), pp. 43–199, 535–627.

Schlick, Moritz, *Problems of Ethics* (New York: Prentice-Hall, 1939).

Sidgwick, Henry, *The Methods of Ethics* (7th ed., London: Macmillan, 1907), Bk. III, Ch. 14.

Sorley, W. R., *Moral Values and the Idea of God* (Cambridge: Cambridge University Press, 1930).

Toulmin, S. E., *An Examination of the Place of Reason in Ethics* (Cambridge: Cambridge University Press, 1950), especially Ch. 2.

13

The Order of Intrinsic Values

BEFORE PROCEEDING FROM the consideration of the meaning of "good" in its intrinsic sense to that of the meaning of "right" in its moral sense, we pause to make some observations concerning the experiences that are found intrinsically good, that is, concerning intrinsic values. Two problems are of special importance here. One is that of the constancy of intrinsic values; the other is that of the levels of such values.

THE CONSTANCY OF INTRINSIC VALUES

A question that must often have been in the mind of the thoughtful reader concerns the extent to which identical experiences have the same intrinsic value, and experiences that resemble one another, similar intrinsic value. Intrinsic value does not, of course, have to be constant in order to be a unique valuational characteristic immediately found in experiences, for each instance of an experience might be found to have just the intrinsic value it does have without regard to the value of any other instance or to the value of any sort of similar experience. But such a high degree of inconstancy among values would render discussion of intrinsic values difficult, to say the least, and while it would not entirely render a utilitarian ethics of achievement of maximum good impossible, it would surely make such an ethics rather impracticable. What, then, is the degree of constancy of intrinsic values? Certainly it is not difficult to find instances of experiences of the same or similar objects that have very different values. Thus, for example, eating steak may be a joy to a well man but nauseating to one who is ill. Robinson Crusoe's discovery of a chest of gold would have been highly prized in England, but it was relatively unimportant to him on an uninhabited island from which he had little prospect of escape. A walk along a lovely lane in the spring sunshine is likely to be delightful, but a walk down the same lane in the autumn rain may be dismal. Enjoyment of the blessings of liberty is among our most cherished experiences in America, but in some places people "spit upon liberty." As a child one likes to hear fairy stories, as an adult he does not. Some people enjoy Beethoven, and others find him dull.

In view of such contrasts as these, it would be foolish to suggest that all experiences of the same or similar *objects* are alike in intrinsic value, or that intrinsic values vary with perfect regularity according to the presence in them of some single ingredient or combination of ingredients. That such an ingredient or ingredients could not in any case be anything other than goodness has already been shown in rejecting the reducibility of intrinsic goodness to anything else. And that intrinsic goodness itself could not give perfectly symmetrical order to intrinsic values is implied in the principle of organic wholes, which shows that the intrinsic value of any whole need not be equal to the sum of the intrinsic values of its parts.

Nevertheless, there seem to be good reasons for thinking that intrinsic values have a rather high degree of constancy in the following sense. If an experience, including not only a major content but the entire content and emotional shading of consciousness at a given time, is once found to be intrinsically valuable for one person at one time and place, and another person has an experience exactly like this one at another time or place, then the two experiences will have the same degree of intrinsic value. Further, if two or more experiences are closely similar to one another, they will also tend to have closely similar degrees of intrinsic value. One might go on to say that if experiences are similar at all in certain crucial respects, they manifest at least some tendency to have similar values, although, as the similarities become less close, the likelihood of the disturbance of value regularity rises rapidly. No sufficient effort to prove these propositions can, of course, be undertaken here; and *proof* of such propositions is in any case hardly possible. What can be done is rather, first, to indicate two considerations that render the constancy of value initially plausible, and then, by closer examination of apparent exceptions, both to remove some major obstacles to the probability of the constancy of intrinsic values and to augment that probability.

One of the two grounds upon which the constancy of intrinsic values in the sense defined above is found initially plausible, though by no means certain, is a principle of analogy that is involved in one way or another in nearly all inductive reasoning. When two things are known to have the same characteristics except for an unknown characteristic, there is at least some initial likelihood that the unknown characteristic will also be the same; and, the more numerous and significant the characteristics that are known to be the same, the greater the likelihood that the unknown characteristic will be the same also. By itself this principle creates at least some presumption in favor of the constancy of intrinsic value. But when this principle is coupled with the previously suggested one of the toti-resultant character of intrinsic value, it becomes very unlikely that two experiences could be exactly alike and yet different in intrinsic value, or very closely similar and very different in intrinsic value. If intrinsic value results, generally speaking, from all of the other properties of an experience, and all of these are in two instances exactly alike or very similar, the intrinsic values involved may surely be expected to be alike or very similar.

The second ground of the initial plausibility of the constancy of intrinsic values in the sense indicated is the fact that, despite discrepancies, one can point to a very substantial number of types of experience that are valued in much the same way all over the world. Everywhere men enjoy their experiences of nourishing food, satisfying drink, and the normal exercise of bodily functions. Everywhere they cherish the ties of family affection, loyal friendships, and community association. Everywhere men have found the unhampered exercise of their capacities, the exchange of ideas, the free play of imagination, the enjoyment of art and music, and some sort of worship good for its own sake. Moreover, the more such experiences resemble one another in details, the more, generally speaking, they tend to be alike in value.

Glaring exceptions to this basic agreement seem to be indicated by such instances as those already referred to earlier in which experiences of the same or similar objects seem to have very different values. Actually, however, careful consideration of pairs of experiences of the same or similar objects that differ in value reveals that while each experience belonging to such a pair is like the other in being directed to the same object or a similar one, the two tend to differ from one another as experiences in precisely such ways as would lead one to expect the differences in evaluation that occur. These differences between experiences of the same objects that render the experiences so different in kind and accordingly also in value are of three main varieties now to be considered.

One kind of difference that makes experiences of the same object sufficiently different to require different valuations consists of differences in the part of each experience constituted by awareness of attendant circumstances. Consider, for example, the case of the well man's experience of eating steak versus the sick man's doing the same thing. To be sure, the central objects of the experiences are the same and the values are different. However, in addition to its central content, each experience includes feelings arising from organic conditions, and these render one experience radically different from the other in such fashion that the values cannot be expected to be the same. Or, consider the case of the walk in the spring sunshine versus the walk in the autumn rain. Each experience is of a walk down the same lane, and the intrinsic value of each experience is different from that of the other. But, in each

instance, the experience as a whole involves awareness of attendant circumstances, and, where sunshine and rain are concerned, this awareness is sufficient to account for the difference
in degree of value in the experiences. A more striking example of the influence of awareness of associated features of
an experience is found in *The Vision of Sir Launfal* by James
Russell Lowell. Sir Launfal makes a gift to a beggar at the
beginning of his pilgrimage and another at the end. The one
act of giving he finds worthless, and the other wonderfully
good. But while both are acts of giving, such are the other
features of the experiences that no inconstancy is involved in the
difference in their degrees of value. The experiences themselves are quite different in that the one is a proud bestowal of a
relatively unwanted coin, and the other is a humble sharing
of a last crust of bread.[1]

A second kind of crucial difference among experiences of
similar objects consists not in differences among awarenesses
of attendant circumstances but in differences among present
anticipations of future consequences. This kind of difference
is found in the case of Robinson's finding gold on the island
versus his finding it in England. In the one instance his perception of the gold is accompanied by a dismaying reminder that
there is nothing that he can do with it. In the other his perception is accompanied even now by glad anticipation of many
gratifying experiences that the gold may enable him to achieve.
The case of attitudes toward liberty is similar. Where liberty
is appreciated, experiences of it are likely to be accompanied by
anticipation of a fuller life as a result of it; and, where liberty
is despised, if indeed it really is, the thought of it is accompanied by foreboding fears of potential threats to security in
its exercise. A further striking instance of the influence of beliefs about consequences upon the specific characters of experiences, and accordingly upon their degrees of value, is the following. In certain primitive tribes it is considered good to kill
one's aging parents before they become enfeebled. Among us

---

[1] See G. E. Moore, "A Reply to My Critics," in P. A. Schilpp (ed.), *The Philosophy of G. E. Moore* (Evanston, Ill.: Northwestern University, 1942), pp. 618–20.

experiences of this kind of action would be viewed with disgust and horror. But closer inspection reveals that the tribes under consideration believe that their parents enter the afterlife in the state of mind and body in which they leave this one, and that parents in these tribes often implore their sons and daughters to speed them on their way before it is too late.[2] Clearly an experience of killing one's parents when the killing is accompanied by such belief is a sufficiently different experience from killing one's parents in a modern community to be very differently evaluated.

A third kind of difference between experiences of the same object, or similar objects, that makes the values of the experiences different consists in differences, neither in awareness of present circumstances nor in anticipation of future events, but in levels of feeling and comprehension. Some people simply are not capable of having the same experiences as others even when confronted by the same objects and the levels of comprehension and feeling of the same person vary from time to time. Thus there is no cause for amazement or for the discrediting of the constancy of value in the fact that, as a child, one enjoys fairy stories that, as a man, he no longer appreciates; that the insensitive man does not enjoy Shakespeare and the man of discernment does; that persons of one level of culture find polygamous marriage satisfactory and those of another do not; or that some people appreciate Beethoven and others do not.

In addition to showing how experiences of the same objects having nevertheless different values are really different kinds of experiences that should be expected to have different values and thereby removing the major objections to belief in the constancy of value, careful reflection upon such experiences also discloses the following fact about them that affords further positive evidence for the constancy of value. The more we are able in memory to recall the specific character of past experiences of objects that now yield very different experiences

---

[2] See Edward Westermarck, *The Origin and Development of the Moral Ideas* (New York: Macmillan, 1906), Vol. I, pp. 389 ff.

and evaluations, the more we realize that if our past experiences could be precisely repeated, we should evaluate them now as we did in the past; and the more we penetrate, through patient listening and sympathetic imagination, into other people's experiences of objects that we ourselves experience and evaluate differently, the more we see that if we had the kinds of experiences other people have, we should evaluate these experiences as they do. Thus, for example, the well man can in some measure see how dis-valuable the sick man's experience of meat is, and the lover of liberty can see how in a slave state experiences of freedom may be spoiled by fear. In beginning to relive his experiences of fairy stories, even the practical man of affairs can begin again to attach the values of childhood to them. Putting ourselves in thought as best we can into the mind of the savage, we catch some glimpse of how he values and begin to see how if our experiences were like his we should value as he values. All this does not, of course, mean that immature values involve as much value as mature ones, that the values of the child should be sought by the man or those of the savage by the sage, for just the kinds of comparisons we have been making permit some values to be placed above others. What all this does mean is that each experience has an immediately felt value and that the existence of other more mature values in no way alters this fact, however much it may change the patterns of wise choices.

LEVELS OF INTRINSIC VALUE

If, now, intrinsic value may be taken to be constant in that the same degree of value is always found in a specific kind of experience and similar degrees of value in similar experiences, the further question may now be raised, What kinds of experiences do people find intrinsically valuable? Since each specific kind of possible experience is a positive or negative intrinsic value, and the number of such possible experiences is infinite, no complete list of intrinsic values could ever be drawn up, even if that were desirable. Also, any list of actually discovered intrinsic values that may be made will from time to time be upset by new value discoveries. Even a partial list of actually encountered intrinsic values must, by virtue of the fact that every experience is likely to involve a wide variety of ingredients, be extremely complicated. Moreover, since, in terms of the organic character of intrinsic value, the replacement of one ingredient of an experience by a new ingredient can produce a new experience whose intrinsic value relative to that of the original experience is not proportional to the difference in value between the original ingredient and the new ingredient, no scale of encountered values is likely to conform entirely to any preconceived pattern.

Nevertheless, if for the present such complications may be set aside, it is not difficult to discern certain broad types of experience that men have in general tended to find intrinsically valuable. Moreover, by referring to the kinds of functions that these types of experiences accompany and the degrees of value found in them, we may arrange intrinsically valuable experiences in a rough order of levels, which may prove illuminating. In calling some such levels "higher" than others we intend only to suggest that a given extent and duration of an experience belonging to a higher level tends, despite many possible exceptions, to be found more valuable than the same extent and duration of one belonging to a lower level. Some other possibly significant relations of these levels may come to light as we proceed. The levels are as follows.

Organic Values

The basic level among the types of experience that people tend generally to find intrinsically valuable consists of those more or less pleasurable experiences that normally accompany the healthy functioning of organic impulses. These experiences we may appropriately call *organic values*. They include the satisfactions of eating, drinking, breathing, sex, exercise, rest, gregariousness, fight, flight, and the like. They are not organic functions as such, nor are they merely pleasures as such; rather, they are those widely varied conscious enjoyments, each with its own peculiar flavor, that are usually *present with* the wholesome exercise of organic functions. Though objectionable in excess or in inappropriate times and circumstances, in themselves and apart from the evil consequences of their abuse, they are almost invariably found not only innocent but intrinsically good.

Fundamental Human Values

A higher level of experiences that most men find intrinsically valuable may be distinguished from the level of the experiences immediately accompanying our basic organic responses, by the fact that it involves a substantial reflective element and, accordingly, cannot for the most part be shared by the lower animals. Valuable experiences upon this level may appropriately be referred to as reflective or *human values*.

1. One type of human values, which also helps to bring to focus the distinction between the human and the organic levels, is what we may appropriately call *human association*. This, of course, involves the animal's gregarious satisfaction in rubbing shoulders with his fellows; but it also involves exchange of ideas, shared intelligent purposes, and sympathetic response to the human feelings of one's fellows such as cannot be enjoyed by creatures less sensitive than human beings. Experiences of human association include a rich variety of domestic and friendship relations, of comradeships in work and recreation, of community feeling, of patriotism, and even in some instances of world fellowship. The intrinsic worth of such experiences has never been seriously doubted. Aristotelians and self-realizationists have extolled these values; egoistic hedonists, as well as utilitarians, have regarded them as among the purest of the pleasures; and even monastic orders have been sensitive to their worth. To be without them, in loneliness, is to seek them, and to participate in them is to possess a substantial share in what all men seek.

2. A second essentially uncontested type of intrinsic value upon the distinctively human level consists in experiences of

aesthetic appreciation, or satisfaction in the awareness of things felt to be beautiful or sublime. Such experiences include the contemplation of multitudes of patterns of line, color, mass, tone, and meaning, compounded with even more varied shades of subjective feeling. They involve the enjoyment of Gothic spires and simple cottages, of expansive canvases and tiny miniatures, of rhythmic sculpture and delicate engravings, of moving symphonies and the soft melodies of love songs, of epics in grand style and lyrics that touch the heart. They include, apart from all the arts of man, awareness of an ever-present natural beauty, in blue sky, green grass, crystal streams, purple valleys, white-capped mountains, and rolling seas.

3. No less esteemed than aesthetic experiences by those who achieve them are the values of *moral integrity,* of experiences of doing what one thinks he ought to do. Such experiences of doing one's duty include not only experiences of moral heroism, such as standing firmly for justice against great obstacles and despite great temptations, but also experiences of routine performance of simple obligations and of that daily fidelity to humbler responsibilities that must enter into the making of every genuinely good life. Moments of good conscience are among life's best, and moments that otherwise might be good are often spoiled by a bad conscience.

4. Closely related to the value of moral integrity, but not quite the same, are the values of *being treated justly* and of *seeing others so treated.* Even when the losses suffered, or impending, through injustice are not in themselves serious, men tend to resent deeply and to suffer from such unfairness. And even when the gains realized or anticipated through being treated justly are inconsiderable, men tend to find profound and intrinsically valuable satisfaction in being treated with the respect due them. Moreover, the just treatment that we demand and find satisfying where we are ourselves concerned we tend to wish to see accorded also to others; awareness of just deeds often yields satisfaction and intrinsic value, and awareness of unjust ones resentment, pain, and dis-value, though we ourselves are neither helped nor hurt.

5. A human value sometimes spoiled by coercive and dull educational methods but deeply appreciated by those who attain it in any considerable measure is that of *understanding*. Valuable experiences of this kind include all manner of cognitions, from intuition of the simplest axioms to comprehension of the most sweeping generalizations and from observation of the most concrete facts to the testing of the most abstract theorems, accompanied by feelings ranging all the way from the modest satisfaction of routine experimentation to the boundless joy of significant discovery. To be sure, knowing sometimes involves a pain so great as to render it, apart from consequences, bad; but, generally speaking, to understand is better than not to do so. To know the nature and background of one's own land and culture, to have some insight into the ways of other peoples, to understand something of the structure and history of the world in which one lives and into the facts and principles of art and morals, all this is, in itself and apart from any further good it may achieve for us, a large part of what makes one prefer to be a man dissatisfied than a pig satisfied, or a Socrates dissatisfied than a fool satisfied. Even the coolest mathematician often finds in his work profound fulfillment. The joy of quest for facts helps keep the detective and the scholar, as well as the scientist, at their tasks; and the great astronomer is at times overcome with an awesome feeling that he is "thinking God's thoughts after him." If spectacular discoveries are rare, less striking experiences of insight lend richness and significance to the life of almost every man.

6. A further type of human value, appreciated perhaps more in the modern Western world than in other times and places, consists of experiences of *constructive achievement*. Quite apart from any pleasures derived from the use of the products of his industry, the awareness of progressive accomplishment through one's efforts commonly carries with it significant satisfactions of its own. Often these satisfactions stimulate the most creative endeavors on the part of the captain of industry, the professional man, the musician, and the artist as much as do the rewards that accrue to these endeavors themselves. Even the

most menial of tasks can be a source of immediate gratification when its constructive character is apparent and frustrating obstacles are avoided or overcome.

Rarer Human Values

The various types of experiences that constitute the level of human values differ widely in their degrees of value in ways that cannot be considered in detail here. However, among these types of experiences are two that occur less frequently and are felt by those who experience them to be superior to any of the six types previously discussed. These presumably higher human values may appropriately be called *spiritual values*.

The first of these is *love* in the sense in which the term is used in the New Testament and in some subsequent Christian literature. It is selfless concern for the genuine well-being of all others, without reference to special claims or merits. Such love knows no distinctions of race or nation or creed. It seeks all possible good for its object. It involves deep feeling yet is genuinely practical. It is utterly impartial yet deeply personal. Its roots no doubt include organic functions and the mutual ties of family, friendship, and community loyalty, but it far outreaches all of these. Its fully developed occurrence is rare and beautiful, but some spark of it is to be found in most men at some time. Those who have experienced it have counted the moments of its appearance among their very best, and those in whom it has become a way of life have carried with them a source of joy above the level that most men ever know. It has uncommon power to break through the hardness of men's ordinary negotiations and to inspire a spirit like its own, but even when it fails to accomplish its objective or to be reciprocated, its own worth seems unsurpassable. It has also a way of lending some of its value to all the experiences it touches.

The other type of spiritual value consists of what may perhaps best be called *reverence*. By this we do not mean either formal worship or doctrinal beliefs or institutional practices.

Rather, we mean humble, grateful awareness of and dedication to all creative cosmic and human sources of value achievement. Such reverence is to be found in some degree in adherents of all of the great religions as well as in some sensitive individuals who acknowledge no special creed or cult. Its full achievement is rare, but those in whom it becomes a vital experience place it beyond all values save love itself. Like love it tends to spread its influence over all associated experiences, but it is in no sense in competition with love, for each of these two tends to enrich the other and, at their best, they tend to coalesce.

Relations of the Levels of Value

The major types of intrinsic values may in the light of what has been said perhaps be helpfully visualized in terms of a pyramid of values (see figure).

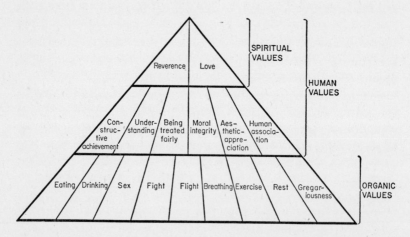

In addition to the fact that the higher values are experiences involving more value for the same duration and extent of experience, four further facts about the relations among the levels of intrinsic value represented in our pyramid may now be noted.

1. The higher values tend to be dependent upon the lower ones and upon the functions with which the latter are associated.

Thus, for example, understanding, aesthetic appreciation, and all other fundamental human values depend upon the eating and drinking that sustain life; and upon the sexual functions that reproduce it; and even love and reverence depend in no small part upon understanding and aesthetic appreciation.

2. Conversely, the lower values are often enhanced by inclusion in the higher ones. Thus, the consumption of food, which may have comparatively little intrinsic value in itself, may become in beautiful surroundings and in the company of interesting and loved companions a delightful experience. Similarly, sexual experience, which by itself may mean little or even yield disgust, may, in association with understanding, human companionship, aesthetic appreciation, and love, become in marriage beautifully satisfying and almost sacred.

3. Since higher values are usually dependent upon lower ones or upon the functions associated with them, sins against the lower values are often considered worse than those against the higher, though little merit is attached to the attainment of the lower ones. Thus, for example, murder, theft, and adultery are considered grievous wrongs, but the normal exercise of organic functions receives no special praise.

4. Since the higher values are more difficult to attain than the lower, no one is much blamed for not achieving them, though those who do merit special praise. Thus, one is scarcely likely to be condemned for not attaining an altruism like that of St. Francis, although St. Francis is greatly admired for his attainment.

READINGS

G. E. Moore, *Ethics*, pp. 138–55; or
Rand, *The Classical Moralists*, pp. 780–90.

QUESTIONS

1. Explain the differences between saying (a) that value is absolute and independent of experience, (b) that the value of any specific variety of experience is constant, and (c) that value is purely sub-

jective. Can one consistently hold (b) and not (c)? If so, how?

2. The spirit of the spy is highly esteemed in his own country but likely to be despised in the country that is injured by his activities. How can this kind of apparent discrepancy between evaluations of the same sort of consciousness exist? Does it mean that value is relative? Explain.

3. List six kinds of experiences that seem to be valued essentially alike throughout the world and indicate how you would deal with exceptions.

4. In some parts of the world the eating of human flesh is, under certain circumstances, a source of great satisfaction; in most places it is looked upon with abhorrence. What, apart from pure relativity of values, could account for this sort of difference?

5. Exceptional skill in operations necessary to the manufacture of munitions is highly prized in wartime but not equally so in peacetime. Absolute fidelity to fact is appropriate in some statements but not equally so in others. How, precisely, do you account for these differences?

6. In ancient Greece manual labor was regarded as degrading. Today we attach much more dignity to it. Does this difference seem to you to refute the doctrine of the constancy of values? Why, or why not?

7. Classify the experiences likely to be associated with each of the following according to the value scale we have suggested: (a) the rhythm of ice skating, (b) the solving of a mathematical problem, (c) the giving of a generous gift for foreign relief, (d) a credible report of someone's noble deed, (e) the sparkling of the moonlight on a clear lake.

8. A recent book entitled *The Open Mind* suggests that Western civilization has unduly stressed active achievement at the expense of contemplation. Do you agree? Why, or why not? Should we act to think or think to act, or what is the proper relation of these two?

9. From your own experience illustrate: (a) the manner in which one intrinsic value may be *instrumental* to another without thereby losing its intrinsic worth, (b) the way in which one value may *contribute* to another without being merely instrumental to it. From what you know of the laws of the land indicate some points at which the law is more concerned with the protection of lower values than of higher ones. To what extent do you consider this preoccupation of the law with lower values justified?

10. Do you think that it would be possible to discover that an experience of pleasant conversation was at all intrinsically valuable without reflecting upon its place in the whole of the experiences of the individuals involved? Does the place of such an experience in total personal experiences have any bearing on its ultimate contribution to the sum of values? Explain. In precisely what sense is personality development the touchstone of value achievement?

REFERENCES

Brightman, E. S., *Moral Laws* (New York: Abingdon Press, 1933).

Everett, W. G., *Moral Values* (New York: Holt, 1918), Ch. 7.

Hartmann, Nicolai, *Ethics,* tr. by Stanton Coit (New York: Macmillan, 1932).

Laird, John, *An Enquiry into Moral Notions* (New York: Columbia University Press, 1936), Chs. 15–16.

—— *The Idea of Value* (Cambridge: Cambridge University Press, 1929).

Lewis, C. I., *An Analysis of Knowledge and Valuation* (La Salle, Ill.: Open Court Publishing Company, 1946), Chs. 14–17.

Martineau, James, *Types of Ethical Theory* (3rd rev. ed., Oxford: The Clarendon Press, 1891), Bk. I, Chs. 5–6.

Moore, G. E., *Ethics* (New York: Oxford University Press, 1912; Reset 1947), Chs. 2, 7.

—— *Principia Ethica* (Cambridge: Cambridge University Press, 1903).

Perry, R. B., *General Theory of Value* (New York: Longmans, Green, 1926), Chs. 19–21.

—— *The Moral Economy* (New York: Scribner, 1909), Ch. 3.

Pratt, J. B., *Reason in the Art of Living* (New York: Macmillan, 1949), Ch. 17.

Roberts, W. H., *The Problem of Choice* (Boston: Ginn, 1941), Chs. 11–14.

Ross, W. D., *Foundations of Ethics* (Oxford: The Clarendon Press, 1939), Chs. 11–12.

Schilpp, P. A. (ed.), *The Philosophy of G. E. Moore* (Evanston, Ill.: Northwestern University, 1942), pp. 43–199, 535–627.

Tsanoff, R. A., *Ethics* (New York: Harper, 1947), Ch. 6.

Urban, W. M., *Fundamentals of Ethics* (New York: Holt, 1930), Ch. 7.

14

The Meaning of "Right"

OUR ESSENTIAL CONCLUSIONS thus far are that intrinsic goodness or value is a unique valuational characteristic immediately found in some experiences and that intrinsic values may be encountered in rich variety upon at least three different levels. We are now ready to begin our systematic inquiry into the central concept of ethics, that of moral rightness.

In general and apart from distinctions of senses, the term "right" seems to refer, as such theories as that of Ross suggest, to a suitability of an act to its situation, although this suitability does not by itself define "right." Some further light is thrown upon the term "right" by its connection with the previously considered term "ought," for except for instances in which more than one act is right, what is right is what we ought to do, and vice versa. But because of the exception noted, as well as for other reasons, the close connections between the terms "right" and "ought" also fails to reveal the meaning of "right."

THE SENSES OF "RIGHT"

Like the term "good," "right" is used in a variety of senses that must be carefully distinguished if confusions similar to those encountered earlier are to be avoided. These senses can be broadly classified for our purposes as nonmoral and moral.

Nonmoral Senses of "Right"

Leaving aside certain geometrical senses of "right," which are scarcely likely to cause any difficulty here, we may further classify the nonmoral senses as theoretical, aesthetic and pragmatic. Each of these senses of "right" refers to suitability, not to human ends as such, but to some subordinate purpose. To say that an act is right in the *theoretical* sense is to say that the act is done in a manner suited to the theoretical purposes in hand. Thus, for example, a method of resolving an equation is right if it yields a result that satisfies all of the formal requirements of the equation. Similarly, a chemical experiment is right if it is such as to yield scientifically reliable results. "Right" in its *aesthetic* sense refers to the suitability of an artistic performance to aesthetic objectives. In painting, a brush stroke is right if it creates precisely the required effect, and in music, a note is right if it is suited to the aesthetic purpose of the musical composition. "Right" in its *pragmatic* sense refers to the suitability of an action to the practical purpose before its agent. Thus, the carpenter's fittings are right if they contribute adequately to the building of a satisfactory house, and the political speech is right if it is suited to bringing in votes without creating needless ill will.

In contradistinction to all these senses of "right," "right" in its *moral* sense refers, as Aristotle's thought properly suggests, to that which is suited to purposes of human beings as such. A morally right act must conform, not merely to what one ought as a scientist, artist, or carpenter to do, but to what one ought as a human being to do. Using Kantian terminology, we may put the distinction in another way by saying that the *ought* accompanying all of the nonmoral senses of right is only hypothetical in being contingent on limited ends, whereas that accompanying the moral sense of the term is categorical in being demanded by nothing less than the ends of humanity. Thus, if we wish to produce satisfactory scientific results, paintings, or houses, we ought not to violate the principles of science, art, or carpentry;

but we ought not to violate the principles of morality no matter what our special wishes may be.

This distinction does not, however, imply that the right in the moral sense need in any way be in opposition to the right in the nonmoral senses. The morally right nearly always requires suitability to more restricted purposes that are included within its requirements, and such limited suitability often constitutes a large part of the morally right. Thus, much of the moral obligation of the painter consists in his fulfilling the aesthetic purposes of painting, and much of the morality of the carpenter consists in his performing well the work of carpentering, although in each case the limited activity is now seen as serving a larger human purpose. But the right in a nonmoral sense may be in conflict with the morally right. For example, efficient burglary is morally wrong even when it is efficient and pragmatically right.

Moral Senses of "Right"

When we have distinguished the moral from the nonmoral senses of "right," the question of the meaning of "right" in the former sense remains to be resolved, for, as our previous studies of Aristotle, Ross, and Kant have suggested, neither the concept of suitability to human ends nor that of a categorical imperative can yield a criterion for distinguishing between right and wrong. But before attempting to interpret right in its moral sense we must notice two more refined distinctions of senses within this sense.

The first distinction, that between subjective and objective rightness, hinges upon the degree of knowledge of the person whose act is being judged. An act may be said to be morally right in the *subjective* sense of that term if, and only if, the agent, after due deliberation, sincerely believes it to be right. That is, the subjectively right in a given situation is what a man having perfect intentions but imperfect knowledge would do in that situation. An act may be said to be morally right in the *objective* sense if, and only if, it is not only believed to be right but really is right. That is, the objectively right in a given situation is what a man having both perfect intentions and perfect knowledge would do in that situation. Thus, if one gives generously to a good cause, sincerely and after careful consideration believing in the cause, even if his money is subsequently unpredictably diverted into the hands of subversives, his act may be said to be subjectively right—but not objectively so.

It is primarily in terms of subjective rightness that the moral integrity of the doer of an act is judged; although a man is held accountable for duly deliberating and doing his best in the light of such deliberation, he can scarcely either be praised or blamed for not acting upon knowledge that, even through such deliberation, he could not be expected to achieve. It is primarily in terms of objective rightness that the act itself is judged; although the doer may be excused for ignorance that he could not help, the act he does is not fully right if more adequate knowledge might have improved it. Those responsible for the late Medieval inquisition may perhaps be partially excused for persecuting honest doubters if they did the best they could in the light of the insights they had or could get, but their deeds can scarcely be said to have been objectively right. The atmosphere of many a dispute about right and wrong could be clarified by keeping this distinction between the subjective rightness of purposes and the objective rightness of acts in mind. For example, if one of two disputants insists that their mutual friend was morally right in undertaking a certain business venture, and the other that he was wrong, the one may in reality be defending the friend as subjectively right in acting in the light of his best knowledge, and the other be condemning his act as objectively wrong on account of its unfortunate, but not adequately foreseeable, consequences. Both may therefore be correct, and the dispute largely verbal. In any case, when the distinction is kept clear, the really substantive issues may more readily be held in focus.

The subjectively right, on the one hand, is the right that one *ought* always to do and is held responsible for doing. As pointed out in the discussion of conscience theories, everyone ought to obey his conscience, to do what after appropriate reflection he sincerely believes to be right. Although reflective conscience may be mistaken, to be guided by it both carries the intrinsic value of moral integrity and yields the most promising prospect of producing maximum good or achieving the objectively right. Moreover, as Kant has convincingly pointed out, *ought* implies *can,* and what he sincerely and after due deliberation believes to be right is all that any man can really know concerning his duty. The objectively right, on the other hand, is the right that deliberation ought to seek and that one ought, insofar as he can find it, to do. When one seeks only the subjectively right, he is caught in a vicious regress of inquiring about his beliefs without ever seeking a proper object for these beliefs. It is thus only through inquiring about the objectively right that one arrives at a subjective belief at all, and one ought at any rate to approximate the objectively right as nearly as possible. In passing it may be worth while to note that the subjectively right is closely related to the morally good in that he who does the morally good nearly always does at least what he sincerely believes to be right.

Cutting across the distinction between the subjectively right and the objectively right is another distinction that hinges upon the degrees of stringency involved in various requirements of the morally right. If the ordinary man is asked what it is to do the right, he is very likely to reply that it is to refrain from such acts as lying, murder, theft, and adultery and to perform such duties as paying one's debts and keeping one's promises. An act that violates the right in the sense that he has in mind is wrong and morally reprehensible, though those who do the right in this sense merit no special praise. For example, he who steals from his neighbor is morally reprobate, though he who refrains from so doing only does his duty. To this sense of right consequences may seem irrelevant. Thus, a businessman may be said to be right if he is honest and fair irrespective of later results; and the deliberate liar is said to be wrong even though he intends good results. The sense of right involved here is what we shall call the strict one in that the observance of its requirements is very stringently demanded of all men in nearly all circumstances. Thus, a moral requirement is *strictly right* if, and only if, although the observance of it merits no special praise, the failure to act in accord with it is wrong and morally reprehensible.

The strictly right does not, however, cover nearly all that may be included in the morally right. Many sensitive persons, including some great religious leaders and moral pioneers, have tended to regard the right involved in the prohibition of lying, murder, theft, and the like as elementary and perhaps only preliminary to a higher right with which men of good will are mainly concerned. The essential requirement of right is, for these persons, not obedience to formal principles but the overcoming of human ills and the achievement of human values far beyond the demands of these principles. Concern with right in this sense is not, however, confined to sensitive persons; nearly all of us, in our efforts to discover the right, at times find ourselves inquiring not about the application of formal moral principles but about how certain human ills can be overcome and values achieved. The sense of right involved here is what we shall call the higher one in that, although its demands are not so stringently insisted upon or so universally applicable as those of the strictly right, the achievement of these demands merits far higher praise than does that of the strictly right. Thus, the *higher right* consists of duties the neglect of which is not necessarily wrong or reprehensible but the achievement of which is worthy of high praise.

As we shall subsequently see, the strictly right exemplifies the moral principle of justice; it is also often accompanied by a moral integrity that is intrinsically valuable. The higher right exemplifies the moral principle of benevolence and is often associated in him who achieves it with the spiritual value of love. The strictly right is what we have a right to expect of others in their dealings with us; the higher right is what we more properly demand of ourselves. The strictly right applies to everyone in nearly all circumstances; the higher right is more variable in terms of individual differences and circumstances. The strictly right is what we have in mind when we say that an act is "all right"—and most of our statements to the effect that an act is right are likely to be of this kind—to suggest simply that the act is in no way fundamentally wrong; the higher right is what we have in mind when we seek for the best that can be done. It is the strictly right—though not by any means all of it—that the law undertakes to enforce; it is to the higher right that the best in religion calls men. As in the case of the distinction between subjectively right and objectively right, much confusion and many empty verbal issues could be avoided or resolved by keeping the distinction between the strictly right and the higher right in mind. For example, a discussion of whether or not a man's refusal to give generously to a certain cause was right may go on endlessly if the disputants forget this distinction. In the light of the distinction, however, each of the disputants may readily see that, although the refusal to give was indeed a failure to live up to the best a human being might do and so was in the higher sense not right, willingness to give was hardly something that could be stringently demanded of the man and so was not required by the strictly right.

To distinguish between the strict and the higher senses of "right" is, however, already to demand a further sense. Since neither of these two senses depends upon the other, both must from a theoretical point of view be embraced in a more comprehensive sense if our moral experience is to be intelligible. Moreover, in practice, the man who must decide what to do cannot be content with the assurance that his act is right in the strict sense and wrong in the higher one; he needs to know about the rightness of his act when *all* moral requirements are duly considered. Actually we do often think in these terms, asking not merely whether the act in question violates basic principles or is a good deed but whether or not it is right when all claims are duly considered. The sense of "right" involved here is what we shall call the comprehensive one, an act being *comprehensively right* if, and only if, it is right when all the claims of both the strict and the higher senses of "right" are duly and coherently considered.

THE MEANING OF "MORALLY RIGHT"

In the light of the preceding accounts of the principal types of moral theory, the meaning of "intrinsic good," and the senses of "right," we are ready to come directly to the central problem of the *meaning* of "right" in its moral sense. The theories we have considered fall, as we have seen, into three major groups, namely, the approval theories, the formal ones, and the teleological ones. Each of these major groups is, as we are now to see, especially associated with a different sense of "morally right," and it is partly because this fact has not been fully perceived that so many theories have so long continued in apparent contradiction to one another.

Insofar as we are concerned with the subjective sense of "right," the approval theories are essentially correct. To be approved is in general to be right in the sense of being sincerely believed to be right; and each of the approval theories has thrown some significant light on a special aspect of the subjectively right. These insights are very important from the standpoint of the psychology and sociology of morals and from that of the evaluation of character and motives. However, the rightness of *acts,* with which we are primarily concerned, is determined not by the subjectively right but by the objectively right; and we have seen that moral inquiry must be directed toward the objectively right if it is to avoid infinite regress. Hence the focus of our attention here must be the objectively right. Actually, the approval theorists themselves have not always confined their attention to the subjectively right; they have often undertaken to tell us about all the right there is. Concerning the objectively right they cannot, however, say anything constructive since in principle they deny its existence; and here they seem, for reasons previously indicated, to be on the wrong track.

Insofar as one is concerned with the strictly right, the formal theories are especially illuminating. The right in this sense consists largely of the kind of duties Ross has referred to as *prima facie* obligations, such as refraining from lying, murder, theft, and adultery, keeping one's promises, and paying one's debts. All such duties as these tend, moreover, to be, as Ross says, morally suitable; and if they are to be put into a single formula, the Kantian imperative bidding one act as if his principle were to become a universal law is about as close an approximation as can be achieved.

However, even with reference to the strictly right, the formalists' interpretations of "morally right" are, for reasons previously considered, inadequate. Their *prima facie* duties remain disconnected illustrations of the right, affording no explanation of its meaning and often in conflict with one another. Ross' "moral suitability," though characteristic of the right, is too indefinite to be of much use as a criterion, and the Kantian categorical imperative is practicable only if certain values are already presupposed. Formal theories supply no satisfactory answer to the reasonable question why the duties they demand ought to be done, nor do they suggest a sufficient motive for doing these duties. The role of scientific fact in moral judgment is ignored, and no explanation or criterion is offered for exceptions to moral rules or for differences in alleged intuitions. Besides, ethics cannot be limited to the strictly right. Both the Christian and the Greek streams of morality, whence our own moral experience emerges, have been concerned with demands of the good that reach far beyond the observance of basic principles, and nearly all of the great moralists have shared this concern. Indeed, no man who takes ethics at all seriously can confine his conduct to the nonviolation of formal principles, and each must go beyond mere obedience to rules to be responsive to all of the claims of the good. Thus the right with which we are concerned includes not only the strictly right but the higher right as well; it is, in fact, nothing short of the comprehensively right. Actually the formal theorists have not entirely ignored the claims of the comprehensively right; but, insofar as they have taken the comprehensively right into account at all, they have tended either to assume that their own formal principles embraced all that there was of this right or else merely to add to these formal principles some of the requirements of the higher right as a sort of appendage. The first procedure is entirely untenable for reasons already noted, and the second scarcely promises much for a *coherent* account of moral experience.

Coming now to the comprehensive sense of the objective moral right, which for our purposes is crucial, we must ask, What interpretation of "right" in this sense best accords with the actual intentions of usage and affords the most illuminating account of moral experience as a whole? The entire drift of the preceding historical and systematic studies is toward the following conclusions. The central key to the meaning of "right" in the sense in question is to be found not in either the approval or the formal theories but in the teleological theories, which hold that right is to be interpreted in terms of conduciveness to good. The best clue to the more specific application of the teleological approach is to be found in the kind of utilitarian method developed by Bentham, Mill, and Sidgwick, and subsequently more satisfactorily by G. E. Moore, the main lines of whose thought the interpretation of "right" to be presented here follows.[1] And the best account of the meaning of "good" is to be found by regarding intrinsic good as a unique value quality immediately found in some experiences. In the light of these clues we may suggest that a *voluntary act is right in the comprehensive, objective, moral sense if, and only if, it is conducive to the most intrinsic good, or the least intrinsic evil, possible in the circumstances for all concerned.*

What, specifically, is meant by this definition may perhaps be somewhat clarified by the following remarks. (1) By *"conducive* to the most intrinsic good" is meant actually tending to produce the most good, not merely being thought likely to produce the most good, for it is the objective sense of moral right and not the subjective one that is here being interpreted. (2) In speaking of the *"most* intrinsic good," we stress the fact that it is not merely Bentham's balance of good over evil that

---

[1] See G. E. Moore, *Principia Ethica* (Cambridge: Cambridge University Press, 1903), especially Ch. 1; *Ethics* (New York: Oxford University Press, 1912; Reset 1947), especially Chs. 1–5.

is meant but the production of as much good as possible, for to act so as to produce only a little good when much more might have been achieved is never fully right.   (3) In speaking of *"intrinsic good,"* we emphasize the fact that it is not the maximizing of good in just any sense that is wanted but the maximizing of experiences having that unique characteristic referred to as intrinsic value.   It should also be noted here that the good that is to count in determining maximum good includes not only the good in the immediate consequences of the act but also that in the act and in all its other consequences, however remote.   (4) Sometimes choice of actions is confined to alternatives any one of which will produce more evil than good, and in such cases the right act is the one that will produce the least evil; hence the phrase, "or the *least* intrinsic *evil.*"   (5) By *"possible* in the circumstances" we mean possibility of actual achievement; for, although the objectively right may in any given instance not be known, what could not be achieved, even if it were recognized to be right, can scarcely be required by the morally right in any sense.   (6) By referring to "the *circumstances"* we suggest that, although the objective rightness of an act is not relative to people's judgments of it, such rightness is always relative to the situation in which the act is performed, so that an act that may be right in one set of circumstances may be entirely wrong in another.   Even criminal law has long recognized this in, for example, condoning killing in self-defense as justifiable homicide while condemning killing with malice aforethought as murder.   (7) In referring to *"all concerned"* we stress the important fact, emphasized in discussing Perry's desire theory and elsewhere, that, in calculating maximum good, everyone's good is to count equally, and that the good of no one in any way affected by the act is to be left out of consideration.

Since this interpretation is presented as a resultant of the preceding historical and systematic inquiry, it must for the most part stand or fall on what has already been said.   However, a few further comments in its defense may be useful.   Like the approval theories, this view sees the subjectively right as the approved; but it goes on to give to both approval and sincere moral belief their only ultimately plausible object—conduciveness to maximum intrinsic good. Like the formal theories, this interpretation recognizes the importance of the forms of consistency and moral suitability; but the form that for it is central, instead of being empty, is an applicable reference to values, and the suitability that it stresses, instead of remaining vague, is the only kind specifically appropriate to the ultimate ends of man as such—suitability to the achievement of intrinsic value. Unlike the formal theories, this interpretation, without neglecting the strictly right, gives full scope to the claims of that higher right demanded by the saints and sages and by us all at our best. Instead of allowing the various rules of the strictly right to remain in disjointed conflict, it brings both these and the claims of the higher right into a single coherent system; and instead of building upon alleged moral intuitions that in fact often clash, it seeks the right through coherent rational judgment that gives appropriate places to both immediate apprehension of good and scientific calculation of consequences. Accordingly, it is able to supply a plausible account of historical growth in moral insight, in terms of advancing knowledge of what tends to produce most good, and of cultural differences, in terms of varying beliefs concerning what serves this same end. Such occasional exceptions to moral rules as must in any case be morally approved are now justifiable upon principle, as special cases in which the maximum good that sustains a general adherence to the rules requires unusual procedures. The theory further recognizes, as no other sufficiently does, the apparently basic moral facts that no act can ever in the end be morally justified save by reference to that which is good in itself, and that we find ourselves ultimately unable to regard an act as fully right if some other possible act could have produced intrinsically better results. Hence this theory is able, by reference to a maximum good that alone can entail maximum obligation, to offer valid reasons for moral judgments. In terms of a self-interest that seeks good for one's self and a love that seeks good for others, it also suggests sufficient motives for acting upon such judgments.

In the light of our account of the comprehensively right, which is our primary concern here, we may now look back to see more clearly the place of the strictly right in the whole moral economy. Instead of being a set of disconnected arbitrary demands, it is now seen both to be supported at every point by the maximum good principle and to constitute the very core of the requirements of that principle. The strictly right, the violation of which is wrong or morally reprehensible, thus constitutes a sort of minimum demand of the maximum good; whatever else one must do to promote the maximum good, at least he must avoid lying, murder, theft, adultery, and, in short, be, as the strictly right requires, basically just.

Sometimes it is suggested that the maximum good principle fails sufficiently to sustain these duties because in its terms the end justifies the means; but when the end is maximum intrinsic value for all human beings, these duties seem not only to be sustained but to be sustained in the most adequate way possible and placed at the very heart of morality. The ends or consequences taken into account here include not only the values, near or remote, that are specifically aimed at but all of the experiences associated with or resulting from the act, however near or remote and whether aimed at or not. These experiences include the tendency of every unjust act to disintegrate the character and reputation of him who does it, to bring discomfort and pain upon others, and, by bad example, to create distrust and to break down moral standards, thereby rendering human life disorderly and irresponsible. They include the sense of betrayed moral integrity and of the failure of human consideration that often accompanies the act, the painful sense of injustice felt by the victim over and above the injury to him, and the disconcerting sense of outraged justice felt by all those who learn of the act. They include also the opposite results of just acts. If the end were less than the maximum good of all human beings, many kinds of unjust means could indeed be justified; but since the end is the maximum good of every human being and the pyramid of the good includes near its peak such values as those of moral integrity, justice, and love, the end cannot justify unworthy means but demands just means as an essential part and a foundation for all its other parts.   In the quest for maximum good, the good of every human being must, as the phrase "of all concerned" reminds us, be considered; and since no man can possibly measure another's good, the best hope, in practice, of attaining the most good is to give the fullest consideration to everyone's good and even, insofar as possible, to seek in fairness to secure the agreement or concurrence of all concerned.

Historically, people have often learned in time to place in the category of the more stringent obligations of the strictly right duties that formally were thought to belong only to the more flexible requirements of higher obligations.   Thus, for example, refraining from the torture of prisoners and paying a living wage to workers were at one time thought of as noble and good though by no means strictly obligatory; but today both are seen to belong to the category of duties that cannot be rejected without being wrong and morally reprehensible, and neither is now thought exceptionally noble.   The law, as well as less formal moral codes, tends progressively to take over larger areas of basic morality.   This development has led some people to suppose that the scope of the strictly right should be constantly expanded until it encompasses the whole of morality, and that the law should follow along as rapidly as possible. However, although it is undoubtedly true that the expansion of the scope of the strictly right and of the law is often useful, there seem clearly to be limits beyond which this process can never wisely be carried.   The strictly right tends to be essentially the same for all people and to be on the whole fairly definitely knowable, but the farther removed a duty is from basic requirements, the more it hinges upon individual differences that no one can fully comprehend and the more difficult it is to know.   Moreover it is highly important for the attainment of maximum good that individuals should retain certain cita-

dels of freedom into which neither the law nor the requirements of strict moral rules may follow them.

READINGS

Moore, G. E., *Ethics,* pp. 50–121.

QUESTIONS

1. Which of the senses of "right" is suggested or implied in each
of the following statements: (a) The eyes in the portrait seem to be
wrong. (b) No doctor would be right to collect his fee in that
manner. (c) The composition of the cement in the building was
found to be precisely right. (d) The defense of freedom is always
right, for only if it is, is human happiness secure. (e) The ancient
sages were right, according to their lights, in approving polygamy.
(f) Pacificism will undoubtedly be right when men come to behave as
they should.

2. To what type of problem is each of the moral senses of "right"
appropriate? What special importance attaches to the objective
sense of "morally right"? Why, then, must some attention also be
given to the subjective sense of "morally right"?

3. When we say that an act is right in the moral sense, what is our
usual meaning? What more can anyone mean by right? Why
shouldn't ethics be confined to the "strictly right"?

4. Why should a definition of right require a reference to evil?
Indicate some specific instances in which such a reference is needed
in order to make the definition applicable. What is the difference
between relativity to circumstances and relativity to attitudes? Why
is this distinction important in ethical theory?

5. What is the role of ethical rules if the theory developed here
is correct? How is one to know when an exception is justifiable?
Illustrate.

6. What, precisely, is the relation of the "strictly right" to the
"comprehensively right"? In what ways are the grounds for doing
the strictly right the same as those for doing the higher right? In
what ways are they different?

7. Does the claim that the maximum good principle would require
one to rob Peter to pay Paul, seem to you a valid objection? a con-
clusive one? Is the claim that this principle would permit one

to leave his bills unpaid so long as he was charitable justifiable? Explain. In what ways could the maximum good theory claim to meet these objections? Are these answers adequate? Why, or why not?

8. Does the theory of right adopted in this chapter imply that the end justifies the means? If so, in what sense? Would a proof that the theory implied that the end justified the means constitute a serious criticism of the theory? Explain.

9. To what extent is it possible to legislate morals? Why should a person be more severe in judging his own conduct than in judging that of another?

REFERENCES

Broad, C. D., *Five Types of Ethical Theory* (New York: Harcourt, Brace, 1930), Ch. 7.

Dewey, John, and Tufts, J. H., *Ethics* (rev. ed., New York: Holt, 1932), Ch. 12.

Drake, Durant, *Problems of Conduct* (2nd rev. ed., Boston: Houghton Mifflin, 1935).

Everett, W. G., *Moral Values* (New York: Holt, 1918), Ch. 1–6.

Ewing, A. C., *The Definition of Good* (New York: Macmillan, 1947), Ch. 6.

Hare, R. M., *The Language of Morals* (Oxford: The Clarendon Press, 1952), especially Pt. III.

Hartmann, Nicolai, *Ethics,* tr. by Stanton Coit (New York: Macmillan, 1932), Vol. I; Vol. II, sec. 1.

Laird, John, *An Enquiry into Moral Notions* (New York: Columbia University Press, 1936), Pt. II.

Moore, G. E., *Ethics* (New York: Oxford University Press, 1912; Reset 1947).

——— *Principia Ethica* (Cambridge: Cambridge University Press, 1903).

Patterson, C. H., *Moral Standards* (New York: Ronald, 1949), Ch. 8.

Perry, R. B., *The Moral Economy* (New York: Scribner, 1909), Chs. 1–4.

Pratt, J. B., *Reason in the Art of Living* (New York: Macmillan, 1949), Chs. 14, 17, 19.

Ross, W. D., *Foundations of Ethics* (Oxford: The Clarendon Press, 1939), Chs. 1–8.

Sidgwick, Henry, *The Methods of Ethics* (7th ed., London: Macmillan, 1907), Bk. III, Ch. 13; Bk. IV.

Toulmin, S. E., *An Examination of the Place of Reason in Ethics* (Cambridge: Cambridge University Press, 1950), especially Pt. III.

Urban, W. M., *Fundamentals of Ethics* (New York: Holt, 1930), Pt. I.

Wheelwright, Philip, *A Critical Introduction to Ethics* (rev. ed., New York: Odyssey Press, 1949), Ch. 7.

PART THREE

Practical Ethics

15

Principles and Methods of Practical Ethics

PRACTICAL ETHICS IS, as was suggested at the outset, primarily inquiry concerning the kinds of acts that are right. To have arrived at an understanding of the meanings of "right" and "good" is already to have made substantial progress toward a satisfactory account of practical ethics, for we may now deduce from the definition of "right" that a right action must always be conducive to the maximum good for all and we may know from the nature of intrinsic goodness how to recognize the good when we encounter it. However, these advances are only a beginning, for what is right in the sense of being conducive to maximum good for all will depend not only upon the definition of "right" and the nature of the good but also upon the facts of life by virtue of which one event leads to another. Moreover, guiding principles somewhat less general than the demand for the production of maximum good as well as tested methods of practical inquiry are often also needed.

A *nonethical causal statement,* such as may nonetheless be involved in ethical inquiry, indicates a connection of constant conjunction between one event and another. A *singular ethical judgment* affirms that a particular act at a certain place and time is right or wrong. An *intermediate judgment* indicates that a certain kind of act is right in certain circumstances. An *ethical*

265

rule asserts that a certain kind of act is right in most circumstances. *Ethical principles* stand between the definitions of ethical theory and the ethical rules of applied ethics and indicate that in all or virtually all circumstances a right action will have certain characteristics. And an *ethical method* is a procedure for determining whether or not the characteristic meant by "right" applies to a particular act or kind of act.

The rightness or wrongness of *kinds* of acts varies with circumstances. Nearly all moral rules have exceptions, and so—at least conceivably—do moral principles except the most general principle that a right action is always conducive to maximum good. Strictly speaking, the only thing that can be said unconditionally to be objectively right is a *particular act* whose circumstances have already been taken into account in defining the act, and the variety of the possibilities of such particular acts is virtually infinite. However, since similar situations tend to recur and moral decisions must usually be made at times at which the opportunity to deliberate is limited, moral principles may serve as valuable guides to practical decisions, and moral methods may well be worked out and applied in advance to kinds of situations. Hence, in saying subsequently that certain *kinds of acts* are right, what we shall mean is simply that such acts tend in situations likely to occur to promote the maximum good for all. What each individual ought to do remains, of course, to be worked out by each individual in his particular circumstances.

The two major branches of practical ethics are those of personal ethics, which is the ethics of actions whose effects fall largely upon the doer of the act, and social ethics, which is the ethics of those acts whose consequences fall significantly upon others as well as upon the doer of the act. Since no effort even to sketch the whole field of practical ethics can be attempted here, what we shall endeavor to do is to set forth in the present chapter, some basic principles of personal and social ethics and then, in the succeeding chapters, to deal with some selected problems in each of several areas within these major divisions of practical ethics.

BASIC PRINCIPLES OF PERSONAL
ETHICS, PRUDENCE

With reference to that area of activity in which the consequences of an act fall mainly upon the doer, the most general of all principles is one that may be referred to, in Butler's language, as self-love or, in the language of the ancient philosophers and of Sidgwick, as prudence. This principle indicates that where other people's good is not affected, to seek one's own greatest intrinsic good on the whole, or in the long run, is the right course of action. As a basic orientation of personal conduct, such a principle is of considerable significance. However, this principle remains somewhat too general to tell us much about the specific kinds of personal activity that are right. Accordingly, we shall be less concerned with the general principle of prudence as such than with certain principles that are involved in it in the actual conditions in which we live. Among these at least five—foresight, self-exertion, self-discipline, value sensitiveness, and fortitude—should be listed.

1. If one is to achieve a satisfying life, he must come to understand what manner of creature man is, what he himself in particular is, and what kinds of events and activities tend to yield experiences that are most valuable to him. Hence a principle that may be referred to as that of *foresight* indicates that if one is to attain maximum value, he must learn to predict the probable value consequences of the courses of action that are open to him and plan his conduct in the light of such predictions. No one realizes maximum value blindly, and he who seeks the good even for himself must see where he is going and watch his step. This demands of us no anxious brooding, for that only hampers the achievement of value, but it does require of us patient observation, thoughtful adaptation, and occasional long-range planning with ends in terms of intrinsic values in view.

2. Even when foresight has indicated the way to the achievement of values, we are still unlikely to attain them unless we

actively exert ourselves along the lines suggested by foresight.
Hence a principle of *self-exertion* reminds us that in order to
realize maximum value we must stir ourselves to that initiative
and effort necessary to overcome our natural inertia and bring
our cherished goals within reach.   The good life is no product
of mere passivity and cannot be fully attained solely by routine.
Rather, it requires, as Aristotle long ago pointed out, sustained
activity along many humanly satisfying lines.   This requirement does not mean that such a life has no place at all for in-
activity or for idleness, for some values are best achieved by
waiting; but it does mean that idleness is incidental and activity substantive.   It does not mean that there are no activities
to be avoided; but it does mean that foresight is to be as much
followed when it bids us stir ourselves to strenuous endeavor for
the good as when it bids us refrain from the evil.

3. The negative counterpart of the positive principle of self-
exertion is the principle of *self-discipline*.   This principle requires the subordination or sublimation of impulses and inclinations that stand in the way of maximum value achievement.
One of the misfortunes of human life is that the selection of
some values often means the rejection of others.   Every choice
is also a renunciation, and he who refuses to forego some present satisfactions in the interest of more significant future ones
may attain little satisfaction at all and almost certainly will
not attain the maximum good possible for him.   Sane self-
discipline requires no prudish rejection of any value as such,
for by definition no value can be evil in itself; but it does require a sane husbanding of energies on behalf of those ends that
are most highly valued.

4. The principle of *value sensitivity* refers to the fact that
the cultivation and exercise of sensitivity to such values as
are offered at any given time is just as important as previous
endeavors to realize the conditions of these values.   Every
worth-while exercise of forethought, energy, or self-disciplne on
behalf of value must have somewhere its consummation; and
unless one is open and receptive to the enjoyment of valuable

experiences as they become available to him, his best endeavors will be thwarted in the end.

5. No matter what the degree of one's foresight, self-exertion, self-discipline, or value sensitivity, every man is confronted at times by dis-values over which he has no control. Thus the principle of *fortitude* requires us to accept without dismay such misfortunes as we cannot help and to turn with cheerfulness from them to matters in which our thought and efforts can be effective. This Stoic principle demands of us no bending before ills that can be removed, nor any premature assumption of our own incapacities; it does require us, as someone has said, to "shake hands with the inevitable." The past is certainly beyond our control, so is our own eventual death. Many other things are beyond any practicable control. To suffer undue remorse or frustration in face of these inevitables is always folly, and to rise above despair in their presence is a foundation of wisdom. He who broods upon unavoidable adversity and, in self-pity, bewails inescapable sufferings poisons with bitterness such satisfactions as might help sustain him in his sorrow. But he who with quiet dignity receives the blows of misfortune and goes on to do his best in what is left to him to do rediscovers a part of the best that he had before and adds to it new, and perhaps deeper, values that he otherwise would not have known.

BASIC PRINCIPLES OF SOCIAL ETHICS, JUSTICE

Apart from the comprehensive but largely formal principle that one ought to act in ways that are conducive to the maximum good of all, the fundamental principles of the part of ethics that deals with actions that significantly affect others fall into two groups, corresponding roughly to what we previously referred to as the strictly right and the higher right. The one is commonly called *justice,* and the other *benevolence.* Each of these groups involves a number of subordinate principles. As in the case of all other moral principles, save the comprehensive requirement to promote maximum good for everyone, the principles of social ethics are relative to circumstances.

The principle of justice, which formulates the demands of what we have called the strictly right, has long been taken to consist in rendering every man his due or in meeting the claims that others may legitimately make upon us. The problem of working out more specific principles in terms of which justice is applicable is largely that of determining what claims of others are in fact legitmate or, in terms of our theory, belong to the central core of the demands of the production of maximum good. Fortunately, despite many detailed variations, considerable agreement—even among people of different cultures— has been attained concerning the major principles of this kind. Of such principles we shall discuss five that would seem to embrace the essential features of justice.

1. If human beings are to have any significant opportunity to achieve intrinsic values at all, they must attain at least a minimal security with reference to life, the use of the physical means of sustaining life, and the conditions in which children are conceived, born, and reared. Hence, from time immemorial, a principle of *basic security* forbidding such acts as murder, theft, and adultery has been rightly recognized. What specifically this principle requires varies somewhat with the particular expectations created by the customs and laws of different societies, but the essential demands involved in it are found to be almost everywhere. Although these demands are largely negative, and corresponding positive ones are usually thought of as benevolence, in recent centuries there has developed an increasing tendency to include in justice some positive requirement of mutual assistance in the meeting of basic needs.

2. Nearly all of the values connected with human communication in matters of fact, including most of those dependent on science, industry, and human fellowship, are contingent upon the reliability of discourse. Hence a principle of *honesty* requires that, insofar as men speak, they speak truly and that, insofar as they can, they fulfill their agreements and promises.

Truthfulness cannot, of course, require that one's words conform to the objective truth, for with the best of intentions a man may be mistaken; it does require that such words as a man uses conform to beliefs of his that are supported by evidence. Departures from truthfulness may, perhaps, be permissible on occasion, as when an innocent life may be saved by a misstatement; but they must be, at most, rare exceptions undertaken with utmost caution, for even white lies depreciate the gold of trust on which the currency of communication depends. The duty to keep one's contracts and fufill one's promises may at times encounter limits through the claims of other duties, but so vital are agreements to value achievement that exceptions to this duty also are only very rarely justified.

3. Every human being tends to be biased on his own behalf and that of his friends. But, if incessant quarrels are to be avoided, and if each individual is to have the opportunity to achieve values and to contribute to the achievement of values as his capacities permit, men must deal with one another *disinterestedly* and *impartially*. Similar cases must, as Sidgwick puts it, be treated similarly. Thus a principle of *impartiality* requires that in meeting the claims of others, we refrain from favoritism and give to the claims of all the same consideration. This principle involves a disinterested refusal to ask special consideration for oneself as well as a fair-minded rejection of favoritism and preferential treatment in dealing with others.

4. Even when the importance of treating similar cases similarly is fully recognized, the question remains, How are dissimilar cases to be treated? In certain areas of human achievement we seem in fact to encounter dissimilarities such that the greatest good for all appears to be promoted by distributing advantages and restrictions in proportion to actual and promised achievement rather than equally and without regard to merit. The requirement that we deal with such differences in this manner constitutes a principle of *proportionality* in justice. Thus, for example, flagrant violation of the law seems to suggest such indifference to the achievement of the common good as to demand restrictons upon the freedom of the offender somewhat

in proportion to the gravity of his offense. Similarly, in the distribution of responsibilities and of honors, a proportion to achievement must be observed if the public interest is to be served. Evidence seems also to be available to the effect that strong incentives to material productivity, on which many of man's values depend, are produced by the preservation of some proportion between one's effectiveness in producing the material means of value and the share of these means that is made available for his personal use. Moreover, in the granting of advanced educational opportunites, the common good seems best promoted by the awarding of the greater opportunities to those most able and willing to live up to them.

5. In the light of such facts as the foregoing, and under the impetus of the mores of his time, Aristotle wished to press the principle of proportionality much farther. He and some more recent writers, such as Nietzsche, inclined toward the view that a sort of general merit attaches to each individual according to his special merit, or even according to his status. Thus, for example, in Aristotle's view, a slave should receive far more severe punishment for the same crime than a free citizen, and a free citizen than a nobleman. Among the most important discoveries of the succeeding centuries under the impact of Christianity, however, were the insights that status is no true measure of merit, that in certain basic respects all men are equal, and that such in fact are the incalculable potentialities of each human being that no differential initial treatment can be justified concerning the essential interests of men. Hence, we have come to see that, in certain fundamental matters, all men ought to be treated alike. This is the principle of *equality* in justice. Thus, for example, because no man's basic value capacities can in the end be satisfactorily measured by his fellows, and because every man's value stake in the civic order under which he lives is very great, every man ought in the interest of the common good to have ultimately an equal voice in the determination of the laws of his land. For similar reasons the protection of the laws ought to be accorded equally to every man,

and no man presumed guilty or inferior unless proved so. Other areas in which the importance of equal justice is coming increasingly to be recognized are initial, educational, economic, and social opportunities; for, whatever differences may be justified in these areas by demonstrated personal merits or failures, none at all seem to be warranted at the outset by reason of accidents of economic status, or color, or creed.

BASIC PRINCIPLES OF SOCIAL ETHICS, BENEVOLENCE

Principles of justice such as those indicated in the preceding list constitute, as we have seen, the central core of the requirements of the right. Although none of them is completely without exception, they apply in nearly all circumstances; and any endeavor to go beyond them without first meeting their claims is likely to be hypocritical and ineffective. They do not, however, exhaust the requirements of the comprehensively right. The demands of the higher right must also be met, and the principle that requires that they be met may properly be called "benevolence." Thus the principle of benevolence demands of us effort to avoid the evil and seek the good, especially on behalf of our fellows, beyond any legitimate claims that anyone may strictly make upon us.

More precise principles involved in benevolence are more difficult to indicate than the basic principles involved in justice, for benevolence is far less restrictive in its application than is justice. That some kind of obligation to benevolence exists is sufficiently clear, but to whom one is to be benevolent, and when, and under what circumstances are matters of comparatively free choice. Nevertheless, answers to some questions about the nature of benevolence must be attempted.

One such question is why benevolence is required at all. Some people hold that if all men were perfectly just, benevolence would not be required. Actually, all men are not, and will never be, perfectly just, and the benevolence of some will always be needed to make up for the injustice of others. But quite apart from injustices, at least four other important reasons may be listed for the ever-present need for benevolence in the interest of maximum good. (1) The frailty of human beings, who, in infancy, illness, old age, and economic distress through no fault of their own, are unable sufficiently to care for themselves, often requires the help of others. (2) Positive achievements for human good, far beyond anything that can or will be done merely by meeting the just claims of others, can be accomplished in industry, in the professions, and indeed in almost every human activity by constructive effort for human good that declines to limit itself to fulfilling the legitimate claims of others. (3) Love itself is at the same time one of the most rewarding and one of the most contagious of all types of experience. It holds thus within itself a dynamic beyond all calculation for human betterment when it is intelligently and effectively released in benevolent action. (4) For many people, reverent appreciation of the unmerited gifts of the cosmic and social orders to their own value realizations is at the same time a convincing evidence of the need for, and a powerful incentive to the exercise of, benevolence.

A second important question with reference to benevolence is one regarding the kinds of favors those who act in accord with it seek to bestow. Two extremes are evidently to be avoided. One is unthinking indulgence of the whims or wishes of the person who is being helped, as in giving candy to the child whenever he asks for it or a dollar to the beggar whenever he stretches out his hand. Such activities may satisfy the agent but they may also do more harm than good to the recipient and to society. Equally mistaken, however, is what we might call "do-goodism," which consists in pressing upon its supposed beneficiaries favors that they have not asked and do not want, without consulting either their legitimate pride or their preferences. A genuinely useful benevolence will retain its own understanding of the deepest human needs and at the same time give full consideration to the feelings and preferences of its beneficiaries. It will thoughtfully cultivate the art of gracious giving and, for the most part, direct its efforts to helping others help themselves.   It will directly aid those who need such help, but it will also see that most men wish and need to stand upon their own feet.

A third question concerns the choice of recipients of benevolence.   This question refers to one of those matters in which the right exercise of benevolence involves considerable freedom of choice; for, whereas opportunities for service are everywhere present, there are few definite rules to determine where service ought to be bestowed.   Nevertheless at least two factors seem worthy of special mention, nearness and need.   Other things being equal, one's own family and the people of his own neighborhood, town, county, state, and nation would seem to merit some special consideration because they are within easier reach, are better understood, and can be more effectively helped, if for no other reason.   Other things are not, however, always equal, and very often the magnitude and urgency of the need, even in very remote places, outweigh the demands of lesser needs nearer home.   In determining the point at which this outweighing of nearer needs occurs, we have, of course, to fall back upon the more general principle of maximum good for all in the long run.

A final question, and to many the most pressing of all in the matter of benevolence, is the relation between the duties of benevolence and one's duties to himself.   No rigid rules can be laid down here, and much will depend on the disposition toward others that one has been able to develop.   A grudging gift yields a dis-value at least to the giver; but most of us could, to the advantage of ourselves and all others, develop much more benevolent dispositions than we ordinarily do.   Most men may rightly do more for themselves than they do for any other individual; for there is much that a man can do for himself that no other man can do, or do so well, for him. On the other hand, perhaps every man ought to do more for all others than he does solely for himself, since there are so many more of the others.   One of the best ways to exercise benevolence is to learn to find one's own deepest satisfactions in activities that also benefit others. Nevertheless, benevolence will always also require self-sacrifice, for no man will ever become so good or so independent of personal needs—nor will society ever become so well ordered—that one's interests will be at all times in perfect harmony with those of all others.

METHODS OF PRACTICAL ETHICS

Even if we now knew all of the general principles of practical ethics, we might still know nothing at all of what was right in any particular instance. In order to know this, we should need to know how to apply the principles in specific circumstances, which vary from one instance to another. Indeed, ethical principles are at best only general guides to that which tends in most circumstances to be conducive to maximum good, and, if we could know in any particular instance what really was conducive to maximum good, that would in such a case carry more weight than a principle. Hence, what we now need are methods to guide us, with, or perhaps at times even without, the aid of principles, in the discovery of the right in particular cases.

If we are correct in holding that "right" refers to conduciveness to maximum good, then the general character of the manner in which one knows what is right or wrong is already essentially clear. In the main what one must do is determine the probable consequences of each alternative course of action and then to make a comparative evaluation of these sets of consequences. The set of consequences that proves to have the most total value over dis-value for all is the one whose causative act will be right. But if our method is to be practically helpful, it must be more specifically worked out. For this purpose we distinguish two rather different kinds of instances, depending on whether or not the problem to be considered is new or involves special difficulties.

Recognition of the Right in Ordinary Cases

In the vast majority of instances in which voluntary choices must be made, no significant novelty or serious difficulty is encountered. In such cases the sort of moral principles we have been discussing, together with the customs of the race, the ideals and traditions of one's nation, community, family, and religion, and the requirements of one's profession and one's chosen patterns of personal life, tend to converge upon some types of action rather than others. All of these sources of moral insight represent a great deal of experience concerning what is likely to promote the greatest good for all. They also are in large measure reflected in that moral orientation which we call conscience in the ordinary sense of the term, thereby making our duty doubly plain, especially since the general types of action that conscience approves and disapproves repeat themselves over and over again. Hence, in the kind of instance under consideration, one can proceed without undue anxiety to act directly in accord with the prevailing mores and his own conscience in considerable confidence that in so doing he is acting in ways that are right or conducive to maximum good. In such instances extensive weighing of *pros* and *cons* is neither necessary nor desirable. The attempt to engage in it may both destroy the capacity to act with the decisiveness that effective contribution to the achievement of good requires and cloud moral insight by one's refusal to act upon the sufficient demands of such insight. Thus, for example, in nearly all circumstances one neither must nor should debate with himself whether or not he ought to lie or steal or be considerate of other people's feelings; the path of duty is in such matters fairly plain to him, and hesitation may only obscure it. Fortunately the vast majority of our choices are roughly of this kind, else we should be too much torn between fear of making moral mistakes and dread of frustration. Nevertheless, one must be wary of being too complacent about keeping some decisions in the category of the nonproblematical, for it not infrequently happens that the grossest social injustices are those that the participants have allowed to be glossed over by custom and a rationalizing conscience. For this reason, one needs from time to time to reconsider his fundamental moral principles and to re-examine his usual patterns of action. By so doing, moral pioneers have sometimes seen new light; and, if there are those in one's society who see duties in ways other than the usual ones, their insights may constitute proper demands that we reassess some accepted customs.

Discovery of the Right in Novel and Difficult Cases

In many instances in which voluntary choices must be made, such is the novelty of the circumstances or the apparent validity of the claims of two or more conflicting alternatives that the usual approaches to moral problems require supplementation. Accepted principle, custom, and conscience do not seem to suffice. Consciences may, as we have seen, be found to be in conflict, and so also may principles and customs. New situations often render old ways inapplicable, and current customs are frequently inadequate to cope with novel circumstances. Nearly all moral problems have some unique features, and in some instances these are far too prominent to permit sole reliance on fixed patterns of behavior. How, then, shall we approach the resolution of those new and difficult moral problems that require serious deliberation?

The following is a procedure that is suggested by the moral theory we have adopted and is often approximated in actual deliberations concerning difficult problems. Five stages are included, of which the first two are preliminary and the other three essential. The stages indicated represent, of course, only a rough outline, for in actual fact many considerations may prove relevant that cannot be strictly classified, and thought will move freely back and forth among the various stages of the deliberative process.

1. The most serious obstacle to sound moral deliberation is self-interested bias, and many an alleged moral inquiry turns out to be largely a rationalizing search for reasons for doing what one was already determined to do. Hence the first preliminary step in genuine moral deliberation is to *acquire a frame of mind suited to such deliberation.* One must replace self-centered bias by that disinterested impartiality on which just decision depends, but without losing that warmth of

human feeling on which benevolent action, and perhaps, ultimately, even justice, rest. This objective may be achieved in part by frank recognition of the existence of biases and the deliberate direction of attention and resolution toward the rationality and rightness of the demand for impartiality. But since biases are personal emotions, as well as thoughts, the objective is often better attained by focusing thought, and with it feeling, upon the value potentialities of all the persons involved in the decision. In thus taking the roles of others, one may come to set appropriate limits upon his own claims and become genuinely aware of those of others. Many persons are also helped at this point by attitudes of religious devotion in which they begin to see human conflicts in that impartial, benevolent perspective that is attributed to Deity.

2. A second preliminary step in the attempt to determine what one ought to do in a morally difficult situation is to *bring the existing facts into clear focus.* Just what has been said or done, to whom, under what circumstances? What commitments or agreements have been made? What are the present circumstances? What persons are involved, and what are their relations to one another and to one's self? What claims and expectations are, in the light of prevailing laws and customs, properly involved in these relations? What is the evidence for the actual assumptions that are being made, and what further facts or evidences would be needed for an adequate decision? All too frequently it is for want of sufficient care in considering such questions as these, rather than because of lack of moral earnestness as such, that our deliberations go astray. But mistakes based on misjudgment of fact may be as grave as any others, and carelessness concerning fact may be itself a moral weakness.

3. If one has achieved such balance of perspective and adequacy of knowledge as he can, he is ready to begin the process of deliberation as such, although he may need during this process to return more than once to the preparatory stages. The first deliberative step is analogous to the formation of hypotheses in science. Since the number of possible lines of conduct

in any situation is almost infinite, one must *select for further consideration the possible courses of action that seem most promising*. As in scientific hypothesis-formation, no fixed rules can be laid down. Frequently an open-minded common sense will suffice to single out two or three lines of action that are most likely to produce maximum good. But when all of these courses promise considerable evil, and none promises much good, one must be wary of too readily confining deliberation to them. Often the most promising course of action is not among those that come readily to mind at all, and sometimes patient and creative reflection is called for in order to disclose possible lines of action that promise to avoid major evils and preserve and augment major values.

4. The next step in moral deliberation is the vital and enormously complex one of endeavoring to *ascertain the probable consequences, in terms of experiences, of each of the more promising alternatives selected*. One must seek to determine the effects of each proposed course of action upon his own immediate and eventual experiences, upon the thoughts, feelings, and purposes of his friends, upon the moral standards of his community and nation, and, ultimately, upon the experiences of all mankind. In this inquiry one dare not confine his attention to ends aimed at. He will need to recognize that means adopted will invariably have other consequences than those intended, and that even achieved ends tend, instead of being final events, to become causes of further experiences. For the most part common sense, based on past experience, will be one's guide in determining probable consequences. But, as problems become more complex, and as the physical, psychological, and social sciences advance, these sciences can, and should, increasingly aid this phase of moral deliberation. Indeed, all available relevant scientific information should be sought out and used in this factual inquiry.

5. The final step in the quest for the right, which will normally proceed in part simultaneously with the preceding one, is to *make a comparative evaluation of the experiences that are expected to result from each of the selected alternative courses*

of action. Thus one must, for each proposed course of action, try to determine the intrinsic values involved in the experiences that are expected to result to him and to all others. If he actually had these experiences, their evaluation could be immediate and intuitive; but since they are only prospective, he can only imagine them as vividly as possible and surmise the value that would be found in them if they were actually had. Thus to project and evaluate comparatively substantial sequences of expected experiences requires considerable patience and skill, but almost anyone who will make the effort can achieve a modest degree of success in it. In time one may even acquire a capacity for rapid survey of the total values involved in a probable set of consequences without extensive consideration of details; but one must not attempt altogether to substitute this capacity for more specific examination of the valuable experiences of individuals, lest one come all too easily to omit consideration of the value experiences of some who will be deeply affected by his proposed acts or become insensitive to possibilities of new and unfamiliar values.

With the comparison of the intrinsic values involved in the probable consequences of each possible course of action, the quest for the right is in principle complete. That set of consequences which contains the greatest balance of intrinsic value, or the least, of evil, indicates the act that, as its cause, is right in the circumstances. But the wise inquirer will not confine his deliberation to his own private reasoning. Even though he was led to undertake his quest through the inadequacy of direct application of custom and conscience, he will nevertheless compare his findings with these sources of moral insight. He will also seek the advice of trusted counselors. If all of these approaches to his problem tend to converge, he may proceed to act with somewhat increased confidence. If not, although he will not necessarily regard his own findings as wrong, he will be ready to re-examine them; for he who proposes to violate custom, the advice of others, or conscience ought at the very least to know exactly what he is doing. But if, after all sources of possible insight have been duly considered, one remains confident that a course of action, even though unconventional, will in the end be conducive to maximum good for all, then such a course of action is presumably as near the objectively right as his thought and experience can lead him.

The prediction and evaluation of probable consequences of alternative courses of action in full detail would obviously be enormously complicated, and no one has in practice either the time or the wisdom to carry it through completely. Fortunately, such impossibly comprehensive inquiry is not necessary; for, even when custom and conscience are insufficient guides, the rough estimates of consequences and their values that we are capable of seem usually to be sufficient to enable us at least to approximate the apprehension of the right, and the demands of the maximum good itself require that limits be set to the deliberative process. In any case no more definitive method seems available to us, and insofar as the problems we encounter are difficult and time permits, we ought presumably to deal with them in some such way as that of the suggested five-stage procedure. Even problems that we have not yet encountered, but are likely subsequently to meet, we may often do well to try to think through in advance in this way, for the occasion of problems is often too pressing to permit extensive inquiry.

Some people are disturbed by the thought that no more assurance is possible concerning the objectively right than that permitted by our calculations of probable consequences. But this lack of certainty need not unnerve moral action and may indeed be a ground for gratitude. We can be virtually certain of the subjectively right in terms of which our moral integrity is judged; the probability of that part of the objectively right that we call the strictly right is usually so great as to amount almost to certainty; and even of the higher right we can often be very nearly sure that, if we have not quite found it, we are quite near to it. To fall short of certainty in important matters is a part of being human. Even science attains no certainty, and the gap between the degree of probability attained in science and that attained in ethics is being narrowed. The element of uncertainty that at best remains in ethics gives zest to the human quest and encourages a becoming tolerance and openness to progressive improvement in our ideals.

READINGS

Justice

Melden, *Ethical Theories,* pp. 44–61.
Rand, *The Classical Moralists,* pp. 20–34.
Clark and Smith, *Readings in Ethics,* pp. 124–33.

Benevolence

Melden, *Ethical Theories,* pp. 247–64; *or*
Rand, *The Classical Moralists,* pp. 427–42.

QUESTIONS

1. What is a moral principle? What moral principle, if any, is absolute? In what sense are most moral principles relative? Of what use are principles that are relative in this sense?

2. Is a man morally wrong in being shortsighted about his own future? If so, how? If not, why not? What function, if any, does idleness have in the good life? Are there any matters in which a person should yield to misfortune? If so, in what? In what sense? And why?

3. The claim is often made that no moral issue is involved where one's conduct does not affect others. In what sense is this true? In what sense is it false? Support your position.

4. A middle-aged woman asked a doctor to examine her thoroughly and give her the whole truth about her condition. Taking her at her word, the doctor, having discovered a cancer that would soon bring about her death, told her his findings. She then went to another doctor, who, observing the same condition, assured her that nothing was seriously wrong with her. The unfortunate woman left this doctor's office in great joy and proceeded to praise him highly among all her friends while bitterly condemning the incompetence of the first doctor. Which doctor was right, and why?

5. If one is in a "tight spot" on account of having failed to do a

part of his duty, a lie will often relieve the tension. What is wrong with lying in such a case?

6. A young girl, having received strict orders from her father to be in by midnight, arrived at 3:00 A.M. The next morning, on being queried, she stated that she had come in at a quarter of twelve (3 being a quarter of 12).[1] Did she lie? Why, or why not?

7. Shortly after a moving address in opposition to all medical lies, Dr. Richard Cabot was demonstrating a diabetic diet that included appetizing bread containing no nourishing ingredients. A fellow physician deeply embarrassed Dr. Cabot by inquiring whether this bread was not a medical lie. Was it? Why, or why not? What is the chief danger in medical lies? On what occasions, if any, are they justified?

8. Two persons have become liable for damages in an automobile accident involving a third party. One of the two is a respected citizen of the community; the other is a newcomer. Should this difference have any bearing upon the judge's apportionment of the damages between the two? Suppose the newcomer were known to be a shiftless fellow who regularly spent most of the money at his disposal in worthless or even harmful amusements. Would this fact make a difference? Justify your answer in terms of the maximum good principle.

9. A cotton plantation owner verbally agreed early in the season to sell his cotton at a given price, but before delivery was made the price of cotton rose substantially. The courts refused to sustain the merely verbal contract, and the owner claimed that he ought not to be called on to take so substantial a loss on the basis of a casual agreement. Was the owner right? Why, or why not?

10. A wealthy mine owner was on the point of making a donation of $100,000 to a liberal arts college that was very much in need of the money when his son, who had been due to graduate, failed an important course. The dean of the college, well aware that refusal to recommend the boy for graduation would prevent the gift, none the less refused. Did the dean act rightly? How can his conduct be justified on maximum good principles?

11. The Medieval theologians had a good deal to say about just prices. We are well aware today that prices must of necessity change

---

[1] From F. C. Sharp and P. G. Fox, *Business Ethics* (New York: D. Appleton–Century, 1937), cited in H. H. Titus, *Ethics for Today* (2nd ed. rev., New York: American Book, 1954), p. 292.

according to circumstances, and many economists scoff at the whole conception of a just price. Do you think that in any given situation such a thing as a just price can be discovered, or do you hold that the price should be whatever can be obtained? If you think there is a just price, how would you go about arriving at it?

12. If justice is giving every man his due, how can justice be said to require the fulfilling of needs whose satisfaction has not been earned? The basis of the right to a reward for work is clear, but on what ground may a right to work be claimed?

13. Immanuel Kant once asserted that if everyone were perfectly just and no one were benevolent the world would be far better off than it is now. Do you agree? What purposes does benevolence serve when justice is already being done?

14. A young man who works hard and provides for his family evidently has no strict obligation to do Boy Scout work in his community. But if he has ample leisure and special talent in this line, may these facts in some instances create a higher obligation to do such work? In what kind of instances?

15. The argument is frequently advanced with reference to supporting charities or missions that one should see to it that everyone in his own country is amply cared for before giving anything for persons in other countries. What is your moral evaluation of this argument?

16. Indicate some instances in which you have felt reasonably sure of what was right without any considerable reflection upon the matter. What do these instances suggest concerning the manner in which right is known? Are you ever very uncertain about what is right? If so, give examples. What do these instances suggest about knowledge of the right? If you can recall instances of both kinds, how can their apparently contradictory suggestions be reconciled?

17. One of the directors of a business concern who cannot morally approve the policies of the concern is debating whether or not he should resign his post and "clear his conscience" or stick to the job and try to improve the procedures of the business. Outline a procedure that he might well follow in trying to settle the issue.

18. A group of citizens are convinced that the management of the schools in their town is hopelessly entangled in "politics" and thoroughly corrupt. How, according to the suggestions of this chapter, should they go about discovering the best line of action to take? Suppose certain political short cuts, such as manipulating

the registration lists, offer the quickest route to better schools.
Should these measures be used? Why, or why not?

REFERENCES

Prudence

Aristotle, *The Nicomachean Ethics*, tr. by Harris Rackham (Cambridge: Harvard University Press, 1934), Bks. III, IV, VI.

Broad, C. D., *Five Types of Ethical Theory* (New York: Harcourt, Brace, 1930), especially Chs. 2–3.

Garvin, Lucius, *A Modern Introduction to Ethics* (Boston: Houghton, Mifflin, 1953), Chs. 12–13.

Pratt, J. B., *Reason in the Art of Living* (New York: Macmillan, 1949), Chs. 9, 20.

Titus, H. H., *Ethics for Today* (2nd ed. rev., New York: American Book, 1954), Chs. 12, 28.

Wheelwright, Philip, *A Critical Introduction to Ethics* (rev. ed., New York: Odyssey Press, 1949), Ch. 9.

Justice

Aristotle, *The Nicomachean Ethics*, tr. by Harris Rackham (Cambridge: Harvard University Press, 1934), Bk. V.

Cabot, R. C., *Honesty* (New York: Macmillan, 1938).

——— *The Meaning of Right and Wrong* (New York: Macmillan, 1933), Ch. 7.

Dewey, John, and Tufts, J. H., *Ethics* (rev. ed., New York: Holt, 1932), Ch. 16.

Drake, Durant, *Problems of Conduct* (2nd rev. ed., Boston: Houghton Mifflin, 1935), Ch. 19.

Hartmann, Nicolai, *Ethics*, tr. by Stanton Coit (New York: Macmillan, 1932), Pt. II, Chs. 19, 25, 26.

Hobhouse, L. T., *Morals in Evolution* (5th ed., New York: Holt, 1915), Pt. I, Ch. 3.

Hume, David, *A Treatise of Human Nature* (Everyman ed., New York: Dutton, 1940), Bk. III, Pt. II.

Kant, Immanuel, "Fundamental Principles of the Metaphysic of Morals," *Kant's Critique of Practical Reason and Other Works*, tr. by T. K. Abbott (London: Longmans, Green, 1879), pp. 24–27.

Mill, J. S., "Utilitarianism," in Burtt, E. A. (ed.), *The English Philosophers from Bacon to Mill* (New York: Random House, 1939).

Paulsen, Friedrich, *A System of Ethics* (New York: Scribner, 1899), Bk. III, Chs. 9, 11.

Plato, "The Republic," *The Dialogues of Plato*, tr. by Benjamin Jowett (New York: Random House, 1937), Bks. I, IV.

Robinson, D. S., *The Principles of Conduct* (New York: Appleton-Century-Crofts, 1948), Chs. 15–19.

Spencer, Herbert, *Principles of Ethics* (New York: D. Appleton, 1893), Vol. II, Pt. IV, Chs. 1–6; Pt. II, Chs. 8, 9.

Titus, H. H., *Ethics for Today* (2nd ed. rev., New York: American Book, 1954), Chs. 15, 18.

Urban, W. M., *Fundamentals of Ethics* (New York: Holt, 1930), Ch. 10.

Westermarck, Edward, *The Origin and Development of the Moral Ideas* (New York: Macmillan, 1906), Vol. I, pp. 141–45.

Wheelwright, Philip, *A Critical Introduction to Ethics* (rev. ed., New York: Odyssey Press, 1949), Ch. 10.

Benevolence

Aristotle, *The Nicomachean Ethics*, tr. by Harris Rackham (Cambridge: Harvard University Press, 1934), Bks. VIII–IX.

Brunner, Emil, *The Divine Imperative, A Study in Christian Ethics*, tr. by Olive Wyon (Philadelphia: Westminster Press, 1947), Chs. 23–26, 29.

Dewey, John, and Tufts, J. H., *Ethics* (rev. ed., New York: Holt, 1932), Ch. 15.

Hartmann, Nicolai, *Ethics*, tr. by Stanton Coit (New York: Macmillan, 1932), Pt. II, Chs. 24, 30.

Hyde, W. D., *The Five Great Philosophies of Life* (New York: Macmillan, 1932), Ch. 5.

Paulsen, Friedrich, *A System of Ethics* (New York: Scribner, 1899), Bk. II, Ch. 6; Bk. III, Chs. 7, 10.

Pratt, J. B., *Reason in the Art of Living* (New York: Macmillan, 1949), Pt. III.

Spencer, Herbert, *Principles of Ethics* (New York: D. Appleton, 1908), Pt. I, Ch. 11.

Westermarck, Edward, *The Origin and Development of the Moral Ideas* (New York: Macmillan, 1906), Vol. I, Chs. 23–26.

Wheelwright, Philip, *A Critical Introduction to Ethics* (rev. ed., New York: Odyssey Press, 1949), Ch. 8.

Method

Broad, C. D., *Five Types of Ethical Theory* (New York: Harcourt, Brace, 1930), especially Chs. 6–7.

Hare, R. M., *The Language of Morals* (Oxford: The Clarendon Press, 1952), especially Pt. III.

Laird, John, *An Enquiry into Moral Notions* (New York: Columbia University Press, 1936), especially Pt. III.

Moore, G. E., *Ethics* (New York: Oxford University Press, 1912; Reset 1947), Ch. 5.

Ross, W. D., *Foundations of Ethics* (Oxford: The Clarendon Press, 1939), especially Ch. 8.

Sellars, Wilfred, and Hospers, John, *Readings in Ethical Theory* (New York: Appleton-Century-Crofts, 1952), especially Pts. III, IV, VIII.

Sidgwick, Henry, *Methods of Ethics* (7th ed., London: Macmillan, 1907), especially Bks. III, IV.

Toulmin, S. E., *An Examination of the Place of Reason in Ethics* (Cambridge: Cambridge University Press, 1950), especially Pts. II, IV.

16

Personal Ethics

HAVING NOW CONSIDERED SOME of the basic principles of ethics and sketched a method by which particular practical moral problems may be resolved, we are ready to look directly at some of the areas in which such problems arise. We begin with personal ethics, in which consequences of an act fall largely on the agent and problems are relatively uncomplicated by obligations to others.

Since the kind of personal activity with which we are here concerned is mainly a quest for such intrinsic values as can be obtained by the individual primarily by his own effort, an adequate survey of personal ethics would include consideration of activities in which the individual achieves for himself values of each of the types of values indicated in our pyramid of values. It would also deal with problems concerning the relations of all these activities with one another and endeavor to show what kind of blending of these activities would tend to produce the best life on the whole for the individual. Obviously what can be undertaken in this chapter must be much less comprehensive than this. What we shall try to do is simply to touch briefly upon one or two selected problems from each of several areas chosen for illustrative purposes.

At the level of activities yielding organic values, instead of attempting to deal with the ethics of each of the organic functions separately, we shall focus attention upon some ethical problems concerning the life and health factors that sustain all or-

ganic functions.   The activities that yield human values include
the cultivation of intelligence, aesthetic appreciation, and character, as well as the activities of work and recreation.   Work at
its best is directed, among other things, to the values of constructive achievement and supplies, in addition to its practical
fruits, an essential integrative factor in a satisfactory human life.
Recreation is directed toward many different values and gives
needed expression to a variety of otherwise neglected impulses.
However, since the roles of both of these factors are usually sufficiently stressed in Western culture, we shall focus attention
with reference to the level of human values especially upon the
cultivation of intellect and of aesthetic appreciation.   The development of moral character involves activities yielding values
at the levels both of the ordinary human values and of spiritual
ones, and is, of course, of special importance to us.

LIFE AND HEALTH

Some philosophers, including the famous musician, physician,
missionary, and philosopher Albert Schweitzer, contend that life
is not only intrinsically valuable but the only thing that is.   This
belief may, for reasons already suggested, be doubted, for only
conscious experiences can be intrinsically valuable; and, even
among these, some are and others are not valuable.   Nevertheless, the claim that life alone is valuable appropriately calls attention to a basic fact that cannot well be doubted, namely, that
not only organic values but all intrinsic values whatever depend
upon life.   As all value is rooted in consciousness, so all consciousness as we know it is grounded in life.   Thus, the preservation of one's own life is not only a natural impulse but a duty of
utmost importance.   Most people, fortunately, do not need to
be reminded of this duty with reference to any immediate future,
for when death is seen to be imminent most men will do all in
their power to ward it off.   But many people are not nearly so
ready to preserve themselves against slow death.   By failing to
adhere to certain readily ascertainable and observable requirements, they permit their lives to be cut far short of their at-

tainable spans and so deprive themselves of years of possible happiness and usefulness.

Health is almost as essential a foundation for the good life as is life itself. Although many kinds of values are attainable in illness, and a few, such as certain kinds of fortitude, are attainable only under adverse conditions, nearly all types of values are attainable in vastly fuller measure in health than in sickness. That this is true of the organic values goes without saying, for neither eating, nor drinking, nor rest, nor physical exertion, nor any other organic function can be fully enjoyed apart from basic soundness of body. That physical vigor is also a vital root of other values becomes readily apparent when one reflects how the worth of companionship, work, thought, the enjoyment of beauty, and even worship is enhanced by the glow of physical well-being and depreciated by physical enervation. Blows of misfortune that would be crushing in sickness can often be borne with equanimity in health, and prospects that elicit great enthusiasm in physical soundness leave us listless in illness. Although youth is disposed to think that its reserves of health are boundless, maturity discovers that, given reasonable steadfastness of purpose and development of skills, what one is able to accomplish in life may be largely measured by the physical vigor and stamina he is able to conserve. Hence, the preservation of health, like that of life, is not only a duty but among the most fundamental of all duties, and he who seeks really to do the right must train for living, in a different way perhaps, but just as assiduously as any athlete trains for his sport.

So long as the requirements of life and health are in harmony with other moral obligations, as for the most part they surely are, the path of duty concerning them is fairly plain. But when these requirements come, as they occasionally do, to be at cross purposes with other obligations, serious problems begin to emerge. With regard to the preservation of health, for example, it not infrequently happens, in times of special stress, that the demands of the health of the physician's patients are not in harmony with those of his own health, or those of the sick child with those of his parents. Similarly, the soldier in wartime and the workman on a tough job in the tropics may in the interest of other ends be called upon to operate under conditions that are far from healthful. Although the health of the individual never ceases, even under such conditions, to deserve full consideration, it may, for the sake of more comprehensive values involving other people, have to yield a part of its demands. At times even one's own personal interests may demand some subordination of health claims. For example, many scientists, teachers, students, physicians, lawyers, farmers, and laborers could perhaps be a little healthier if they gave somewhat more time to their health and less to their work. But, apart from those who actually undermine their health by overwork, the slight gain in health that might be achieved by substantial reductions in work would probably, in most instances, not be worth the cost. Physical culture, like most other activities, is subject to a law of diminishing returns by virtue of which to press the activity beyond a certain point is not worth the cost. Fortunately, the area of conflict between most of our personal objectives and the demands of health is usually very small; for nearly all that we do is best done by keeping health at a level very near the maximum, and, conversely, health itself tends on the whole to be greater when most of our attention is directed to other matters rather than preoccupied with health itself.

Cases in which there is conflict between the duty to preserve one's own *life* and other duties are less frequent than conflicts involving health, but they are more serious. For example, what the soldier in battle or the physician in an epidemic is called upon to place in jeopardy may be not only health but life as well, and situations sometimes occur in which the maintenance of one's principles may demand the surrender of his life. To risk one's life in a good cause may become not only an obligation but a *strict* obligation. Such an obligation presumably occurs, for example, when one's society is in mortal danger and calls upon him to do his share of dangerous military duty. It may also occur when the life of even a single other individual is in danger and one is in a position to help. That a person ever has a *strict* obligation to go beyond *risking* his life and actually voluntarily to *surrender* it may be less likely, but that a man, when he must either surrender vital principles or give up his life, sometimes ought in a *higher* sense to do the latter will hardly be doubted. Some of the best and in the end most constructive of human deeds have been of this sort.

We come next to the related but basically different problem of whether or not a person is ever morally right in taking his own life. In the ancient world suicide was considered in some circumstances honorable and good, and a number of admirable persons of antiquity ended their lives in this way. Such acts, it could be held, relieved individuals of suffering and shame, their families of humiliation, and their states of embarrassment. Some writers of this period argued that when the conditions of life became intolerable, the situation was a sign from nature, or the gods, that it was time to depart. The early Christian attitude toward suicide was much more severe. Life was a gift of God and a call to His service, and every individual life was of infinite worth in His sight. To take one's own life was to depreciate God's gift and to disobey His command. The Medieval attitude went even further and regarded suicide as an unforgivable sin. Unable to punish the suicide himself, Medieval law heaped indignities upon his body and penalized his family by prohibiting their inheritance of his goods. The modern attitude lies between the extremes of the classical and Medieval ones.

Generally speaking, the attitude suggested by the application of the maximum good principle to the actual conditions in which suicide is likely to occur is somewhat as follows. Since nearly all acts of suicide are presumably performed in moments of deep depression in which the victim is not quite himself and in which in any case the motives can never be fully known to anyone else, to condemn the suicide as a person or to think his act subjectively wrong or evil is not only futile but unfair. However much we deplore his act, it is not for us, who have not known his sufferings, to condemn his motives or his character. Moreover, in some peculiar combinations of circumstances suicide may possibly be objectively right or even praiseworthy, as in the case of the soldier captured in war and justifiably convinced that, under the influence of drugs, he would almost certainly reveal information that would be used to destroy his regiment.

Nevertheless, in the vast majority of those circumstances in which suicide occurs, the action seems to be objectively wrong. Being a product of exceptional depression, it usually results from a moody misreading of the facts; but, being final in its results, it precludes all possibility of seeing or participating in the improvement of either facts or moods. It destroys those prospects of the further realization of value that can remain, even in the worst of circumstances, so long as conscious life exists. Its effect upon the morale of friends and loved ones is likely to be devastating far beyond any conceivable gain that might be hoped for on their behalf. It also tends seriously to undermine that respect for the value of every individual human life upon which much that is most humane in Western civilization depends and with the undermining of which inhuman brutality may, as we have tragically seen of late, be all too easily unleashed again.

We come next to the problem of the legitimacy, not of taking one's own life, but of consenting to its painless extinction at other hands, the problem of mercy killing or euthanasia. Although the motives of some who have taken the lives of others to spare them pain have been legitimate or even admirable, such acts involve, apart from other serious hazards, grave violations of the basic laws of almost every land. Under these circumstances, euthanasia must be regarded as at present almost always objectively wrong. But to point out the evils of mercy killing in violation of law does not settle the whole moral issue of euthanasia. Even if the total results of mercy killing are bad when the ill effects of violating basic law are added to the other evils involved, one still has to ask what the total effects would be if the law were altered, for example, to allow the painless administration of a lethal dose of morphine upon request of the person involved, his family, and a board of competent physicians. Such mercy killing would be free of at least two serious evils attaching to suicide. For one thing, it could hardly result solely from sudden impulse or morbid lonely brooding and, for another, it would scarcely involve the painful, bungling, inefficient, and cruel methods often employed in suicide attempts. Further it could sometimes relieve both the individual and his family of needless suffering and expense; and it would permit some to die with dignity whose diseases might otherwise prohibit this.

Nevertheless most of the objections to suicide would still hold even against legalized mercy killing. Mistakes are possible on the part of physicians as well as patients, and new discoveries are constantly being made. In addition to the loss of a loved one, a family that consented to euthanasia might be tortured by guilt feelings, and physicians might be repeatedly called upon to suffer excessive pangs of conscience. The social sense of the value of life would be depreciated perhaps even more by legalized euthanasia than by occasional suicides, for in the former case killing not only occurs but also receives society's stamp of approval. Perhaps the most serious objection to legalized mercy killing is the danger of abuses, of which the memory of Nazi atrocities initiated under the guise of euthanasia is grim reminder.

On such grounds as these, although the genuine mercy killer is rarely convicted of crime, euthanasia is, perhaps justifiably, rejected by most people at the present time. However, the problem of euthanasia remains one of the open moral questions of our era. It is hardly for those who do not suffer categorically to deny the right to relief to those who do. The debate concerning mercy killing will no doubt go on for a long time, and the day may come when society can risk legalizing a carefully safeguarded euthanasia without endangering its basic respect for life. Meanwhile, even now we do not condemn physicians who sometimes decline to use all available means to prolong for a few days or weeks the lives of hopeless sufferers but we do insist that their task, and that of all others, with reference to life is primarily to preserve it.

INTELLIGENCE

Among the many personal ethical problems involved in one's cultivation and use of his intelligence are the questions of whether or not one is obligated to cultivate his intellect and skill at all, and if so, to what extent, what the relation of theoretical capacities and practical skills in this connection is, and how obligations to cultivate intelligence are related to other obligations. A variety of social problems is also involved, concerning, for example, the support and control of public education, the desirability of developing a special class of intellectuals, the social status to be accorded and the degree of freedom to be permitted to intelligence, and other related questions. Our primary interest here, of course, is in the personal questions, and among these our attention will be confined almost exclusively to a single comparatively simple one.

Almost everyone today would acknowledge some obligation on the part of all who can, at least to become literate. Everyone would probably also acknowledge an obligation to develop sufficient intelligence and skill to perform one's vocational function and the basic duties of a man and citizen. But whether one has any obligation to develop his intellectual capacities or increase his knowledge beyond this point is a matter of considerable controversy. Moreover, this question is a very practical one, which both young people and adults are often called upon to face in making decisions regarding the use of their leisure time.

A tradition of long and respectable standing holds that the development of knowledge beyond basic requirements is not only not obligatory but tends to be evil. Expressed in earlier times in such varied modes as the Genesis connection of man's original sin with the eating of the fruit of the tree of knowledge, the Medieval tendency to link science with the devil, Carlyle's preference for activity over understanding and Kingsley's "Be good sweet maid and let who will be clever," this tradition still lives in contemporary tendencies toward extreme pragmatism and anti-intellectualism. Advanced cultivation of intellect, this tradition contends, is a useless diversion of man's attention from his proper business. It destroys his contentment with his lot. It makes tedious pedants of some men, furnishes others with tools to do irreparable damage, and undermines social institutions. It may also, some people would add, create an aristocracy of intellect that is inconsistent with democracy. Besides, those who seriously endeavor to excel in it are likely to find the task arduous and incompatible with many other things that they would enjoy, or perhaps even prefer, doing.

In face of such an indictment, the first thing that must be said is that there is in fact some foundation for the charges, that the cultivation of intellect does sometimes have such unfortunate results as those suggested. But one must go on to add that in each case cultivation of intellect is only the instrument or the occasion of the evil and that the basic difficulties lie elsewhere in distorted human purposes. Moreover, in each instance at least a part of the cure of the evil is to be found in more, not less, cultivation of intellect. Given adequate breadth and placed in proper perspective, such cultivation can overcome discontent, resist crime, strengthen sound social institutions, prevent tyranny, and become an exciting human adventure. One may further concede that if the question were whether or not such cultivation is strictly obligatory, the answer would probably be in the negative; for, while all men need some knowledge in order to perform their basic duties, the further development of knowledge can hardly be said to belong to that central core of right the violation of which will likely cause great harm and is morally wrong and reprehensible.

However, the question that primarily concerns us is neither whether or not cultivation of intellect beyond functional necessity can be used for good or evil purposes—obviously it can be used for either—nor whether or not such cultivation is a demand of the strictly right but whether or not such cultivation is a requirement of the comprehensively right or is essential to the achievement of maximum good for all. In this sense, every man does seem to have an obligation to develop his intellect far beyond basic functional necessities. The reasons for this obligation concern the avoidance of evils, the achievement of values, the knowledge of the right and the intrinsic value of understanding.

The first reason, then, is that substantial cultivation of knowledge is an indispensable instrument in the conquest of evils that could not otherwise be avoided. These include all those evils

of hunger and thirst, heat and cold, drudgery, disease, and premature death that science and technology have enabled man,
both collectively and individually, to overcome, and many others
that the steady advance of knowledge promises soon to conquer.
They include also many superstitious and groundless fears concerning himself and his fortunes to which every individual is
almost certain to be subjected unless he attains considerable
knowledge for which no specific use is immediately in sight.

A second reason for insisting upon a higher obligation to cultivate intellect beyond the requirements of vocational and social
necessity is that such cultivation is an instrument to the positive
achievement of values otherwise beyond our reach. The fruits
of knowledge are by no means always apparent upon the surface.
Through discoveries of facts whose functions could not at first
be seen man has been able to erect magnificent buildings, to
bridge rivers, and in large measure to conquer the sea and the
air. In so doing he has gained undreamed-of comforts and
conveniences and vast new wealth of experience of the world and
of his fellows. The growing knowledge of each individual
makes possible for him increasingly satisfying constructive
achievement. It brings within his reach new ranges of beauty
in literature, art, astronomy, and botany. It links him in a
brotherhood of understanding with his fellows and gives content to his friendships. It even opens doors of insight through
which the beneficent influences of love and reverence may enter
his life.

A third, and possibly the most significant, reason for urging
an obligation to enlarge the range and depth of intellect and
knowledge is that such achievement is necessary specifically to
some phases of that discovery of the objective right that everyone ought to seek. If the right is that which is conducive to
maximum good, then there can be no moral substitute for knowledge of what a proposed act is in fact conducive to. So long as
moral problems remain relatively simple, good intentions and a
little information about fact and moral tradition may serve to
keep one's ethical decisions sound; but when conditions become
complicated, the best of intentions may, in the absence of de-

veloped insights, leave one hopelessly bewildered. Some of the worst wrongs have been done by men with good intentions. The pages of history are littered with the mistakes of men who wanted to do good but were misinformed, and the biographies of multitudes of men and women are rendered pitiably sad by the misdeeds of those who intended to do the right but did not know how. One must cultivate his mind, if for no other reason, because otherwise he will never see beyond the merely conventionally right to the really right in new and complex situations.

Our final reason for contending for a duty of development of intelligence consists in the sheer delight that can be attained by doing so, in the previously indicated fact of the intrinsic values of understanding. It is, of course, true that the first steps in liberal education are often painfully slow, and unfortunately those who guide them are all too often persons who themselves have lost the zest of learning. Perhaps it is for these reasons that many people never get beyond the preliminary stages to where the joy of understanding outweighs the effort. But as the process acquires momentum, as fact begins to dovetail with fact and theorem with theorem, as new discoveries illuminate old generalizations, and as new thoughts replace old fancies, the whole moving panorama of cosmic and human history begins to come alive. Adventure with reality may become more fascinating than the most romantic fiction. Moreover, in addition to being themselves valuable, the intrinsic values that one enjoys in understanding have the practical merit of being relatively independent of other human beings. In these days of ample books and other records of intellectual achievement one can, at least after the introductory stages, to a considerable extent make his own way in the world of knowledge. Nor indeed does anyone's pursuit of knowledge interfere with that of any other. Rather, each one's efforts serve as stimulus and incentive to those of the other, and in the exchange of insights, each one profits by the other's advances.

The precise extent and character of the knowledge beyond the strictly functional level that any given individual ought to seek depend on many factors including capacity, time of life, pressure of other duties, and inclination. Because of the slowness with which interest in liberal knowing begins and its vast potentialities, once it has begun to gain momentum, almost everyone owes it to himself at the very least to press the effort far beyond the limits of initial inclination. Although youth is usually the time of maximum opportunity for the kind of learning we are discussing, the young are unfortunately not always ready to receive the best that is being offered. But even when youth's opportunities have been missed, the maturer judgment, deepened interest, and longer span of the years of adulthood still often offer opportunities for a range and penetration of knowledge far greater than any that can be gained in the years of formal education alone.

AESTHETIC APPRECIATION

When we turn from the ethics of the intellectual quest to that of the aesthetic one, the crucial question for many people will not be whether or not one has a duty to cultivate aesthetic tastes beyond functional necessity but whether or not one has any duty to cultivate them at all. Such suspicion is deeply rooted in the Puritan and frontier tradition of America, which was perhaps justly distrustful of the socially irresponsible gaiety of the European courts of the seventeenth and eighteenth centuries. The suspicion lingers on in a strong feeling among ordinary people that concern with aesthetic culture is somehow effete and altogether lacking in wholesome robustness. The cultivation of taste, one is told, diverts attention from scientific pursuits and useful activities. It relaxes the usual moral inhibitions, and leads to irreparable mistakes and degrading lethargy. Art itself is, as Plato suggested, a mere imitation of nature. It may all too easily be put to low commercial uses or even employed for base subversive purposes. Artists themselves are often notoriously loose in their personal morals. Even when art tries to be religious it only succeeds, one may hear, in a blasphemous attempt to make "graven images" of that which can never properly be represented.

Now it is certainly true that individuals and nations can be weakened by misplaced emphasis upon some aspects of the aesthetic, and that art can be used for all manner of evil ends, but these facts in themselves tell us little about the ethics of the aesthetic; anything can be used for bad purposes, and the aesthetic surely can lead to good as well as to evil. One may add that there is no reason to think of the cultivation of taste as a strict obligation, but that this also reveals little concerning the ethics of the aesthetic, since such cultivation, if it a requirement of the right at all, is a requirement of the higher right rather than the strictly right. Perhaps the attitude of most people, including those who find nothing especially suspect about the aesthetic, is that, while anyone who so desires should be free to cultivate his awareness of the beautiful as fully as he can, such cultivation is, for the vast majority of us at any rate, not a requirement of the right in any sense. However, if a certain type of activity could substantially enrich the life of an individual to an extent not possible without it, even though he does not yet know that this is so and could in fact get along very well without ever engaging in it, he remains none the less under a certain requirement of the objectively and comprehensively right to enter upon this sort of activity. To refuse to acknowledge this fact is perhaps to confuse the objectively right and the subjectively right, for, in this latter sense, ignorance of a value possibility sometimes excuses the failure to seek it. Even so, due consideration of the contribution of cultivated capacity to appreciate beauty to the good life will in most instances sufficiently reveal the importance of this kind of development to render it subjectively as well as objectively right.

The grounds on which the cultivation of taste is said to be a requirement of the objectively right are, in the main, as follows.

1. The intrinsic values of aesthetic enjoyment are perhaps the most abundantly available of all values at the least cost. They are virtually everywhere to be had through nature, in blue sky, purple flower, or rosy sunset, in towering mountain and quiet stream, in lofty trees and tiny blades of grass, in open fields and tidy lawns, in rolling seas and quiet lakes. They meet us often

through the things that our hands have made for other uses, and the constructs of the mind are for the most part not less but more beautiful than those of our hands. People, too, can be beautiful, in character as well as in face and form. In addition, there are the virtually inexhaustible treasures of art, in which man is not merely reproducing nature but ever creating new sources of value, and all these treasures are now increasingly made available to nearly all who will seek them out—if not always in the original at least in excellent reproduction. Unlike that of the organic values of eating, drinking, sex, and sport, which have low saturation points and cannot be enjoyed beyond very limited periods of time without weariness or even disgust, the enjoyment of aesthetic values becomes for many people a sustained source of almost inexhaustible satisfaction. Instead of creating barriers of weariness or satiety that inhibit the subsequent enjoyment of other values, it adds to the likelihood of achieving such values and often unites with them to enrich their actual realization. Moreover, instead of interfering with like appreciations by other persons, it also tends to enhance these appreciations.

2. Quite apart from the intrinsic value of aesthetic experiences, such experiences are instruments and ingredients of intrinsic values of virtually all other kinds. In his aesthetic appreciations man begins to find what he himself is. In artistic creation, as philosophers from Plato to Schopenhauer have reminded us, genius envisions an ideal and so embodies it in sensuous media that the beholder glimpses something of the original vision; and in the beauty of nature, the sensitive spirit feels something of the grandeur of first creation. In the deeper moments even of tragic enjoyment ordinary people sometimes so break through the crust of their habitual responses as to sense the vast untapped potentialities within them; and in the mirth of comedy men's deepest woes, though never completely submerged, lose much of the sharpness of their sting. Even villainy, as Aristotle reminds us, sometimes spends itself harmlessly on the stage instead of wrecking the lives of men and women; and the lowliest organic functions are by the touch of artistry clothed

in a goodness far higher than their own. Aesthetic appreciation is the special friend of human fellowship, for, unlike intellectual communication, it is able to leap at once across linguistic barriers. In this respect art is peculiarly well adapted to serve as a means to the creation of that world community on which man's survival seems now to depend. Although awareness of beauty sometimes breaks down useful inhibitions, it more often inspires moral ideals; and for the most part, the artist need not and should not specifically endeavor to preach to us, since the more genuinely he fulfills his own function in creating beauty the more he also rectifies our moral sensibilities. Beauty has always been a doorway to the holy, and he who holds Deity in reverence can in the end do so only in the "beauty of holiness."

3. Many of the most satisfying aesthetic experiences cannot be achieved without cultivation of a kind that, though within reach, requires effort. At the very least, the attainment of aesthetically valuable experiences demands of us that we break through the hardness of our preoccupation with the practical and see and hear what is around us as it is. Such appreciation never asks of us that we pretend to like what we do not enjoy, but it may suggest that we learn what others like and at the very least turn favorable attention toward it. We shall surely need to go where beautiful things are and to beautify our ordinary surroundings. We shall also need to master certain intellectual tools without which some experiences of beauty, as, for example, in literature and science and some kinds of music, can never come to us. Perhaps we shall often be helped by the mastery of the elements of artistic performance in some field of our choosing, in order that we shall feel at least at second hand some of the power of creativity. But at any rate, we shall all be required, beginning with the beauty we can now enjoy, gradually to cultivate our more refined sensibilities until larger ranges of beauty come within our reach. These are relatively simple askings; but multitudes of people go through life without responding to them, and, in so doing, tragically deprive themselves of a very large part of the richness of experience that might be theirs. Hence their mistake is not merely an error,

but a failure to follow a requirement of the objectively right that would claim for them the maximum good available to them.

MORAL CHARACTER

A *virtue* is a disposition to do the right. A disposition is like a habit in being a reliable tendency to do a certain thing, but it may be less mechanical than a pure habit in that it may involve thought, feeling, and deliberative decision as well as more mechanical responses. Character is the whole pattern of one's dispositions, and good character is a character made up predominantly of virtues. In terms of our theory such character is a total pattern of dispositions to do the kinds of acts that tend to promote the greatest good for all, and in terms of any theory it is a pattern of dispositions to do the right.

Where those personal activities that develop character are concerned, the question of primary importance is not whether or to what extent they should be undertaken. Everyone who takes ethical obligations at all seriously will agree that one ought to develop his character to the full extent necessary to attain a high degree of dependability in doing the right. The important question is not, therefore, whether or not character should be cultivated but how this can best be done.

The basic roots of character lie, of course, beyond the control of the individual, in hereditary factors and especially in early training. How such training is to be undertaken is one of the most vital problems facing any culture. That it should be grounded in ethical ideals goes without saying, but there remain many very difficult problems concerning which educational psychology has only begun to make progress. Always required will be common sense, sympathetic understanding, and worthy example, but the rest of these matters we shall have to leave to the experts in the field.

The question to which we shall direct our attention here is what, when a person has reached sufficient maturity to want to develop character, he can do to assist in the wholesome growth of his own character. What he can do includes clarification of thought, reorientation of emotion, realignment of habit, and re-enforcement of will. We shall consider these possible processes in the order indicated.

As one emerges from the period in which his character formation is almost completely dominated by others, he can—and should, if he is to attain strength of character—begin to develop his own philosophy of life. Very important here is clarification of ethical ideals. Coming to see the life of man as a quest for values, one must begin to work out for himself some order of values, to see what is more and what less worth striving for. One must also continuously deepen his insights concerning how values are attained, what a man's obligations and rights with respect to others are, and what modes of conduct in particular fulfill or violate these. One needs especially to arrive at some understanding of what his own special place within the community of persons is, and what special duties this position entails for him as a member of an economic order, a state, and an international order.

In addition to ethical ideals, a philosophy of life involves also at least tentative answers to some broader questions about life and the world without which ethical questions themselves often remain unanswerable and practical ethical motivations and adjustments are difficult and insecure. One needs some insights concerning what life is, what manner of creature man is, and what sort of individual he himself is. One requires some answers also to questions concerning the kind of universe in which he lives. One's answers to all these questions may turn out to be pessimistic and gloomy; they may be optimistic and confident; or they may be melioristic and hopeful. What the answers should be is a question that belongs more to general philosophy than to ethics; but whatever they are, they will have important bearings on attitudes, and one must face them sufficiently frankly to adjust to them if the attitudes that constitute his character are to be firm. If one's answers are pessimistic he will need to develop moral courage to stand against the human and cosmic tide; if optimistic, he will need to cultivate caution to avoid indifference to actual evils; and, if melioristic, he will need to increase his resolution to help in the achievement of the better world for which he hopes.

A satisfactory philosophy of life is not something that one sits down one fine day and dreams up; but neither is it something that is likely to emerge altogether without deliberate thought. Rather, it is in the making in every successful personal undertaking and every failure, in every satisfying and every unsatisfying experience, in all our thinking, working, worshiping, loving, and living. To be constantly preoccupied with it is to become excessively introspective and to distort experience by too much brooding, but not to reflect at all upon it may be to lose the meaning of experience altogether. A sound philosophy of life is perhaps best achieved by being preoccupied most of the time with the business in hand and then pausing at intervals to consider the significance of what has been going on and may subsequently happen.

Although some people manage to get through life without much thought about life, if one's life is to be more than the "tradition-directed" kind that follows outmoded folkways or the "other-directed" [1] kind that follows the prevailing climate, one must build upon considerable reflection. Indeed, if one is to avoid being weak, vacillating, and bewildered in new situations of any sort, he must have deep philosophic foundations, not necessarily in terms of a technical philosophy, but at least in terms of a reflective way of life. The study of the philosophies of life of others in all significant literature can be helpful here; for essential to a satisfactory journey is intelligent choice of objective and itinerary, and to this end an understanding of the pertinent possibilities is indispensable. Yet even this is no substitute for one's own continuous observation and repeatedly renewed reflection.

A second phase of the contribution that one can make to the cultivation of his own character consists in reorientation of his emotional adjustments or the building of sound sentiments. No philosophy, however correct, can create moral goodness or by

---

[1] See David Reisman, *The Lonely Crowd* (New Haven: Yale University Press, 1950), Ch. 1.

itself lead a man to do the right.   Action springs at least as much
from emotion as from thought, and, as the psychologists remind
us, thought itself is often shaped by emotion.

A *sentiment* is a system including an idea or ideal of some
objective around which are organized certain sustaining emotional drives.   A sound moral character will, if our general
theory is correct, have as its dominant sentiment a supreme devotion to all possible human value realization.   Since every man is
naturally disposed to be peculiarly devoted to his own value
realization, such devotion will involve a special offsetting emphasis on altruism or devotion to the good of one's fellows.   Perhaps
the best-balanced formulation of what is required is a very old
one, in terms of love for one's neighbors as for one's self.   To
this dominant sentiment, which in terms of our theory is similar to devotion to the right, should perhaps be added some
special determination to do justice or adhere to the strictly
right; one needs, of course, always to guard himself against violations of the very core of right, although a whole-hearted concern
for all human welfare will normally suffice to prevent all such
violations.   That love for all men is to be dominant does not,
of course, mean that other sentiments are to be excluded.   Those
associated with eating, drinking, exercise, rest, constructive work,
wholesome companionship, marital devotion, parental care, and
many other natural human activities are each to receive its
own expression, but always in such ways as also to contribute
to the fulfillment of the dominant concern for all human beings.   Only sentiments in conflict with this dominant orientation need be resisted, the resistance being not so much in terms
of denial as in terms of redirection of basic drives.   One needs
to learn to find his partial satisfactions in those ways that also
contribute to his total satisfaction, and his personal satisfaction
in ways that contribute to the satisfaction of all.

This deliberate reorientation of emotional life is the most
difficult of all the phases of the development of character.   Not
only has nature endowed us with a larger original preponderance
of impulses directed toward our own well-being than is compatible with good character, but the reshaping of our emotions

has for the most part taken place under doubtful direction other than our own. Fortunately, however, reason operates on the side of character to the extent that anyone who will can understand the rightness of equal consideration for all. And while emotion often leads thought and action, it also sometimes follows upon them, so that in altering our thought we may change our emotions. Hence emotion itself, if not always directly controllable, is in the long run at least indirectly subject to a rational control that may be ethically oriented.

Precisely what we can do in the process of reorienting emotion is hardly subject to simple rules, but some suggestions may be worthy of consideration in this connection. (1) Having clarified his moral ideals, one can repeatedly hold before his mind the image of what he wishes to be like, both in general and in detail, until by self-suggestion it penetrates below the cognitive surface, and his deeper feelings give it power. (2) Even when his emotions do not yet prompt wise or considerate action, one can sometimes act as though they did, and, by the law in terms of which emotions at times tend to follow actions, our feelings may come in time to fall in line. (3) In dealing with other persons, one may school himself to watch for and respond to whatever lovable and admirable qualities they have, and where these are wanting one may focus his attention upon the better potentialities that even the worst of men possess. (4) One may choose as his most intimate acquaintances, both in immediate contact and in literature, those who manifest the kind of character that he himself seeks to cultivate. (5) One may repeatedly rededicate himself to cooperation with those value-sustaining qualities that he finds in Deity. (6) One may join with other like-minded persons in occasional reaffirmations of moral purposes. Herein lies the essence of the ethical aspect of worship, and those who can no longer engage in worship as such are still likely to need to find some moral substitute for it.

A third phase of one's effort to improve his own character may well consist in an attempt to enlist habit in the cause of right conduct. No matter how clear one's philosophy of life, or how well integrated his sentiments, if feeling is to be sufficiently free to enjoy other values and thought to consider other significant matters, including the really difficult moral decisions, many— perhaps even a majority—of one's actions must become largely habitual. To achieve a good character is no small measure a matter of overcoming habits that are injurious to our own and other people's interests and of substituting for them habits that are helpful.

No better account of how in practice this goal may be achieved has ever been set forth than that of William James in his essay on "Habit." The essential features of his recommendations are as follows: First, "We must take care *to launch ourselves with as strong and decided initiative as possible.*" [2] This injunction means: "accumulate all the possible circumstances which shall reinforce the right motives; put yourself assiduously in condi- tions that encourage the new way; make engagements incom- patible with the old; take a public pledge, if the case allows; in short, envelop your resolution with every aid you know." [3] Second, *"Never suffer an exception to occur till the new habit is securely rooted in your life."* [4] Uninterrupted success from the beginning is needed. "Tapering off" does not suffice. "Abrupt acquisition of the new habit is the best way . . . *provided one can stand it.* . . . A desire will die of inanition if it is *never* fed." [5] Third, *"Seize the very first possible opportunity to act on every resolution you make, and on every emotional promoting you may experience in the direction of the habits you aspire to gain.*[6] It is only as they produce *"motor effects"* that resolutions really get through to the brain; only as we act on them do they become rooted in us.

Neither sound philosophy of life, nor integrated personality, nor good habits, nor any combination of them are sufficient in

---

2 William James, "Habit," reprinted in William James, *Selected Papers on Phi- losophy* (Everyman ed., New York: Dutton, 1917), pp. 60–61.

3 *Ibid.*, pp. 60–61.

4 *Ibid.*, p. 61.

5 *Ibid.*, p. 62.

6 *Ibid.*

themselves to assure satisfactory responses in situations in which novel factors render the usual responses inappropriate. One has accordingly also to learn how to apply his moral assets to new situations with due deliberation, and to act with decision upon his best insights even when he cannot be sure they are entirely correct. That is, one must, as a fourth phase of the development of character, cultivate what James calls soundness of will.

Many people, even when they have ample opportunity for deliberation, are disposed to rush headlong into important choices. Unwilling to bear any burden of serious thought or temporary indecision, they no sooner begin to weigh the issues than they hasten to act upon the factors that first seem favorable, without ever really looking at the other side. In doing so, they often bring untold grief upon themselves and others and exclude the best opportunities that come to them. Even more tragic is the case of other persons, of the best of intentions, who seem unable to bring the process of deliberation to a close at all. They habitually weigh all available factors on either side of an issue, but somewhere in the process they lose their perspective and find themselves incapable of choosing; they vacillate back and forth until the time of choice has passed. Sound will steers a steady course between these two extremes. It looks candidly at both sides of an issue, and, seeing how much thought the problem is worth, it makes its choice and acts in the light of what can fairly be found in the available time.

The surest way of securing reliable resoluteness in action is in fact regularly to act with resolution as soon as the deliberative process has been completed. In this fashion decisive action upon one's soundest insights becomes itself a kind of habit. Not only is such a habit valuable for its direct bearing upon character-building but it is also a necessary adjunct to all of the other phases of character-building. New moral thought becomes clear only as one acts decisively upon the old. Desired emotional patterns are confirmed only as they are lived out, and one cannot break an old habit or build a new one save by emphatic action upon his decision so to do.

READINGS

Intelligence

Clark and Smith, *Readings in Ethics,* pp. 215–27; *or*
Rand, *The Classical Moralists,* pp. 277–85.

Moral Character

Clark and Smith, *Readings in Ethics,* pp. 25–52; *or*
Rand, *The Classical Moralists,* pp. 394–417; *or*
Sellars and Hospers, *Readings in Ethical Theory,* pp. 451–63.

QUESTIONS

1. So long as one isn't hurting anyone else, is his conduct subject to moral criticism?   If so, on what grounds?   What is wrong with laziness?   Apathy?   Rebellion against the inevitable?

2. In reply to the suggestion that he ought to restrict his diet if he wishes to be healthy a fat man may reply, "Yes, but I don't want to be healthy."   Is there any other basis of moral appeal to him?   If so, what?

3. In Shakespeare's *Hamlet,* because Ophelia's death seemed to be by her own choice, even though she had been driven to insanity, the priest refuses the usual burial rites, declaring:

> "We should profane the service of the dead
> To sing a requiem."

In just what ways if at all would you say that this Medieval attitude was mistaken?   How would you answer a person who claimed that since his life was his own he was justified in taking it when he pleased?

4. In a much-discussed trial a few years ago a physician admitted injecting air into the veins of a patient suffering from cancer in order to hasten her death.   Was he justified in doing so?   What difference would a law permitting euthanasia have made in the morality of his action?

5. The family of a patient who can never regain consciousness puts the decision up to a young doctor whether to remove her to a hospital to prolong her life for a week or so and in so doing deplete

the family's meager resources or to let her die quietly at home within a few days. Which should he do, and why?

6. What would you say of the conduct of a doctor who puts a week's supply of morphine by the side of a hopeless cancer sufferer, telling the patient that if he takes one pill it will relieve him, that if he takes two he will go to sleep, and that if he takes all of them he will never wake up? What bearing does the legal aspect of the problem of euthanasia have on this situation?

7. Would one be justified in temporarily disregarding the rules of maximum health in the effort to excel in an important examination? If so, why? Would one ever be justified in permanently impairing his health in the interest of his vocation? Consider this problem carefully and explain your answer. Why is this sort of problem comparatively rare?

8. Modern science has produced weapons of mass destruction by comparison with which those of the armies of ancient Rome are like children's toys, and it could create bombs that are yet many times more destructive than those now available. Does this situation imply that scientific knowledge is an evil thing? If not, how not? How can any conscientious man morally justify himself in becoming a scientist? Does modern science entail any special moral responsibilities? If so, what?

9. Some knowledge, such as that of the number of letters on a printed page or that of the number of feathers in a pillow, is not very significant, and some knowledge, like that of the sordid details of a sex crime, cannot be wholesomely dwelt upon. What are the implications of these facts with reference to an alleged duty of seeking knowledge?

10. The man who quietly and efficiently attends to his business is normally more likely to be moderately successful than the one who is in constant quest of new ideas. A patent office lawyer is recently quoted as saying that "a genius is a successful lunatic"; but, then, the percentage of success among lunatics is very low. Would people then be better off if everyone would stick more closely to his job? How can one justify any other conclusion?

11. Knowledge of astronomy will not ordinarily help the doctor or the businessman or the politician to do a better job, nor will insight into Greek philosophy or Roman law enable the carpenter to drive more nails or the mason to lay more bricks. Since such knowledge is not functional to the groups indicated, should it therefore not be

sought by them? Does any man have a duty to seek any knowledge that is not functional for him in the sense suggested?

12. A financially successful father argues with the younger of his two sons that he himself has done well without an education, that his elder son is already substantially established in the business, and that a suitable place awaits the younger also. The younger son nevertheless insists that, although he does hope to settle down in the family enterprise, he feels it to be his duty to go to college or, if not, to win for himself the equivalent of a college education. How could the son's position be justified?

13. In your opinion, who should receive how much education? What bearing, if any, does economic status have on the matter? How much responsibility does the public have in the matter?

14. To appreciate beauty is not to pretend to like what the high-brow critics say you should but to enjoy what you yourself find beautiful. What, then, is the purpose of *training* in aesthetic appreciation and how indeed is such training possible?

15. A freshman reasons thus with his student adviser concerning the humanities requirement of the college: "I can see the value of mathematics, chemistry, biology, psychology, and even a little philosophy, for these give one laws of thought and life, but I can't see that this so-called cultivation of taste in literature and the fine arts gives one anything at all. If you will please explain, I will listen, but I don't want to take courses just to meet the recommendation of the catalogue." In what way could you come to the rescue of the poor adviser?

16. What further individual or class studies, if any, in literature and the arts would you recommend to the average college graduate who has majored in other fields? On what grounds?

17. Plato once remarked that while you could later throw away poisoned food that you had brought home in a basket, poisoned ideas to which you had listened could not be so easily disposed of. On this ground, among others, he favored censorship of art and literature. How would you answer him? Should the writer or artist censor himself? If so, why, and to what extent?

18. In Plato's *Protagoras* Socrates suggests that since in public assemblies, where moral issues are often resolved, the unlearned and the learned have an equal voice and since good men rarely succeed in making their sons virtuous, perhaps virtue cannot be taught. Can it? If so, in what sense, and how would you answer Socrates?

19. Aristotle, John Dewey, and many other educational philosophers agree that we learn by doing. To what extent do you think this is true? Defend your position.

20. Of what use is a philosophy of life? Could a person get along just as well without one? Explain. Does the good life need religious motivation? Discuss.

21. In terms of what we have said about the limitation of morality to voluntary activity, purely habitual action would seem to have no moral value, but nearly all moralists agree that good habits are indispensable to morality. How can these apparently conflicting claims be reconciled? What is the proper role of habit in the good life?

REFERENCES

Life and Health

Drake, Durant, *Problems of Conduct* (2nd rev. ed., Boston: Houghton Mifflin, 1935), Chs. 15, 17.
Everett, M. S., *Ideals of Life* (New York: Wiley, 1954), pp. 344–58.
Patterson, C. H., *Moral Standards* (New York: Ronald, 1949), Ch. 14.
Titus, H. H., *Ethics for Today* (2nd ed. rev., New York: American Book, 1954), Ch. 16.
Westermarck, Edward, *The Origin and Development of the Moral Ideas* (New York: Macmillan, 1908), Vol. I, Ch. 17; Vol. II, Chs. 35, 38.

"Euthanasia, Right or Wrong," *Survey Graphic*, XXXVII (May, 1948), 241–43.
"Goodbye, How G. R. Long Killed His Daughter," *Time*, XLVIII (Dec. 2, 1946), 32.
"Make It Legal," *Time*, XLVIII (Nov. 18, 1946), 70.
"Thomas Moore, The Mercy Killer," *Catholic World*, CLXIII (April, 1949), 3.
"The Trial of Benedetto," *Time*, LXV (March 28, 1955), 64.
"1000 Doctors Urge Mercy Death Law," *The New York Times*, Dec. 15, 1947, p. 63.

Aesthetic Appreciation

Drake, Durant, *Problems of Conduct* (2nd rev. ed., Boston: Houghton Mifflin, 1935), Ch. 20.

Gibran, Kahlil, *The Prophet* (New York: Knopf, 1948), pp. 83–86.

Hartmann, Nicolai, *Ethics,* tr. by Stanton Coit (New York: Macmillan, 1932), Vol. II, Ch. 16.

Langer, Susanne K., *Philosophy in a New Key* (New York: New American Library, 1948).

———— *Feeling and Form* (New York: Scribner, 1953).

Perry, R. B., *The Moral Economy* (New York: Scribner, 1909), Ch. 5.

Cultivation of Understanding

Aristotle, *The Nicomachean Ethics,* tr. by Harris Rackham (Cambridge: Harvard University Press, 1934), Bk. VI.

Dimnet, Ernest, *The Art of Thinking* (New York: Simon and Schuster, 1928).

Erskine, John, *American Character and Other Essays* (Chautauqua, N.Y.: Chautauqua Press, 1927), Ch. 2.

Fosdick, R. B., *The Savage in the New Civilization* (New York: Doubleday, 1928).

Hartmann, Nicolai, *Ethics,* tr. by Stanton Coit (New York: Macmillan, 1932), Vol. II, Ch. 20.

James, William, *The Principles of Psychology* (New York: Holt, 1890), Vol. II, Ch. 22.

Paulsen, Friedrich, *A System of Ethics,* tr. by F. Thilly (New York: Scribner, 1899), Bk. III, Ch. 5.

Robinson, J. H., *The Mind in the Making* (New York: Harper, 1921).

Stebbing, Susan, *Thinking to Some Purpose* (Baltimore, Md.: Penguin Books, 1939).

Wheelwright, Philip, *A Critical Introduction to Ethics* (New York: Odyssey Press, 1949), Ch. 9.

Character

Brande, Dorothea, *Wake Up and Live* (New York: Simon and Schuster, 1936).

Brunner, Emil, *The Divine Imperative, A Study in Christian Ethics,* tr. by Olive Wyon (Philadelphia: Westminster Press, 1947), Ch. 15.

Charters, W. W., *The Teaching of Ideals* (New York: Macmillan, 1927).

Dewey, John, and Tufts, J. H., *Ethics* (rev. ed., New York: Holt, 1932), Ch. 15.

Drake, Durant, *Problems of Conduct* (2nd rev. ed., Boston: Houghton Mifflin, 1935), Chs. 21, 31.

Everett, M. S., *Ideals of Life* (New York: Wiley, 1954), Chs. 9, 13.

Fosdick, H. E., *On Being a Real Person* (New York: Harper, 1943).

Franklin, Benjamin, "His Autobiography," *The Harvard Classics* (New York: P. F. Collier & Son, 1909), Vol. I, pp. 5–174.

Hocking, W. E., *What Man Can Make of Man* (New York: Harper, 1942).

James, William, *The Principles of Psychology* (New York: Holt, 1890), Vol. I, Ch. 4.

Overstreet, H. A., *The Enduring Quest* (New York: Norton, 1914).

Plato, "Protagoras" and "Meno," *The Dialogues of Plato,* tr. by Benjamin Jowett (New York: Random House, 1937), Vol. I, pp. 81–130, 349–80.

Robinson, D. S., *The Principles of Conduct* (New York: Appleton-Century-Crofts, 1948), Ch. 31.

Sorokin, P. A., *The Reconstruction of Humanity* (Boston: Beacon Press, 1948).

Titus, H. H., *Ethics for Today* (2nd ed. rev., New York: American Book, 1954), Chs. 28–30.

Tsanoff, R. A., *Ethics* (rev. ed., New York: Harper, 1955), Chs. 8–10, 19.

Urban, W. M., *Fundamentals of Ethics* (New York: Holt, 1930), Ch. 14.

17

The Ethics of Economic Activity

THE TRANSITION FROM a personal ethics that is concerned with activities primarily affecting the agent to a social ethics that is preoccupied with activities significantly affecting others beside the agent cannot, of course, be abrupt; as we have indicated, every personal act has social consequences and every social act has personal ones. Some of the various areas of social ethics are closer to personal ethics than others in affecting the individual more directly and in being more directly affected by him, although all of the areas of social ethics, in the end, derive their significance from their bearings upon the experiences of individuals. If we begin with the areas that are closest to personal ethics, the major areas of social ethics may be said to consist of those concerned with the family, free associations, economic activities, politics, and international relations. Within each of these areas, in turn, some phases are much more directly linked with individual activities and feelings than others. Since it is impossible to deal here with all of these areas or with all phases of any one of them, and since the more personalized parts of social ethics are more often discussed and more amenable to obvious application of such principles of social ethics as we have presented, we have chosen to consider here the least personalized areas, that is, the three last named. In discussing each we shall, moreover, without ignoring personal applications, concentrate upon the broader aspects, which are more likely to be neglected by moralists and treated in nonethical ways by others. Obviously, the determination of the specific ethical requirements of each of the areas in question needs a great deal of detailed reflection by people actually preoccupied with the activities involved. Our present inquiry is a more modest preliminary attempt to indicate some of the basic problems and to sketch in outline the manner in which the principles we have developed may be applied to them.

ETHICAL OBJECTIVES FOR ECONOMIC ACTIVITY

Economic activity may be said to consist of the things that people do in the production and distribution of the material means of value achievement. Because of an excessive interference with economic progress by Medieval moral rules and because of a firm confidence in the philosophy of mechanism, many people in the eighteenth century began to think of economic activity as subject, like nonvolitional nature, to iron laws of its own and so beyond the sphere of ethics. Under such slogans as "business is business," some such view is still frequently encountered. However, although the Medieval moral rules may have been wrong in detail and economic activity fortunately does manifest some regularities, the view that economic activity is essentially nonmoral is almost certainly mistaken. Virtually all of our values depend in one way or another on material means, and the production and distribution of these means are activities in which human conflicts of the kind that concerns ethics are extremely likely to occur. Moreover, whereas physical nature as such seems to be nonvolitional and not subject to ethical demands, the manipulation of even physical law for human ends *is* volitional and subject to human control, hence, also to ethical demands. This relation of laws and human volition is obviously at least equally applicable to the use of economic laws, which in any case are themselves in part products of human volitions and subject to alteration through changes in such volitions. The sphere of economic activity is, then, one in which ethics can operate and perhaps the one in which, among all others, it most needs to operate.

What is the objective of economic activity when such activity is guided, as all activity ought to be, by ethical, or value-oriented, aims? This objective can scarcely consist either in ascetic shrinking from economic functions, as though the production and use of material goods were in itself evil, or in materialistic dedication to such activities, as though they were primarily good in themselves. In terms of an ethical outlook economic activities are merely means to, and constituents of, a whole of human good. The ethical objective of economic life is so to regulate the activities of the economic sphere that they will contribute as fully as possible to the maximizing of all intrinsic values for all people. Somewhat more specifically this objective involves the following: (1) Since all organic values depend directly on material means in certain quantities and qualities and all other values do also at least indirectly, ethical economic activity will endeavor to *produce* material goods in those ample quantities and those satisfactory qualities required for maximum value realization for all. (2) Since the productive process may involve in itself certain important intrinsic values and dis-values, an ethical economic activity will endeavor to produce the requisite material goods in such *ways* as yield the least intrinsic evil and the most intrinsic good for those involved in the productive process. (3) Since no amount of production can assure human value realization unless the goods produced reach those who need them, ethical economic activity will endeavor to *distribute* material goods in those ways that will, in keeping with the requirements of production, secure ample fulfillment of human need. In the light of such comprehensive objectives as these, the objective of the economic activity of the individual will be to find and occupy himself to these ends with that part of the economic process to which his own needs and aptitudes best suit him.

Three major problem areas in the ethics of economics now emerge. One concerns the value potentialities of the general framework in which economic activity takes place. A second concerns the ethical problems of the productive phase of economic activity; and a third, the ethical problems of the distributive phase of economic activity. Each of these is now to be briefly considered.

THE ETHICS OF ECONOMIC SYSTEMS

By an economic system is meant a prevailing pattern of the ownership and control of property. Although economic systems depend mainly upon customs and attitudes, they also have political bearings that must be taken into account. What an individual can and ought to do in the economic sphere depends in considerable part upon the kind of economic system under which he lives, and although most individuals can do little by themselves to alter their economic systems, such systems are in the end constituted largely by complexes of individual decisions. Every choice has a bearing upon the existing system, and the concerted choices of many people can in time considerably alter a system. Hence ethics is ultimately applicable to systems as well as to individual and corporate economic decisions.

After describing what he took to be the primitive conditions of man's existence, Rousseau once suggested that the point at which social evils began was the one at which some man staked out a plot of land and said, "This is mine." However, since the use and consumption of material goods is a kind of human activity in which conflict is very likely to arise, human beings must, as Rousseau himself eventually acknowledged, reach some understanding concerning the use of material goods if they are not to live in a state of perpetual strife. Some kind of system of property ownership is necessary to any satisfactory life in society at all. Our question is what kind contributes most fully to maximum value achievement for all. With this question in mind let us look briefly at some of the major kinds of systems that are being advocated and practiced today.

Pure Capitalism

The relatively pure *laissez faire* capitalism that was set forth by Adam Smith, Ricardo, and other classical economists and exemplified in considerable degree in western Europe and America in the late eighteenth and early nineteenth centuries is still present in parts of our economy, and many people would like substantially to extend its domain.   The system is very roughly as follows: Mixing their labor with material things, men produce economic values, which some men, instead of consuming, save to invest as capital, in tools and in the employment of other men's labor.   All commodities, including labor, are bought and sold in a free market in which each bids on an essentially equal basis. Each buys as cheaply and sells as dearly as possible; but the force of free competition keeps prices, wages, and rents at the levels required for economic efficiency.   Hence although each is, within the rules of the game, seeking only his own interest, the whole process operates, as though guided by an invisible hand, in such a manner as to promote the interests of all.

In terms of certain of the objectives of economic activity, the advantages of this system, when it works according to its theory, are very great.   To begin with, the system creates powerful incentives to industry and ingenuity, and its champions are not far from the truth in saying that the astonishing economic growth of western Europe and America in the past two hundred years has been in very considerable part due to the predominantly free enterprise character of the economies of these regions.   In the second place, the relatively pure capitalism under consideration maintains an intimacy of relations between production policies and consumers' wants that apparently cannot be matched by any sort of planned economy.   Manufacturers make just what they expect to be able to sell, and such is their sensitivity to buyers' demands that the market is rarely either flooded with unwanted goods or very short on wanted ones.   Equally important with these economic advantages is the accompanying political one that economic freedom tends to promote and sustain political freedom.

Nevertheless, pure *laissez faire* capitalism is confronted with virtually insuperable obstacles.   At best it was always too much disposed to foster selfishness, neither sustaining such modest altruism as was natural to man nor encouraging the growth of more.   It never offered to the worker much beyond a bare subsistence, and, in times of temporary economic lags, it forced him into a position of intolerable hardship.   Moreover, as Keynes has shown, the depressions incipient in its processes are very likely to be more than temporary. The savings withheld from circulation by some people may depress the purchasing power of others, and this depression may in turn reduce production. Curtailed production may then reduce wages and purchasing power, and the process may continue thus until the economy has settled at a relatively permanent low level, as apparently the American economy might have done in the thirties save for new modifications of *laissez faire* and the incidence of war. The most devastating obstacle in the path of *laissez faire* capitalism, however, and the one that makes return to it impossible today is the fact that the free competition upon which the feasibility of the system was predicated simply cannot, without support from outside, be maintained under modern industrial conditions. Such is the superior efficiency of large-scale production over small in many instances that *laissez faire* tends almost inevitably to pass over into monopolistic conditions in which prices, wages, and rents can all too easily be fixed against the interest of the worker, the potential competitor, and the public alike. All these disadvantages do not mean, of course, that free enterprise must be abandoned. They do mean, as most even of the staunchest supporters of the capitalistic system are now ready to acknowledge, that free enterprise cannot be sustained unless considerable checks are brought to bear upon the *laissez faire* principle.

Communism

Over against pure *laissez faire* capitalism, at the opposite extreme, is the communistic type of economic system. Under such a system all of the means of production are confiscated by violent revolution for collective ownership and operation. Ideally, and ultimately, the system is intended to be associated with a classless society in which the state "withers away." However, in the interim the means of production as well as the lives of the producers are to be rigidly controlled by a powerful dictatorship of Communist Party leaders, who act in the name of the workers both to govern and to plan in detail production and consumption. Actually this interim form is the only one in which communism has yet manifested itself upon any considerable scale and the only one to be expected to do so in any foreseeable future. Hence it is to this phase of communism that attention is here directed.

Such a system no doubt has some merits that deserve consideration; otherwise it could scarcely have lasted as long as it has. Ostensibly, it aims directly rather than obliquely at the general welfare, basing its appeal for the good of all not primarily upon the selfish interest of the individual but mainly upon the importance of the general interest itself. Its careful planning and systematic controls permit the avoidance of some of the worst features of economic depressions and of unemployment. At the same time, while availing itself of some of the efficiency of monopoly, it avoids at least some of the disadvantages of *private* monopolies.

Nevertheless communism entails disadvantages such as to make it an unthinkable alternative for most men who have once tasted freedom. It has to surrender nearly all the powerful incentives involved in free enterprise and so is often obliged to drive both workers and managers to their tasks by the oppressive force of a police state. Its planning, which must provide in advance for all of the interlocking aspects of the whole economy, is of necessity too rigid to be sensitive to consumers' needs, so that all too often the market is overstocked with unwanted goods while genuine needs go unmet. Worst of all, instead of enhancing liberty and integrity, it has been and remains a mortal enemy of freedom and justice, utterly ruthless in destroying individuals or groups that stand in its way.

Socialism

In the days of its earlier champions socialism was a somewhat doctrinaire system of rather comprehensive public ownership, which in its purely economic aspects—though by no means in its political ones—resembled the communism we have been dis-

cussing. As it was later advocated in Fabian societies and subsequently adopted and practiced in Great Britain and the Scandi-
navian countries, however, it came to be a much more practicable
and moderate system characterized by the following central
features. First, the government owns and operates key transportation, mining, and industrial facilities in the name of and
for the benefit of all the people. Second, most of the remainder
of the economy is on an essentially free enterprise basis but subject to substantial checks through governmental control and
well-developed labor and cooperative movements. Third,
through graduated taxation and welfare programs a very substantial effort is made to provide basic security for all and to narrow
the economic gap between wealth and poverty. Fourth, these
economic reforms are attempted through strictly democratic and
constitutional means, in which civil liberties are carefully
guarded and such properties as are taken over by government
are bought at fair prices rather than confiscated.

Over against communism, socialism has the advantage of preserving, through its moderation, some of the individualistic incentives and sensitivity to market conditions found in capitalism.
It also has the more important merit, which renders it radically
different in spirit from communism, of persistent recognition
and protection of the dignity and rights of individual persons.
Over against pure capitalism, it has the advantages of appealing
beyond egoism to social responsibility, of mitigating the evils of
unemployment and depressions by planning and counter-
measures, and of insuring the basic welfare of all its people without resort to such repressive police measures as prevail under
communism.

The only disadvantage of socialism by comparison with communism is a lack of power to enforce its plans by arbitrary decree,
but such is the essential place of liberty and human rights in the
achievement of intrinsic values that this must actually be regarded as a gain rather than a loss. Socialism has, however, certain considerable disadvantages by comparison with capitalism.
One is its loss of a certain part of the force of individual initiative.
Another consists of the administrative difficulties that beset a

government when it takes over control of key industries. Perhaps the most important is the fact that, although personal liberties can and are being maintained under democratic socialistic systems, they become at some points more difficult to maintain as more economic power is taken out of private hands and vested in government.

Modified Capitalism

The economic system of the United States is somewhat to the right of that of Great Britain and the Scandanavian countries and may appropriately be called a modified capitalism or mixed economy. Although it differs from the British system in preserving a somewhat larger capitalistic element, the similarities are much more marked than the differences, and each differs far less from the other than does either from Russian communism on the one hand or pure *laissez faire* capitalism on the other. In American modified capitalism, most economic activity—including transportation and mining, which in Britain are socialized —is on a free enterprise basis, and American taxation and welfare programs are not so comprehensive as their British counterparts. Nevertheless, the socialization of many aspects of the American economy is now well established and rather generally recognized. This socialization includes, for example, public ownership and operation of the postal system, highways, public schools, many utility and municipal transport systems, and some strategic manufacturing concerns. It also includes the partial subsidization of air and sea transportation and of farming, numerous controls over business and commerce, a steeply graduated income tax, a vast social security program, and a "whole arsenal" of weapons in the form of fiscal procedures and public works projects for use against depressions. Although the cooperative movement has not come to play so important a role in America as in Great Britain, it nevertheless exercises considerable influence, and the influence of the American labor movement, though more directly economic than political, is enormous.

The virtues of the American economy have often been extolled

and need not be detailed again here.   Clearly they include somewhat more of the powerful individual incentives and economic
freedoms of pure capitalism than do socialistic economics.   They
also include an increasing sense of social responsibility, substantial checks upon excessive greed, and provision for welfare.
The productive efficiency of our economy is strikingly attested
in the remarkable growth, the present health, and the promise
of even better standards of living in the economy.   These merits
do not indicate that the American economy is without weaknesses, and certainly not that one precisely like it would be best
for all times and places.   As we are presently to see, substantial
areas of tension and injustice remain, and improvements will
always be called for.   The merits of our economy do indicate
that something involving excellent value prospects has been
achieved here, and that this fact ought never to be lost sight of by
any who might contemplate a general abandonment of the prevailing system for something else.

SOME ETHICAL CONCLUSIONS CONCERNING
ECONOMIC SYSTEMS

The ultimately moral problems relating to economic systems
are exceedingly complex and difficult, and little progress toward
their solution is likely apart from the cooperative good will and
intelligence of many people, including not only moralists but
also economists, business and professional men, laborers and consumers.   Nevertheless, even so cursory a survey of systems as the
foregoing would seem to involve several broad suggestions that
may be worthy of consideration.   One is that no single property
system seems to be best for all situations, but that patterns of
ownership—which historically have always differed widely—
must be suited to the circumstances of the society in which they
operate with reference to such factors as geographical conditions,
population density, technological skills, and prevailing mores.
Another is that, under the conditions in which we live, both of
the more extreme systems presented above must be excluded.
By reason of the drift toward monopoly, pure *laissez faire* cap-

italism is now quite unworkable; and, by reason of the essential values rooted in liberty, communism is ethically unthinkable. A third suggestion is that any economic system that is to make reasonable claims to be conducive to maximum good for all must give due recognition to the fact, emphasized by capitalism, of the powerful incentive of self-interest and at the same time to the facts, emphasized by socialism, that self-interest is not always self-adjusting and that social responsibility is essential to the soundness of an economic system. A fourth suggestion is that, although workable ideals for the economic order ought to be sought out and kept in view, the most satisfactory method of economic reform is not to attempt to work out in advance doctrinaire systems and then to apply them all at once, but, rather, to look for crucial weaknesses and possible improvements and to endeavor to advance a step at a time as democratic procedures allow. No man is wise enough to see the whole pattern of the best future in advance and every man's ideas and purposes must be taken into account if readjustments are to be fair to all. A final suggestion is that however excellent the prevailing economic system may be, it will need constant readjustments in the light of changing conditions and that gradually these may improve not only the details but also the general complexion of the system. In view of such suggestions as these the wisest course for all those who are genuinely interested in establishing the best kind of economic order would seem to be largely to abandon preoccupation with economic *isms,* which all too often serve only as catchwords in irrational ideological warfare, and to concentrate instead upon more manageable issues within the general type of economy under which they live and work. To some such problem of our own type of economy we turn, first with reference to some issues connected with production and then to some relating to distribution.

ETHICAL PROBLEMS OF ECONOMIC PRODUCTION

Generally speaking, the major issues of the ethics of production fall into two groups. One is concerned primarily with the efficient organization of the industrial process, and the other with potential human conflicts involved in that process. Selected problems of each variety are now to be considered.

Conflicts Involved in the Organization of Industry

From the very outset of man's attempt to organize his productive efforts, a conflict, implicit in the basic aims of ethical economic activity, has been apparent. This is the conflict between man's desire to get the things he needs and wants produced efficiently and his resistance to the humanly unattractive features of sustained effort in work; it is the conflict between disciplined technical efficiency and immediate satisfaction. This conflict has been greatly intensified through the rise of industrialism. Prior to the modern period each worker ordinarily produced whole products, often designing them, selecting their materials, and selling them himself, as well as making them. Though the process was slow, there was ample employment for all among friends and neighbors, and each could find some creative satisfaction in his work. But with the growth of the division of labor and factory and machine techniques, each worker came to have a smaller and smaller part in the making of a given product and virtually none at all in its planning or distribution. These changes carried with them enormous increases in efficiency, so that the product of a group of workers might be five, ten, or even hundreds of times that of a similar number of individual workers in earlier periods. At the same time these changes often brought to workers themselves deadening monotony in endlessly and unimaginatively repeating the same operations day in and day out; dreary, unhealthful, and impersonal conditions of work; and occasionally ruinous unemployment. The new situation also marred many a theretofore lovely countryside with unsightly chimneys and filled its pure air with smoke and smog.

Gloomy economists sometimes suggest that we are caught here in an inescapable dilemma between inhumane efficiency and human inefficiency, but this conclusion we ought not to accept unless in fact there is no way out. Actually, on the one hand, despite real merits in the earlier ways, the benefits of modern productive efficiency are far too substantial in terms of security, comfort, and leisure for cultural growth to be easily abandoned, and, on the other hand, there are numerous ways of mitigating the worst accompaniments of modern technological progress without undermining that progress itself. (1) Many producers are finding that they can shift a worker from one phase of the process to another and assign to him a larger responsibility for the planning of his work without any appreciable loss in efficiency and often with considerable gain. (2) Such is the marvelous progress of late in "automation," the controlled operation of machines by electronic devices, that the end of much industrial drudgery and the achievement of new satisfaction and interest in remaining processes of attending machines is actually in sight. (3) Industrialists, laborers, communities, and governments can cooperate in the elimination of needless hazards in industry and in the improvement of the health and aesthetic conditions in which it takes place; and in this connection numerous industrial communities have already splendidly exemplified what can be done. (4) As standard-type machines and automatic devices are developed further, unemployment may be avoided and valuable leisure gained by further reductions in the hours of labor. (5) If these reductions are to be useful, new education for leisure both at the level of youth and in adult education programs will of course be required; and this in turn will open up vast new possibilities of cultural and human enjoyment, of creative activity, and of the sharpening of industrial skills themselves, provided the new leisure is well employed and not merely squandered. (6) Meanwhile, and indeed with reference to such routine work as will always remain to be done, every human being owes it to himself and to others to develop a genuine appreciation of the dignity, and even the potential intrinsic value, of labor that, though unprompted by inclination, is productive of good for himself and others.

A second major issue of industrial organization with important bearings upon human value realization is the conflict between monopolistic, or quasi-monopolistic, control and full and free competition. As we have previously suggested, there is, under modern technological conditions, a constant drift toward the domination of a given industry or group of industries by a few giant corporations or even by a single one. The trend toward monopolistic control may have considerable advantages in terms of efficient production, for it eliminates much useless overhead and machine cost and permits planning and mass production on so large a scale as substantially to reduce unit cost. At the same time it tends to exclude the stimulus of competition and to make a travesty of the idea of equality of economic opportunity.

All sorts of solutions have been proposed, ranging from Woodrow Wilson's demand that monopolies be relentlessly broken up, through Theodore Roosevelt's appeal for big government to control big business, to John Knox Jessup's suggestion that responsible corporations be allowed to grow indefinitely and to take over many of the functions now performed by the states of our federal union.[1] None of these proposals can by itself solve the problem, nor is any other simple solution in prospect. For example, the first of the above proposals would, if rigorously enforced, seriously disrupt the present economy and make for needless inefficiency. The second leans farther than seems to be wise toward bureaucratic socialism and is in any case impracticable apart from the aid of other controls in addition to governmental ones. The third represents an unthinkable return to a kind of feudalism, in which the rest of society is made dependent upon the good pleasure of a relatively few industrial barons. The problem remains, in fact, one of the very live, and as yet quite unsolved issues, of the ethics of present-day production.

Nevertheless, in line with certain aspects of the foregoing and the other proposals that have been made, it is possible to offer at least a few suggestions from the standpoint of ethical, or value-oriented ends. (1) Vast corporations must somehow be kept in check on behalf of all the people, and at present there seems no prospect of doing this apart from some such strong governmental

[1] See M. W. Childs and Douglas Cator, *Ethics in a Business Society* (New York: New American Library, 1954), pp. 95 ff.

intervention as was intended in the proposals of Wilson and Roosevelt. (2) No matter how strong governmental checks are, government itself is all too likely to become subservient to corporations, unless its efforts are sustained by other forces of a more directly economic character. In this connection J. K. Galbraith has appropriately called attention to the fact that "countervailing" economic forces are already at work in our economy. In addition to the partial competition among the few surviving giants in each industry, these forces include the competition between parallel industries such as steel and aluminum, the demands of organized labor, and the pressures of suppliers and consumers. Instead of being discouraged as harmful to a free economy, such checks upon monopoly ought to be encouraged and further organized as helpful substitutes for the stimulating and balancing forces of full and free competition in earlier economies.[2] (3) No matter what checks upon monopoly are achieved, a tremendous weight of moral responsibility will continue to rest upon the managers of corporations themselves, and if giant corporations are to continue to exist, they must not operate solely in terms of profit objectives but in adequate orientation to the social objectives for which the vast powers permitted then render them responsible. (4) Provided reasonable public controls over, and genuine responsibility in, corporations can be achieved, there is no reason why industries that use their power in the public interest should not be allowed to grow to very considerable size. Thus the courts are increasingly finding that it is not mere size but restraint of trade and abuse of power that constitutes harmful monopoly.

A third issue of the organization of industry that has vital ethical bearings is the conflict between the incentive of initial advantage and the demands of rapid dissemination of technical knowledge and skill. If, on the one hand, an inventor who devises a new technique or a manufacturer, or even a nation of manufacturers, who develop it, have no prospect of gain thereby, the incentive to inventiveness and resourcefulness may tend to

---

2 See J. K. Galbraith, *American Capitalism and the Concept of Countervailing Power* (Boston: Houghton Mifflin, 1952).

decline. But, on the other hand, if the new technique is confined to a relatively small group of producers, its usefulness is likely to be very restricted.

Fortunately, at least the broad outline of an ethical solution to this problem is not difficult to find, although the requirements involved differ somewhat from usual practices. It is, of course, quite natural for the favored inventor or manufacturer, or nation of manufacturers, to want to preserve the advantage gained by being the first to employ an efficient device or technique. But, generally speaking, the inventor has ample incentive in patents of limited duration and the honor accorded him, and the manufacturer or nation that first develops a new technique profits sufficiently by the time advantage gained. For the rest, the public interest is by far best served by as rapid dissemination of productive potentiality as is possible. For this reason, the practice of some corporations in bottling up unused patents can scarcely be ethically justified and the length of the period of exclusive rights allowed by our patent laws themselves may need some re-examination. Perhaps the example of medical discoveries that are rapidly made freely available to all cannot always be followed, but it could well be much more nearly approximated than at present.

Many people, however, who can readily see the importance of the rapid spread of technical knowledge within a nation fail to see the parallel on the international plane. Actually the importance of such dissemination is even greater here. A highly industrialized nation may, if it chooses, endeavor to keep its technical "know-how" within its own borders in order to avoid creating competition in undeveloped countries. But while some immediate gains may result, this is a shortsighted policy, even in purely economic terms. So long as the producers in underdeveloped countries are working, as they often are, in extremely inefficient ways, what they have to exchange with more highly favored nations must be very meager, and the markets of the latter consequently limited. If, on the other hand, men everywhere are enabled by dissemination of knowledge and wise use of capital to produce in the most effective ways, then vastly more goods are available for exchange and the scope of markets widens. Meanwhile each group comes more and more to produce what its special conditions best facilitate, and since all are then producing at higher rates of efficiency, higher standards of living can be attained by all. Indeed, in the light of techniques now available, not to mention vastly more productive ones immediately upon the horizon, the total produce of world economy could in a single generation be at least doubled and possibly trebled or quadrupled. The duty implicit in these potentialities, to share industrial "know-how" as rapidly as possible, should already be amply recognizable without consideration of international rivalries; but if further stimulus is needed, it is powerfully present in the fact that if free nations fail to help in the development of backward nations, other powers will quickly fill the vacuum and alienate these potential friends from the free world.

Human Conflicts Involved in Industrialism

From ethical problems relating to the efficient organization of the productive processes we turn now to some of the potential *human* conflicts involved in industrialism, especially between capital and labor. Among the fundamental theses of Marxism is the doctrine that the relationship of owners and workers in any industrial society is necessarily one of irreconcilable conflict of interests that can only result in the violent overthrow of the owners. Generally speaking, this thesis has long since been disproved by the actual experience of a number of highly industrialized nations, and each passing decade seems to bring an increasing realization of a mutuality of interests of owners and workers and a growing ability of these two groups to get along harmoniously with one another. Workers are more and more aware that their jobs depend on the capacity of industry to survive and prosper, and that the flow of the goods that they need at prices they can pay is dependent upon the productivity of industry. At the same time, owners are seeing more clearly than before that available markets for their goods depend on the maintenance of substantial wage levels, and that the degree of productivity of workers depends upon their health and morale. Nevertheless, areas of tension remain that can be disruptive unless properly resolved, and serious ethical problems result. These problems include, apart from the problems of distribution, subsequently to be considered, the problem of the method of determining wages, that of closed and union shops, that of the use of the strike, that of the control of industrial policy, and that of legislation relative to industry and labor.

1. We begin with the problem of the method by which wages are to be equitably agreed upon. The most natural method is, of course, the *laissez faire* one of direct bargaining between employer and the individual employee. However, when the worker brings to the bargaining process only his own strength and skill while the owner brings the accumulated power of an established business organization and perhaps the vast resources of a giant corporation, the process tends to become unbalanced in ways that may be damaging not only to the worker but to the whole economy. A second suggestion may then be offered, that the industrialist ought to see his responsibilities and that sound bargaining could be achieved through his sense of duty. Now certainly a sense of fairness is needed on both sides, and each party to a bargain ought always to treat the other as an end and never as means only. But unfortunately human beings are so constituted that no group is likely fully to perform its economic duties to others without the prompting of pressure from these others and no group should be left without the means of applying some such pressure on behalf of its own rights. At third suggestion is that patterns of wages should be determined by government; but while government undoubtedly has some responsibility in this area, to make it the basic determiner of wages would entail endless cumbersome and insensitive machinery and considerable loss of liberty on the part of free workers and industrialists alike.

A fourth proposed method of determining wages that has tended increasingly to be adopted in Western civilization, namely, the determination of wages primarily through collective bargaining between industry and organized labor unions. This method, also, involves serious deficiencies and undoubtedly needs to be supplemented by some reliance on the other methods; but under modern conditions it seems to be by all odds the method that holds most promise of justice for the parties principally concerned and of maximum benefit for all. Unlike individual bargaining, it backs each worker with sufficient strength to give him some prospect of a fair agreement. Unlike governmental decision, it enables industrialists and laborers to meet face to face to work out their own specific problems. Unlike the appeal solely to the industrialists' sense of fairness, it enables the interested parties to meet not as petitioner and petitioned but as equal human beings discussing their mutual interests and rationally ordering their differences. Besides, it has in fact achieved marvelous results, as anyone can see who will compare present wage and hour scales with the fourteen-hour days and few pence a day wages of the early years of the Industrial Revolution.

2. Acceptance of collective bargaining as the principal mode of determining wages inevitably gives rise to the problem of closed and union shops, or of the rightness of agreements accepting a given union as the bargaining agency for a given company in such fashion that only those who are or will become members of the union may be hired by the company. Opponents of such arrangements argue that they are illegitimate infringements of the freedom of the company to hire whom it will and of the worker to work where he can, and certainly considerations relating to freedom always have substantial ethical import. Accordingly, many of our states have passed "right to work" laws forbidding closed and union shops and guaranteeing the right to hire or be hired regardless of union membership. Proponents of closed and union shops answer that agreements to hire only actual or prospective union members are simply an effective implementation of the principle of collective bargaining, which tends to break down if companies can fill their ranks with nonunion workers; that workers have far more freedom with union benefits than without them; and that just as participation in the benefits of citizenship demands acceptance of its

responsibilities so participation in the benefits achieved by unions requires acceptance of the responsibilities of union membership.   This is an extremely difficult issue and we shall have to leave the reader to sift for himself the bearing of the various factors upon the maximum good of all.   With special reference to "right to work" laws, however, it should be remarked that the term involves a propagandist slant in that for the most part the proponents of such laws are not workers seeking to defend their rights but persons wishing to employ workers without union restrictions and communities hoping to attract new industries through the prospect of relatively low labor costs.

3. The process of collective bargaining occasionally breaks down in strikes, and such are the economic loss, the suffering, and the disorder likely to accompany a strike that all strikes have come in many minds to be thought of as illegitimate and even vicious violations of the peace.   As a matter of fact, strikes have sometimes been used to press irresponsible claims, and many of the accompaniments even of justifiable strikes are deplorable. Nevertheless, these organized interruptions of work, or threats of them, often remain the only means by which workers can exert pressure in favor of any of their claims to counterbalance the pressures supporting the claims of their economically more powerful employers.   The effectiveness of actual and potential strikes in improving the lot of the worker may be readily seen by comparing the present lot of white-collar and government workers, who do not engage in them, with that of often less skilled workers who do.   Nor, indeed, is the force called into play here merely that of economic pressure, for whereas reason and moral insight often lie dormant when they are not prodded into action, they are not infrequently significantly stimulated by pressures on behalf of claims to which they ought to have in any case responded.   A sound ethical attitude toward strikes would therefore seem to be not forthwith to regard them and their participants as wicked but, rather, while helping in the removal of maladjustments that lead to them and in the elimination of their abuses, to accept strikes that cannot be avoided without injustice as necessary aspects of the kind of unregimented

economy under which free men prefer to live. Meanwhile, one of the very difficult moral problems facing all participants in a free economy is that of the improvement of the economic situation of persons in positions of public responsibility in which the strike is either illegal or highly undesirable.

4. Just as their enormous power places upon modern corporations a heavy load of responsibility that has been often emphasized but frequently unfulfilled, the growing power of labor unions places a tremendous weight of social responsibility upon these organizations and their leaders. Often this responsibility has not only not been met but flagrantly violated in arbitrary, unjust, and even violent methods of labor leaders, in racketeering, in injustice in the use of funds, and in other types of lawlessness and even crime. A great deal of commendable progress has been made in checking such abuses and much more is now in the making. What is required of labor in terms of social responsibility is, however, something more than simply a correction of irregularities. Labor, like all other segments of society, must, as it has begun to do, refrain from demands injurious to the whole economy and think and act in statesmanlike fashion with the interests of the whole in mind. Indeed so intimately interwoven are the interests of every segment of our present economy that no organization, whether of business or professional men or of laborers has a moral right to exist solely for its private ends, and every member of every such organization has an obligation to exercise the functions of membership in this association or union with a view not alone to its interests but also to those of the whole economy.

5. The tension between ownership and labor is not confined to wages and hours but bears also in some measure upon other conditions of work, and upon the determination of industrial policies themselves. The first of these two additional issues is now often conceded to be a matter for collective bargaining. Upon the second industry is for the most part extremely reluctant to make concessions. That owners should have a very substantial share in the determination of industrial policy is, of course, implicit in the fact of their investments, for such invest-

ments are means of value achievement that owners may not be expected to give up without maintaining some degree of control. That the details of management likewise are best placed in the hands of managerial experts responsible to boards is also evident in view of the vast complexity of modern industry and of the need for decisions that are beyond the direct competence of large groups either of workers or of owners. At the same time considerations both of justice and of expediency would seem to suggest that workers also ought to have some voice in the determination of the broad policies of the industries in which they are employed. If the investment of their funds by owners entitles them to be heard, so it would seem, does the investment by laborers of their lives. Moreover, since workers are daily preoccupied with problems of the industry in which they are employed and since their fortunes rise and fall with its successes and failures, they may surely be expected to have something worth saying concerning its policies. Actually, some companies are already finding that by giving labor some representation upon their governing boards improvement in their own perspectives as well as in the morale of their workers is being gained.

6. Since the prices and qualities of goods are affected by industrial relations and the whole economy is helped by industrial harmony and hindered by want of it, every consumer—which means everyone—has some stake in the sort of problems we have been considering. Perhaps in the end the most powerful expression of this interest lies in the force of public opinion, which each party to an industrial struggle accordingly tries to win over. For this reason, if for no other, everyone's ethical attitudes in these matters are important. However, the major organ for the overt implementation of this public interest is government. The functions of government in this connection are, in our sort of economy, not fixed and definite but have a sort of stand-by character intended to meet special needs that cannot be met as well in other ways as by governmental action. Many such needs are fairly regularly encountered, and some of the resulting governmental functions have already been indicated. Among the functions particularly pertinent here are

the placing of floors under wages and working conditions, the prevention of all manner of industrial abuses, the control of labor unions, the preservation of the balance of bargaining power so that neither side comes to dominate the other, the assembling and dissemination of statistical material, the allocation of materials in dangerously short supply, the control of monopolies, the regulation of strikes threatening the national wealth or security, the assurance of standards of quality of goods that affect health and safety, and the stimulation of industry in periods of depression.

There are, of course, those who fear any sort of governmental intervention in matters of production on the grounds that it interferes with private property, is an invasion of economic freedom, and constitutes a menace to economic prosperity. However, although governments can, of course, be excessively intrusive, property, economic freedom, and prosperity remain instrumental to the greater end of achievement of the maximum good of all, and their security and development to this end are in any case far better sustained when democratic governments can, subject to constitutional guarantees, act to correct economic abuses than when governments are obliged to keep hands off no matter what happens. Indeed the very survival of property, freedom, and prosperity seems today to depend in no small measure upon constructive governmental action.

THE ETHICS OF ECONOMIC DISTRIBUTION

Although the general standard of living may be more effectively elevated by increasing production than by further distribution of what is being produced, unless the fruits of industry are adequately distributed, many people remain excluded from them in such fashion that maximum good for all cannot be even remotely approached. Moreover, vast differences in wealth tend to be morally degenerating both to those who hold great wealth without putting it to work in the fulfillment of need and to those who suffer such poverty that their basic needs are not met at all. Even those in the middle brackets who fail to help to rectify maladjustments in distribution must bear a heavy burden of moral responsibility.

The moral principles of the ethics of economic distribution are primarily those of justice, although those of benevolence are also involved. It will be recalled that among the most important principles included in the principles of justice are those of disinterestedness, impartiality, honesty, proportionality, basic security, and equality. Each of these principles has significant bearings on the ethics of economic distribution.

Disinterestedness, Impartiality, and Honesty

The principles of disinterestedness, impartiality, and honesty, are primarily applicable to the manner in which business transactions are conducted; they demand the exclusion of all manner of cheating and the grosser forms of injustice in economic activity. They involve no peculiarly difficult problems of theory, although in practice they are by no means always easy to apply. (1) Although no one is expected to be disinterested in the sense of being totally unconcerned about economic goods, every man is morally responsible for being disinterested in the sense of asking for no economic privileges that he is not willing to accord to others in similar circumstances and of making no demands of others that he would not be willing to fulfill if situations were reversed. (2) Similarly every man is ordinarily expected to exclude favoritism from his economic transactions and deal with each of two other persons on a basis of impartiality. Although the matter was seen in a different light by earlier civilizations, this is now widely taken to mean, for example, that a given merchant should make his prices the same for all his customers. Such practices facilitate the flow of trade and tend to conserve harmony and good will. Whether or not the principle should be extended to mean that all merchants should agree on a single price scale is a much debated question at present. So-called "fair trade laws" designed to facilitate this practice have actually been enacted in many states; but, in an economy designed to be mainly free and to serve the interests of customers, the practice would hardly seem to be ethically justifiable. (3) Upon conformity to the principle of honesty, the whole pattern of communication through which a sound distributive process must operate depends, and where honesty is absent the process has to be drastically curtailed. One of the points at which these facts are especially apparent, is that of the keeping of contracts, for a very large part of modern business is conducted on the basis of contractual promises to deliver goods or services. Fortunately, our economy has on the whole encouraged the growth of a fairly high sense of responsibility on this point; and, whether or not people always live up to their obligations, nearly all are convinced that a business agreement made ought to be carried through even, if necessary, at a loss, unless either a release is obtained or conditions so drastically change as to render the contract meaningless.

Another area in which the demand for honesty is important is that of the factual representation of goods and services. In some economic systems and in some phases of our own the "buyer beware" principle, that the purchaser is responsible for the discovery of the flaws in the goods he selects, is accepted as satisfactory. This principle involves a crude kind of honesty in that the seller tacitly admits that his merchandise may not be what it seems, but a genuinely efficient transfer of goods, not to speak of other moral considerations, demands a higher level of honesty. The necessity for the buyer to scrutinize every purchase in detail tends excessively to slow down the volume of trade, needlessly to divert attention from other more useful activities, and generally to disintegrate the character of both buyer and seller.

At the present time, as never before, the representation of goods and services takes place through the complex process known as advertising, which has now become almost a separate industry. This process involves a number of comparatively new ethical problems, including problems of honesty as well as others, and some of these are worthy of mention in passing even though no answers can be attempted here. To what extent is an advertiser obligated to represent the facts concerning his products with literal accuracy? Does the fact that his competitors are making extravagant claims and that his own honest statements may cause his product to be taken to be relatively inferior make any difference? How far, if at all, are irrelevant illustrations that confuse issues and suggest social values not actually achieved by the product legitimate? Is the effect of advertising upon the general level of intelligence any concern of the advertiser? In what degree is an advertiser responsible for the aesthetic consequences of his billboards and other advertising? Does he have any obligation to consider the tastes of the artists he employs apart from results in terms of sales? Are the vast expenditures for advertising and correspondingly increased costs passed on to customers justified in terms of increased employment and flow of trade? What are the rights and responsibilities of advertisers with reference to products that are useless or even possibly harmful to large segments of the public? What responsibilities do the media of advertising, such as newspapers, magazines, and broadcasting companies, have with reference to the products they advertise or the integrity with which these products are represented? What responsibilities does government have in these and related matters? To what extent, if any, can advertisers legitimately bring pressure to bear upon the editorial and news reporting policies of media that carry their advertising? Is compliance with such pressures compatible with the proper functions of these media? To what extent can success in advertising be measured by sales records? For the most part no satisfactory codes covering these issues have yet been worked out; but although an ethical individual can to some extent recognize his own duties in this area the achievement of common codes is urgently needed in order both to lift general standards and to give to the individual who tries to do the right thing the fair chance that he deserves.

Proportionality

As the first three of the principles of justice named above are primarily applicable to the problem of the manner of a just distributive process, the fourth, that of proportionality or value-compensation, is primarily applicable to the more difficult problem of the scale of just distribution or of fair shares in the material means of value achievement. This principle requires that economic value received should be in proportion to value given, not necessarily in the numerical sense that he who gives twice as much should receive double compensation—for such strict proportionality is not always either possible or desirable—but at least in the looser sense that he who supplies the greater means of value realization should receive the greater compensation in kind. Two important facts in the human situation persistently suggest adherence to this principle. One is the fact that, human self-interest being as it is, one tends naturally to *expect* to enjoy at least a substantial part of the fruits of his own labor and to feel frustrated and even cheated if he is deprived of them without receiving compensating means of value achievement in return. The other is the fact that general prosperity, which is in the interest of all, is facilitated by and partially dependent upon keeping self-interest motivation at work by compensating a person in proportion to what he contributes.

The crucial question is, of course, how economic value compensation is to be measured. In the absence of any scientific formula, one can at best only offer certain incompletely coordinated criteria.

The classical economists felt that just compensation could properly be determined only in the open market where the laws of supply and demand determined values at any given time. Moreover, since the price he pays is presumably of a little less value to the purchaser than the goods or services he buys, and since the goods or services are presumably worth a little less to the seller than the price at which he sells, the general economic values of the price and the goods or services presumably tend to approximate one another in the open market. Hence the open market often does facilitate something like just value compensation, and at many points it does so better than any other device. Nevertheless, contemporary markets are never entirely open, and situations often occur that give some groups peculiar advantages and place others under grave disadvantages in such fashion that market prices come to be far from fair. Further, other factors than market conditions, including government policies, corporation agreements, executive decisions, and labor union demands concerning pay scales, enter into the setting of the prices of goods and services. Even where the market does determine prices, it allows considerable margin for decision, for example, between the lowest prices at which a merchant can afford to sell and the highest he can get, or the lowest wages at which a manufacturer can secure workers and the highest he could afford to pay. The problems of just value compensation are therefore not automatically settled by the ordinary processes of trade but require further practical policy-decisions, not only by governments and corporations, but by virtually every executive, proprietor, stockholder, union member, job seeker, or consumer.

What specific factors ought to be taken into account in making such decisions? A very important one is cost. What a man has to pay for goods or services must at very least be some measure of what he may hope to receive from them, and he may ordinarily not be expected to part with them without being compensated for his expense. Nor indeed, when all costs are fully accounted, may a man justifiably expect to gain a great deal more from goods or services than he has put into them. How costs are, in justice, to be accounted is, however, not an easy question to answer. They include prices paid for goods and for transporting them; wages paid to labor; risks of loss; dangers and hardships endured; the strain of work; the wear and tear of administrative burdens; expenses incurred in training, education, research, retooling, and retraining to keep abreast of the times; the satisfactory maintenance of the producer, worker, or merchant and his dependents; as well as many other factors difficult to detect and to measure. However, even though all who seek to work out wages and prices fairly must take all such factors as these into account, costs alone cannot fully determine scales of economic value compensation. Some individuals and some businesses are maladjusted to the work they have undertaken, and, despite considerable effort, produce inefficiently. The economy can scarcely afford to pay them altogether according to costs, and must use failure to do so as a means of guiding their efforts into other endeavors better suited to their talents. Moreover, as an incentive to some especially productive efforts, the economy can sometimes afford to offer compensation substantially beyond full costs, though whether or not gifted individuals who are able to produce in such fashion should ask for or accept such compensation is another question.

Another factor that may well be taken into account in estimating economic value compensation is the *extent* of the contribution made. Thus, for example, the merchant who brings a large volume of goods to market should presumably receive more than the one who brings a small volume and the manufacturer who produces more goods should receive more reward, though not necessarily more, or even as much, per unit. Similarly, groups of workers who produce more goods should ordinarily receive more than those who produce less. Moreover, although costs of machines have, of course, to be taken into account, this principle should also hold when the increased product is due to the improvement of machines. Otherwise all of the profits of scientific and technical advance will accrue to the advantage of the favored few against the less fortunate many, and the whole economy will eventually bog down through imbalance and unemployment.

Yet another factor is skill, for presumably, of two services equal in cost, the one requiring the greater skill contributes more to the community and should be better paid. Certainly it is likely to be much rarer and therefore more in need of incentives to call it forth. On this basis, work of precision is properly better rewarded than crude operations, the skilled management of complex machines than the ordinary manipulation of simple ones, and competent intellectual, artistic, managerial, and executive work than routine operations. Many administrators in both government and industry as well as many labor organizations are increasingly endeavoring to take this sort of principle into account in determining pay scales, but a great deal remains to be done and new adjustments are required with every significant technological advance.

Closely associated with the principle of extent of service, though by no means always strictly proportional to it, is that of degree of responsibility. Thus, for example, the weight of responsibility of the surgeon, in whose hands are placed human lives, is greater than that of the watchmaker, whose work may require equal precision and make a substantial contribution but deals only with inorganic materials. Similarly, the work of the commercial air pilot or the railroad engineer perhaps requires no more skill than that of the operator of some industrial machines but it usually involves much more responsibility. Many kinds of administrative workers must bear a weight of responsibility not equally shared by those who work under them. Such responsibilities usually merit, and for the most part receive, compensation in material terms.

Although no formula for value-compensation is, of course, achieved here, the endeavor to gain progressively clearer insights suited to changing situations is one of the foremost tasks of ethico-economic inquiry in every generation. Even without any specific formula it is not difficult to see that considerable inequities exist in our own economy in terms of the factors indicated. For example, unskilled workers, having relatively little responsibility, often receive considerably more than office workers whose jobs require a great deal of skill. Similarly semiskilled workers, such as plumbers and bricklayers, often receive substantially more than research scientists or teachers whose work involves expensive preparation, skills of a high order, and very great responsibility. Workers in dangerous jobs are often not compensated for their risks, and many a solid contributor to economic welfare receives an income that represents only a small fraction of the income of a playboy son of a wealthy father. Such injustices are partly due to differentials between organized and unorganized work and partly to the free enterprise character of our system. The remedy does not lie either in diminishing organization or in abandoning free enterprise. Rather, essentially it lies in further extension of labor organization; in a growing sense of responsibility on the part of industrialists, merchants, and labor leaders concerning the obligation to arrive at and put into operation scales of compensation in terms of such factors as costs, skill, responsibility, and extent of service; and in efforts on the part of the public as well as the groups involved to achieve adequate compensation for groups of workers who in the nature of the case cannot effectively organize.

The principle of proportionality does not by itself, however, determine fair shares in the material means of value achievement. For example, children, the aged, and the unavoidably unemployed contribute little in terms of the material means of value achievement, yet surely ought to share in these means. At the other extreme, some military leaders, statesmen, and scientists make contributions to the general welfare for which they could never be sufficiently paid in material terms, and society properly refrains from making the attempt to repay them solely in this manner. These situations in which the principle of proportionality is obviously inadequate brings to mind those aspects of justice to which we have referred as "basic security" and "equality of opportunity" and also the principle of benevolence.

Basic Security, Equality of Opportunity, and Benevolence

The same principle of justice that demands that the basic security of the lives of all men be protected from murderous attack demands, in only slightly less stringent degree, that all men should be protected from want of the fundamental necessities, that their basic needs be met. It is for this and related reasons that needs of the young, the aged, and the unavoidably unemployed are to be met regardless of their inability to contribute in equal degree; and, for similar reasons, even the most shiftless persons, though perhaps at some points properly prodded by the pinch of want, ought not to be allowed to starve. The maximum good of all can never even be approximated as long as some have little chance to share in or to contribute to the good and are constantly hounded with the threat of unendurable evils.   Nor is any society or individual that avoidably allows an individual to starve or otherwise to remain in grave want adequately just or benevolent.   Indeed one may go on to say that so long as the basic needs of many still are not met, no one is fully justified, in the higher sense of the term, in living in great personal luxury; and that every man who has more than enough to meet his own basic needs is, in the higher sense, obligated to share either directly or indirectly in carrying the burden of meeting the basic needs of all.   To fail to realize and act upon this obligation is to produce callous indifference on the part of those who have, misery and frustration on the part of those who have not, and grave tension and conflict in society as a whole.

Like the principle of basic security, that of equality of opportunity is deeply rooted in the demands of maximum good and essential to the determination of fair shares.   No man's abilities to achieve or contribute to values can be known until they are tried, and this surely is at least as important where the material means of value are concerned as elsewhere.   This implies that every child and youth is entitled to decent surroundings, such educational opportunities as his abilities and inclinations warrant, an opportunity to find work, and a chance essentially similar to that of all others to advance in the economic sphere. Like most other ethical ideals this cannot perhaps at present be fully achieved, but all men surely ought to endeavor to contribute to an approximation of it.   To what extent such equality of opportunity now prevails is a matter of considerable debate; but deplorable departures from it are often seen, for example, in the virtual economic disenfranchisement of the children of some slum areas, the inadequate school facilities of other children, and, by way of contrast, in the initial opportunities—far beyond need, merit, or ability—of some children born to substantial wealth.

Just how the objectives envisioned in the principles of need and equality of opportunity are to be met within the framework of a free society is a difficult problem.   To some extent the usual processes of production and trade operate to this end, in every normal man's inclination to meet his own need and in the tendency of competition to check excessive power. But owing to illnesses and misfortunes of many other kinds as well as to the growth of monopolies, the usual processes simply cannot alone achieve these ends, and other factors have to be introduced. Among these are included union activities demanding basic sustenance, marginal benefits, and equitable opportunities for all union members. Others include voluntarily adopted profit-sharing and welfare programs that have not only spread the fruits of industry further and helped to meet basic needs but also materially improved morale. Also extremely useful to the ends in question have been splendid programs of individual and organized charities that have developed within the framework of free economies as in many ways their finest moral flower. Nevertheless, a very substantial part of the burden of meeting basic needs and equalizing opportunities must of necessity rest upon governmental activities designed to serve these ends by means of graduated income and inheritance taxes and extensive welfare programs.

Some serious-minded people fear the kind of procedures mentioned here on the ground of interference with the effectiveness of the profit motive, which they take to be the basis of the whole economy, and this sketch of the ethics of economics may well be concluded with some comments upon this much-discussed motive. As we suggested in discussing both systems and the principle of proportionality, considerable reliance upon wholesome self-interest stimulates prosperity and is ethically commendable. Everyone is entitled to at least sufficient profit to sustain himself and his dependents, and each should have as much more as the economy can afford and as his efforts merit. At the same time, the building of a whole system or the action of an individual wholly upon profit motivation is both ethically contemptible and practically unworkable. Material means are necessary to many values, but when decisions are made and success measured solely in terms of profits, the order of values has been turned upside down. Profits are at most only means of attaining some values. They are not the only means; nor are the values attainable by them the only values or indeed the best values. A ruthless contest to gain material means at the expense of important personal end values or of other people's values is often degrading both to him who wins and to him who loses.   No one wishes to patronize the physician or lawyer or even the businessman who operates solely in terms of profits, and the society that builds upon economic gain alone tends quickly to lose those principles of workmanship and integrity that in the long run make such gain possible.   He who best seeks to promote the good of all often does not in doing so directly seek for reward at all, but, insofar as he receives it, much of the best of what he does receive is often in terms of internal satisfactions and external expressions of gratitude that have little connection with monetary reward.   Without attempting to abandon profits or even its principles of proportionality, a good society will then encourage the growth of these other rewards and will never obscure the noneconomic intrinsic value ends to which every economic device must be subservient.

READINGS

Heffner, R. D., *A Documentary History of the United States* (New York: New American Library, 1952), pp. 154–65, 178–93, 240–69.

QUESTIONS

1. Do you consider valid the argument that, since it is futile endeavor to tamper with laws of nature, one ought not to try to alter the prevailing economic system?   To what extent are the laws of economics like the laws of nature?   Are technical procedures ever successfully altered in order to utilize the laws of nature more effectively for human ends?   Why, and to what extent, is ethics concerned with economic laws at all?

2. What is wrong with regarding general prosperity or the "wealth of nations" as the sole objective of economic activity?

3. Do you think it possible for a nation to maintain free political institutions with a socialistic economic system, or does socialism inevitably tend, as is often said, to totalitarian government?   What are the chief threats to political freedom involved in socialism?   How, if at all, can they be met?

4. What do you consider the principal weakness of socialism from the point of view of economic efficiency? Do you think socialism would require a different kind of moral education? Do you think that the moral virtues needed under a socialistic system would differ at all from those needed under a capitalistic one? If so, how? Do you think that the reorientation of children's attitudes toward thrift, work, competition, and social responsibility could in time overcome the major weaknesses of socialism? How so, or why not?

5. G. B. Shaw once remarked that if proper distribution of wealth could really be achieved by the slaughter of a few thousand persons, men of good will ought to be ready to commend this sacrifice. What is your opinion of the ethics of this attitude?

6. Provided a Communist in America is sincere in so doing, do you think he is morally justified in disregarding ordinary moral standards in order to further what he takes to be genuinely humanitarian ends?

7. Is a person who believes the accepted American "free enterprise" system ethically inferior justified in making his living as a merchant? Why so, or why not?

8. What is wrong with pure *laissez faire?* In what sense can the American system be called a "mixed economy"? What are the principal merits of such an economy from the point of view of specific promise of value realization?

9. A gigantic corporation discovers that to adopt a new and useful device would involve expensive changes and temporary curtailment in profits. But if competitors adopt the device it will give them an advantage. Accordingly the corporation buys the patent in order to prevent its use. (This has actually been done with reference to literally thousands of devices.) Is this sort of action right? If not, what should be done about it?

10. A state medical association protests vociferously against the idea of compulsory health insurance, but the same association has for years blocked every effort to expand facilities for the training of doctors. Comment upon the ethics involved. What is the way out?

11. Why not let monopolies become as big as they can? What good do laws against monopolies do? What do labor unions accomplish by way of checking the power of monopoly? Do labor unions themselves ever manifest evils akin to those of monopolies? If so, how? What are the requirements and limits of proper government regulation of labor unions?

12. In what senses is being a member of a union in a closed shop arrangement like being a citizen of a country, and in what senses are these two different? In what sense is the closed shop an infringement upon individual freedom? What do your friends among owners think of the closed shop? What about your friends among workers? How could one arrive at a balanced perspective on such a matter?

13. Should workers be informed concerning broad company policies? Why, or why not? Do the principles of democracy commonly adopted in politics have any proper bearing on matters of industrial relations? To what extent ought human relations in the areas of politics and of industry be alike and to what extent different?

14. What are the ethical grounds for a graduated income tax? What are the objections? Should the graduation be more severe or more moderate? Why? Are inheritance taxes ethically justifiable? If not, why not? If so, why, and on what principle should the amount be determined?

15. As an executive of a railroad or a member of a union committee having a voice in the determining of wages, how would you apportion the wages of porters, engineers, brakemen, conductors, maintenance men, ticket agents, and clerical workers? On what principles?

16. Just what is meant by equality of opportunity? Why is it desirable? What can be done toward achieving it?

17. What are the principal merits and defects in the profit motive? What other motives specifically could adequately stimulate people for productive work? Illustrate.

REFERENCES

Arnold, T. T., *The Folklore of Capitalism* (New Haven: Yale University Press, 1937).

——— and Associates, *The Future of Democratic Capitalism* (Philadelphia: University of Pennsylvania Press, 1950).

Berle, A. A., Jr., *The Twentieth Century Capitalist Revolution* (New York and London: Harcourt, Brace and Macmillan, 1954).

——— and Means, G. C., *The Modern Corporation and Private Property* (New York: Macmillan, 1933).

Bernstein, Irving, *The Arbitration of Wages* (Berkeley: University of California Press, 1954).

Boulding, Kenneth, *The Organizational Revolution* (New York: Harper, 1953).

Bowen, H. R., *The Social Responsibility of the Business Man* (New York: Harper, 1953).

Burnham, James, *The Managerial Revolution* (New York: John Day, 1941).

Brunner, Emil, *The Divine Imperative, A Study in Christian Ethics,* tr. by Olive Wyon (Philadelphia: Westminster Press, 1947), Chs. 33-35.

Childs, M. W., and Cator, Douglas, *Ethics in a Business Society* (New York: New American Library, 1954).

Dewey, John, and Tufts, J. H., *Ethics* (rev. ed., New York: Holt, 1932), Chs. 18-22.

Drake, Durant, *Problems of Conduct* (2nd rev. ed., Boston: Houghton Mifflin, 1935), Chs. 24-26, 28.

Ebenstein, William, *Today's Isms* (New York: Prentice-Hall, 1954).

Galbraith, J. K., *American Capitalism, The Theory of Countervailing Power* (Boston: Houghton Mifflin, 1952).

George, Henry, *Progress and Poverty* (New York: Random House, 1938).

Glover, J. D., *The Attack on Big Business* (Cambridge: Harvard School of Business Administration, 1954).

Glueck, Sheldon, *The Welfare State and National Welfare* (Cambridge, Mass.: Addison-Wesley Press, 1952).

Hayek, Friedrich, *The Road to Serfdom* (Chicago: University of Chicago Press, 1944).

Hayes, H. G., *Spending, Saving and Employment* (New York: Knopf, 1945).

Heermance, E. L., *The Ethics of Business* (New York: Harper, 1926).

Hoyt, E. E., and Others, *American Income and Its Use* (New York: Harper, 1954).

Keynes, J. M., *General Theory of Employment, Interest, and Money* (New York: Harcourt, Brace, 1936).

Kilman, E. W., and Wright, Theon, *Hugh Roy Cullen, A Story of American Opportunity* (New York: Prentice-Hall, 1954).

Kornhauser, A. W., and Others, *Industrial Conflict* (New York: McGraw-Hill, 1954).

Kuzneth, Simon, *Shares of Upper Income Groups in Income and Savings* (New York: National Bureau of Economic Research, 1953).

Lilienthal, David, *Big Business: A New Era* (New York: Harper, 1953).

Lodge, R. C., *Philosophy of Business* (Chicago: University of Chicago Press, 1945).

Mumford, Lewis, *Techniques and Civilization* (New York: Harcourt, Brace, 1934).

Osborn, Fairfield, *Our Plundered Planet* (Boston: Little, Brown, 1948).

Oxnam, G. B., *Labor and Tomorrow's World* (Nashville: Abingdon-Cokesbury, 1945).

Perry, R. B., *Realms of Value* (Cambridge: Harvard University Press, 1954), Ch. 15.

Potter, D. M., *People of Plenty* (Chicago: University of Chicago Press, 1954).

Scarlett, William (ed.), *The Christian Demand for Social Justice* (New York: New American Library, 1949).

Schumpeter, J. A., *Capitalism, Socialism and Democracy* (rev. ed., New York: Harper, 1947).

Sharp, F. C., and Fox, P. G., *Business Ethics* (New York: Appleton-Century, 1937).

Soule, George, *Men, Wages, and Employment* (New York: New American Library, 1954).

Tawney, R. H., *Religion and the Rise of Capitalism* (New York: New American Library, 1947).

Titus, H. H., *Ethics for Today* (2nd ed. rev., New York: American Book, 1954), Chs. 22–23.

Toucks, W. N., and Hoot, J. W., *Comparative Economic Systems* (rev. ed., New York: Harper, 1943).

Tsanoff, R. A., *Ethics* (rev. ed., New York: Harper, 1955), Chs. 14–15.

Urban, W. M., *Fundamentals of Ethics* (New York: Holt, 1930), Ch. 12.

Veblen, Thorstein, *Theory of the Leisure Class* (New York: New American Library, 1953).

Ward, A. D. (ed.), *Goals of Economic Life* (New York: Harper, 1953).

Woytinsky, W. S., and Associates, *Employment and Wages in the United States* (New York: Twentieth Century Fund, 1953).

Weber, Max, *The Protestant Ethic and the Spirit of Capitalism*, tr. by T. Parson (New York: Scribner, 1930).

18

The Ethics of Politics

ALTHOUGH MOST PEOPLE ARE much more preoccupied with economic activity than with political, what can be accomplished by the former depends in no small measure upon what has been achieved by the latter. Indeed, throughout the centuries, the progress or retrogression of peoples in every sphere of activity has been closely linked with the laws and political institutions that they have been able to develop. Hence the intrinsic values that individuals can realize hinge in considerable degree upon what they do or fail to do with reference to the political order, and political choices are virtually always matters of ethical significance.

A *community* may appropriately be said to consist of a group of people bound together by common interests and mutual concerns. A *state* is a group of people, usually consisting of one or more national communities, having a single *government* that is authorized to enforce at least certain basic requirements. The most important questions of the ethics of politics may accordingly be grouped under the following broad issues. (1) What are the objectives in terms of which the existence of states can be ethically justified? (2) What kind of state can best be justified in terms of these objectives? (3) What are the principal rights and duties of an ethically justifiable state? (4) What are the special responsibilities of agents of governments?

JUSTIFYING OBJECTIVES OF THE STATE

What kinds of ends can justify people in surrendering the liberties that they must surrender in order to form a state and live under the authority of a government? Some philosophers have replied that the state is really a natural growth that needs no further vindication. Others have suggested that, if not natural, it is at any rate the inevitable product of habits of obedience incurred in times of crisis. Still others have agreed with Hobbes that the state is justified by its protection of the security of its people, to which all else must be subordinate; and many have been inclined to say that the state exists primarily to defend property. The first two theories take the state to be inevitable and really offer no justification for it. The other two are very narrow views that must be included in larger perspectives if they are to be considered valid at all.

Unless our whole account of ethics up to this point is drastically wrong, ultimately to justify anything is to show its relation to the realization of values, and only that is fully justified which is conducive to maximum realization of value for all. The major channels through which political institutions may be expected to contribute to the good of all would seem, as advocates even of widely divergent political systems tend to agree, to be primarily the following, which may be taken to be the principal justifying aims of the state. (1) Since life apart from states is, as Hobbes insisted, always precarious, men properly expect the state to defend their basic *security* and at least in some degree to support their quest for *material well-being*. (2) Since justice is often violated by crimes and threatened by quarrels, and, as Locke insists, no man is a good judge of his own case, the *administration of justice* is an important function of the state. (3) Since man does not live by bread alone, and cultural growth depends to some extent upon cooperative activity, the state is expected at least not to hamper and, as far as possible, to help in the *education* and cultural advancement of its citizens. (4) Whereas all values are greatly enhanced by liberty and depreciated by lack of it, and the unrestrained liberty of some tends to destroy the liberty of others, the state is expected to defend the *freedom* of its citizens and to perform its own functions in such fashion as to interfere as little as possible with liberty.

THE MOST PROMISING KIND OF STATE

The question that we have now to consider is what broad type of state can be most fully justified or is best in terms of the foregoing objectives by which any state must be tested. If the question required a specific form of state that was best under all circumstances, it could scarcely be answered; for, as political philosophers ever since Aristotle have seen, the particular kind of state that is best suited to any given situation depends upon the situation, and no single form of state can be imposed upon every situation with uniformly good results. However, since human situations in which fairly high levels of civilization have been attained are much more alike than different, it is reasonable to suppose that at any rate some broad type of state will be more promising for most situations of this kind than others.

Among the possible specific kinds of states there are at least as many as there have been states and political philosophers, and many more besides, but broad types of states can be reduced to relatively few. They may for purposes of ethical evaluation be classified according to the questions concerning *for whom* and *by whom* government is conducted. Regarding the first question, some states have existed for the favored few, and others for all or nearly all of their people. As candidates for the best type of states, those that exist for the favored few may be eliminated at the outset, as avowedly incompatible with the moral objective of conduciveness to the maximum good of all and in any case not openly advocated by any considerable group in the contemporary world.

With reference to the second basis of classification, four major types of states demand attention. Two of these place the ultimate control of the state in the hands of limited groups and may appropriately be called authoritarian. The other two place this control in the hands of the people and may properly be referred to as democratic. The first of the authoritarian types gives all of the authority to a single ruler or to a small group of rulers who rule in the name of and in accountability to no other human beings. This type, which may appropriately be called *absolute authoritarianism,* is exemplified to some extent in ancient Oriental absolute monarchies and is supported in theory in later European doctrines of the divine right of kings. The second type of authoritarian state places the authority in the hands of a limited group who ostensibly rule in the name of, and in line with the purposes of, the people, but not in accountability to the people. This type, which may be called *ideological authoritarianism,* is advocated in theory by Plato, Hobbes, Lenin, Mussolini, Hitler, and many others. It is exempliefid in the contemporary world both by fascism and by communism—despite drastic differences in social and economic theory, these systems are essentially similar in political structure and operation. In the first of the two types of democratic states the people, in whom the ultimate authority resides, exercise their sovereignty through representatives chosen by majorities to govern but restricted by constitutional guarantees of the rights of individuals and of minority groups. This type, often called *constitutional* or *representative democracy,* is exemplified, though at many points imperfectly, by Great Britain, France, the United States, and other nations with similar political systems. It is championed in theory by liberal political philosophers, such as John Locke, J. S. Mill, John Dewey, and A. D. Lindsay. The second type of democratic state places both ultimate sovereignty and active governmental control in the hands of all of the citizens, who vote directly upon every issue and take turns in holding office. This type, often referred to as *pure democracy,* is exemplified by the ancient Athenian state.

The more extreme of these four types, the first and the last, scarcely require elaborate consideration. On the one hand, little prospect for the general good is contained in the natural self-centeredness of those who claim to rule solely in their own right, and even those who have claimed sovereignty in the name of God have for the most part manifested too much of human egotism to be very sensitive to the needs of their subjects. On the other hand, pure democracy is too cumbersome to operate under conditions of the modern national state, and even when it could function in the Greek city-states, it was disastrously prone to rash decisions and to majoritarian tyranny. In any case, neither of these two systems as such is now seriously advocated by anyone, and neither seems to offer substantial value prospects. The two middle types of systems, ideological authoritarianism and representative or constitutional democracy, are the systems actually contending for supremacy in the contemporary world. We shall henceforth refer to them, for brevity's sake, simply as authoritarianism and democracy.[1] The practical question for our purposes is, Which of these two is, generally speaking, best suited to the achievement of maximum intrinsic good for all under modern conditions?

Many people tend to regard this kind of question as one that cannot be resolved rationally and accordingly need not be confronted. Everyone's political preferences, they contend, are so much a part of his social conditioning that each will take his own political system to be best and will invent reasons for thinking it so. But despite the impossibility of attaining absolute impartiality, the refusal to examine as impartially as one can such questions as the one before us is a dangerous and unwarranted retreat into irrationalism. If one's own cherished political system is discoverably inferior, the sooner he can understand this fact and go to work for the improvement of the system the better; and if it is superior, rational recognition of this fact may save him from persuasive misleading propaganda and enable him worthily to defend and advocate the better system. Moreover, if the objectives of political activity consist in conduciveness to maximum good along the lines of the ob-

---

[1] The term "democracy" is often used by Communists to refer to their own system, but while the argument that follows depends in no way on usage of the term, we adhere for convenience to the traditional usage.

jectives earlier indicated, some political systems do in fact
promise more value realization than others, and the more
promising ones should be fairly clearly discernible by comparing the actual and probable consequences of the functioning
of systems in these terms. Accordingly, while recognizing the
difficulty of overcoming bias and without attempting exhaus-
tive comparison, we must place the contributions of the contending systems to the justifying objectives of political activity
alongside one another as best we can.

With Respect To Security and Material Welfare

Insofar as it is the function of government to sustain the
security and material welfare of its citizens the case for authoritarianism is somewhat as follows. Being government by experts, unhampered by the interference of incompetent citizens
or of restrictive constitutions, this system is able to provide
both for the security of its citizens against aggression and for
their general welfare with admirable efficiency. It may conduct its diplomacy; levy, maintain, and deploy troops; and
mobilize industry without consulting or reporting to anyone.
It may plan and organize the whole production and distribution of goods so as to avoid unemployment and to provide
equitably for all. It may alter its manner of life to meet any
emergency, without being hampered by scruples concerning
property and without revealing its intentions either to inquisi-
tive citizens or to potential enemies. Moreover, in actual practice, authoritarian states have often proved militarily powerful;
and, under enlightened and benevolent rulers, they have sometimes even achieved astonishing material progress within brief
periods of time.

This type of argument is very convincing as it stands, but
it overlooks at least three important considerations that, when
duly taken into account, strongly suggest the superiority of
democracy even in matters of security and material welfare.
One is the fact that intrinsic values are conscious experiences.
Another is the tendency of every man to be partial to his own

interests in the absence of accountability to other people. And the third is the possibility of bringing expert knowledge and skill into the service of popular sovereignty. Because intrinsic values occur and are only directly apprehended in individual consciousness, the value requirements of each citizen, either for security or welfare, can scarcely be adequately known to government unless each is represented by persons politically accountable to him. Moreover, such is the selfishness of man that even needs of the people that are known are rarely given due consideration by rulers who are not accountable to their people. Never in the history of the world has a government not responsible to its citizens consistently continued for any very considerable period of time to act primarily for the good of all its citizens, and none is likely to begin to do so now. However enlightened and benevolent authoritarian rulers may be, in time either they or their successors begin to misuse public power for private ends. When such misuse occurs that very efficiency which authoritarianism can employ in the interest of the security and welfare of its people is directed against its people, and the threat to the people's security and welfare becomes greater from their own governments than from foreign powers.

However, even the efficiency of authoritarian governments tends in the long run not to be nearly so great as that of democracies. While people can be driven, as unwilling workers, to tasks over which they have no control, they will when so driven, as the Russians have found in dealing with their farmers, put no heart into their work. But when people work at jobs of their own choosing, even if job allocation is for some purposes less efficient, they work with a willingness and enthusiasm that more than compensates for possible deficiencies of organization. The people's power can be fully called forth only at the people's command. Nor indeed need the efforts of democracy in the fields of security and welfare or any other be blind surges of brute strength; democracy can place in positions of responsibility men of creative intelligence such as it alone is likely to develop, encourage the growth of such intelligence in all its people, and call forth the full expression of such intelligence in both public and private affairs as no other political system can. Thus, genuinely united under the leadership of able men devoted to the people's causes both through training and through accountability to the people, democracies may, as they often have in the past, develop a stability and a power for action in the public interest that authoritarianisms of equal size and natural resources can never match.

With Respect to the Administration of Justice

The case for authoritarian administration of justice is essentially as follows. In apprehending criminals and enemies of the state, authoritarian governments are unhampered by such restrictions as those concerning warrants, searches and seizures, and wiretapping, which often retard law enforcement in democratic countries. Similarly, in securing confessions from wrongdoers, authoritarian police are allowed to use the methods they find most effective without undue regard for the accused who, as enemies of the state, deserve no special consideration. Court procedure in authoritarian systems is conducted largely by experts without hindrance from ignorant juries, rigid rules of evidence, or needless assumptions concerning the innocence of those not yet proved guilty. Thus, authoritarian justice moves swiftly and surely toward its objective, the single-minded service of the ends of the state, to which the ends of individuals must always be subordinated. Like a wise surgeon the state promptly removes from the body politic those members who by their own degeneration threaten the health of the whole organism, for it is the life of the whole, not that of separate members, that counts.

Now, while the administration of justice in constitutional democracies need not be as slow and cumbersome as it sometimes is, it can scarcely ever, in the nature of the case, proceed with the dispatch possible under authoritarian systems. However, the fact is that most of those very procedures that, in democratic jurisprudence, delay the apprehension and conviction of the guilty have been shown to be necessary for the protection of the innocent; and the protection of the innocent turns out in the end to be far more vital to the value achievement of all than the punishment of the guilty. The state is not a biological organism that the individual members must serve; it is, rather, a man-made organization intended to serve the ends of its individual constituents, for never in states as such but only in individuals are intrinsic values realized at all. Lightly to dismiss the claims of the individual even when he is accused of a grave crime is to defeat the basic ends for which the state exists, and to insist upon the recognition of these claims is the very foundation of justice in the administration of the law. If persons may be sacrificed for the ends of the state, not only do some innocents suffer unjustly but all must live in constant uneasiness, never knowing who will be the next victim. Even when authoritarian judges attempt to administer the law impartially, they are likely, being out of touch with ordinary people, to be unsympathetic with the ends of ordinary people; but when, as usually happens, they become simply the agents of the all-powerful state they become the ruthless oppressors of the people. Authoritarian "justice" has in recent years, in Germany, Russia and China, sacrificed literally millions of innocent persons to its special ideological schemes, and the end of the slaughter is not yet. The lesson is daily more deeply confirmed that the innocent cannot be duly protected apart from sincerely and effectively sustained, if sometimes awkward, guarantees concerning police methods, rules of evidence, open trial before a jury of one's peers, independence of the judiciary of other branches of government, and the ultimate accountability of the whole judicial process to a sovereign people. However imperfectly applied or at times cumbersome procedures protecting civil liberties may have been, they are the characteristic procedures of the administration of justice in constitutional democracies that render democratic jurisprudence vastly superior to any achieved in authoritarian systems.

With Respect to the Education of Citizens

The educational advantages that have been claimed for the authoritarian state from Plato on down include the following.

Those in charge of the educational process can be experts who are not obliged to conform their policies to the wishes of an uninformed public. They know what the truth is, how much of it should be taught, and how to teach it. Since all educational processes are concentrated in the state, private individuals or institutions are not permitted to poison the minds of citizens with subversive doctrines. Each individual may be amply indoctrinated in the correct ideology and efficiently trained for his special function with no needless concern for extraneous matters. Moreover, in terms of actual performance authoritarian systems have to their credit some remarkable records in the rapid development of literacy, for example, in nineteenth-century Japan and in twentieth-century Russia. Their success in training special agents and scientists has also been notable.

However, in education and culture, as in the administration of justice, the major source of authoritarian strength is even more significant as a source of weakness. By its very nature authoritarian cultivation of citizens must consist largely of indoctrination and training that have no place for those liberal studies essential to education at its best. Authoritarian systems can never, for fear of implanting ideas that threaten their rigid regimes, allow free inquiry in the fields of social thought, art, literature, and philosophy, in which much of the best in human culture has been achieved; even scientific imagination begins in time to decline under the deadening demands of their ideological rigor.

Representative democracies, however, have no incentive to discourage free inquiry. Rather they have every reason to encourage it, for only in its light can there develop a leadership sufficiently enlightened and flexible to carry on under the conditions of open debate in changing times. Only so, also, can a citizenry intelligent enough to choose and support competent leaders be evolved. Under democratic systems citizens have educational incentives that simply do not exist under authoritarianism, for when citizens are charged with making the basic decisions, the very fact that they must repeatedly make political choices and live with the consequences of these choices calls forth efforts to understand the issues such as are entirely lacking under authoritarian systems. Indeed, even some who criticize democracy have thought this great stimulus to its citizens the most significant of the merits of democracy. The appeal to the people's choices is, at the same time, quite as consistent with the use of expert leadership in education as elsewhere. Indeed, as responsibility breeds intelligence, intelligence will increasingly demand the most competent leadership available for the vital and difficult task of developing the minds of each new generation in the tradition of tolerance and the atmosphere of freedom. Moreover, although the public, to which educational leaders remain responsible, must be careful not unduly to hamper the work of the experts, the awareness of accountability to the public often serves to make the experts themselves sensitive to a wider range of values and needs than would otherwise be likely. Finally, and by no means least, since education in democracies is not all concentrated in the state but constantly operating through many different agencies, the culture of the people continuously receives fresh impulses from a variety of sources, and the range and freedom of state institutions themselves are sustained by the free inquiry of other institutions. If, therefore, only indoctrination and training are wanted, authoritarian education may be superior; but, if the growth of the enlightened and open mind and of the liberal spirit are also desired, then democratic education is far superior, and from the point of view of the cultivation of those capacities on which maximum value realization depends, the indispensability of the open mind and the liberal spirit is abundantly apparent.

With Respect to Freedom

Authoritarian systems differ considerably from one another in their attitudes toward freedom and our comparison of authoritarianism and democracy must take such differences into account. Some authoritarian systems, like that of Mussolini, have little regard for *freedom*, indeed, to quote their own advocates, they "spit upon freedom." Others, like the one advocated by the Nazis, claim that the individual's freedom is best attained in his participation in an authoritarian state which expresses the spirit of a superior race. Still others, like the communistic ones, contend that they alone can liberate men and women from the slavery to which capitalism subjects them.

Since the first of these three types of authoritarian systems admittedly has no use for any sort of freedom and the second presents only a very doubtful and perhaps ever self-contradictory concept of freedom, it is the third or communistic type of authoritarian system that we shall be concerned to compare with democracy with respect to contributions to freedom. Communism emphasizes economic freedom; democracy stresses political, juridical, and religious freedom. From the point of view of the ethical ends of the state all of these kinds of freedom are of vital importance.

With reference to each of the last three kinds of freedom the facts as well as the claims of democratic states seem to place the advantages fairly clearly on the side of democracy. Politically, whereas in authoritarian states people may neither speak nor write nor assemble freely, nor choose their candidates, nor vote their preferences, all these privileges are cherished in democracies. Juridically, whereas in authoritarian systems neither one's person nor his goods are safe from arbitrary seizure or destruction, in democratic systems one's person and property are, in principle, inviolable so long as he observes the law of the land. Religiously, whereas in authoritarian states worship is considered an instrument of the state and independent worship, if tolerated at all, is severely penalized, in democratic systems freedom of religion is encouraged as essential to the good life and a source of wholesome criticism of governmental activities.

The question that remains is that of the effect of communistic authoritarian government upon economic freedom versus the effect of democratic institutions upon such freedom. Now there can be no doubt that in some capitalistic democratic systems some people are in effect economically disenfranchised and deprived, even amid free political institutions, of effective freedom. However, since genuinely democratic governments are responsible to all of their people, they are more competent in the long run both to cope with restrictions upon the freedom of those now suffering special economic disabilities and to preserve the freedom of all others than are the governments of any other kinds of states. Even when political democracy is very inadequately achieved and government tends to be dominated by capital, the state in which democracy is even seriously attempted is likely to maintain a greater degree of economic freedom for its people than any authoritarian one, and the prospect of progress in this area is surely far better. Authoritarian states tend to determine for worker and producer alike where he shall operate and what he shall do, and for the consumer what he shall buy and how much he shall pay; in democratic states, on the other hand, although the need for some regulation is recognized, all these matters are kept as free as the interests of all permit.

In no one of the areas in which government ought to nurture freedom is any existing democracy perfect, nor has any system ever been devised in detail that can perfectly defend all of the basic freedoms, but so vital is democracy's support of freedom that even if democracy were less satisfactory elsewhere the general superiority of its conduciveness to value achievement would be sustained by this support. People who are on the whole favorably disposed toward democracy sometimes suggest that an authoritarian government would perhaps be the best form of government provided one could be assured of finding invariably good authorities, but such is the indispensability of freedom to the fullest value realization that government even by the best of dictators remains inferior to representative democracy.

Such considerations as the foregoing do not of course carry the argument concerning the best form of government through to detailed value consequences nor do they deal directly, with certain more specific questions concerning the best forms of government, such as the currently debated question whether the next steps in democratic government should be toward making government agents more independent of the people or toward making them more responsible to the people. In passing it may be remarked concerning this illustrative question that, although considerable scope must always be allowed for the recommendations of experts, the whole logic of the argument for democracy would seem to tend to encourage a greater degree of accountability to the people than has yet been attained in the modern world, and that modern means of communication would seem to make growth in this direction increasingly feasible. But, however this may be, the foregoing argument should at any rate be sufficient to suggest that the great current controversy between ideological authoritarianism and constitutional democracy is amenable to reasonable discussion and that when the main facts are duly considered in view of objectives of political activity, the overwhelming advantage is on the side of a form of government resting upon the consent of the governed and, though operating through representatives of majorities, maintaining effective constitutional guarantees of the rights of all individuals. If this much may now be at least tentatively assumed, we may pass on to the consideration of some problems of the ethics of democratic political orders.

RIGHTS OF CITIZENS OF DEMOCRATIC STATES

Basic to every democratic state, and quite as important as its majoritarian principle, is its insistence upon the protection of the rights of all its individual citizens. Without provision for the protection of the rights of minorities, majorities can become, as they have often done, as tyrannical as dictators.

The attempt to discuss rights almost invariably leads, however, to an apparent paradox. On the one hand, it seems absurd to talk about rights that are unsupported by the laws of the land and are not, and perhaps cannot be, realized. Yet, on the other hand, one can scarcely avoid thinking that people have rights that, though not sustained by the law or supported by citizens, ought to be so sustained and supported. For example, there seems to be a sense in which even the peasant farmers of Russia have a right to liberty, which in a legal and functional sense they surely do not have.

The paradox is intensified by the opposition of two frequently encountered theories of rights, each of which, while properly insisting on a significant aspect of rights, neglects the aspect stressed by the other. Thus, the theory of *natural rights* contends that rights are eternal and inalienable but fails to apprehend their temporal and institutional aspects, whereas the *conventionalist* theory properly recognizes the latter aspects but ignores the former.

The most satisfactory resolution of this paradox would seem to lie in taking the basic character of rights to be a moral one that involves a certain dependence of rights on circumstances but makes ample provision both for eternal and inalienable and for temporal and conventional aspects of rights. In terms of this approach a right of an individual is a privilege that, in the existing situation, other people *ought* in the strict moral sense to permit and would be morally wrong in preventing. More specifically, an objective moral right is a privilege such that, under existing conditions, for others to hinder its exercise would clearly tend to interfere with the achievement of maximum intrinsic value for all.

If this account is correct, some moral rights are eternal at least in the sense that since certain of the basic conditions of human life remain essentially constant, to hinder the activities requisite to the realization of value with reference to these conditions always tends to be wrong. Thus, for example, since certain activities are always necessary to the maintenance of life, and certain liberties to the good life, these activities and liberties would seem to be eternal rights. Other rights, though inalienable in the sense of being moral and neither created by the state nor removable by the state, are temporal in the sense that they are actually realizable only when certain conditions have been achieved. Thus, for example, although in any age every man has a right, which no state can justly prevent, to an equitable share in the material goods that are then available, it would be absurd to say that in a given period every man had a right to a standard of living technically impossible for that age to achieve. Some rights, though moral, are neither eternal nor alienable but are conventional and legal in that, in the implementation of more basic rights, customs and laws have been chosen that, though not in themselves better than alternative ones, ought, having been chosen, to be conformed to in the interest of harmony. In this category would fall, for example, many of the rights involved in traffic laws and some of those regarding property relations. Finally, it should be noted that privileges can be legal and conventional, though not moral and possibly even immoral. They are sometimes called rights but are hardly properly so named. An instance of one variety of them occurs when an unjust law giving special privileges to some people interferes with the moral rights of others.

No complete list of rights can be drawn up for all time, for no one can foresee all future conditions. However, useful lists have been worked out for our own times upon which rather remarkable unanimity has been attained, at least in principle. An illustrative list, intended to apply impartially regardless of color, race, or creed, and composed largely by combining elements of three of the best-known statements, the American Declaration of Independence, the Bill of Rights of the Constitution of the United States, and the United Nations Universal Declaration of Human Rights, follows.

General: Right to life, liberty, security of person, and pursuit of happiness.

Expression: Freedom of speech, press, and other means of communication and of assembly.

Religion: Freedom of belief, teaching, ecclesiastical organization, and worship.

Movement: Freedom to move within the boundaries of one's own state, and to leave and return to one's state.

Political: Right to a nationality, to political asylum, to vote, and to hold office.

Juridical: Freedom from involuntary servitude, arbitrary arrest, torture, cruel or degrading punishments; right to recognition as a person before the law, to trial by impartial jury in open court, to security against unwarranted searches and seizures, to be confronted by one's own accusers, and to be assumed innocent until proved guilty.

Domestic: Right to marriage, the protection of the home, and special care of motherhood and childhood in cases of need.

Economic: Right to own property and not to be arbitrarily deprived of it, to work, to equal pay for equal work, to join a trade union, to a decent livelihood.

Recreation: Right to rest, leisure, holidays, and recreational facilities.

Education and culture: Right to education, to enjoyment of the arts, and participation in scientific achievement.

Some of these rights are eternal in the sense indicated above in that they tend to apply to human beings in all times and places. Such is, for example, clearly the case with the general rights; with the rights of freedom of religion; and with the rights of freedom from involuntary servitude, torture, and arbitrary arrest. Many of the rights listed, however, depend upon the ability of society to achieve them for the manner of their application, if not for their very existence. Thus, for example, what care of motherhood or childhood can be given, what property or work can be had, and what standard of living can properly be claimed depend upon the extent to which a civilization has achieved mastery over its environment.

No individual right is absolute in the sense that it may not in some dire emergency have to be suspended in the interest of all individuals. Thus, for example, the state sometimes justifiably calls upon a man to place his life or property in jeopardy for the sake of the whole community. But such a situation only suspends—it does not destroy—the rights in question for the sake of other rights; and on the whole the good of all demands a scrupulous observance of rights and only rare suspension of any of them.

Problems concerning which rights should be supported by laws, and which should not, at a given time are constantly occurring. For example, a major problem at the present time is that of the degree of freedom of speech and of assembly to be allowed to those whose avowed purpose is the overthrow of the existing mode of government. A classic statement upon this point is that of the late Supreme Court Justice, Oliver Wendell Holmes, who resisted all limitations upon freedom of speech save where a "clear and present danger" could be proved. Holmes wrote:

The ultimate good desired is better reached by free trade in ideas. The best test of truth is the power of the thought to get itself accepted in the competition of the market. We should be eternally vigilant against attempts to check the expression of opinions that we loathe and believe to be fraught with death, unless they so imminently threaten immediate interference with the lawful and pressing purposes of the law that an immediate check is required to save the country.

This answer, however, only brings the problem to focus; for, even when the "clear and present danger" principle is accepted at full value, debate continues as to the extent of the present danger. Another closely related problem is that of the right of a person under examination by a loyalty review board to be confronted by his accusers. On this point another Supreme Court Justice has suggested that perhaps "in choosing a hearing method, the Government is then stuck with a due process hearing, and nothing short of a due process hearing." On one side of this issue are those who claim that adherence to usual civil rights in security cases would dry up sources of government information and jeopardize the nation. On the other side are those who say that disregard for such civil rights involves even greater jeopardy to the nation. And in fact the security of the nation is scarcely worth preserving unless the nation protects the rights of the individuals who constitute it. A third current problem concerning moral and legal rights is that of the degree of rigor and speed with which the rights of children to desegregated schools should be pressed in areas in which customs of another sort have long prevailed.

Even though no individual or group ought in the strict moral sense to be hindered in the exercise of rights, an individual or group is not necessarily right in the higher moral sense in insisting upon all that he takes to be included in his rights or even upon all that is in fact included in his rights. For one thing, he may be mistaken about his rights, and such is each man's tendency to overrate his own rights that, if all men seriously pressed all the rights they thought themselves entitled to, harmonious social life might become virtually impossible. Further, even when one is correct about his rights, temporary suspension of them may at times be better than pressing them against possibly valid counterclaims. A man sometimes has a right, and in the higher sense even a duty, to forego his rights. However, generally speaking, individuals and groups are right in standing up for their rights for the sake of the interest immediately involved, for the sake of the lasting establishment of their own rights, and for the sake of similar rights of others. Rights long neglected tend to be obscured. The one initially most likely to support an individual's rights is that individual himself, and the obligation to defend his rights is primarily his own. But others also have an obligation to support the rights of each, and the impartiality of the support of the rights of one man by other parties sometimes gives this support an influence substantially greater than that of a man's defense of his own rights.

DUTIES OF CITIZENS OF DEMOCRATIC STATES

Since the ability of the state to secure the rights of its citizens or to perform any other significant function depends upon the activity of its citizens, the duties of citizens are quite as important as their rights; and, since people are more inclined to stress their rights than their responsibilities, emphasis upon the latter may even be considered more important. For the most part one's duties as a citizen are not very different from his duties as a man. In general, the best that a man can do for his country is to be an intelligent man of upright character, an honest contributor to his country's economy, and a good husband, father, friend, and member of community groups. Nevertheless the specific character of the state as an organized national community is such as to require at least some duties of citizenship beyond the more general ones of manhood.

The Defense of the Nation

If a principal function of the state is the security of its citizens against foreign aggression, then one of the chief duties of citizens is participation, either directly or indirectly, in the defense of the nation. Such defense must in the nature of the case be a joint enterprise, and, under modern conditions, it requires virtually unanimous cooperation. Any individual or group that stands aside to let others carry the load unbalances the burden, creates disunity, and tempts others to do likewise in a manner that can quickly undermine the security of all. Unless such a person sincerely believes that armed defense is morally wrong, his conduct seems to be an irresponsible shirking of duty; and even if he does have such scruples, he would appear, however subjectively innocent or even praiseworthy, to be objectively wrong. We shall, however, return to this subject.

Obedience to Law

As the state's support of security against foreign aggression involves a duty of defense, so its maintenance of internal order through the administration of justice entails a duty of obedience to law. Only where habitual respect for and obedience to law is sustained can there be a state at all, and only where these are deeply ingrained can harmony be attained or progress be freely made. Every act of disobedience to any law tends by so much to break down obedience to all law and hence to destroy both the usefulness and the very existence of the state. That one disapproves of some laws by no means by itself excuses breaking them, for, since laws are scarcely needed at all in areas of life in which there is no disagreement, the breaking of disapproved laws would jeopardize nearly all laws. Many laws, in fact, that should never have been made are better obeyed than disobeyed; for, although the attempt to change them may be wholly beneficial, the willful violation of them is likely to damage the basic fabric of society.

Nevertheless, at times laws not only may—but ought—to be

disobeyed. When their enactment and enforcement is tyrannous, arbitrary, and without provision for fair reconsideration, or when their demands are for action in violent opposition to human decency and basic morality, despite the evil involved in their violation, even greater evils may be entailed in obedience to them. In such cases violation of laws would seem to be justifiable. Constitutional democracies are scarcely likely to demand extreme immoralities, and when their laws are unjust or unwise, peaceful remedies are nearly always available. For this reason, occasions for justifiable disobedience rarely, if ever, occur in such states. But where no peaceable means of rectification is available, democratic theory has always recognized a right of disobedience and even, in extreme cases, of revolution. If no such rights exist, the oppressed are thwarted by both physical and moral force, a situation that is scarcely compatible with the greatest good for all. Any who consider the exercise of such rights, however, take upon themselves a heavy responsibility and have to contemplate the probability of serious consequences both for themselves and for others.

Defense of the Rights of Minorities

Since, in claiming his own rights, one legitimately expects his fellow citizens to come to the support of these rights, he must, in the interest of the common good, be ready to do the same for the threatened rights of others. In democratic systems constitutions and laws are intended to defend the rights of all, but when, as often happens, existing laws prove insufficient supports of rights, merely to obey these laws is not enough. Good citizens must demand the enforcement of old laws defending conceded rights and the enactment of new laws covering neglected rights. What is sometimes even more important, good citizens must also bring the force of their personal words and works to bear in private and community life on behalf of the rights of oppressed minorities. To fail in these duties is to acquiesce in situations that may bring all rights—including one's own—into jeopardy and to share responsibility for avoidable suffering of others that is incompatible with maximum human good.

Payment of Taxes

Since nearly all of the state's services to its citizens depend upon the use of material means, the payment of taxes is an essential duty of citizens. In an authoritarian state, where taxes are levied without representation and often arbitrarily for the benefit of rulers rather than people, such payment may justly be complained of and even perhaps justifiably avoided. But in a democratic state all have some voice through their representatives in determining tax and budget policies, and each is morally as well as legally responsible for his assigned share. Under favorable conditions the payment of his taxes may be among the most useful of all the contributions that a citizen makes to the common good; but when tax money is wrongly collected or misused, the remedy lies not in avoidance but in participation in reform movements. That the payment of taxes should be in proportion to income seems, despite occasional complaints, quite as it should be, for those who gain most draw most fully upon the resources, capacities, and protection of the community and should return most to it. Moreover, having essentially the same needs as others less fortunate, they have greater ability beyond need. Even so, the real burden of taxation tends to fall more heavily, not upon him who pays more, but upon him who is left with less when payments have been made.

Political Activity

By no means least among the duties of citizenship in a democracy is that of intelligent participation in political life. Where citizens become apathetic, power almost invariably falls into the hands of bosses who make their decisions in their own rather than the people's interests. The only remedy lies in intelligent public interest in political affairs. This involves a duty not only to vote but also to keep informed concerning current issues, to share in discussions, and, if possible, to participate actively in the making of party choices at the local level as well as at higher ones. It also involves a duty of qualified citizens to seek elective office and enter government services. Failure of able and good men to shoulder these responsibilities leaves them to the less qualified and morally questionable, to the detriment of all. The financial rewards of public service are often less than elsewhere, but the contribution to the common good can be extremely significant.

SPECIAL RESPONSIBILITIES OF AGENTS OF DEMOCRATIC GOVERNMENT

In the democratic state agents of the judicial, legislative, and administrative branches of government have essentially the same duties, as men and citizens, as anyone else; they are bound by the laws of the land and are accorded no special privileges save such as are required by the performance of their duties. Nevertheless, by virtue of the fact that as agents of governments, they are entrusted with the direction of major interests of the people and that the existence and satisfactory functioning of government depend on their meriting the confidence of the public, certain special duties devolve upon them that do not fall upon ordinary citizens in quite the same way. As governmental structures grow increasingly complex, these duties often become somewhat specialized and technical. For these reasons some states are working out extensive codes to guide their officials; but, in any case, public servants will always need sensitive discernment to keep in sane paths of justice, between the extremes of dangerous looseness and harsh rigidity. Although we cannot here enter upon problems of detail, a few broad principles may be profitably suggested.

Financial Integrity

Agents of government must, upon pain of forfeiting their rights to office and doing serious damage to the community, scrupulously avoid using public office for private gain. Thus the acceptance of gifts conditioned upon special favors is almost everywhere condemned by law as bribery. The acceptance of any sort of gift, whether conditions are stipulated or not, where the donor has a matter pending before a public official is also suspect, and so is the acceptance of large gifts even where no issue is at the time pending. These considerations do not mean, of course, that the public official may not accept ordinary untainted gifts from personal friends, for participation in public life does not forfeit the rights of private life; but they do mean that he must keep every aspect of his conduct above suspicion. A special sort of gift that may lead to difficulties consists of expensive entertainment by persons whose interests are deeply involved in an official's decisions. Limited contacts with a variety of interested parties may, of course, be useful in keeping administrators and legislators informed concerning the needs and wishes of their constituents, but when entertainment by a single interest becomes extravagant or frequent it tends to pass over into illegitimate persuasion. Even worse than the wrongful acceptance of gifts are demands by public officials for special favors or financial rewards from contractors with whom the government is dealing. Less serious, perhaps, but none the less damaging to public confidence, is the "padding" of expense accounts and the charging of costs of private undertakings to government expense. Correlative with the duties of the public servant to avoid all the abuses indicated here are duties on the part of citizens not only to refrain from offering bribes but also to provide, through tax programs and support of appropriate legislation, such pay for public servants as will enable them to perform their duties without undue financial loss to themselves or excessive temptations to abuse their privileges; but failure of citizens to do these things is not, of course, to be construed as excusing looseness in the conduct of officials.

Freedom from Questionable Involvements

A second special duty of a public official is the careful avoidance of involvements that, though ordinarily proper enough, might in the particular capacity in which he serves entail special temptations to disloyalty or favoritism or create suspicion of these offenses. For example, although membership in organizations, or frequent association with persons, not outlawed but

generally considered subversive is not a crime or even necessarily wrong, a public official who accepts such memberships or
engages in such associations may cast doubts upon his loyalty
in such fashion as to undermine his usefulness. Similarly, although business leadership is quite proper in its own sphere, a
public official who holds extensive interests, or retains board
membership, in a concern with which his branch of government
deals calls his impartiality in question in such a way that, ordinarily, either the business connection or the government position
must be surrendered. Other cases in point occur, for example,
in the secret or illegal acceptance of funds from special interests
either for the winning of an election or for the support of interests favorable to one segment of the official's constituency
against others.

Impartiality

A third special duty of public officials is the avoidance of
favoritism. Nepotism, which gives coveted appointments to
members of the official's own family, has always been a source of
legitimate complaint, and the conscientious official will lean over
backward to avoid it. Appointments of personal friends whose
qualifications are inferior can be equally damaging and is more
difficult to prevent. The spoils system, though defensible insofar as it puts into policy-making jobs members of the elected
party, becomes a favoritism prejudicial to good government
when it makes appointments to which political views are irrelevant on the basis of party labels instead of competence.
Civil service systems are designed to overcome these evils and to
place people of proved ability in appropriate positions of responsibility. In view of their notable contributions in this connection such systems deserve maintenance and even extension.

Respect for Citizens

The other side of the duty of avoiding favoritism is that of
respecting the dignity and rights of every ordinary citizen. Elec-

ted public officials often scarcely need this warning, for they know that re-election depends in part on respect for constituents. But appointed officials, from cabinet members to policemen, often come to behave with arrogance and disregard of the worth and dignity of individuals, forgetting that they are the servants of the people rather than their masters.

Diligence in Office

Alongside the duty to respect the dignity and rights of ordinary citizens should be placed another homely and apparently obvious but often neglected duty of every public official, that of diligently, and, if possible, creatively, attending to the functions assigned to him. The responsibilities of public officials today are both large and extremely complex, and even routine duties are often demanding. Nothing short of constant inquiry and faithful performance all along the line will do, and such negligence and repeated absenteeism as often occur—for example, in legislatures—are morally as well as politically culpable. With the significant honors of public office go significant responsibilities, that no official can neglect without dishonor.

Political Fairness

A duty of governmental officials upon which the very existence of the constitutional democratic state hinges is that of political fairness or willingness to abide by the spirit as well as the letter of the constitution and laws. No constitution or law can be so constructed as to be proof against men who are determined to have their way regardless of it; and even the best of constitutions necessarily contain various devices that can be used to nullify their intent and ultimately to overthrow them. For example, if at election time each party is determined to win at any cost, public confidence may be so undermined by smear tactics as to make good government difficult and even, if the process be often repeated, impossible. Again, if a party once having gained power is determined so to do, it can use its advantage to break the power of the opposition and virtually to exclude the beneficial resistance of a loyal opposition.   In actual legislative and judicial procedures dozens of ways can be found, even within the letter of the law, to thwart the will of the people and break down constitutional government.   The defense of democratic government cannot, then, depend on codes alone but always requires, and fortunately has in this country on the whole found, a certain political restraint that is in the main willing to accept the limitations of law and political fair play.   But such restraint is not infrequently threatened, and every public official must seek to preserve it both in himself and in his associates.

Responsibility and Self-Reliance

The last of the special duties of government officials to be mentioned here must be approached, not from the point of view of an assertion, but from that of a problem of apparently conflicting responsibilities.   Consider the case of a United States Senator. Is he primarily responsible to his party, to the whole constituency of his state, to all the people of the United States, or in some sense to all mankind?   When the question to whom he is responsible is settled, is he responsible for the use of his own best judgment concerning their interests or is he to be expected to follow their specific mandates in each instance?   Leaving aside for the present other aspects of the matter, let us consider the single conflict between responsibility to the wishes of his state constituency and responsibility to use his own best judgment in their interests.   If his policies are determined solely in the light of his own judgment, they cease to be democratic; whereas, if they are guided only by his constituents' desires, democracy loses most of the advantages of representation by persons chosen for their special competence and of genuine legislative deliberation.   In this problem is epitomized a basic dilemma of democracy, for the problem repeats itself in connection with every elective or appointive office, and upon its resolution depends the drift of representative democracy in the direction of authoritarianism on the one hand or pure democracy on the other.   Insistence that officials at the same time adhere, concerning broad policies, to the platforms on which they are elected and retain considerable scope, concerning implementation, for their own enlightened judgment tends to preserve the benefits both of popular sovereignty and of enlightened leadership. How, specifically, the problem involved is to be worked out is one of the most difficult problems confronting present-day political science. In any case, it should be clear that the solution should be such as to facilitate the achievement of what the sovereign people upon due deliberation really want, and neither on the one hand an arrogant substitution of one's own purposes for those of the people nor on the other hand a demogoguery that tends eventually to defeat the purposes of the people. To this end an excellent constitution is a blessing of incalculable worth; but, since in democracy it is ultimately the people who decide, there can be no substitute for an enlightened people.

READINGS

Heffner, R. D., *A Documentary History of the United States*, pp. 13–16, 21–28, 70–79, 144–49, 204–23.

QUESTIONS

1. Aristotle thought that the end of the state was the good life, but many thoughtful people have been inclined to say that the least government is the best government. Are these statements contradictory? What truth, if any, is involved in each? How, if at all, can the apparent opposition between them be resolved?

2. In the course of a recent political campaign one of the candidates defined a "welfare state" as one in which the government attempts to take over economic functions intended to remain in the hands of Almighty God. Comment on the ethico-political assumptions implicit in this definition.

3. The claim is sometimes set forth that preference for democracy is only a prejudice of Western culture and that if one happens to have been reared in another kind of culture a different type of government would be seen to be better. Sketch the answer that you would give to such an argument.

4. What do you consider the strongest argument in favor of authoritarian government? How, if at all, can this argument be met?

5. Plato argued that as in illness one wants the aid of a competent doctor and in travel that of an experienced pilot, the conduct of affairs of state should be entrusted to political experts. What flaws, if any, can you see in this analogy? How can democracy make use of its best brains without losing its distinctive merits?

6. How would you answer the claim that since effective rights are created only by the state, to speak of a duty of a state to defend rights that it does not recognize is idle talk?

7. Does the right of freedom of speech exist in Russia? If so, in what sense? In what sense, if at all, does the right to adequate medical care exist in America?

8. How would you reconcile the apparent conflict between the right to property and the right to work?

9. Ever since the time when Cain asked, "Am I my brother's keeper?" people have been inquiring why they should be responsible for the rights of their fellow citizens. Why should they? Why not leave the protection of rights to the government?

10. Persons who have on occasion defied the authority of the state include some of the worst criminals and some of the greatest moral heroes. How does one know which is which? What should be the attitude of a government toward the consciences of its people? What are the chief evils of disobedience to law?

11. Why shouldn't a person disobey a law that he knows to be useless or even harmful? If a person ever should disobey a law, indicate some circumstances under which he should.

12. In order to protest against an unjust city ban on all political activities of teachers a group of teachers deliberately sent to certain councilmen a signed petition advocating the re-election of those councilmen. The ordinance was subsequently withdrawn, largely as a result of this action. Was this disobedience to law justified? Why, or why not?

13. How would you distinguish between a bribe and a friendly gift to a government official? What precisely is the difference between one's duties as a friend and his duties in public office? When does the awarding of a government contract to a company owned by a friend become questionable favoritism?

14. If government properly rests on the consent of the governed, how can the adoption of the policies against which a minority has

voted be justified?   How can the threat of tyranny of majorities best be avoided?

15. A Senator has been elected in good faith by a constituency to which he acknowledges responsibility.   A Gallup poll has revealed that a majority of his constituents would vote for a pending piece of legislation.   However, in the light of his special training and knowledge the Senator sincerely believes the measure to be against the people's interest.   How should he vote?   Name some questions that you think should be decided by the people and some that should be left to experts.

REFERENCES

Appleby, P. H., *Morality and Administration in Democratic Government* (Baton Rouge: Louisiana State University Press, 1952).

Aristotle, *Politics,* tr. by Harris Rackham (New York: Putnam, 1932).

Ascoli, Max, *The Power of Freedom* (New York: Farrar Straus, 1949).

Becker, Carl, *The Declaration of Independence* (New York: Harcourt, Brace, 1922).

Bosanquet, Bernard, *The Philosophical Theory of the State* (New York: Macmillan, 1899).

Brunner, Emil, *The Divine Imperative, A Study in Christian Ethics,* tr. by Olive Wyon (Philadelphia: Westminster Press, 1947), Chs. 36–39.

Cabot, R. C., *Honesty* (New York: Macmillan, 1938), Ch. 7.

Cahn, Edmond, *The Moral Decision: Right and Wrong in the Light of American Law* (Bloomington, Ind.: Indiana University Press, 1955).

Carritt, E. F., *Ethical and Political Thinking* (London: Oxford University Press, 1947).

—— *Morals and Politics* (London: Oxford University Press, 1935).

Castell, Alburey, *An Elementary Ethics* (Englewood Cliffs, N.J.: Prentice-Hall, 1954), pp. 200–17.

Catlin, George, *The Story of the Political Philosophers* (New York: McGraw-Hill, 1939).

Clark, G. H., and Smith, T. V., *Readings in Ethics* (2nd ed., New York: Appleton-Century-Crofts, 1946), Ch. 9.

Commager, H. S., *America in Perspective* (New York: New American Library, 1947).

Croce, Benedetto, *Politics and Morals* (New York: Philosophical Library, 1945).

Dewey, John, *Freedom and Culture* (New York: Putnam, 1939).

―――― and Tufts, J. H., *Ethics* (rev. ed., New York: Holt, 1932), Ch. 17.

Douglas, P. H., *Ethics in Government* (Cambridge: Harvard University Press, 1951).

Douglas, W. O., *An Almanac of Liberty* (Garden City: Doubleday, 1954).

Drake, Durant, *Problems of Conduct* (2nd rev. ed., Boston: Houghton Mifflin, 1935), Chs. 23, 26, 27.

Ebenstein, William, *Great Political Thinkers* (New York: Rinehart, 1951).

Garvin, Lucius, *A Modern Introduction to Ethics* (Boston: Houghton Mifflin, 1953), Chs. 17, 18.

Hobhouse, L. T., *Metaphysical Theory of the State: A Criticism* (New York: Macmillan, 1918).

Hocking, W. E., *Present Status of the Philosophy of Law and of Rights* (New Haven: Yale University Press, 1926).

―――― *The Spirit of World Politics* (New York: Macmillan, 1932).

Hofstader, Richard, *The American Political Tradition* (New York: Vintage Books, 1954).

Lindsay, A. D., *The Modern Democratic State* (New York: Oxford University Press, 1947).

Lippmann, Walter, *The Public Philosophy* (Boston: Little, Brown, 1955).

Locke, John, "An Essay Concerning the True Original Extent and End of Civil Government," in E. A. Burtt (ed.), *The English Philosophers from Bacon to Mill* (New York: Random House, 1939), pp. 403–503.

MacIver, R. M., *The Web of Government* (New York: Macmillan, 1947).

Meiklejohn, Alexander, *Free Speech and Its Relation to Self-Government* (New York: Harper, 1948).

Mill, J. S., *Representative Government* (New York: Harper, 1867).

Niebuhr, Reinhold, *The Children of Light and the Children of Darkness* (New York: Scribner, 1950).

―――― *Faith and History* (New York: Scribner, 1949).

Ortega y Gasset, Jose, *The Revolt of the Masses* (New York: New American Library, 1952).

Orwell, George, *Nineteen Eighty-Four* (New York: Harcourt, Brace, 1949).

Padover, S. K., *Thomas Jefferson on Democracy* (New York: New American Library, 1953).

Patterson, C. H., *Moral Standards* (New York: Ronald, 1949), Ch. 18.

Perry, R. B., *Realms of Value* (Cambridge: Harvard University Press, 1954), Chs. 13, 14, 16.

———— *Shall Not Perish from the Earth* (New York: Vanguard, 1940).

Plato, "The Republic," *The Dialogues of Plato,* tr. by Benjamin Jowett (New York: Random House, 1937), pp. 591–879.

Popper, K. R., *The Open Society and Its Enemies* (Princeton: Princeton University Press, 1950).

Pound, Roscoe, *The Relation of Law to Morals* (Chapel Hill: University of North Carolina Press, 1926).

Pratt, J. B., *Reason in the Art of Living* (New York: Macmillan, 1949), Ch. 25.

Riesman, David, *The Lonely Crowd* (New Haven: Yale University Press, 1950).

Robinson, D. S., *Political Ethics, Political Ideals* (New York: Crowell, 1935).

Rousseau, J. J., *The Social Contract* (Everyman ed., New York: Dutton, 1913).

Russell, Bertrand, *Freedom versus Organization, 1814–1914* (New York: Norton, 1934).

Smith, T. V., and Lindeman, Edward, *The Democratic Way of Life* (New York: New American Library, 1953).

Spitz, David, *Patterns of Anti-Democratic Thought* (New York: Macmillan, 1949).

Tead, Ordway, *The Case for Democracy, and Its Meaning for Modern Life* (New York: Association Press, 1938).

Titus, H. H., *Ethics for Today* (2nd ed. rev., New York: American Book, 1954), Chs. 24–26.

Tocqueville, Alexis de, *Democracy in America 1835–1840,* tr. by Henry Reve (New York: Vintage Books, 1954).

Tsanoff, R. A., *Ethics* (rev. ed., New York: Harper, 1955), Ch. 16.

Wahlke, J. C. (ed.), *Loyalty in a Democratic State* (Boston: Heath, 1952).

Weldon, T. D., *States and Morals* (New York: McGraw-Hill, 1947).

Wheelwright, Philip, *A Critical Introduction to Ethics* (rev. ed., New York: Odyssey Press, 1949), Ch. 12.

Wilde, Norman, *The Ethical Basis of the State* (Princeton: Princeton University Press, 1924).

19

The Ethics of
International Relations

THE AREA OF ETHICS with which we are now to deal differs from those thus far considered in at least two important respects. First, the relations of the international area are not primarily among persons or even among persons and organized bodies but mainly among nation-states. Second, whereas activities in all the other areas are for the most part already subject to established law, only limited aspects of international relations are as yet subject to effective legal control. Partly as a result of these two differences the conduct of international relations, though in some instances carried on with a fairly high sense of moral responsibility, has often been a chaos of moral irresponsibility. The most elementary rules of ethics, which statesmen and diplomats would not think of violating in their personal relations or in dealing with their own governments, are often almost completely disregarded in transactions between nations; and diplomacy and morality are not infrequently thought of, in Machiavellian terms, as irrelevant to one another.

In the past nations could afford, while deploring this sort of amorality in their relations with one another, to let it pass without being seriously challenged; when warfare was limited and nations could function in relative isolation, they could survive even when relations between them broke down in armed conflict. However, of late two new factors have drastically altered this situation. One is the growth of determined world revolutionary movements willing to stop at nothing in the effort to spread their ideologies and ways of life. The other is an amazing growth of technology that has suddenly brought all the world very close together and placed in men's hands weapons capable of obliterating entire nations. In such a situation whether or not ethics applies to the international situation is no longer in any sense a merely academic question. The cultivation of a morality for relations among nations becomes an imperative necessity that must now in some respects take precedence over all other areas of moral development.

The current problems of a morality of international relations are of two somewhat different kinds. Owing, among other things, to the radically new features of the international situation, sound ethical development in the international order requires that some of the old accepted patterns be broken and some new ones established. The problem of possible new patterns will concern us in the last section of this chapter. Until such patterns are worked out, however, international relations have to be conducted within the framework of existing ones, and it is with the ethics of international relations within this framework that we shall be primarily concerned in the next three sections.

OBJECTIVES OF AN ETHICAL FOREIGN POLICY

The foremost ethical question with regard to any area of conduct is that of its ultimate aims; and, since the conduct of international relations operates mainly through foreign policies, our first question here will concern the ethical aims of such policies. What, when all the relevant factors are considered, *ought to be* the aims of a foreign policy? To what end would a nation conduct its relations with other nations if its policies were fully ethical or morally right?

To the question, on what bases *are* the foreign policies of a nation such as ours usually debated, the answer is fairly plain. The characteristic issue discussed, for domestic audiences at any rate, is simply whether or not a proposal under consideration furthers the interests of the nation, the interests in question being not necessarily limited to short-term gains but often including the long-term interests of security and sustained prosperity as well. Trade agreements; technical, military and financial assistance; and other programs helpful to other nations are indeed at times considered and adopted, but almost the sole basis of discussion is likely to be whether or not these programs further our own military and economic interests. Arguments largely in terms of national self-interest are characteristic not alone of ultraconservatives and superpatriots but also of leaders of all shades of political opinion. Thus, for example, the conservative representative Bruce Barton rejects all crusades and wishes to build foreign policy solely upon "cold self-interest." Similarly, our middle-of-the-road President argues for reciprocal trade largely as a matter of "enlightened self-interest"; and the more liberal diplomat George F. Kennan argues that "our national interest is all that we are capable of knowing." Even the Socialist Norman Thomas was recently heard to say that in seeking a settlement with the Russians he would inform them that we cared nothing for them but that our self-interest and theirs demanded some agreement. Such statements as these do not mean that either national leaders, such as those cited, or people generally have no other concern in international affairs than national self-interest. They do mean that self-interest has become the dominant touchstone and almost the sole basis of appeal in debating international issues. All other approaches are likely to be shouted down as mere sentimentalism or even treason. Even leaders who adhere in their own thought to broader objectives are well aware of this trend and so, like others, tend to support even their more generous programs almost exclusively in terms of national self-interest.

Our suggestion at this point is that, although national self-interest, like personal self-interest, has its proper sphere, attempts to determine foreign policy exclusively in terms of it are morally inadequate and wrong, and that the only kind of objective that is either morally adequate or ultimately practical is one that embraces the interests of all human beings of all nations and involves willingness if necessary to make some material sacrifices for the end of human welfare. That the moral objectives of international relations must be thus universal in scope would scarcely seem, in the light of our whole previous discussion, to need arguing. No man is ever right in attending to only his own interests when the interests of others are involved, and the involvement of the interests of others does not suddenly cease at national boundaries. In the light of current economic interdependence and of the mutual capacities of nations to obliterate one another, the interests of people are at some points even more deeply affected by events that occur outside their borders than by what goes on within them. To act, or even to think, in disregard of the interests of people of other lands is wrong in any age; in the present age it may result in the commission of unbelievably horrible crimes against humanity.

Is our suggestion, however, practical? If it really is moral in the objective sense that we have treated as basic throughout this book, it certainly is practical in the broadest sense, for the right is by definition the conduct that is best in the circumstances. Morally to aim at human welfare is not to be duped by cynical propaganda or frightened into appeasement by display of force. It is, rather, to size up every situation in terms of utter realism and then direct one's conduct toward a clear humanitarian objective in the full light of the facts as they are. Nothing could be more practical. But many people demand practicality also in the special sense of preserving one's own interest. Even here, however, the broader humanitarian ideal is on the whole more practical than the narrower nationalistic one. The greatness of a nation, in which its citizens share, does not consist alone in wealth and military power but even more in moral and spiritual stature, and only in action guided by humanitarian ends does a nation gain such stature. Yet even in terms of wealth and military security such a nation as ours will apparently lose nothing by directing its efforts to world order rather than national interest only. For example, if promotion of world order requires the fuller growth of world production and the freer flow of world trade, whatever our contributions to these may cost us in the short run seems almost certain to be more than repaid to us, even financially, in the long run. Moreover, our own military security, already demanded for world security, will be greatly enhanced by the growth of that of other free nations. Most of all, however, broadly humanitarian ends are more practical than coldly self-interested ones in terms of international good will toward the nation that acts in the light of them. No nation can debate international programs at home purely on the basis of self-interest and expect other nations abroad to be impressed with its generosity; and other nations are not particularly interested in supporting any nation's cold self-interest. In the long run the purposes that direct actions are felt by the recipients. Cold self-interest that may be turned, when convenient, against a now-benefited nation breeds similar self-interest in that nation; but good will, even in less costly actions, breeds reciprocating good will; and only with the aid of the good will of other nations can any nation remain great or strong.

The objection may of course be raised that no matter how good an ideal the welfare of all may be, the ideal of national interest is the only one that the people of a nation will support. Even here, however, humanitarianism is more practicable than it may seem. Latent in the whole Judaeo-Christian orientation of the culture of Western civilization, as well as in human nature itself, is a vast reservoir of potential good will that need not be confined within national borders. Moreover, most people in the main desire to do what is right; and if leaders of thought and action can begin to direct people's attention to the rightness of humanitarian ideals and so to link these ideals with the substantial resources of this rational desire, there is no reason why the sort of social purposes that influence interpersonal relations should not come to play a more significant role in international ones.

Until there is a reorientation of the objectives of foreign policies to include larger elements of avowed purpose to promote human ends as well as national ones, nations will continue to make tragic mistakes that could have been avoided through broader objectives, and even when they make the right choices they will not reap the best rewards if they act for wrong reasons. The obligation to orient national policy to humanitarian ends does not, of course, give the statesman the right forthwith to begin to direct his action to ends not approved at all by the people whom he represents.   It does indicate that candidates can stand for election on the basis of broader platforms, that those already in office can enlarge their purpose to the extent that their constituencies already would approve, and that ordinary citizens who see the larger right in these matters can support policies in accord with it.   Broad humanitarian ends, though indispensable to sound international morality, do not, however, in themselves dictate specific policies, and we must now seek some insights concerning what rights and obligations of nations these ends involve in existing circumstances.

RIGHTS OF NATION-STATES

Before considering any particular rights or duties of nation-states we must consider the sense in which nation-states may be said to have rights or duties at all.   An individual has moral rights in that, being a conscious center of intrinsic value realization, he may justly make claims the nonrecognition of which is clearly incompatible with maximum value realization for all. Similarly, he has duties because, as a responsible agent, he makes voluntary choices that either contribute to or hinder the achievement of maximum good.   Since the state is an effectively organized collection of human individuals, rather than an individual, it neither constitutes a center of consciousness nor makes voluntary choices, and hence has in the strictest sense neither rights nor duties.   Nevertheless, such is the importance of the state in the life of man that many rights of individuals depend on the recognition of something like rights in the state; and such is the capacity of individuals to coordinate their choices through the state that the state also acquires something like duties.   Provided then one keeps in mind that what are called rights and duties of states are entirely contingent upon those of individuals, considerable light can be thrown on the problems of international relations by thinking in terms of quasi-rights and quasi-duties of states. Such quasi-rights include among others the following.

Sovereignty

Prominent among the rights claimed by nation-states is sovereignty, or independence of any other authority. This right in the state may be thought of as being somewhat analogous to the right of life in the individual, in that when sovereignty is destroyed the state as such no longer exists. Historically the concept of sovereignty emerged along with the rise of the modern nation-state and in many ways exercised a wholesome influence. It tended to limit an ecclesiastical domination over nations that had often been disruptive, to end confusions of conflicting political authorities within nations, and to give to at least some rights of individuals the support of more or less stable government. At the present time the concept of sovereignty remains an important part of the functioning international order, and any nation that arbitrarily interferes with the sovereignty of another wrongs not only that nation but the whole family of nations, the tranquillity of which depends in considerable part upon the maintenance of a stable balance of sovereign powers.

Nevertheless, the right of sovereignty is not only not absolute but has less moral finality than the right of individuals to life. If the individual is destroyed, his capacity to achieve intrinsic values comes to an end, but if the sovereignty of the state, which even at best enjoys no intrinsic values, is destroyed, the individuals who compose the state may still realize values and indeed may suffer no loss in this respect. In any case, however valuable sovereignty may be at present, changes in the human situation may in time render it partially obsolescent. Indeed voluntary abridgments of it often take place even now, for example, whenever the authority of international law is acknowledged, a treaty signed, or an international organization joined. Instead of constituting the ruin of world order, as some fear, these modifications of sovereignty could even be the beginning of the making of a better world order but other aspects of this problem must wait for subsequent consideration. Meanwhile, one or two problems concerning application of the sovereignty in the world as it now is must be touched upon.

One such problem concerns the question: What groups of people are entitled to sovereignty? For the most part, what groups have in fact achieved and maintained sovereignty has depended on who had the purpose and power to do so. Nearly always, however, ethical considerations have been at least in some degree brought to bear upon disputes concerning these matters and sometimes these considerations have exercised a substantial influence. That ethical principles ought in fact to have a significant bearing here is sufficiently plain, but just what the required principles are is not easy to say. During World War I President Wilson proposed a doctrine of the self-determination of peoples that, if appropriately implemented, seems to be close to the ethical core of the matter. If democracy is ethically the most promising form of government, then presumably it ought to be in terms of essentially democratic principles that states should be instituted. This suggestion must not be taken to mean that numbers of other factors do not also need careful consideration in determining statehood. For example, ethnic, cultural, geographical, economic, and historical factors should all play significant roles. The difficulties of maintaining excessively small groups or of holding together very diverse ones, and the disruptive influence of frequent or sudden changes ought also to be duly considered. But when all such factors have been fully taken into account and all dangers adequately safeguarded, it is difficult to see how the determined purpose of the preponderance of the inhabitants of any considerable geographical area to constitute a sovereign state can ethically be thwarted by others unless such sovereignty can be shown, for some very special reason, seriously to jeopardize the security or well-being of all nations.

An important problem closely related to that of the determination of sovereignties is the problem of colonialism, or the maintenance of political authority by one nation-state over the people of another area. Actually, colonialism in the old style can scarcely be said to be advancing anywhere in the world. However, a new kind in which a nation is infiltrated and thus dominated both from within and from without by the agents of another nation is being extensively practiced by Communist countries. Most political moralists and most people of the free world are inclined to agree that in view of the rights of peoples to self-determination, no advancement of colonialism of any kind is now justified. This position, however, leaves unresolved the question of colonialism already in existence, which is at present the crucial issue.

Generally speaking, we may say with considerable confidence that the right of peoples to determine their own political destinies at present requires the fastest feasible withdrawal by colonial powers, for this is almost invariably what colonial dependencies now want and are demanding. There are, to be sure, complications. A third power may be already poised to step in as soon as the evacuation is complete to use the unfortunate colony for its own purposes. The colony may be deeply torn by internal conflict or for some other reasons not yet ready for self-government. Or the colony may have some strategic importance of world-wide significance such that at least the temporary maintenance of colonial status seems imperative for the security of all. A colonizing power may, whether it wishes to do so or not, have obligations to take such factors as these into account in the timing of its withdrawal. But such factors as these are all too often used as mere excuses for postponement; and, wherever there is a genuine and determined independence movement, no colonial power would seem to be justified in remaining any longer than necessary. Nor would any seem to be justified in remaining at all without genuine effort to assist in the rapid removal of those conditions that required its temporary presence.

Recognition

Closely related to the right of sovereignty and roughly corresponding to such personal juridical rights as that of equality before the law is the right of a nation-state to be recognized as sovereign by other nations. This refers both to formal recognition of its government and to the kind of factual recognition involved, for example, in respecting its territories and its territorial waters, according its agents and nationals the privileges of representatives of sovereign nations, respecting its air and sea rights, and giving it a status of equality before all international tribunals. That such recognition should be accorded to sovereign nations is essential, not only to the smooth flow of diplomatic relations, but also to that proper regard for the dignity of the various peoples of the earth to which they are entitled and to the maintenance of peace with justice throughout the world.

In this connection the question arises, When should formal recognition be granted a new government and when withheld? During most of modern history the usual practice has been, while not altogether ignoring the moral qualifications of the candidate for recognition, eventually to recognize any government that could in fact firmly establish itself as the ruling power in a given territory. In this matter, as well as in that of the determination of sovereignty, President Wilson undertook to inject a distinctively moral element. Since his time the policy of the United States in dealing with governments outside this hemisphere has tended to be to reserve recognition for those governments that seemed genuinely to represent their people and to have established themselves as reliable members of the family of nations. However, while sovereignties ought to be determined by the people's own choices, once they are determined, the ethically best policy with regard to formal recognition would seem to be in general a somewhat more realistic one analogous to our recognition of persons rather than the more moralistic one proposed by Wilson. In dealing with persons, while extreme moral perversions might cause us to withhold some privileges, we ordinarily recognize one as a person by virtue of his having certain broad human traits, reserving the question of the quality of his character for consideration as a separate question. A new government lacks initial status analogous to that which the very existence of an individual human being entails, and new governments flagrantly embroiled in belligerent or irresponsible action may scarcely be said to merit recognition.   Nevertheless, the analogy of the individual human being holds concerning governments in the sense that governments, like persons, are active policy-making realities that are actually encountered and must be practically dealt with for the good of all.   A government that is in fact firmly established as the ruling authority in a nation and has begun to show reasonable signs of international responsibility, would seem, in the interest of international order, to be best recognized even though it be not yet fully representative of its people or as responsible as might be wished.   On the one hand, refusal of recognition in such cases does not often change the facts but does render negotiations difficult and create serious tensions.   On the other hand, granting of recognition in such cases keeps the channels of international communication and adjustment open, avoids placing each individual nation in the impossible role of judge of the moral quality of all other nations, and carries no implication of moral approval with reference to such doubtful governments as must in any case be recognized.

Effective Voice in International Councils

Corresponding to the political rights of individuals to vote and to hold office is a right of every nation to be heard in the councils of nations in world organizations, and in the determination of treaty alliances.   A strong tendency has always existed for great nations to dominate and push their smaller neighbors about for their own ends as pawns in a sort of international game of chess, as is said to have been done, for example, at the Yalta Conference.   This tendency is, moreover, accentuated by the present concentration of atomic and hydrogen weapons in the hands of a few great powers.   However, if the legitimate self-respect of peoples is to be sustained, and peace and justice upheld every sovereign nation must be duly represented and heard.   Moreover, the influence of smaller nations, when duly felt, has often furnished a broadened perspective and a stabilizing ballast amid the more aggressively ambitious struggles of the great powers. These considerations need not of course imply that, as every individual has one vote in his nation, every nation is to have an exactly equal voice in the councils of the nations. All individuals are equal as centers of value-realization and of potential capacity to contribute to the value realizations of others, but nations consist of vastly different numbers of these personal centers of value-potentiality. Hence the roles of nations in international organizations must bear some relation to their sizes and capacities to contribute to the ends of such organizations. Some political philosophers have proposed that, like the United States Congress, an international organization should have one house, in which all nations would be represented according to population—and perhaps also power —and another in which each would be represented equally. Specifically this proposal is no better than some others, but the principle embodied in it, equal representation for some purposes and proportional for others, would seem to be in line with the facts of the situation as well as the ends of justice.

Industry and Trade

Roughly corresponding to such economic rights of individuals as those to ownership of property, to decent standards of living, and to equality of opportunity are rights of nations to produce, to trade, and to enter freely into agreements with other nations concerning these matters according to their potential capacities. Rights of this sort are infringed by positive action in interference with shipping upon the high seas and in all manner of discriminatory tariff and trade restrictions. They are also infringed by neglect whenever a nation is allowed to remain unable, through want of capital or technical knowledge, to develop its own natural and human resources. The evil involved in failure to sustain these rights is in some ways even more grievous than that involved in the failure of individuals to realize parallel rights; for, whereas the worst inequities among individuals tend in some degree to be overcome by birth and death in each generation, nations live on to perpetuate vast inequities and, in so doing, to produce untold suffering among backward peoples and to detract from the prosperity of the whole world economy through the unproductiveness of such peoples. The full exercise of these rights need not entail either removal of all tariffs or precise equality of economic opportunity for all nations, for tariffs may be justified in special cases, and it is individuals rather than nations that need full economic opportunity. Nevertheless these rights do require the removal of all but essential trade barriers and the cultivation of opportunities for each nation to develop materially to the full extent of its natural and human resources. The remedy of injustice in this area depends partly upon enlightened actions of individual nations in removing hindrances and in projecting extensive programs of economic and technical assistance, and partly upon unilateral and multilateral trade agreements; but, like the securing of most other national rights, it also depends partly upon the development of effective international organization.

Security of Citizens Abroad

A right of nations much discussed of late is that of the security of their citizens traveling or residing in other countries. On the one hand, that every nation owes its citizens some protection wherever they are and accordingly has a right at very least to bring its moral force to bear on behalf of justice for them is entailed in the citizenship relation as such and is beyond dispute. That a nation may also at times be justified in enlisting the aid of other nations in bringing moral and even economic pressures to bear in the interest of justice for its citizens abroad will also be widely acknowledged. On the other hand, that no nation has a right to claim for its citizens in other countries extraterritorial privileges, or exemption from the tribunals of those countries, is implicit in the sovereignty of those countries and is now rather generally recognized. These considerations, however, leave unsettled the difficult question, whether, when citizens of a nation are treated with gross injustice in other nations, that nation has a right to use force or the serious threat of it on behalf of its mistreated citizens. If the lives and liberties of the citizens in question and the correction of a certain type of international injustice were the only factors involved, the answer would surely be in the affirmative, for every human being is of inestimable worth and the doing of justice is always important. The fact is, however, that war, or the serious risk of it, involves comparatively little promise of saving the individuals in question, unjustly jeopardizes thousands of other innocent individuals, and perpetuates in its brutal methods a kind of injury to humanity that may far outweigh the injustice it sets out to correct. Hence we seem compelled to say that the right of a nation to intervene even on behalf of its unjustly treated nationals is limited by the potential injuries and injustices inherent in the procedure proposed for the enforcing of this right. This brings us to some general remarks about the whole problem of war itself.

Self-defense

Does a nation-state have a right to engage in warfare against other nations? For the most part an affirmative answer has been taken as axiomatic, though not always without qualms of conscience. What, one may ask, would a nation be, or how could it be sovereign, if it could not make war?

Nevertheless, it may be seriously doubted that a moral right to engage in *aggressive* warfare or to use war as an instrument for the furtherance of national policies at the expense of others has ever really existed. Some material gains have indeed accrued to some nations through such warfare; but even the victors have suffered great material and spiritual losses, and the vanquished have been subjected to horrible injustices and irreparable devastation. Throughout the centuries man's whole material and spiritual growth, his development of democratic institutions, and his orderly enjoyment of virtually all intrinsic values have been constantly undermined and destroyed by wars and threats of war, which have constituted probably the greatest of all preventable sources of human misery. If the wars of the past have been thus devastating, what shall we expect of those of an era in which the means are within reach to reduce the whole of human civilization to ashes and to preclude the effective survival of either victor or vanquished?

In view of the overwhelming evils of aggressive war, the tendency of each nation to regard the other as the aggressor, and the havoc unjustly wrought upon innocent people even by defensive war, many conscientious persons of pacifist persuasion have come to believe that not only aggressive war but even defensive war and all manner of military defensive measures are morally wrong, and that the whole effort of a nation in respect to other nations should be devoted to peaceful cooperation. Now in their strong and sometimes sacrificial protest against aggressive war and in their positive insistence upon the importance of peaceful cooperation, the pacifists have helped to drive home lessons that for human good or even survival can scarcely ever be too well learned. Moreover, such is the importance of the maintenance of free conscience and its criticism of governmental policies to the whole democratic way of life that even those members of the state who thoroughly disagree with pacifists ought to support their right to stand for what they believe.

Nevertheless, despite the wrongness of aggressive war and the service of pacifists in stressing this, the pacifist rejection of all military effort seems clearly to be ill-balanced and even at some points harmful in the present world situation, and the right of nations to military defense of humanity and justice must remain, at least until effective international order can be established. While seeing clearly enough the horrible consequences even of defensive war and the cost of military preparedness, the pacifists do not seem sufficiently to have envisaged the effects of full unilateral abandonment of arms. Even if enough people could be persuaded actually to bring defensive measures to a halt in a strong nation, the almost inevitable result would be that aggressive powers would immediately step in to fill the power vacuum. In the light of previous experience of modern totalitarian powers, the result would be the liquidation of enormous segments of the population of the occupied nation including most of its moral and intellectual leaders, the virtual cessation of the free flow of ideas, the rigorous control of its economy for foreign advantage, the elimination of all freedom of worship, and—worst of all—the domination of its entire educational system in order to impose upon the rising generation an enslaving ideology. The suggestion is sometimes made that eventually the captive nation would emerge from its bondage, and this suggestion may be correct, but even so the suffering and the degradation of the human spirit that would have to be endured during the period of enslavement stagger the imagination. Even the risk of war and the cost of preparation for it do not entail evils so great as these. Actually, there is little prospect that pacifist views will come to be sufficiently widely accepted in any great nation to bring about unilateral disarmament; and, this being so, advocacy of these views may in fact—despite the best of intentions —result in a weakening of the will of free nations to resist aggression and thus encourage aggression.

Concerning the difficult question, when war in self-defense or in defense of international justice is justifiable, we can here offer only a few general remarks. Such are the devastating consequences even of defensive war that a major end of every nation's activity, even when no war is imminent, should be so to conduct its affairs as to remove tensions that lead to war and to preserve peace. Even self-defense is not a sufficient moral justification for war if the total probable consequences of the war for all are worse than those of yielding. Only when even the tragic evils of war and all its consequences are outweighed by the prospect of even greater evils in refusing to fight is war ever justified; and such today are the unbelievable horrors of war that almost anything is better than war. For the nations fully to renounce the use of force apart from international policing would be to put the peoples of the world at the mercy of any nation that might choose to turn gangster, and unfortunately there are always nations willing to be persuaded to assume that role in the absence of external deterrent forces. The practicable alternative to war in our era would accordingly seem to be not the absolute renunciation of force but the maintenance of reasonable defenses together with patient concerted efforts to achieve world community until such efforts render both war and vast armaments altogether obsolete.

DUTIES OF NATION-STATES

Since the rights of any nation are secure only as every nation adheres to its responsibilities, and men's duties are always more within their control than their rights, the duties of nations are at least as important as their rights.   Remembering that the duties of nations, like their rights, depend in the end upon individual relationships, some instructive insights concerning the duties of nations may nevertheless be gained by observing parallels between them and the duties of individuals.   Some of the major duties of nations are as follows.

National Self-interest

As the individual is obligated to be prudent, or to act, other things being equal, in accord with the demands of his own best interest in the long run, so also is the state.   To such an extent is national self-interest ordinarily taken to be an obligation, or even the supreme obligation, of the state that the need for concern with this interest requires little further vindication, although prudence on the national scale is far from being satisfactorily achieved.

Usually national self-interest is interpreted largely in material terms of security and prosperity, and the interests of the present and immediate future often tend to obscure essential long-term interests.   Actually, not only are the spiritual values associated with national policy quite as important as material ones, but, as Toynbee has so forcefully pointed out, the survival of a civilization depends in the end primarily upon the spiritual caliber of that civilization.   Moreover, that self-interest should be construed in terms of the long as well as the short run is even more essential where nations are concerned than where individuals are.

The course of each separate life is relatively quickly run, but the life of a nation goes on to shape the destinies and determine the value realizations of generations of individuals yet unborn.

Justice

Is there a duty of nations not only to promote their own national interests but also to be just in dealing with other nations? The reply of Machiavelli, who expressed the spirit of a large part of modern diplomacy, was somewhat as follows. It is the primary business of the sovereign—which in a democratic state is the people—to preserve the state whatever may be the cost. Such preservation will often require seeming just but not necessarily being so. A nation must be gentle or severe, fair or unfair, straightforward or devious as suits its interests. It must play other nations off against one another, weakening the strong and strengthening the weak according to its own purposes, having, as a later writer puts it, no friends but only interests. Essentially, therefore, justice is irrelevant in international affairs, and the attempt to achieve it at the expense of more pressing national interests may be not only not right but even culpable disloyalty.

This somewhat cynical approach to the subject calls attention to at least one important fact about international relations that no sane ethics of the subject can afford to ignore. Since international affairs are conducted, not in an orderly framework in which legal authority stands ready to secure justice for aggrieved parties, as are personal affairs, but in a lawless chaos of conflicting sovereignties, international relations cannot at present be accompanied by quite the same spirit of full openness and mutual trust that often prevails in personal relations. In today's world a nation must preserve essential safeguards, proceed with caution, and be prepared to deal with the bad faith it may encounter.

Neither this consideration nor any other, however, affords a legitimate reason for neglecting the claims of justice in international relations. These claims do not rest, as Hobbes and others have supposed, upon the prior existence of a political authority to enforce them; rather, they are rooted in the basic demands of the maximum good for all in the actual conditions of human life. Indeed, they constitute, as we have seen, the very core of the demands of the maximum good for all; and, because the consequences of their violation are vastly more severe on the national scale than on the personal one, their importance on the national scale is at least as great. In view of the size of the units and the lack of a fully effective international authority, specific applications of justice in international relations must often be very different from those of the personal relations; but that disinterested and impartial integrity, basic equality before international tribunals, and distribution of rewards in some proportion to services ought to be maintained among nations is scarcely subject to doubt on ethically plausible grounds.

The moral demand for justice does not entitle statesmen to conduct the foreign relations of their nations purely in accord with their personal codes of justice. Statesmen, at any rate in democratic societies, are agents of sovereign people. They are delegated to use their own judgment only in the implementation of broad policies determined by the people and hence are not entirely at liberty to act as they as individuals would think best. The demand for justice in international relations does mean, however, that the people of a nation ought to be aware of the claims of international justice and conform their purposes to them. It means also that statesmen ought to adhere as fully to demands of international justice as the purposes of the people permit; and this would seem to be a good deal more closely than their usual practices would suggest, for ordinary people are often as much concerned with international justice as are their more expert leaders.

Conciliation

When two individuals are at odds with one another, they ought to endeavor to come to some agreement, either alone or with the aid of others; and when the attempt fails, the state still forbids their fighting and stands ready to mediate their dispute. When two great nations are at odds with one another, they also ought to seek agreement; but when they fail, no international organization is as yet able to prevent their fighting or to enforce its recommendations. Therefore the duty of conciliation or effort to arrive at agreement through mutual concessions and voluntary arbitration is much more important in international than in interpersonal relations. Conciliation as it is conceived here is a proper mean between a self-righteous rigidity that presumes the possession of a monopoly upon justice and is ready to fight all who disagree and an appeasement that, in the interest of peace and regardless of justice, yields to the other whatever he demands. Unlike the belligerently rigid nation, the conciliatory one recognizes, as any man or nation must, that its views could conceivably be wrong and it stands ready to offer reasonable concessions in exchange for comparable ones of other nations. At the same time, unlike the appeasing nation, the conciliatory one refuses to ignore the claims of justice and, adhering to its principles, makes such concessions as it does make with the claims of justice as well as those of peace in mind. It seeks agreement both unilaterally and multilaterally, by open discussion and *mutual* understanding, and failing that, it turns to the best available international arbitrational machinery, knowing full well that no party, whether individual or nation, is altogether a fair judge in its own quarrel.

Responsibility

A nation may at the same time promote its own long-term interests, be just and properly conciliatory, and still endeavor to implement its broad foreign policy along any one of three major lines. A nation that follows a policy of *isolationism,* while fulfilling international agreements and other previously established responsibilities, endeavors, as far as possible, to avoid entering into new agreements or taking on further responsibilities and concentrates all its energies upon building up to its own economic and military forces. A nation that follows a policy of *containment* enters into agreements with all friendly nations with the single-minded purpose of keeping potential enemies strictly in check and hindering their further advances. A nation that follows a policy of *constructive international cooperation* endeavors not only to avoid infringements upon its national rights but actively to achieve harmonious relations among nations. Both of the first two policy lines are hopelessly inadequate to the ends of a genuinely ethical foreign policy in such an age as ours. The first completely ignores the interests of people of all other nations and in doing so does dangerous disservice to its own interests also. Whether they will or no, all nations are now bound together by unseverable bonds of interdependence, and the nation that does nothing to surround itself with friends is likely to find itself shut in by enemies that threaten its swift destruction or slow strangulation. The second policy is broader than the first but still falls short of ethical ends by leaving out of account at least the interests of its potential enemies. It may also, in the very effort to contain its enemies, jeopardize its own security and that of others; for nations encircled by threatening foes tend sooner or later to find it necessary to fight their way out, and in an era of hydrogen bombs the result may be universal destruction.

The third broad major line of foreign policy roughly corresponds in the affairs of nations to benevolence in the sphere of interpersonal relations. The kind of constructive cooperative effort referred to here involves neither any neglect of the nation's own internal strength nor any hesitancy in joining other free nations in checking aggressive policies of potential enemies. However, it involves much more. It includes, for example, constant positive effort to strengthen ties of mutual understanding and friendship among peace-loving free nations, and generous efforts to build up the economic potentials of underdeveloped nations. Regardless of international crises such efforts ought to be undertaken in the interest of humanity, for in no nation can the fullest values be achieved while in other nations men suffer want; but in a time of world revolution like our own, such efforts are the more imperative as bulwarks against the inroads of ideologies that threaten the enslavement of all nations. The kind of constructive cooperation among nations required for peace and justice, however, involves yet more. It includes a constant willingness to enter into negotiation and cooperation with actual or potential enemies whenever such relations do not plainly jeopardize peace and justice. Those who are thought hostile to peace often in fact want peace quite as much as anyone. No matter how diabolical a potential enemy may seem to be, nothing will be lost by readiness to talk with him unless national leaders are either less intelligent or less cautious than he; and it is always possible that great mutual gain will be achieved. Indeed, every gesture of friendship and every joint undertaking that does not jeopardize security tends, whether fully successful or not, to enhance mutual trust and further the emergence of a world order in which nations can live and let live.

NEW PATTERNS OF WORLD ORDER

Thus far we have been concerned with rights and duties of nations within the actual functioning framework of international relations. However, as we suggested at the outset, the achievement of ethical ends in international relations may demand not only ethical activity within the existing patterns but also modification of these patterns. Some of the needed changes are already emerging and perhaps others are on the way. Specific answers to the question, what new patterns are needed, must wait upon united efforts of economists, political scientists, statesmen, psychologists, and sociologists, as well as moralists. The suggestions offered here are of necessity rather broad, general, and tentative, but they represent, as any satisfactory approach to this problem must, an effort to bring ethical objectives to bear upon the harsh realities of the actual situations.

World Community

The primary development in the framework of international relations required for world peace and justice is not, as some suppose, the emergence of new international and political institutions as such, but the sound and rapid growth of .world

community.   Community is harmonious association in terms of
shared interests and mutual respect and consideration.   If
people are to live together in peace and justice, they must learn
to understand and appreciate one another, to become aware of
their initially shared interests, and to cultivate their interests in
the furtherance of one another's interests.   They need to confront external nature with a sense of common heritage and purpose, a well-developed "we" feeling, a united devotion not to
nationality alone but to humanity as well.   Apart from world
community, neither world political institutions nor any other
special devices, however cleverly conceived, can be effective or
indeed long sustain themselves.

Community is of course a matter of degree, and men have
moved a very long way in the direction of world-wide development of it since the days when the earth was peopled largely by
hunting tribes who were scarcely aware of the existence of any
other groups beyond their near neighbors.   But the degree of
world community achieved up to now remains tragically inadequate to the demands of a period in which irresponsible armed
conflict threatens to bring calamity upon all.   Some nations
are primarily interested in agriculture, others in industry; some
in low tariffs, others in high; some in raw materials, others in
manufactured goods; some in free trade, others in restricted
trade.   Even those with similar interests are often in ruthless
competition and bitter struggle against one another for survival.
Some nations cherish freedom; others think it the root of evil.
Nations are often deeply divided concerning religion and morality; and even drastically different artistic tastes separate them.
Peoples remain under crude misapprehensions, often deliberately fostered, concerning one another, and international negotiations are constantly clouded by fundamental misunderstanding and mistrust.   Individuals often take loyalty to their
own nations to be incompatible with interest in the welfare of
mankind, and national leaders tend to be more concerned with
holding office than with world order.   No power outside this
planet threatens the world's peoples in such a way as to create
common bonds like those formed within a nation when another

nation threatens its people.   Moreover, insofar as the peoples of
the world grow together at all they tend to form, not a single community that might make them secure, but two hostile ones that
threaten to annihilate one another.

Nevertheless, conditions have already been realized that bring
mankind within sight of a degree of world community scarcely
even dreamed of in the past.   The bases of such community
in the fundamental similarities of the needs and natures of
human beings, always present, are now better understood than
ever.   The specialization and complexity of modern industry
have created a new economic interdependence.   Modern transportation has broken down barriers of distance and brought nations closer together than their own cities once were.   Modern
means of communication enable news to travel with such rapid-
ity that the people of one nation may now know within minutes
or even seconds the daily events and even the thoughts of people
of other nations of whose very existence their ancestors had
scarcely heard.   Codes of morality and religion no longer remain in isolation, and the free flow of ideas creates new understanding even when it does not produce assimilation.   Artificial barriers cannot altogether stop the process of cultural inter-
change, and the gathering of the nations into hostile camps could
be a prelude to their eventual unification.   Besides, the very
destructiveness of modern warfare creates a common bond between potential enemies.   The fear of sudden death and mass
destruction is not a national fear but a human one.

These favorable conditions do not, of course, render the
growth of world community inevitable.   They create a more
promising possibility of such community than has ever existed
before and they bring that possibility within reach, but they
guarantee nothing.   The same forces that draw men together
can be used to intensify the conflicts between them.   The
manner in which these forces are to be used depends upon human
decisions.   To direct the new conditions into channels of cooperative community rather than destructive conflict constitutes
the major challenge of our age.   Required to this end are concerted effort to disclose the common foundations of human na-

ture and to break down the barriers of class and race prejudice, the elimination of every needless obstacle to the free exchange of thought and news, open-minded endeavor to understand alien cultures, and scrupulous maintenance of respect for other cultures even when they are not understood. More specific efforts will need to be directed toward the elimination of obstacles to trade and the stimulation of its free flow, and toward a re-examination of the teaching of social studies in order to eliminate chauvinism and narrow nationalism and to focus upon the common interests of all human beings. Exchanges of students, professors, editors, farmers, and merchants, as well as of government officials, could well be undertaken on a far larger scale than at present; and cooperation in all manner of cultural, health, and scientific enterprises ought to be considerably stepped up; for it is most of all in face to face meetings and in working alongside one another that people come to know and esteem one another. If the cost of efforts of this sort seems large, it nevertheless remains small by comparison with the human and financial costs of war and the preparation for war.

International Organization

Although the growth of world community is the most important type of development needed for world peace and justice, it is not the only one or even by itself a sufficient one. The complex relations of modern nation-states at best require some administrative machinery. Moreover, just as world political institutions cannot function adequately save in a matrix of world community, so world community can scarcely survive apart from the cohesive force of world political institutions. Hence, to such world community as can be achieved must be added such world political and legal institutions as are suited to the existing stage of community development. The achievement of any sort of international political or legal organization at all requires, of course, some relinquishing of national sovereignty, but the gains to be derived from well-considered advances along this line will increasingly prove to be more than worth their cost, and no really satisfactory alternative seems to be available. The most promising types of international political and legal institutions would appear to be the following.

1. One type of international political structure already to some extent in use but capable of considerable expansion in the near future, within the already existing matrices of community among nations, consists of regional treaty organizations such as the North Atlantic and South East Asia organizations, various groupings of American states, and even certain Communist blocs. Although such alliances as these of course involve real dangers in the possible spreading of local conflicts to larger areas, their present tendency to inhibit conflict would seem to be far greater than their tendency to cause it. These alliances tend to provide protection to each of the separate nations participating in them from external aggressions to which any one nation individually might be subject. They adjust disputes among their several members, facilitate trade agreements and cultural exchanges, and provide experience in the administration of international law. Moreover, through interlocking patterns, the increasing extension of these treaty organizations tends to bring the various groupings together in larger units and sometimes even in ways that cross the boundaries of the two major power groups. Even when these broadest extensions fail to mature, the mere existence of opposing groups of nations tends to provide a more equitable basis for negotiations between the groups that could be achieved if each of the member nations of each group attempted similar negotiations with each of the member nations of the other.

2. Equal in importance to the development of regional organizations, and ultimately even more important, is the development of a genuinely effective world political organization. Such an organization can serve as a forum for the full and free discussion of international agreements and differences. It may facilitate the organization and flow of trade, promote world health, and encourage cultural exchange. It may also make recommendations concerning the settlement of international

disputes and, given sufficient authority and power, it may in time come to be able to enforce its recommendations.

Such an organization has, of course, been initiated in the United Nations, which has begun to perform with considerable success all of the above functions, save the last. Even in the enforcement of its demands, the United Nations has achieved some success on a relatively limited scale. Although this organization remains far from perfect, because it is the only comparable organization in the field, and because some such organization seems to be indispensable to that adjustment of the affairs of nations on which the good or even the survival of the members of each depends, the United Nations would seem to deserve the support of all men of good will.

Whether or not the Charter of the United Nations should be altered and the organization's powers extended to permit enforcement of its decisions against great powers as well as small ones is a very difficult question. Such extension of United Nations powers would obviously entail considerable surrender of sovereignty on the part of member nations, and no powerful nation either will or should make such a relinquishment unless there are very strong controls to assure that all other nations will do likewise. Ordinarily any such drastic step would be expected to wait upon further growth both of world community and of regional and world organizations. But such is the present build-up of fission and fusion weapons, not to speak of biological and chemical ones, that no thoughtful person can rest easy while two nearly equal sovereign hostile powers remain fully armed and unchecked by any authority save their own decision. However difficult the undertaking, therefore, statesmen must continue to press the quest for "foolproof" reduction of all national armaments to a level at which no single nation or group of them will have as much power as that at the disposal of an organization genuinely representative of all nations.

3. The third development required for international peace and justice is closely related to both of the two preceding ones. It consists of a growth, both within and outside the United Na-

tions, of a clear and respected body of international law.   To
some extent, of course, international laws have been recognized
by the courts of nations almost as long as there have been such
courts, and the usefulness of such laws is already great.   However, in the main, the growth of international law is recent,
the important areas of possible friction not covered by it are
many, the confusion in those areas that are covered is considerable, and the prestige of decisions made in terms of it often leaves
much to be desired.   Until legal development can be further
extended in this area much needless uncertainty and ill-will are
sure to remain even when a high degree of world community and
political organization has been achieved.   Legal development is
at best slow, but, if the urgency of the problem is sufficiently recognized, much can be done both through legislation and in the
courts to achieve the acceleration of the process that the present
era demands.

READINGS

Heffner, R. D., *A Documentary History of the United States,* pp.
    80–84, 224–39, 270–87.

QUESTIONS

1. What is meant by saying that our nation has no friends but
only interests?   Is the attitude expressed in this statement more or
less justifiable than a parallel attitude concerning personal relations?
Is the objective of human welfare compatible with patriotism?   How
so, or how not?

2. Is it fair to the people of the United States to ask them to reduce
their high standard of living in the effort to help other countries to
raise their lower ones?   How so, or why not?

3. Can a nation be held guilty or be justifiably punished in the
way an individual can?   What differences, if any, are crucial at this
point?

4. In what sense does a nation have moral responsibilities?   What
is the duty of a statesman who is urged by a substantial majority of
the electorate to adopt a policy that in his judgment involves serious
risk of unjustifiable war?

5. Would the United States be justified in deliberately attempting

to create discontent and ultimately rebellion among the people of the Soviet satellite nations or even in the Soviet Union itself? On what ethical grounds can present "Voice of America" policies be defended?

6. Does the strategic importance of Gibraltar have any bearing upon the claim of the British to retain their hold upon it? If so, what? How about the island of Cyprus?

7. Is war necessarily worse than submission to aggression? How would you define aggression for the purpose of determining right with reference to war? How far should a moral nation press peace efforts before engaging in war?

8. What should an individual do if he is drafted to fight in a war that he considers aggressive and unjust? What bearing does his tacit agreement to obey the law have on this problem? What bearing does his obligation to humanity have upon it?

9. The hydrogen bomb threatens the life of man on earth, but all previous attempts to negotiate workable disarmament have ended in failure. Would further attempts represent appeasement or humanitarian effort? Explain. Illustrate the difference between appeasement and conciliation.

10. Should the United States role in world affairs be one of dominance or of partnership with allied nations? What can be said for "go it alone" policies? What is wrong with them?

11. Plato once remarked that the more closely two unjust men associate with each other, the more they will hate one another. How much truth is in this remark? How does it apply to international relations? Can individuals be brought to unite their efforts only by a hostile third party? Discuss the bearing of this question on international relations.

12. In what ways, if any, do you think we are now nearer world community than at the beginning of the century? What would you consider the chief requirements for the furthering of world community?

13. To what extent must world community be achieved before world government is feasible? In what ways can world government contribute to world community?

14. By what right could governments be asked to surrender their sovereignty to a world government? Could a world government justly claim sovereignty over a nation that refused to enter it as does a national government over individuals living within the na-

tion's boundaries who are unwilling to accept national sovereignty?

15. Under what circumstances should the right of political asylum be supported by international law? Does this right apply to criminals? To mutinous crews of ships?

REFERENCES

Aristotle, *Politics,* tr. by Harris Rackham (New York: Putnam, 1932).

Brunner, Emil, *The Divine Imperative, A Study in Christian Ethics,* tr. by Olive Wyon (Philadelphia: Westminster Press, 1947), pp. 469–82.

Bryn-Jones, David, *Toward a Democratic New Order* (Minneapolis: University of Minnesota Press, 1945), Chs. 14–15.

Dolivet, Louis, *The United Nations* (New York: Farrar, Straus, 1946).

Drake, Durant, *The New Morality* (New York: Macmillan, 1928), Ch. 19.

Ebenstein, William, *Today's Isms* (New York: Prentice-Hall, 1954).

Finletter, T. K., *Power and Policy* (New York: Harcourt, Brace, 1954).

Heffner, R. D., *A Documentary History of the United States* (New York: New American Library, 1952), Chs. 4, 7, 19, 21, 24, 25.

Hobhouse, L. T., *Morals in Evolution* (5th ed., New York: Holt, 1915), Pt. I, Ch. 6.

Holloway, V. H., *Power Politics and the Christian Conscience* (New York: Council of Social Action, 1950).

James, William, "The Moral Equivalent of War," in *Memories and Studies* (New York: Longmans, Green, 1911).

Kant, Immanuel, *Perpetual Peace* (New York: Columbia University Press, 1932).

Kennan, G. F., *American Diplomacy, 1900–1950* (Chicago: Chicago University Press, 1951).

——— *Realities of American Foreign Policy* (Princeton: Princeton University Press, 1954).

Leighton, J. A., *The Individual and the Social Order* (New York: D. Appleton, 1927), Chs. 40–41.

Leys, W. A. R., *Ethics for Policy Decisions* (New York: Prentice-Hall, 1952), Ch. 21.

Loos, A. W., *The United Nations and the Disciplines of Peace* (New York: Council for Social Action, 1954).

Machiavelli, *The Prince* and *The Discourses* (New York: Random House, 1940).

Myrdal, Gunnar, *An American Dilemma* (New York: Harper, 1944).

Niebuhr, Reinhold, *Christianity and Power Politics* (New York: Scribner, 1940).

Patterson, C. H., *Moral Standards* (New York: Ronald, 1949), Ch. 19.

Perry, R. B., *Realms of Value* (Cambridge: Harvard University Press, 1954), Ch. 16.

Reissig, H. F., *Christian Faith and World Upheaval* (New York: Council for Social Action, 1952).

Reves, Ernest, *The Anatomy of Peace* (New York: Harper, 1945).

Robinson, D. S., *The Principles of Conduct* (New York: Appleton-Century-Crofts, 1948), Ch. 24.

Sidgwick, Henry, *Practical Ethics* (New York: Macmillan, 1898), Ch. 3.

Sorokin, P. A., *The Reconstruction of Humanity* (Boston: Beacon Press, 1948).

Titus, H. H., *Ethics for Today* (2nd ed. rev., New York: American Book, 1954), Ch. 27.

Tsanoff, R. A., *Ethics* (rev. ed., New York: Harper, 1955), Ch. 16.

Weldon, T. D., *States and Morals* (New York: McGraw-Hill, 1947).

Westermarck, Edward, *The Origin and Development of the Moral Ideas* (New York: Macmillan, 1908), Vol. II, Ch. 33.

Wright, Quincy, *A Study of War* (Chicago: University of Chicago Press, 1942).

Index